ANTIGONE, IN HER UNBEARABLE SPLENDOR

SUNY series, Intersections: Philosophy and Critical Theory

Rodolphe Gasché, editor

ANTIGONE, IN HER UNBEARABLE SPLENDOR

New Essays on Jacques Lacan's
The Ethics of Psychoanalysis

CHARLES FREELAND

Cover image: © Can Stock Photo Inc. /Frankix

Published by State University of New York Press, Albany

For information, contact State University of New York Press, Albany, NY
www.sunypress.edu

Production by Eileen Nizer
Marketing by Michael Campochiaro

Library of Congress Cataloging-in-Publication Data

Freeland, Charles, 1947–
    Antigone, in her unbearable splendor : new essays on Jacques Lacan's the Ethics of psychoanalysis / Charles Freeland.
        p. cm. — (SUNY series, Intersections: philosophy and critical theory)
    Includes bibliographical references and index.
    ISBN 978-1-4384-4649-3 (hbk. : alk. paper)—978-1-4384-4648-6 (pbk. : alk. paper)
    1. Lacan, Jacques, 1901–1981. Ethique de la psychanalyse, 1959–1960.
2. Psychoanalysis—Moral and ethical aspects. I. Title.

    BF173.L1463F74 2013
    150.19'5—dc23   2012023540

10 9 8 7 6 5 4 3 2 1

CONTENTS

PREFACE

"To essay" means "to attempt." Hence, the following may be read as "attempts" at a philosophical reading of a difficult subject: namely, the place, the role, and the function of "ethics" in Lacanian psychoanalysis. Such a subject is best approached with a hypothesis, and my hypothesis is that especially in his seventh seminar, entitled *The Ethics of Psychoanalysis,* Lacan's psychoanalytic teachings became more closely and more urgently "philosophical." The European traditions of philosophical ethics provided Lacan with a range of concepts and vocabularies that helped him to shape his own ideas and ideals concerning the ethics of psychoanalysis. In this regard, Lacan's seventh seminar was in constant dialogue with one of philosophy's most classical and perennial concerns: the questioning of the conditions, the limits, the scope, and the hopes of ethical thought and ethical life.

To test this thesis, the following essays take up key questions and perspectives in Lacan's work where his psychoanalytic practice both confronts and opens the philosophical traditions of ethical thought to new dimensions. The ethical ideals of self-search and of self-knowledge, the ethical challenge that one must "take care of one's soul," the very question of who or what is the ethical subject, are examples of such intersections between the great European ethical traditions and the work of Lacanian psychoanalysis. Likewise, the limit experiences of death, truth, desire, transgression, and the human quest for happiness and the moral-ethical good, are all crucial areas of ethical experience transformed by the Lacanian conceptual approach. One pathos, if I may so call it, that Lacan's seminars and the great European traditions in ethics have in common is the notion that the human being comes into being as a subject, an ethical subject, somehow defined by a lack, as a "soul" in search of an "object" from which it has been separated, an object that has been lost, that shall be forever sought but never found or fully attained. The idealizing classical European philosophical tradition might have called this the True, the Good, and the Beautiful. But, guided by the Freudian hypothesis of the unconscious, Lacan began to think of it as the price, the gatekeeper's fee that had to be paid for this very coming into being of the subject. He has a term for this "lost object": he calls it *objet petit a*, and in various other guises and formulations that we shall be examining, he calls it the Thing (*das Ding*) and the Real, objects of fantasy and foreboding. In any case, it is the key to understanding human desire and the essential horizons of human moral and ethical life. The following essays thus ask whether or not Lacan's teachings on ethics so obviously and directly constitute an "anti-philosophy" or whether they succeed in putting the philosophical questioning of moral and ethical life on a wider stage.

A couple of notes regarding the text: These essays were first presented as lectures given over the course of three seminars, the first of which was held at Thammasat University, Bangkok, Thailand, in 2006; the second, a three-day seminar to which I was invited by of the Department of Comparative Literature at the State University of New York at Buffalo in October of 2007; and the third, another seminar that again convened at Thammasat University, Bangkok, in December of 2008. The participants in those seminars, Krzysztof Ziarek, Ewa Ziarek, David Miller, and David Johnson, to name just a few, provided much valuable criticisms and questions that helped enormously in the development of this project. I especially thank Distinguished Professor Rodolphe Gasché, not only for his part in organizing the SUNY Buffalo seminars, but also for his encouragement in getting these lectures rewritten for their eventual publication as a book.

Because I do not take Lacan to have been a systematic thinker, I have decided to present my readings in the form of a collection of essays rather than as chapters in a continuously and systematically developed narrative. Each essay takes up the question of the philosophical or "anti-philosophical" dimensions of Lacan's ethics of psychoanalysis in terms of certain key concepts, sources, and texts to which he returned again and again over the course of his seminars. An overall chronological approach has been adopted in the order of presentation of these essays. The first essays concern the earlier seminars, especially *Seminar VII*, and the later essays deal with seminars and essays from the late 1960s and early 1970s. The essays try to develop working definitions of some of Lacan's terminology as it is pertinent to the perspective under discussion, so readers unfamiliar with such terminology might benefit by reading these essays in the order of their presentation. Readers more familiar with the Lacanian discourse may read the essays in any order they wish.

Please also note that references to Lacan's published seminars have been given in the text and not as endnotes. The references appear in the following example: (S7: 35). The "S" refers to "Seminar," the number to the numbered book of the seminar. In this case, S7 refers to Lacan's seventh seminar, *The Ethics of Psychoanalysis*. The number(s) following the colon refer to the page number. I have used the standard English translations for Lacan's seminars where they are available. In some of these translations, the pagination in the French text is also given. Where the French pagination references are available, I have also given them. For the convenience of the reader, references to Sophocles' plays are also given in the text.

I have also chosen to italicize the word *jouissance* to show that it is a foreign word, in this case, a French word. I realize that many English translations of Lacan's terminology do not do this, but I have chosen to do so because there is no exact English translation for this overdetermined French word, and so I have left it as a French word and have accordingly italicized it.

Finally, I would like to extend my heartfelt thanks to the editors and staff at SUNY Press, Albany NY, for all their efforts and patience in working with me in the preparation of this volume. If the devils are in the details, then it took the angels at SUNY Press to help me find a way to overcome them.

ABBREVIATIONS OF WORKS BY JACQUES LACAN

S1: *The Seminar of Jacques Lacan, Book I, Freud's Papers on Technique, 1953–1954.* Edited by Jacques Alain Miller, translated by John Forrester. New York and London: W.W. Norton & Company, 1988.

S2: *The Seminar of Jacques Lacan, Book II, The Ego in Freud's Theory and in the Technique of Psychoanalysis, 1954–1955.* Edited by Jacques-Alain Miller, translated by Sylvana Tomaselli. New York and London: W.W. Norton & Company, 1988.

S7: *The Seminar of Jacques Lacan, Book VII, The Ethics of Psychoanalysis, 1959–1960.* Edited by Jacques-Alain Miller, translated by Dennis Porter. New York and London: W.W. Norton & Company, 1992.

Le Séminaire, livre VII, L'éthique de la psychanalyse. Texte établi par Jacques-Alain Miller. Paris: Éditions de Seuil, 1986.

S8: *Le Séminaire, livre VIII, Le Transfert.* Texte établi par Jacques-Alain Miller. Paris: Éditions de Seuil, 2001.

S11: *The Four Fundamental Concepts of Psychoanalysis.* Edited by Jacques-Alain Miller, translated by Alan Sheridan. New York and London: W.W. Norton & Company, 1977.

S17: *The Seminar of Jacques Lacan, Book XVII, The Other Side of Psychoanalysis, 1969–1970.* Edited by Jacques-Alain Miller, translated by Russell Grigg. New York and London: W.W. Norton & Company, 2007.

Le Séminaire, livre XVII, L'envers de la psychanalyse. Texte établi par Jacques-Alain Miller. Paris: Éditions de Seuil, 1991.

S18: *Le Séminaire, livre XVIII. D'un discours qui ne serait pas du Semblant.* Texte établi par Jacques-Alain Miller. Paris: Éditions de Seuil, 2006.

S20: *The Seminar of Jacques Lacan, Book XX, Encore, On Feminine Sexuality: The Limits of Love and Knowledge, 1972–1973*. Edited by Jacques Alain Miller, translated by Bruce Fink. New York and London: W.W. Norton & Company, 1998.

Le Séminaire, livre XX, Encore. Texte établi par Jacques-Alain Miller. Paris: Éditions de Seuil, 1975.

INTRODUCTION

There is a yearning (*Sehnsucht*) that seeks the unbound (*Ungebundene*).

—Hölderlin, "Mnemosyne"

Antigone, in her unbearable splendor: My title speaks from the heart of this book. These words, taken from Lacan's seventh seminar, *The Ethics of Psychoanalysis*, not only comprise the title to one of the central essays in this collection, they are also the words, the image and the enigma, the epiphany, one might say, to which my thoughts kept returning as I attempted to understand the direction and ideals of Lacan's teachings on ethics. Rather than contemporary clinical case studies, why did Lacan instead place this tragic yet electrifying image, drawn from classical, literary sources, at the climax of his famous seminar? Was Lacan merely emulating Freud's adaptation of the sufferings of the son of Laius? Or was there some other, perhaps darker, purpose at work in this "splendor"? Is a tragic dimension the key to understanding Lacan's ethics?

Understandably, Lacan does not portray Antigone as darkened by mourning and melancholia over the death of her brother. His Antigone is neither muted nor defeated in the finality of the dark silence of the tomb that awaits her. In his reading of the play's final scenes, we see instead an Antigone bathed in transgressive and defiant colors. She becomes an unappeasable force crushing the pale of human law. It seems indeed something larger and more explosive is being brought to center stage in this evocation of her "unbearable splendor." Is there a link between Lacan's ethics of psychoanalysis and the sort of transgressive ethics one finds in the writings of Georges Bataille, a latent complicity perhaps with the Bataille who described himself as being not a philosopher, but a mystic or a madman? But such a solar Antigone, eloquent in the grips of an impossible desire, would certainly have darkly and dramatically shaded the project of a psychoanalytic ethics. Would this not end up promoting an unspeakably violent and singularly transgressive act as an ethical paradigm?

1

Why, indeed, this death-stalked poetic climax to Lacan's seminar? Would not all that is here "unbearable" also be unspeakable? What would the consequences of this be for an ethics presumably rooted in speech and speaking? What new directions in ethical thought might be heralded by this recourse, elaborated at length in Lacan's seminar, to the ancient tragedy of Antigone? But what is the upshot of all this? What new ways of thinking emerge from the shadows of this "unbearable splendor"?

Such are the questions and perplexities to which the following essays are an attempted response and elaboration. Allow me now to briefly survey four main perspectives that shall be taken up in this regard.

The first of these concerns the overall critical relation between Lacan and the classical philosophical tradition. In terms of such great themes as those of "death," "truth," and the "good for a human being," the following essays question and examine the critical relationship between Lacan's ethics of psychoanalysis and the classical European traditions of ethical and political philosophy. The term "philosophy" names an essentially classical Greek tradition of ethical and political thought, the tradition that defined itself by posing and sustaining such fundamental questions as: "What is the being of a human being?" "What is True and the Good for a human being?" Regarding this tradition we shall ask, is Lacan an "anti-philosopher"? Lacan makes many efforts and many statements that would seem to support this position. Especially his insistence on the unconscious as a dimension fundamental to human experience would seem quite enough to distance his psychoanalytic ethics from the horizons of the classical European philosophical tradition. Throughout his seminars, he often seems to be searching for a way through philosophy, a way toward its limits, its outside, its "Other," or its "after." But Lacan never simply rejects philosophy outright. He seems rather to be attempting something more troublesome and paradoxical: a philosophy of "anti-philosophy," the effect of which is to enlarge philosophy and to possibly enrich it. What is Lacan's strategy here? While it is a strategy that looks for moments, angles, questions, dimensions of thought and experience that question and indeed tear at the philosophical canvas, the critical effect of all this is to offer philosophy a new language and new ways of thinking the being and the limits of human language and experience. Lacan thus enlarges philosophy rather than rejects it. His position with regard to the classical traditions of ethical and political thought can perhaps be thus characterized as both inside and outside that tradition, a relation of both belonging to and separation from "philosophy." Lacan's anti-philosophy is thus a position that is both intimate and yet also "extimate" to philosophy. It is both within philosophy and, at the same time, it is a movement to its limits, its "outside," its "Other."

If Lacan is an anti-philosopher, he is so in terms of two key assertions. First, he asserts the truth of the unconscious; and from this he develops his second important assertion: a human being is a "speaking" being. His conceptions of the human bearing toward death, his definitions of truth and of the human good all arise from the fundamental way he conceives the structure of both the unconscious and speaking being. Setting aside the dimension of the unconscious, it would seem that with all its privileging of the voice and speech, the classical tradition has a place already cut out and prepared for such an ethic as this. But, it is his way of formulating speaking being as a *structure*—a generalized structure of language linked with bodily, sexual needs and desires—that also distances Lacan's ethic from that tradition. It is along these general lines that Lacan's ethic is both "Greek" and "anti-Greek." The question of a possible "ethics of psychoanalysis" indeed seems the place or the scene where Lacan's relation with "philosophy" is best presented, where his critical questioning of a philosophical tradition unfolds and where it is most crucially tested, and, too, where all the risks, the stakes, and the exciting new possibilities for such a position are most acutely felt. And if we were to put a face on this anti-philosophy, or better yet, a mask as worn in the performances of ancient Greek tragic dramas, no doubt the mask of the tragic heroine Antigone—Antigone in her "unbearable splendor"—would be one of the most daring and far-reaching.

Second perspective: Antigone is the central figure linking Lacan's anti-philosophy to the classical Greek tradition. Thus, it is not only his reading of Plato's *Symposium* in his eighth seminar, but also and most spectacularly his reading of Sophocles' *Antigone* in his famous seventh seminar that shall situate for us Lacan's ethics vis-à-vis the Greek ethical tradition extending from Socrates through Plato and Aristotle. While the eighth seminar—where Lacan takes up an extended and detailed reading of Plato's *Symposium,* and does so in order to formulate his conception of the psychoanalytic transference—indeed offers not only a plethora of references to the classical Greek traditions, but also its own intriguing and important ethical dimensions, dimensions pursued in the last of the essays in this collection, nonetheless it is first his reading of the play *Antigone* in the seventh seminar that is most captivating, and where his early ethical positions are most engaging. It is here that he holds up before the tranquil, paternal countenance of Aristotle's *kalos kagathos* the wild grimace of Sophocles' Antigone, "in her unbearable splendor."

Arising anamorphically across the surface of his seminar, Lacan's Antigone thus emerges as the tragic image of a woman whose doomed desire has carried her beyond the limits of life and death. Nothing like it has ever before appeared in any other book on ethics. From the midst of a very measured discourse, a discourse on "ethics," which, after all, in a traditional and very Greek way, is itself a discourse on the measure of life, on the measured life and the good and beauty that measure brings, in the midst of this, at this limit-point, something immeasurable is brought forth, traced by her splendor. She surpasses everything the ancient Greek philosophers had said about the beautiful, happy life. She makes the old philosophical-ethical heroes, especially the Greek aristocratic gentleman, the famous *kalos kagathos*, seem pallid ideals, beautiful illusions, whose dreams of self-knowledge and self-mastery served more to mask and to impede access to the truth of desire than to reveal it. No doubt, Lacan's portrayal of Antigone in her immeasurable and unbearable splendor was precisely his way of shattering such beautiful illusions. Antigone thus exemplifies and embodies the ethical force of his teachings. She spearheads his guiding task, which was to demystify the illusions of the classical European philosophical ethical tradition.

There is thus an important critical link between Lacan's ethics of psychoanalysis and the fifth- and fourth-century BC Greek "Enlightenment," especially the tradition of "the care of the soul," current from Socrates through Aristotle to Epicurus and Epictetus. If Lacan is an anti-philosopher, it is this tradition that he especially targets. This tradition seems a guiding dimension of Lacan's thought. It is the touchstone to which he continuously returns in the course of his seminar. But it is also a tradition he strenuously resists. How, through his reading of the tragic drama *Antigone*, for example, does he seek to question it and to suggest a whole new orientation for any philosophical reflection on the interrelationships between ethics, politics, and aesthetics?

In the Socratic-Aristotelian tradition, ethics was seen as a way of curing the sicknesses of the human soul, and it did so by orienting the ethical measure of human life on the transcendent Beautiful and the Good such that "taking care" of the soul always meant "taking the right measure" of the soul, finding its proper balance, a balance that is both Good and Beautiful. This was the true path to human happiness and well-being, one that led from the semi-darkness and confusion of Plato's cave upward to the sunlight of the True, the Good, and the Beautiful. As a psychoanalyst, can Lacan not also seem to be a philosopher-priest, confessor, and healer? Is he not a "doctor" of the human soul? But here the ethical path does not have a transcendental bearing. It is not an ethic that turns the soul upward away from the world and toward the supramundane triumvirate of the True, the Good, and the Beautiful. Rather, Lacan's ethic unfolds across the surfaces and folds of three interlaced and very worldly fields: the Symbolic, the Imaginary, and the Real. A new domain and strategy for ethics emerges here: neither the ideality of the summits nor of the hidden mysteries of the depths, rather, this is an ethic of surfaces, the surface of language, of images, of bodies and desire; the surfaces of a voice; surfaces that are acoustic, that are felt, touched, and embraced; surfaces that double and twist, that turn and tangle one upon another. While it is said that splendor arises from the heart, Antigone's very Greek "splendor" is the scintillation of a surface. Lacan is a Greek in the Nietzschean sense: superficial out of profundity.

Thus, one of the most original and truly powerful moments in Lacan's seminar lies in the way it evokes Antigone's beauty, calling it "unbearable," because it is the beauty and splendor of diremption and destitution, the beauty of a *jouissance*, as Lacan shall call it, a *jouissance* that shimmers across a surface of word and flesh, a *jouissance* that is the paradoxical knowledge (*savoir*) of the truth of desire.[1] However she may be a figure drawn from the repertoire of classical Greek theater, however she may have been a contemporary of Socrates and Plato, for Lacan, she is as much anti-Socratic as she is "pre-Socratic." Her pathway in life leads not to the Platonic sunlight of the Good, but to the darkness of the tomb. Her desire is not for salvation, but is described as criminal. Her beauty is not a reflection of an Eternal, Ideal Beauty, but a paradoxical surface that is both a lure and a barrier unto evil.

Such an ethic cannot promise falsely to heal the human soul when it has come to know too well the yearning for the impossible that binds human life and death in a torsion always torn, open, infinite. In Lacan's reading of the play, Antigone's splendor is the radiance of a desire not for a healed soul but for something lost, the tender surfaces of an object lost because cutaway and forbidden, something that can be recovered only through dreams and disguises. After Freud, Lacan shall call this object, "the Thing," (*das Ding*). And in the course of the seventh seminar, Sophocles' tragic drama then becomes the romance of Beauty and the Beast of *das Ding*, a romance set "outside" the philosophical ethical and political theater of the Good.

Bound by the law, Antigone yearns for the unbound. And while her desire for a "lost object" may recall the Platonic reminiscence, the philosophical and erotic desire for a dimension beyond the stars that the human soul desires to recover from within the limitations of its incarnate finitude, she must be seen instead as the crucial point of resistance to all of that. For Lacan, Antigone embodies a drive not toward the transcendent eternality of the Good, but toward death, the death that is always at work in the heart of human life. This is Antigone's impossible desire and her tragedy. It is also the generalized tragedy of our human situation: bound with death, yet, always seeking the unbound; always hoping for the eternal life that shall defeat death, yet never gaining insight into the nonduality of life and death that is as fundamental to the Buddhist vision of samsara as it is to Sophocles' plays. His refusal to pursue either the ideality of the summits or a hermeneutics of the depths, his acknowledgment of the tragic dimension of human life and its desire for the impossible, thus emerge as the key dimensions of Lacan's seventh seminar.

A third key perspective in the following essays: the figure of Antigone also situates Lacan's ethic vis-à-vis Hegel, Kant, and Sade, the tradition of the European Enlightenment and the dialectics of negativity, death, and transgression. Particularly the Hegelian dialectic sought to inscribe her as but a moment in a nomic conflict of universality and particularity, of law and subjectivity that would find its eventual reconciliation in the dialectic of Absolute Spirit. As in Hegel's *Phenomenology of Absolute Spirit*, or even in Hölderlin's "Notes on Antigone," Lacan's evocation of Antigone also seems to heroize her. But for the way she resists all reconciliation in the Lacanian ethical and political theater, she perhaps plays the role not just of an anti-philosopher, but of an anti-hero, as well. Her act is heroic insofar as it is singular and transgressive, a violent and unholy union of god and woman, anticipated in Sophocles' play by the figure of the goddess Niobe and furthermore linked in Lacan's seminars with the figure of the goddess Diana, who, for Lacan, is the very lethal personification of Truth.

Indeed, Lacan's more general "anti-Hegelianism" crucially turns on this denial of dialectical reconciliation and healing. Thus, his refusal of a key ideal of late eighteenth-century German Idealism, the ideal of a union with totality, a union that achieves the overcoming of time, particularity, and finitude, the overcoming of ethical and political culture in a culminating union with nature. Hölderlin's tragedy, *Empedocles*, is a prime example of this ideal given dramatic form in the self-immolation of its hero. Lacan's reading of *Antigone* gives this a new direction by placing its heroine, Antigone, not on the stage of dialectics but rather on the stage of linguistics and psychoanalysis. She is a woman, but she is first a signifier and an image of the death drive. Unlike Hölderlin, where tragedy is a metaphor of an intellectual intuition that realizes this union with nature, tragedy for Lacan promises neither union nor the resolution of dialectical oppositions. Rather, the tragic heroine is a rending image of the death that stalks language and desire. For Lacan, these are dimensions fundamental to human ethical life that cannot readily be resolved in or reinvested back into a dialectic of Absolute Truth.

It is along these lines that Antigone's "unbearable splendor" becomes one of the ways Lacan approaches the starting point for his seventh seminar: a deeply human need for transgression, a transgression that knows no reconciliation. Transgression is a dimension both approached and distanced in the Greek and German philosophical tradition extending from Socrates to Hegel. Indeed, Lacan might have been satisfied with calling this transgression "a will to destruction," except that he resists using this term, *Wille*, precisely due to its inscription in a philosophical heritage of the *Wille* that culminates in Schopenhauer and Nietzsche. Thus, he prefers to speak the Freudian language of the drives, *Trieb* (*pulsion*), in particular, defined as a drive beyond any destination in pleasure, beyond any instinct for a return to an initial state of unity, of equilibrium and measure. More than a "yearning," the death drive is a drive unbound and immeasurable, a drive that defines human life. In excess of the resources of philosophical language, Lacan thought it was perhaps best approached by way of poetry and drama. In the Lacanian theater, Antigone is, thusly, a woman who is "not one," for she is first of all a work of poetic art. Since the days of Schelling, poetics has been called the highest art. As a work of poetic art, Antigone's work is thus the work of truth, where truth in this case is the truth of desire, the death drive. Lacan's reading of *Antigone*, which never loses sight of the poetic dimension, shows the play's heroine—like desire itself—as situated along the surfaces and folds of the Imaginary, the Symbolic, and the Real. She is both word and image. Not only word and image, in the Lacanian universe of discourse, Antigone is more properly speaking a signifier, and in this she is an image of the death drive, a "drive" Lacan situates not so much in "nature," but in the "historical domain" as something that obtains at the level of signifiers and the symbolic (S7: 211). From the standpoint of classical philosophical discourse, Antigone's transgressive beauty and splendor thus comprise what may also be said to be a "zero point" of word and image, a point where the word equals zero, where signification stumbles and comes to a halt, where someone, the hero—or the heroine, as in this case of

Sophocles' *Antigone*—must die, and not just once, but twice, a heroic "double death," as it were.[2] Such beauty and splendor, such a double death, have no productive role to play in the Hegelian dialectic, for they mark a moment of unemployable excess, a moment that cannot be reinvested back into the production of the dialectical reconciliation of opposition promised by Absolute Truth.

Fourth, and finally, via Lacan's extensive use of tragedy there is a theory and a practice of "catharsis" at work in his ethics. However much Lacan might have wished to distance his concept of tragedy and the "tragic" sharply from that found in both the Greek and Germanic philosophical traditions, there are nonetheless elements from especially the Greek understanding of tragedy that survive in his work. Especially one of these elements is crucial for the question of ethics: the Greek medical notion of *Katharsis*, most prominently brought into service in Aristotle's *Poetics*, is still pertinent in Lacan's readings of tragic drama and in his considerations on ethics. Lacan's audience at the 1960 seventh seminar was mostly made up of analysts. There were even a few philosophers present. Through his evocation of Antigone in her tragic splendor, Lacan might have wished to purge them of any desire as analysts and philosophers to maintain the philosophical and psychological ideal of the "care for the soul." Not only because he harbors deep suspicions regarding the existence of a human "soul," but also because he might, in this regard, have wished to purge them of any illusions they may have held about bringing a healing unity and reconciliation to the wounds and the tragic dimension that he always maintained as essential to human experience.

Lacan's engagement with tragic drama, especially with the play *Antigone*, and the way he linked it with new critical readings of Kant and Sade and the whole classical European philosophical tradition of ethics from Socrates to Hegel, thus comprises a crucial moment in the legacy of his seminars, a moment of catharsis, perhaps, that defined the purpose of his projected ethics of psychoanalysis, namely, to purge the fear and pity that the highest ideals and the ultimate promises of that tradition had instilled in the philosophical spectator.

In his later seminars, Lacan goes beyond the death-bound and transgressive figure of Antigone, which he eventually came to see as an impasse. Yet, his reading of the play remains a pivotal moment in his seminars. It was the initial shock, the daring experimentation and interpretation that not only took the classical treatment of Sophocles dramas but also the tradition of philosophical ethical and political thought to a new level, one that both deepens that tradition and critically opens it to new directions and possibilities. His efforts in this regard constitute a body of work and reflection that philosophical ethics cannot ignore without depriving itself of some of the most fertile ways and means necessary for its creative transformation.

Thus, the little phrase "Antigone, in her unbearable splendor," seems a vision and a poem, a work of art and thought. It also marks a limit-point where the ethical measure and the measure of ethics are transgressed, where the immeasurable arises. At that limit where a tragic, unspeakable dimension of human experience is brought to light, such splendor points not only toward the shadows of death and finitude, but also toward a way of transfiguring ethics through an encounter with the infinite that opens like a wound at the heart of thought, language, and desire.

To conclude, two additional notes:

First, the interpretative task for the following study shall not so much concern the possibility of situating Lacan's work historiographically. Rather, the task is to continue in the present a philosophically grounded and critical questioning of the ethical and political traditions of the classical and modern European Enlightenments, something that is already at work in Lacan's seminars, and, on this basis, to show how Lacan's teaching has helped to open contemporary philosophical thinking on ethics and politics to new directions and new possibilities of conceptualization. The crucial question now is to see how and in what ways Lacan's work has an important philosophical dimension and how his thought resonates with a philosophical effect—not despite all of his efforts to distance himself from philosophical reflection—and to show how this has been important and on what levels and in what ways Lacan's dialogue with philosophy has been enacted.

Thus, the hermeneutic principle invoked for the following reading of Lacan's seminars and essays is similar to the one Lacan adopted for his own studies of Freud: the task is not so much to situate Lacan in the history of thought and ideas as it is to gauge whether the questions Lacan raises in his teachings concerning the ethics of psychoanalysis have or have not been superseded by the larger questions he raises and the perspectives he opens for contemporary philosophical concerns for the foundations and limits of ethics and politics more generally.[3] In the most general terms, the questions Lacan raises concerning the classical philosophical discourses on ethics and politics—and not despite their pronounced "anti-philosophical" bias—are yet still philosophical insofar as they ask, what is this Reason, what is this thinking, what is this desire for the Good, the True, and the Beautiful—what is this desire for human "happiness," in short—that the classical philosophical tradition has placed at the center of the domains of ethics and politics? What are its limits and its effects? What are its dangers? How and why must it be challenged? Is this challenging not philosophical in both its letter and its spirit?

Second, in this regard, it must be said that this ethic is an ethics of resistance. This is something that must be kept in mind in any reference to an alleged "anti-philosophy" at work in Lacan's thought. Throughout his seminars, his teaching takes the form of an ethic that ceaselessly sounds a warning against a persistent danger he keeps recalling to our attention. As Nietzsche's madman tells us in the parable of the death of God, God may be dead, but word of that death has yet to reach our ears. In other words, even if "God is dead," certainly the demand for God, the demand for new masters, like the demand for happiness, have not yet died, and no doubt, never will. Hence, the resistance that unfolds in *The Ethics of Psychoanalysis* is a resistance against all the new masters that might arise so as to fill-in the emptiness traced and left by their now dead predecessors. Lacan's ethic resists the return of the masters, resists the dominant shadow cast by all the old "absolute masters," even that of death itself, "*the* absolute master," death, whose role as a signifier in the contemporary ethics of finitude is always questioned by Lacan. We "modern men," Lacan warns us, yet live on under the shadow of ever more ferocious fathers, imaginary and religious. Ever more cruel masters, they all have their role to play and their work cut out for them. It echoes in every promise they make to heal the wounds and overcome the pathos of human suffering, contingency, and finitude. These monsters are always there, waiting as though in the depths of every human longing for whatever irretrievably lost objects that may define the limits of human desire; they wait behind every hope for a happiness that seems always promised yet never attained. *The Ethics of Psychoanalysis* is, thus, a book haunted and stalked by such monsters. It bears witness to a forbidding and unforgiving reign of the Fathers, those "eminent personalities," as Lacan calls them in a reference to the "Great Man," the legislator, politician, and rationalist Moses, for example, foregrounded in Freud's *Moses and Monotheism*, figures who are far more powerful dead than they ever were when alive (S7: 142/173 and 173/205). There is also the dark allure of what Lacan calls—in reference to Freud—the "Thing" (*das Ding*), for example, and that insatiable, tortured love called "courtly love," where something—a hole, a void, something impossible—is glimpsed but never touched. Here is where he shall situate the "splendor of Antigone," as the numinous other side of the darkness of the unapproachable and forbidden. Through the prism of such darkly heroic and tragic figures, Lacan's *Ethics* focuses a beam of moral light, displays it in the spectrum of its many colors, and so hazards an ethics for "our time." From under the illusory ideals of the European traditions in ethical thought, he brought to an always hesitant articulation something that that tradition had always approached but missed or misrecognized: the "gap" (*béance*), the wound, the failure, the lack, the crime and the truth that tears at the surfaces of human desire, as at the heart of the human condition itself. Lacan traces both the reign of the Fathers who command from high atop their proverbial mountaintops and the superegos and the moral laws that reign from within back to this gap. Week by week, his seminars thus unfolded a tragic and magnificent view of humanity. As piece by piece, bit by bit, the seminars unfolded a tireless probing of the truth of human desire, his hearers, readers, and subscribers were offered an unflinching look at the civilization and its discontents of post–World War II Europe. By turns humorous and grim, Lacan's presentation of the "human condition" was also deeply accented by his heroically imploring his audience against any giving up or "giving way" on desire. And while it may not at first seem to be much, it is also here that he leveraged the only remaining possibilities for human freedom and self-assertion in the face of seemingly implacable necessity. The product of an indefatigable critic and inventor of new ways of thinking, is Lacan's thought ever best summarized as being an anti-philosophy? Indeed, when he says he wants to demystify the European tradition of philosophy, to take it to that point where its eloquence stumbles and a new poetry can be heard, or when he tries to grasp from the stolid and predictable rhythms of the measurable something unexpected and immeasurable, does he not have something to offer our ever restless hunger for new beginnings and new ways of engaging and addressing philosophy's perennial questions: What can we know? What can we hope? What must we do?

Such, in broad outlines, are the questions and perspectives that the following essays take as their starting points. Each of the essays in this collection takes up a theme, question, juncture, or conceptual setting in which the tensions of breaking and belonging between Lacan's teachings and the European philosophical traditions in ethical and political thought are explored. Thus, the first essay shows that insofar as Lacan's psychoanalytic teachings have an important, indeed crucial, place for ethics, they have something that both carries them toward and yet away from philosophy just as they are both anchored in and yet drift away from purely "scientific" and clinical concerns. The second essay takes up the thematic of death and finitude in Lacan's text and shows how this puts Lacan's text in an important critical relation with the philosophical work of Hegel. The thematic of a Lacanian "anti-philosophy" is further explored in the third essay, which takes up the complex ways in which Lacan questioned and pursued "truth"—a seminal philosophical perspective if there ever was one—across the course of his seminars. The fourth essay considers the Lacanian ethic and his definition of human desire in relation particularly to the Kantian concept of "moral law." The central essay on Antigone shows Lacan's ethic in relation to the setting of tragic drama and transgression, while the essay that follows shows how Lacan questioned those perspectives and attempted new directions in both ethical and political thought. The final essay, by returning to question just how Lacan's psychoanalysis may be taken as an "anti-philosophy," considers the Lacanian ethic in terms of the psychoanalytic "pass" and suggests ways of situating Lacan's work in relation to the overshadowing of nihilism in contemporary thought. Throughout, the essays show Lacan as a thinker deeply rooted in the traditions of both the classical Greek and the eighteenth-century European Enlightenments, a thinker who comes to grips with the European traditions of philosophical thought and who is also able to delimit a way of thinking beyond that tradition toward new possibilities for ethical and political reflection.

1

TOWARD AN ETHICS
OF PSYCHOANALYSIS

An alien language will be my swaddling clothes.
Long before I dared to be born
I was a letter of the alphabet, a verse like a vine,
I was the book that you all see in dreams.

—Osip Mandelstam, from "To the German Language"

A CURIOUS LITTLE BOOK

The Ethics of Psychoanalysis is a curious little book. Curious for the way it came to be as a book, and curious, also, for what it attempts to achieve, for the headings, for the ends at which it may be said to aim. Much like Aristotle's *Nicomachean Ethics*, it, too, is based on student lecture notes, stenographer's notes in this case, taken during a seminar Lacan gave, his seventh seminar, at St. Anne's Hospital in Paris from November of 1959 until July 1960. Lacan himself remarked on this some twelve or thirteen years later, in his 1973 seminar, his twentieth, entitled *Encore, the Limits of Love and Knowledge*. He began his session of February 13, 1973, by recalling *The Ethics of Psychoanalysis*, remarking how important Aristotle's *Nicomachean Ethics* had been for the seminar. Lacan had been telling his hearers about the obvious problems translating Aristotle into French when he suddenly turned from this to a reflection on how his own seventh seminar, *The Ethics of Psychoanalysis*, had, perhaps like Aristotle's *Ethics*, been compiled and produced by a student, J-A Miller, in this case. Lacan recalled how Miller, "wrote it up . . . making it into a written text." Of course, Miller had no desire to steal the seminar. He was only regretting that it had never been properly published and wished to do something about it. But, Lacan held the transcript back from publication. He said he would like to rewrite it himself one day and make it into "a written text" (S20: 53/50). But this never happened, not in Lacan's

13

lifetime, anyway. *The Ethics of Psychoanalysis*, its text "established" by J-A Miller, who by that time was Lacan's son-in-law and known as "faithful Acathe," moral guardian of the work and even billed on the cover of the publications as its coauthor, was finally published in 1986 after a lengthy court battle, which Miller won,[1] through Éditions du Seuil as part of a collection, *Le champ freudien*, originally established by Jacques Lacan and now directed by Jacques-Alain Miller. The problem, of course, is that for both Aristotle and Lacan, the circuit from spoken lecture to written notes, and from there to a published book, which is itself then translated into perhaps dozens of foreign languages, in this circuit, something is always lost, bungled, or misinterpreted. The pages that comprise the published book, *The Ethics of Psychoanalysis*, seem to be but a residue of that seminar, its "death mask." In their written form, taken from stenographer's notes, the master's words never reach their destination. They nevermore run, let alone win, that race between speaker and hearer that seemingly parallels that race known through Zeno between Achilles and the tortoise, a race that shall never be won by Achilles due to the infinity that lies between each step of the way. Now that infinity between speaker and reader, that gap, that uncrossable, incomprehensible distance, is the distance of death, time, and the written word, which functions more like a veil than a wall for the way it is always inviting the reader to try and see what is on the other side. As Lacan asked of Aristotle's *Ethics*, so we ask of his own seminars on the ethics of psychoanalysis: How can we understand this discourse, separated from us as it is by time and circumstance? What is Lacan trying to accomplish in this seminar? What is he up to? What is he pursuing? What slippery, shiny fish does he bring up from the depths of his thought? How can we think the revolution this text brings for us to read, like a letter from another world, a revolution in the way the human situation in all its social links can be thought and articulated? Is there any reason why it is not thinkable for the philosopher? But we can never have it all. There always seems "a remainder," something left behind, some fish not brought up from the depths, something that cannot be made-up for, something missed, in short, by *The Ethics of Psychoanalysis*. Perhaps it is the remainder of the voice, Lacan's voice, perhaps it is a certain pleasure, a certain *jouissance*, a great love of truth that should not be and yet also could not fail to be something, a necessity, perhaps, linked to the impossible, something that "does not stop not being written," something that would help us to understand, in other words, why "he got so worked up" (S20: 54–59/52–56). In any case, Lacan's contemporary reader thus inescapably feels that he/she does not have all of Lacan in the written pages of his book, that the body of the text is somehow, "not whole," that, it is not "One," that we, his readers, can never catch up with him, that his truth, the truth that speaks in his discourse, is never quite where one expects to look or to find it, and this but makes us run faster in that impossible-to-win race.

Lacan's seventh seminar, now published in English as *The Ethics of Psychoanalysis*, has since become one of the best known of Lacan's seminars, and the subject of much commentary. It created a stir in the psychoanalytic field of its time. Only three years after giving the seminar, Lacan was forced out of the IPA, the Association psychoanalytique internationale. Since that time, the seminar has become widely read outside of the field and territory of psychoanalysis, especially by philosophers. This is curious. Why would a text that seems on its surface to deal with a highly specialized and questionable field called psychoanalysis be of interest to philosophers?

AN ANTI-PHILOSOPHY?

Lacan's seminars are replete with references to philosophers and philosophical ideas, especially those of Hegel, Kant, Plato, and Aristotle. Nearly an entire seminar, *Seminar VIII*, from the early 1960s, was devoted to a reading of Plato's *Symposium*. Yet, Lacan himself occasionally spoke of his work as being a kind of "anti-philosophy." A growing body of commentary on Lacan's work also concerns the idea that Lacan was a philosopher of an anti-philosophy, that he no longer found the philosophical tradition to be relevant to what he was trying to think through in his seminars, and that he wished to distance himself from that tradition. In light of Lacan's continuous reference to the philosophical tradition, this anti-philosophical dimension of his work seems paradoxical. What does it mean in this case to be an anti-philosophy? The overall thesis of the following essays is that this thematic is not just a metaphysical and epistemological issue, but that it is especially pertinent to and developed in the context of the question of an ethics of psychoanalysis. It is in the domain of what the philosophical tradition called practical philosophy that the Lacanian anti-philosophy is most forcefully developed. Thus, while all of Lacan's seminars reference the philosophical tradition, his seventh seminar, *The Ethics of Psychoanalysis*, with its focus on the tradition of philosophical reflection on ethics running from Aristotle through Kant and Bentham, seems one of Lacan's more philosophically imbued works. It is especially with regard to the question of the possibility of an ethics of psychoanalysis that we find Lacan's deepest engagement with the texts of classical philosophy. In this regard, the Lacanian anti-philosophy might well turn out to be one of the ways Lacan ironically articulates a more profound engagement with the European philosophical heritage. Especially in his work on the ethics of psychoanalysis, Lacan develops a curious philosophy as an anti-philosophy.

This philosophical element in Lacan's work, especially his overall concern for the ethics of psychoanalysis, certainly seems to distance him from the teachings of his master, Freud, who, in his autobiographical study, is quite clear about his disdain for any attempt to link psycho-analysis with philosophy and to make it subservient to a moral system.[2] While these are certainly not Lacan's overall goals, it is nonetheless true that Lacan is much closer to philosophy and to a philosophical reflection on the ethical directions of psychoanalysis than Freud ever was. Lacan's first concern in his seventh seminar is not for determining a set of moral directives and imperatives that would guide action or decide upon its moral worth, nor for determining the "meaning of life." Rather, it seems more concerned with the "directions for a cure," and the questioning of the "ends" of analysis. It is also concerned with the practical task of enabling his patients to answer for themselves the question that hangs over each of their lives: "Why am I suffering?" Thus, Lacan's seminar can be read as being tangent with an important European philosophical tradition, namely, the "care of the soul."

What is the beginning point, that point where the question of an ethics arises, for an ethics of psychoanalysis? Let us begin with Lacan's late seminars of the early 1970s, *Seminar XIX*, entitled . . . *Ou Pire*, and *Seminar XX*, *Encore*. Here, Lacan is discussing what by all appearances seems to be a strikingly classical philosophical proposition: *Ya D'L'UN* ("There is something of the One"). Being is *L'UN*. What is this *UN*, from which Lacan derives, however, not the philosophical foundations of unity and necessary sameness grounding the dominion of the many, but rather "pure difference," and this almost unreadable anagram of *ennui*, Lacan calls *L'UNIEN* ("oneyance," is offered by Marini's *Jacques Lacan: The French Context* as a possible translation of Lacan's neologism).[3] Lacan's invention and usage of such strange new terms arises as a result of his probing a dimension of language hitherto untouched and unthought by the philosophical tradition. The term *L'UN*, for example, is, in Lacan's discourse, an instance of what he calls *lalangue*, which might be defined as the chaotic drift of polysemy that is the both the limit and the "under-pinning" (*supporte*) for language, a dimension especially of speaking that although it is investigated only in and through language nevertheless works against it, turning it, bending into new forms. *Lalangue* is thus a dimension that may be said to "support" language (taken in the sense of being a more formal and grammatical discourse), but in this case, "to support" would mean "bearing up" or "putting up" with language. But more importantly, the invention of such neologisms also shows that Lacan's critical distancing of his work from the philosophical tradition will not be worked out only in the domain of concepts, but that it will also be worked out in the domain and field of language itself. Through the usage of such terms as *L'UN* and *L'UNIEN*, Lacan was playfully bending language so as to think against the philosophical tradition of the One, particularly against the idea that the "One" could provide some sort of ultimate foundation or unity of thought and being.

Lacan's ethics of psychoanalysis develops over the course of his seminars into an ethic that thus has its foundations, its ends and its beginnings, in *L'UN*, taken precisely as a lack of foundations. Throughout his seminars, Lacan takes pains to undercut every possibility of there being any theoretical foundation, any metalanguage or metaphysical grounding for the ethics of psychoanalysis. There is no metalanguage, as he often says in his seminars, there is no transcendental "idea of reason" active here, no moral idea given in consciousness. Ethics arises only in relation to something other, some other source, something other than a pregiven desire for the Good or an *a priori* reign of moral law. Hence, while Lacan's seminars thus may speak of "the One," *L'UN*—"the One which is not just any signifier," as he says—it is always something indeterminate, a "between," located between the phoneme, the word, and the sentence, indeed, between the whole of thought. But, again, Lacan's is not a philosophy of Oneness, but a philosophy—an "anti-philosophy?"—of difference. For Lacan, it is always a question of the signifier, its place, its function, its determining role in the unconscious and so in the whole architecture of thinking and the subject. One might ask in this regard, is "the One" a "master signifier from which the 'whole of thought' emerges"? "It is," Lacan says, "what is at stake in what I call the master signifier" (S20: 143/131). We shall be returning to these themes over the course of the other essays in this collection.

For now, this addresses our question concerning the beginning point for an ethics of psychoanalysis. The "master signifier" is the point of inscription of the subject into what Lacan's 1960 essay "The Subversion of the Subject and the Dialectic of Desire" (published in *Écrits*), calls the "treasure trove" of the signifier. This is the One mark, the "unary trait" (*trait unaire*), the mark of the One that makes "one," that makes one something countable, a "subject," a "person," a solitary "soul." The question at issue in the later Lacan, the Lacan of the twentieth seminar, concerns not only the question of ethics, but also the question of knowledge, of the love of knowledge, and of truth, and the love of truth. "What is knowledge?" Lacan asks. How does one "learn to learn"? What is the significance of these seemingly epistemological dimensions for ethics? We can recall that for Plato, ethics required knowledge, self-knowledge. Such knowledge would defeat self-delusion and ignorance of the Good. Virtue is or requires such knowledge, Plato famously claims. But, Lacan asks, what kind of knowledge is this? Is it knowledge of the truth of desire or does it mask that truth? Whereas the philosopher may puzzle over whether or not such knowledge (in the sense of *connaissance*) can be taught to others, the psychoanalytic Lacanian might wonder if it is even desirable that knowledge of the truth of desire (in the sense of *savoir*) be something that can even be framed pedagogically and transmitted as a doctrine or is it closer to *jouissance*? For, is it ever univocal? Does it speak in one voice? Or is it strikingly individual and polyvocal? What would be the role of a master and of mastery in connection with such knowledge (*savoir*)?

By introducing the stammering, polysemic dimension of *lalangue*, Lacan's work from the early 1970s shows that all such "practical knowledge," insofar as it requires the regulated working of grammar, logic, and univocality, also has as its "other side," as its incarnate edge and lining, the stammering polysemy, the *jouissance* of what Lacan is here calling *lalangue*, a dimension from which communication and articulation arise and upon which they break and shatter. Beyond the question usually asked by ethicists as to whether it is reason or emotions that dominate ethical life, Lacan shows in his account of the genesis of the ethical subject on the basis of the signifier and of the unconscious, how there is a dimension both beyond and beneath the domains of reason and the emotions, something that can only be approached and accounted for from the perspectives of both the structure of the signifier and the embodied, vocal stammering of *lalangue*. Lacan is asking, in other words, as to the emergence of the ethical subject as a subject not just of reason and the emotions, but as a subject of language, desire, and the unconscious. In doing so, he shows the spoken dimensions of polysemy and of disarticulation that are the effects and the affects of the unconscious. What Lacan seeks is to put the question concerning both the beginnings and the ends of ethics on a much wider stage than it has had in the classical philosophical tradition. Lacan's seminars are thereby calling into question the classical philosophical orientations of ethical life as being first of all concerned with the mastery of the emotions, as being bound up with or requiring a kind of ethical "knowledge" or a capacity to reason that will be able to ultimately master the turmoil of the passions and appetites, a "practical wisdom" (*Phronesis*), as it has been called in that tradition. He is calling into question the whole trajectory of the philosophical conception of the ethical subject as being first of all a knowing subject and the subject of such knowledge, one who is a rational hearer/interlocutor of a philosophical-ethical discourse, and who, through his/her ethical choices, will realize his/her potentiality by putting this knowledge into action and so attaining his/her ultimate Good. It is, in short, the tradition of the "care of the soul" that is in question here, a tradition that begins in the early Socrates and Plato, continues strongly through Aristotle and the Stoic and Epicurean traditions, and that has continued down into modernity in the work of the Czech philosopher Jan Patočka, for example. It is this tradition Lacan wishes to "demystify" by showing that it has missed and occluded something deeply fundamental, namely, the dimensions of desire in relation to the functioning of language and the unconscious.

In doing so, the ethics of psychoanalysis puts another, wider perspective into play, a perspective that takes as its beginning point the discovery of the unconscious and the ascension of the ethical subject in and through the reign of the signifier. It shows how the discourses on ethics and the practical wisdom they have to offer both inhabit and yet must always attempt to put at a safe distance the dimension of the effects and affects of language, of desire, the body, and the unconscious. By the time of his twentieth seminar, Lacan is saying that the ethical subject philosophically posited as a knowing subject is but something "supposed," "but a dream," as he puts it, "a dream of the body insofar as it speaks, for there is no such thing as a knowing subject (*il n'y a pas de sujet connaissant*)." Beyond the measured articulations of the philosophical subject "who knows," and who first of all has "self-knowledge," Lacan approached through the neologism *lalangue* another dimension of the enjoyment of speaking that he calls the *jouissance* of speech, "an enjoying of speech qua *jouissance* of speech (*parole jouissance en tant que jouissance de parole*)," that is quite beyond and inaccessible to the measured articulations of the philosophical subject who knows what he/she wants (S20: 127/114). But this reference to *jouissance* requires that not only the enjoyment but also the suffering introduced by language be stressed. The effects of the introduction of language into the living human being are not always so salutary in Lacan's view as they may be for the philosophical ethical tradition, where the measured eloquence of truth brings self-mastery and has a healing effect, for language in the Lacanian universe introduces not only mastery and salvation, it also brings subjection. It can even be seen as a parasite, a disease, virulence, an Other in which the subject, from the day it is named, from the day it is a subject, is captured and defined. The aforementioned *jouissance de parole* is also bound with suffering. Words bring suffering by introducing a primal tear in life ultimately traced in the splendor and misery of *jouissance*. And it is Lacan's teaching that it is from this very binding of pleasure and suffering, of mastery and subjection, that we come to define and attain all that we call "the goods" of life, the goods that are the objects of desire and that are necessary to sustain our being. Thus, Lacan's ethics of psychoanalysis was in many ways an ethics of speech and the speaking subject, an ethic folded and enfolded across the surfaces of *jouissance* and suffering that defines the being of a speaking subject. Not just a theory that looked down, as though from a bird's-eye point of view, on the subject trapped in the maze of language and desire, Lacan's ethics of speech entered into that maze; it was first of all a practice that sprang from the twisting, turning liminal surfaces of speech it both encountered and enacted in the analytic situation.

Such perspectives can also be illustrated and approached by looking for a moment at a little experiment Lacan summarizes in his twentieth seminar (see S20: "The Rat in the Maze," session of June 26, 1973). Again, the question primarily concerns knowledge: "What is knowledge?" Knowledge in the sense of scientific knowledge is always linked to speech; it is a capacity of speaking beings. Speaking is, thus, a kind of limit: it demarcates those beings that have the logos, and those that do not. Studying, investigating this limit is crucial, for Lacan. A speaking being asks, "What is knowledge?" "How does one learn to learn?" In order to answer these questions, a scientist, one who is supposed to know, one who loves to know the truth, invents an experiment. The scientist asks, if knowledge is a capacity of speaking beings, what about those beings that do not speak? What can we learn from them? What do they have to teach us? It is in this regard that experiment shows in connection with language and the symbolic order precisely how and where desire arises.

A rat is placed in a maze. It must find its way to a button that it must learn to push in order to obtain its reward, its "good," the nourishment necessary for the maintenance of its being. For the researcher, the rat is first identified with its body and with its bodily needs for nourishment. These are recognized starting points. But when, in the repeated insistence of its need, the rat learns to find its way and to push that button, a transformation occurs that sparks Lacan's interest. When the rat is placed in the maze as part of the experiment, the rat itself is no longer just a body, but a "rat-unit." It becomes a countable one, a "unit." This marks the first ascension of the rat body into the discourses of science and knowledge, which is the discourse of mathematics. Submitted to the discipline of the maze, the rat becomes a "rat-unit," and so, like all such units, it becomes something repeatable and replaceable. The key moment inside the maze—and the way out—is when the rat extends its paw and touches the button. The button is itself a sign, and when the rat reaches to touch it so that its "good," its reward, will appear, an appearing made possible by the sign, the rat itself becomes a sign. It learned (*appris*) something. It apprehended the sign by learning that it is something to be grasped (*à-prendre*); (*qu'il a appris la façon dont un mécanisme, ça se prend, qu'il a appris ce qui est* à-prendre). It grasps the sign and is itself grasped by the sign. It becomes a sign in that moment of learned reaching/apprehension. This is the moment of the "master signifier." Now the key difference between the rat and a speaking being, something Lacan calls "the subject," is that the subject extends its paw only in its acceptance of the signifying cut of castration, castration here being the operation, the cut, whereby the subject as a speaking being, the subject now defined in Lacan's ways as a signifier represented to another signifier, comes to be through the acquisition of language by occupying a place or position within the symbolic order, and so becomes a speaking subject, a subject that can learn and that can learn to love learning, to love knowledge and truth. This is the moment, the infinite moment, the infinite field where desire insinuates itself; this is the infinite field of the *L'UN*, the first name. There is something called the One (*Il y a de l'Un*) because there is this "infinite" field that opens with the signifying cut of castration. This way of formulating the problem is suggested by the title of an article on Lacan's work published in *Scilicet 5*, in September of 1972, "L'Infini et la castration."[4] What is in question here is the field, the "domain" of the emergence of language and knowledge, and so also of what Lacan is calling *lalangue*, "lalanguage," or "llanguage," for another translation.

   Lalangue, the level of the polysemic, stuttering drift of speech, is an embodied effect of the unconscious, the unconscious by and through which the body speaks and from which spoken language arises; *lalangue* is something that the unconscious, "structured like a language," "knows how" to use as its effect. In this sense, *lalangue* supports and shelters knowledge, here defined as the "know-how" (*savoir-faire*), of the unconscious. Knowledge in this sense "inhabits" *lalangue*. ("Knowledge, insofar as it resides in the shelter of *lalangue*, means the unconscious" [S20: 142/129].) *Lalangue* is there at the moment there is One, at that point of the inscription of the master signifier, where, after so many trials and errors, the subject rises and finally learns to extend its paw, to touch the button, and so get its reward, which is the nourishment necessary for its being. *Lalangue* is there at that point where the rat becomes a being grasping and being grasped by the sign. The experiment shows in small letters the big letters—the letters of the big Other—of that point of emergence of the subject, that point where, just as at that moment the rat extends its paw, so the subject transforms himself into a sign, becomes a sign in an economy of signs that regulates the relations of all knowledge, as of all marriage and exchange. This is the moment, like the rat in the maze, at which the subject is inscribed in the Other, in the lack at the heart of the Other, in the symbolic order and the whole economy of the circulation of goods and rewards by which the subject's being is both marked and sustained. Humans, like the rat, cannot leave their being behind. They must learn to find their rewards, their "goods." In order to sustain their being, to sustain the body of their being, rat and human must both submit, they must subject themselves to the maze of the sign, which is also the maze of desire. This is the point where both language and desire emerge, insofar as desire is what is left over from the articulation of need. This also is the point where "love" emerges, love as the love of knowledge and the love of truth, the kind of love spoken about in Plato's *Symposium* that leads the soul to the ultimate knowledge, the Good beyond being. This is precisely the point Lacan marks as the beginning point of ethics and of the discourse on ethics, the seminar entitled *The Ethics of Psychoanalysis*.

For our purposes, this is why this little experiment is so revealing. It shows not only that moment where the subject becomes a subject in the sense that it becomes a speaking, desiring being, one condemned to always having its being elsewhere, but it also shows how, insofar as this subject reaches for its "good," it becomes an ethical subject. The subject in the maze of language and desire brings into view *lalangue*, the language of the unconscious that "shelters" and supports knowledge and yet itself cannot be an object of knowledge.

The analogy of the rat in the maze brings into view something that is ordinarily missed: the rise of the speaking subject in and through castration and its institution as something represented by a signifier for another signifier. Knowledge implies or requires articulation. As the rat is the rat of the maze, so the subject is the subject of the unconscious. The subject as a speaking, ethical subject, the subject of the unconscious arises through castration, which is that moment it becomes a subject "represented by a signifier for another signifier," just as the rat makes itself a sign, a sign of its presence as a rat-unit, by pressing its paw at the sign of the button. With castration comes repression (*refoulement*), a primary level of repression, that is not so much a psychic structure or the more secondary repression of a specific memory, for example, as it is the effect, the logic of the signifier, which is a logic of differences. The first name, *L'UN*, is the One of pure difference.

Now, the ethics of psychoanalysis also begins with the assertion that there is an unconscious. However the psychoanalyst posits the fact of the unconscious, getting back to this unconscious is not possible for the articulations of knowledge. The truth it seeks, the truth that speaks *lalangue*, can only be half-articulated in the language of knowledge. There are barriers; there are limits. The unconscious, which, for Lacan, is not just a dark bag full of instincts but something structured, "like a language," is no doubt a kind of cause, a cause of the speaking, desiring subject. As a cause, the unconscious has its effects, which are themselves subject to being folded back, reduced (*rabattu*). Since the ethics of psychoanalysis cannot know this cause, since it cannot get back behind the barriers set up against it, it can only know its effects and the affects that arise from those effects. It can only be the knowledge of the affects of the effects of the unconscious, which are necessarily folded back, reduced, pushed back (*un rabattement des effets*) insofar as it they are potentially subversive.[5] This is a paradox of the ethics of psychoanalysis: its knowledge, its shadow-draped, half-said truth, can never be the articulation of a knowledge of causes, as Aristotle said all knowledge must be insofar as it is to be knowledge. Psychoanalysis can only be but an ambiguous articulation of the effects and the affects of an unconscious domain. This is what it pursues, what it must make do with.

So, Lacan says he cannot enter here, cannot enter the domain of the unconscious "without a hypothesis." And his hypothesis is this: The individual who is affected by the unconscious is the same individual who constitutes what I call the subject of a signifier" (S20: 142/130). It is this subject—and not the subject as one "who knows" (*connaissance*)—that must also become the ethical subject caught in the knots of desire and moral-ethical law, a subject that is bound by the limits of language and that is inscribed within the limits of the symbolic order. Among the affects of the unconscious on the subject, would also include a desire to transgress those limits, a desire, and an unavowed passion to get back behind or beyond the limits of language, to exceed the limits of the law. This is a desire for the "Real," which Lacan names as the third field in his interlinked topology of the fields of the Symbolic, the Imaginary, and the Real. With the inscription into the symbolic order comes order, comes regulations, and the reign of moral law. The real is whatever disrupts that order and that law; whatever breaks the operation of the symbolic order. Access to the real is difficult and perhaps dangerous, but also not without a certain enjoyment, a certain *jouissance*. Even the love of knowledge and the love of truth, insofar as they are ways of access to the real, are the ways of *jouissance* as access to the real. Ultimately, as we shall see in the other essays in this collection, for Lacan, this will be a feminine *jouissance*—a *jouissance* of expenditure, distinguished in Lacan's seminars from a "phallic *jouissance*" in that it cannot be put to work in the production of meanings or use values—and a "feminine way." It is this attempt at an access, however indirect, to the unconscious, an access to the "real" of the unconscious and to everything that is at the limits of language, that is so essential to Lacan's discourse on ethics, his teachings on the ethics of psychoanalysis. This makes of Lacan's ethics an ethics of the real and of *jouissance*, the *jouissance*, for example, of the love of knowledge and truth, the *jouissance* of the "extended paw."

We can now take this next step: While the ethics of psychoanalysis is based on the assertion, for example, that "there is an unconscious," this is an assertion of existence that is made and marked from within the horizon of the infinite and of a "beyond of being" Lacan calls ex-istence. Nothing is without it being said that it is, Lacan says: *"Il est évident que rien n'est, sinon dans la mesure où ça se dit que ça est"* (S20: 137/126). The assertions of the existence of castration qua signifying cut, and the infinite, qua mathematically articulated language of the unconscious, are thus, as statements, knotted together in the sense that the conditions for their possibility are in the same hole, the same cut, the same rupture torn in the fabric of the real through which the subject is plunged into the field of the symbolic. At the heart of the ethics of psychoanalysis one finds several such repeated and interrelated statements (*énoncé*), several essential "theorems of existence," as the *Scilicet* article previously cited calls them: "There is castration," "there is the infinite" (*il y a a de l'infini*), or, phrased mathematically, "there exists an infinite ensemble" (*un ensemble infini*), there exists a "paternal function" (*une fonction paternelle*), and, there is the One (*il y a l'Un*).[6] These are all linked to what Lacan calls the "phallic function." As such, they all arise from the same rupture Lacan continues to call castration, which is the rupture, the hole of an infinite lack at the heart of human existence, the lack of desire, marked in the inscription, the signifying cut of the master signifier. Beyond the articulations asserting existence, nothing can be said to exist. The "nothing is" (*rien n'est*) names the ex-istence, the dimension of the "beyond" existence of the subject of the unconscious insofar as its being is also a kind of beyond-being, a radical alterity, the ex-istence of the inarticulable and so inaccessible real.

We have mentioned the "infinite lack." Let us pause and consider this word, the "infinite." For Lacan, the "infinite" has essentially a mathematical definition rather than a metaphorical or a figurative one. This

shows that Lacan's discourse on the ethics of psychoanalysis, its articulations, will tend in, especially in the early 1970s, toward the language of
the *mathème*, toward formalization, as a condition for its discourse, at the
same time that it also leans toward the poetic utterance, toward the plays
of words and spoken language (his use of "*lalangue*," for example), and
toward the psychotic, private languages of a poet like James Joyce. It is
with these perspectives that the ethics of psychoanalysis finds its beginning points and its horizon, and that it returns to this infinite horizon,
the infinite "*milieu élémentaire*," the "elementary inscription" of the One,
the One of pure difference, where desire arises.[7] Its horizon is the horizon
of the infinite field where language and desire arise, and not the horizon
of death and finitude, as one finds in much of the twentieth-century
philosophy of the ethics of authenticity. If this is the case, then Lacan's
ethics, as an ethics of *jouissance* and the real, is however not an ethics of
finitude, for it finds its beginning point at that moment of the "milieu" of
the infinite. Infinite and finite are not opposed here. One might even say
that the *milieu élémentaire* of the infinite enfolds and shelters the finite,
which, in the figures of death, the famous "double death," death qua "the
death drive" (*pulsion de mort*), the infinite of repetition, and desire, open
from within its horizon. Thus, the ethics of psychoanalysis is an infinite
ethics, an ethics of the infinite, and not an ethics of the pathos of finitude.

Regarding this mathematical conception of the infinite, let us in
closing cite the paradox that Lacan says obtains in modern European
science: First, Lacan's work could be thought of as articulating a "theory
of ensembles"; a mathematics of ensembles, a logic of sets, defines his
topography, which might even be characterized as his way of writing a
poetics of the unconscious. Yet, this topography, this theory of ensembles
is not intended to be merely a *model* of the unconscious. Rather, it is
something actually produced in the realm of the unconscious. In other
words, Lacan is not attempting in his ethics of psychoanalysis to produce
a discourse *on* or *about* desire (his shall not be "a discourse *on* semblance"
as he says in the title to his eighteenth seminar [S18]), but rather a discourse that is itself the register of the effects of the unconscious. Here
is where the *Scilicet* article pinpoints a "crisis of European civilization,"
such that mathematics and science are understood to speak and work
on the basis of a terrain, the terrain of the unconscious, which would be
a subversive terrain of breaks, ruptures, and contradictions—the unconscious does not abide by the logic of noncontradiction—but at the same
time, the mathematical-scientific articulation speaks only in the language
of pure entities; it necessarily speaks a language from which all pulsions
have in some sense been exhausted, rendered safely non-contradictory,

with all their breaks and potentially disturbing movements and whirlpools plugged up, their reserves of pulsions effectively reduced, pushed away, such that the "mathematical machine," as one might call it, can finally create and deliver not only a "finished product," but a finished and resolved state of mind, as well. Phrased otherwise, one might say that at the level of the scientific-mathematic statement, the level of the *énoncé*, which is the level of the finished product, there is also a level of *énonciation* that underlies it and circumscribes it, but which has been forgotten. This forgetting, however, is no doubt essential to its being what it is. Behind or within every "said" there is also a "saying" that must be pushed back, reduced, or censored in some way in order to insure the operation of the scientific and mathematical apparatus. And as long as we're at it, let us stress the parallels with truth here: behind every truth conceived as the truth value of a statement, which pretty much defines scientific truth, there is a truth as *aletheia*, a truth, in other words, that both gives and reveals, and in this giving also withdraws and conceals, a truth that cannot be said, a truth only half-said. This truth goes unremarked in scientific statements, but it is there, an unapproachable level of "ex-istence." To characterize this situation as a "crisis," as the author of the *Scilicet* essay claims, shaking the European scientific discourse down to its roots, in some ways obviously echoes the Husserlian conception of a "crisis of the European sciences." Indeed, it is tempting to suggest that both Lacan and Husserl might agree, but in different ways and according to different criteria, that the universality and objectivity of scientific conceptions—and this would be especially true for the so-called sciences of the human soul, the "psycho-logos"—and the regulated functioning of their conceptual apparatuses, have been uprooted, displaced from their sources and origins. Not that this situation is something that could have been avoided, or that things could have been otherwise. Nonetheless, in the spirit of this, Lacan would not wish to repeat the degradation of what one might call the infinite discourse of desire, as the *Scilicet* essay phrases it, which is certainly something one finds in the "master discourses" of philosophical ethics and morality. Instead, Lacan would oppose to any such discourse "*on* truth," or "about truth," a discourse that, like a seismographic needle, registers the trembling effects of the truth of desire, a discourse that is the register of the effects and the affects not of a pure object but of a pure, infinite lack. This would be not an ethics *about* the infinite, but an infinite, or rather, an "in-finite" ethics.[8]

Not only desire and death, the word "love" also returns here within this horizon of the infinite. It must be said at this juncture that Lacan's ethics of psychoanalysis has "love" as its strongest passion and in some ways its guiding ideal. In his eighth seminar, for example, he maintains that he has always been passionately interested in love, one of the oldest and most essential of passions. But, again, this is not the sort of "love" whereby two become One. Lacan made two important remarks in his seminar on "love" and "the limits of love," the seminar entitled *Encore*, given in 1972–1973: First, that "love is the linchpin (*pivot*) of everything that has been instituted on the basis of analytic experience" (S20: 39/40). In saying this, Lacan might well be referring to "doctor love," which he says in his seventh seminar has almost become a guiding ideal for analytic practice, something active in "the transference." In certain circles of psychoanalytic practice that Lacan rejects, such love is highly valued for the way it is essential in their idea of a "cure" as identification with the ego of the analyst. Second, he defines love as "lack," as "giving what one does not have." Now since it is precisely "truth" that one does not have, not the whole truth, anyway—it is the truth that is always lacking—we could say that Lacan's discourse gives the gift of truth, that it constitutes a kind of "love of truth" that at the same time is a questioning of the philosophical "love of truth." Does such an anti-philosophical gesture not yet speak from the very heart of philosophical discourse, which above all others, leaps from the embers of a "love of truth"? Perhaps. In its ethical-practical dimensions, Lacan will situate this passion called love not just in terms of truth, but more importantly in terms of the field of "the Other." But what Lacan is calling "the Other" must not be confused with that enigma-laden field ethical and political philosophers call "intersubjectivity" and "community," whereby the Other is taken to mean the face of the other, of the other as "neighbor," in other words, the "other" as site and source of the moral command to "love one's neighbor." Lacan's seminars distance themselves from such traditional discourses on love. It is not a love for the neighbor as Other that is at issue here. For Lacan the Other qua neighbor is the Other qua "symbolic order" that is in us "more than us." It is a question of a love—like the other passions of hatred and ignorance—that does not originate in us, certainly not in the depths of our souls, but that comes to us and is provided by this "Other" (*Autre*), by the Other as lack and by the lack that is in the Other.

A questioning of truth, a question of making truth speak, is also an important part of Lacan's seminars on ethics, and this both brings his discourse close to philosophy and maintains a distance from it. This is not the sort of philosophical saying of truth whereby truth is opposed to semblance in the sense that truth is opposed to what is in some way false. Truth is semblance for Lacan, where semblance refers to an important function of language and to the play of masquerade, being semblances that are lures, that are "semblance(s) of being," as *Encore* puts it (S20: 84). The whole world knows that there is nothing truer than that truth that speaks in the enunciation, "I lie." An unbreakable truth here speaks. This enunciation is thus far from the shadow of the false. But who or what is it that speaks in this enunciation that says, "I" (*Je*)? It is semblance itself, Lacan says in his eighteenth seminar, *D'un discours qui ne serait pas du semblant* (S18: 14). Moreover, as Lacan continues in that seminar, semblance is continuous with discourse; it a question of a *semblant* that regulates the economy of discourse (S18: 18), an economy that is also an economy of truth insofar as the truth is not only what obtains from within language as something said, but especially insofar as truth is always only "half-said" (*mi-dire*). These are the Lacanian theses and questions on truth that we shall be following in our reading of Lacan's seminars.

In all these ways, Lacan's *The Ethics of Psychoanalysis* is philosophical not only in its passion, but also in its purpose, which is to question the possibilities of and the limits for an ethics today. If Lacan finds those limits in the field of desire, which is to say, in the field of the signifier, then Lacan's discourse on ethics is in some ways a "critique of desire." It seems to ask as to an Other source of ethics, and another heading, as well. How does this relate to a possible questioning not only of ethical discourse, but also to political discourse, and to the relations between ethics and politics, as well?

With these perspectives in mind, let us return now to what was posed earlier: However Lacan's book, *The Ethics of Psychoanalysis*, stirs up philosophical questioning, it is also curious for the way it succeeded in casting Lacan as an "anti-philosopher." Is this correct? Is this a helpful way of characterizing Lacan's confrontation with philosophy? It certainly has the merit of bringing the relationship between Lacan's teachings and those of the European tradition of philosophy more closely into question. Lacan indeed says in his seventh seminar that he wanted to "demystify" the classical European philosophical ethical traditions. It is from Freud's discovery of the unconscious that a whole new ethical domain presented itself throughout Lacan's seminars, one seemingly opposed to philosophy, a domain that might be misunderstood by philosophers, but that could not be ignored. Freud's discovery, to which Lacan returned with a messianic sense of urgency from the 1950s through the 1960s, thus provided him with the hypotheses and the language that made a stark questioning of the European classical traditions in ethical and moral discourse a theoretical and a practical necessity. This questioning is also perhaps his finest philosophical moment.

BETWEEN "CARE" AND "THE CURE": PSYCHOANALYSIS HAS AN ETHIC

So, "Toward an Ethics of Psychoanalysis." As we have seen, the path toward such an ethics is the path of demystification. Just as Plato, for example, had to demystify the sway that the poets held over Greek education and ethical life in order to clear the path toward a philosophical ethics, so Lacan uses the poets Shakespeare, Sophocles, and Claudel, for example, to demystify the sway that the philosophical tradition, especially that of the "care of the soul," has had over the European ethical imagination. He does so in order to clear the path toward a new ethics of psychoanalysis and a new way of articulating the truth of desire. But this is a double path and a double demystification. There is not only the path of the demystification of the philosophy and of "the care of the soul"; there is also the demystification of the practices and theories of psychoanalysis and psychotherapy itself, the path of the demystification of "the cure."

An early essay, "Variations on the Standard Treatment," initially published in 1955 at the request of Henri Ey for the *Encylopédie Médicochirurgicale* and republished in 1966 in *Écrits*, with changes and updates, gives us an important indication regarding the role and place of an ethics in Lacan's teachings and his psychoanalytic practice. In this essay, Lacan makes an important, guiding distinction between psychoanalysis and psychotherapy. The deciding difference between these two is that psychoanalysis has an ethic; it possesses a "rigor that is in some sense ethical, without which any treatment, even if it is filled with psychoanalytic knowledge, can only amount to psychotherapy."[9]

As Lacan continues in this essay, the question of rigor bears on the requirement for a "formalization," a "theoretical formalization," which he says has not been provided because it has all too often been confused with a "practical formalization," which Lacan says would in turn become nothing more than a set of rules regarding what is and what is not to be done during the analytic session.[10] Such theoretical formalization will continue to develop over the course of Lacan's seminars to the point where mathematics and logic become the key discourses for his theoretical work.

An important question for us shall be the bearing of this "theoretical formalization" on philosophy. What is the relation between this theoretical formalization, as Lacan calls it, and "practical philosophy," on the philosophical formalization of ethics and politics?

For Lacan, the concern for a "rigor" and for an "ethics" bears directly on the question of the goals or ends of analysis, something he touches on in the opening pages of *Seminar VII*. What, he asks, is to become of the traditional, guiding ideals of analysis: the ideal of "human love," of "authenticity," and of "non-dependence"? Shall these be maintained uncritically? Clearly, he concludes, the ethics of psychoanalysis will involve an "effacement," a "setting aside," and a "withdrawal" such that the it shall be distanced from the sort of philosophical ethics that preceded it, namely the ethics of "good character," the ethics of "habits, good and bad habits," (S7: 10/19) for that ethical tradition, rooted as it was in the teachings of Plato and Aristotle, is an ethics of "improvement," and so is an ethical tradition that became identified in Lacan's seminars with a kind of orthopedics of the human soul.

In this 1955 essay, Lacan asks whether it is the overall intention of psychoanalysis to evaluate itself in terms of whether or not an "improvement" in the patient has been effected. How can psychoanalysis make its assessments according to such terms as "improved,' "much improved," or "cured?"[11] Even Freud, in Lacan's view, only saw the "cure" as "an added benefit (*la guérison comme bénéfice de surcroît*) of analysis and not its motivation. In fact, Freud expressed caution regarding the "misuse of the desire to cure." Lacan: "This is so ingrained in him (Freud) that, when an innovation in technique is based upon this desire (to cure), he worries deep inside and even reacts inside the analytic group by raising the automatic question: 'Is that still psychoanalysis?'"[12] Perhaps one of the chief reasons for this scruple regarding the desire to cure is an inner uncertainty about precisely what it means to have brought about a "cure." Would it mean to 'normalize'? Would it mean that the patient, in a completed "transference," has successfully identified him/herself with the supposedly active, normal functioning of the ego of the analyst? Would it mean that the patient has finally achieved a "normal" genitally based sex life? Would it amount to "happiness," entailing the "exclusion of the bestial desires," (S7: 13), the telos par excellence of ethical thought since the ancient Greeks? Is psychoanalysis an "orthopedics" of desire? (See S7: 11) Such were some of the goals set by many analytic parishioners, according to Lacan, and it was such perspectives and such performative goals that Lacan questioned throughout his teachings.

Clearly, then, "the cure," at least in the sense of bringing about the realization of human happiness, was not to be the deciding criteria for an ethics of psychoanalysis. Rather, the sought-for ethic in Lacan's work seems to be more concerned with the desire of the analyst in the analytic situation. Would the analyst, in other words, demand a cure that would in some way meet the demand of the analysand for happiness? After all, Lacan's early audiences were comprised for the most part of aspiring or practicing analysts. If the desire of the analyst was not to be chiefly aimed at a desire 'to cure,' in this conventional sense of the term, what, then, was its objective? Perhaps there is an ethical dimension here by which there is more at stake in the analytic act than restoring in the analysand's ego an imaginary sense of well-being and 'happiness.'

Lacan's 1955 essay establishes three criteria that he continued to explore in his subsequent seminars: First, the dynamic of psychoanalysis, which meant that "formalization" would not lead to a static structuralization, but would concern the "pulsation" of the opening and closing of the unconscious. Second, the topography, which in Freud's work first divided the human psyche into the three systems of the unconscious, the preconscious, and the conscious, and in a later topography divided into three agencies of the ego, superego, and the id. Lacan developed his own 'topology' as a way of developing a theoretically rigorous (i.e., nonintuitional) structural differentiation of the three fields of the imaginary, the symbolic, and the real. This is not just a metaphorical expression of the structure of the field of the psychoanalytic adventure; rather the topology is that structure itself. This topology privileges the signifying "cut," or *coupure*, by which a continuous transformation can be distinguished from a discontinuous one. This has an important bearing on treatment. Using the example of a Möebius strip, Lacan shows how the "traversal of a fantasy," as he calls it would be a continuous transformation such that the subject, the analysand, would not have to make a leap from the inside of a fantasy to its outside. A discontinuous transformation, on the other hand, would be brought about when the analyst brings about an interpretation of the subject's desire—and this is what analysis offers, namely, "interpretation"— that would modify the structure of that desire in a radical way, effecting a complete and discontinuous transformation of it.[13] The third criterion named by Lacan in his 1955 essay is that of an economy, which, in Freud, refers to the "economic point of view." This concerns the circulation and distribution of a quantifiable energy that can increase and decrease. In terms of the treatment, this allowed Freud to scientifically understand neurotic symptoms expressed by patients who felt that "there was something in me that was stronger than me," and by the energetics of sexual discharges that often triggered neurotic symptoms.[14] This also relates to the "transformation of the energy of desire, which makes possible the idea of the genesis of repression," that and the "attraction of transgression" that Lacan singles out as an important, indeed decisive ethical dimension of analytic practice (S7: 6 and 2, respectively).

These criteria only sketch the most general levels of conceptualization in Lacan's hands. They were also continuously transformed, enriched, and carried beyond themselves in a movement he calls "the principle of extraterritoriality."[15] Each of them opened a new level—better, a *renewed* level of questioning—that came to define *The Ethics of Psychoanalysis*. A new level and a new way of envisioning the ethical subject, Lacan's was thus an ethic that surpassed, or at least sought to surpass, the limitations of the sort of "ego analysis" and "object relation" theory more typical in the psychoanalytic doxa of his times, thereby taking psychoanalysis in new directions.

Hence, the first criterion, that of the dynamic, not only resists the stultifying effects of a static, structural approach in psychoanalysis, but it also effectively downgrades the "ego" in relation to a new privileging of the unconscious, which is shown to be dynamic rather than static, and so renews Freud's concerns for the importance of the death drive and the "beyond" of the pleasure principle. Speech, desire, and death are thus linked, dynamically entangled. No longer captivated by the "ego" and its trembling before death and finitude, the Lacanian ethics can now take its start from the horizon of the in-finite.

The second criterion, whereby the Freudian topography becomes a Lacanian topology, is of fundamental importance for it occupies a place where the topoi of the imaginary, the symbolic, and the real overlap. It is here that Lacan encounters not only the whole question of the formation of the ethical-political "subject," but the question, as well, of the relation of the subject to the community, the ethical to the political dimensions of human community. This criterion shall allow us to see just how Lacan proposes to completely recast the philosophical perspectives of these domains.

As for the third criterion, that of the economic, this is a level both theoretical and theatrical, a level with its own formalities, rigors, as well as its requisite ethical, political, and poetical dimensions. This is the level of *jouissance*. In that it marks the very limits of what can be said, *jouissance* is the most insistent ethical question and conundrum for psychoanalysis. Where *jouissance* is conceptualized and articulated in terms of a double economy of production and expenditure, it is a *jouissance* that not only simmers across the surfaces of the poetic, tragic, and dramatic discourses, it also infuses the Lacanian psychoanalytic discourse, as well, the discourse of his famous seminars, the discourse that gives voice to the "I who am speaks the truth." Is this articulation of *jouissance* not the central anti-philosophical moment of Lacan's "ethics of psychoanalysis"? And where Lacan speaks of death and desire does he not also transform, "demystify," as he says, a monumental tradition of ethics, that of the "care of the soul," by placing at its center this decentering dimension of *jouissance*, something that tradition must exclude, something that, from the standpoint of a deeply traditional and rational outlook, it was even constitutively necessary to exclude? Where the ethics of the traditions was an ethics of limits, Lacan's ethics of psychoanalysis is an ethics of transgression and expenditures, an ethics of *jouissance*. Demystification is thus the reinscription of *jouissance*, of transgression and expenditure, in the heart of that tradition.

Throughout these criteria, the paths of demystification can always be shown to lead back to a fundamental question in Lacan's work, "What does it mean to speak?"[16] What shall the ethics of psychoanalysis be when it so situates itself in language rather than in the rhythms and process of biological processes? The question of the ends, taken in all its definitive rigor, the question of what Lacan's 1955 essay calls the "endpoints of analysis," is the question of the limits of analysis; thus, the limit of the endpoint, this is what comes into view in Lacan's teachings on the ethics of psychoanalysis.[17] It is here, at the endpoint thus marked, that the "principle of extraterritoriality" becomes most active, for it is here that the sorts of questions the analyst begins to ask can also be seen as fundamental to the great and classical discipline of the question, namely, philosophy, philosophy as found in all its massive weight in the work of Plato and Aristotle, of Kant and Hegel, the philosophy that finds its ethic most importantly in the great tradition of the "care of the soul," or "the self," as it came to be phrased in more modern usages. It then becomes for Lacan the mission of finding from within that tradition the "principle of extraterritoriality," the "extimacy" that lies within it, that is essential to it and that yet brings it to its limits and opens it from within itself, a wound so essential to its very life that must never be closed, "cured," or healed. Thus, Lacan's ethics of psychoanalysis offers not only a new level of practice, a new way of treatment for a particular analysand. It is also where he most acutely defined and gave dramatic shape to his confrontation with philosophy, especially with the philosophical tradition of the "care of the soul/self."

WHAT IS THE ULTIMATE DESTINATION OF THE LACANIAN DOUBLE PATH OF DEMYSTIFICATION?

Two general concluding and summarizing orientations emerge.

First, through the notion of a "variation on the standard treatment," the practice of psychoanalysis, as developed in Lacan's seminars, especially those of the early and middle 1960s, is constructed around a return to Freud. The texts of the "Fathers" and "Masters," Freud, Aristotle, and Hegel, are read side by side. The cure and the "care of the soul" thus interweave in a textual tapestry that seeks to go beyond the limits of each. Moreover, there seems a reversal is operative here: no longer is it philosophy that shall provide the truth about psychoanalysis, rather it is a reconceptualized psychoanalysis that shall tell the truth about philosophy, at least the truth about its relation to the truth of desire. And that truth shall show that the philosophical tradition, in denying or discounting the Freudian truth of the unconscious, never went far enough, that it only dealt in half-truths. Nonetheless, that tradition and its half-truths was something that Lacan never felt he could ignore. Indeed, he was always recommending it to its audiences as essential reading.

Thus, a second question: Does the path toward an ethics of psychoanalysis, the path of demystification, lead Lacan's thought to a point that is somehow outside of philosophy? Is Lacan's teaching an anti-philosophy such that it might be counted among the enemies of philosophy, another of the skeptics and ironists who would like to knell the death of philosophy? There is no easy answer for this, as the other essays in this collection show. Yet, it must be asserted from the outset that Lacan's thought is no doubt subtler than being a simplistic anti-philosophy. It might be more fruitful to read it as a way of listening, perhaps, to what the philosopher has to say, as though the philosophical text is in the position of the analysand, whereby it is then the analyst's role to adopt the position of death, marking a kind of density in the hollow of being, being, a bottomless silence and non-being, and from this position to question philosophy such that it is able to "traverse its own fantasies" of mastery, of Truth and Oneness, and, as though in a "continuous transformation," or, in the midst of yet another breathtaking interpretation, to bring it to the limit, to the "endpoints," where philosophy, where philosophical thought, the great tradition of the question of the meaning of being, undergoes a radical, "discontinuous transformation."

2

PHILOSOPHY'S PREPARATION
FOR DEATH

> Who, as fearlessly as this clinician (Freud-Lacan), so firmly rooted
> in the everydayness of human suffering, has questioned life as to its
> meaning—not to say that it has none, which is a convenient way of
> washing one's hands of the matter, but to say that it has only one,
> that in which desire is borne by death.
>
> —Jacques Lacan, *The Direction of the*
> *Treatment and the Principles of Its Powers*[1]

It might seem that Lacan is not really interested in ethics at all. He says
that he is not looking for a new route to human happiness and well-
being. Nor does he wish to refine Kant's deontological ethic with a new
determination of the moral law and its relation to desire. Certainly, Lacan
does raise these questions, but his purpose is to put the whole question
of the human good and the relation of law and desire—the traditional
frontiers of philosophical ethics—on an entirely new footing and to bring
them to a new articulation.

This position can seem anti-philosophical. In Badiou's reading of
Lacan, for example, we meet a Lacan who presents himself as an outsider
of philosophy, perhaps an anti-philosopher. Alain Badiou describes him
in this way, saying it is even "perilous to approach Lacan from a philosophical point of view."[2] To point out the anti-philosophical dimensions
of Lacan's thought, Badiou focuses on the relation between Lacanian
psychoanalysis and, not Hegel, but Plato, which he describes in terms
of "rivalry," "contestation," and "rupture." But, however set aside, surpassed, or deconstructed, Plato's philosophy in fact remains a reference or
a touchstone for Lacan. His eighth seminar was a long interpretation of
Plato's *Symposium* dialogue, showing the relations and ruptures between
Plato's philosophical usage of the themes of love, desire, and truth and
their usage in Lacanian psychoanalysis. Love and truth may be two of

35

the great Platonic themes, in relation to the soul, that Lacan returned to again and again. Other essays in this collection take up these themes.

For now, let us question the Lacanian demystification of philosophy in terms of a notion crucial to Lacan's *Seminar VII*: the death drive. If, as in Plato, ethical life was in some ways a "preparation for death," whereby death's "sting" was greatly diminished in that it stung only the body and left the immortal soul free, and in fact liberated that soul from its imprisonment in the body, what is the relationship toward death in the Lacanian ethic of psychoanalysis for which there is certainly no immortal soul to care for nor is there any destination of that soul in an afterlife?

As we have seen, far from being an outright enemy of philosophy, Lacan is perhaps better understood as saying that something essential to philosophy has, probably from necessity, been set aside as too destabilizing or unapproachable, something that thus marks the limits for philosophy, a limit beyond which it cannot proceed. For Lacan, this limit is not just death, not just the act of dying, but specifically what he calls "the death drive," the Freudian *Todestrieb*, which Lacan translates as *la pulsion de mort*. Badiou marks this limit and presents the psychoanalytic rupture with Platonic ontology by way of a resonance he brings into view between Lacan and the pre-Socratic philosophers, especially Heraclitus. Retracing the Heideggerian route, Badiou shows how Lacan likewise deconstructs Plato by going back behind him, or before him, to a pre-Platonic thinking, particularly that of Heraclitus, that came before the ontological metaphysics of Plato, and that may have in fact conditioned it, but which was subsequently silenced, left in fragments by the tradition of thought that emerged from Plato. According to Badiou's reading—and it is hardly beyond reproach—where Plato is the philosopher of the greater, higher unity of a transcendental *Eidos*, a true philosopher of the infinite, Heraclitus is a thinker of difference and of the gap, a philosopher of the enigmas of finitude and of the lack of final resolution and closure in being. Heraclitus is the first philosopher to "allow us to think the death drive," something that was foreclosed in Plato's thought. Insofar as Plato identifies or unifies difference through the *Eidos*, "there was no room for it (the death drive)," Badiou writes,[3] despite Plato's declaration, in relation to the great thematic of the care of the soul, that philosophy "is preparation for death."

In this context, it seems that Lacan is not adopting a position outside of philosophy by which to oppose it. Rather, he thinks both with and against philosophy. He marks in philosophical discourse, as within the symbolic order as such, the hole, the absence that opens that discourse from within to what is outside it. If there is indeed an anti-philosophical moment in Lacan's thought, it turns, as we shall see, on the role and place of death in philosophical thought, but also in relation to what he calls *jouissance* and the Thing. Lacan sees traditional philosophical ethics as seeking not only to gentrify the death-drive qua traumatic drive to destruction and "the night of the world," as Slavoj Žižek describes it,[4] to pretty it up, or even to eliminate it altogether by sweeping it under the proverbial carpet, but also to legislate a rule of law, a rule of reason, by which this drive—which Lacan characterizes by an insistence and by repetition as a drive to its own extinction, the drive of all drives—could be thought, could be brought to thinking, presented, yet resisted, revealed, yet absented. As we shall see, it is along this pathway of the death drive marked in *Seminar VII* that we shall encounter what Lacan, following Freud, called "the Thing," *das Ding*. We shall also encounter the death drive's connections with truth, the truth of desire, and so, its connections with what Lacan calls "ex-istence," not the being, but the "eccentric place," the beyond-being of the subject of the unconscious.

Hence, a source for Lacan will be not only the landmark texts from the philosophical tradition stretching from Heraclitus to Hegel, but also tragic drama. It is not philosophy, not even the enigmas of Heraclitus, but tragic drama that best approaches the limits of death and desire. It is by the "oblique" and "imaginary means" of tragic drama—by Antigone's splendor, for just one example—that Lacan finds the way to present not only the interplay of death and desire in our human situation but also the profound hold that the symbolic order—the order of language, of moral law, and knowledge—has on the deepest recesses of the human organism. It is tragic drama that teaches us this, and that shows the unimaginable limits and the beyond of that symbolic order in its intersection with the category of the real. It is in tragic drama, not philosophy, according to Lacan, that one encounters the drive and the distress of death. It is by "digging into verse," as Mallarmé put it, that one encounters the abyss of death and the absence of God, forfeits the sureties of being, and is thereby brought to the limit where one must break with everything, even the traditional horizons of truth and the promise of futurity.[5] It is by digging deeper into desire through literature that one encounters the limits and the question of the outside and the inside (Freud's "*Frage des Aussen und Innen*"), a limit Lacan posed in terms of the limits of the symbolic order, where it gives way to the Thing and the real, dimensions of loss which, like death, have been excised and foreclosed (*Verwerfung*) by the symbolic. It is tragic poetry, not philosophy, that shows us how they are already there in their destructive and creative force, both inside and outside, like the void at the center of a ring, or torus.

This brings us to some key questions that frame our reading of *Seminar VII*: In view of the fundamental character of the death drive for Lacan—and if, as Lacan says, "desire borne by death" is the "one meaning" of life—what are the ends of psychoanalysis?

If the death drive is such a fundamental dimension of human experience, then, clearly, it cannot be merely set aside or overcome such that a higher state of happiness and well-being can be realized. Would not the end purpose of psychoanalytic practice be to confront this "meaning"? But how can this be confronted? How can such a thing as "desire borne by death" constitute a "meaning" of life that could be taken up within life? How is this a "meaning" not only in the bare sense of being a significance, but in the broader sense of giving a human life a purpose, a reason for being? For the existentialist, for Camus, for example, the question of the "meaning of life" was, thus, *the* philosophical question. Is Lacan also in this tradition?

Granted for argument's sake that "desire borne by death" is a "meaning," would this not transform ethical life into being the pursuit of, the desire for, not a "Good" but for "death"? Would not the core of an ethical practice be transformed by this conception of human desire that entails not the fulfillment of human possibilities but rather their destitution? Moreover, if not happiness, as conceived in and by the philosophical ethical traditions, including that of the "care of the soul," if not a wholeness of soul, ego, or self, if not a "normality" promised and anticipated, then what is the goal and end of psychoanalysis where "desire borne by death" is the "one meaning" of life?

Perhaps in saying that "desire borne by death" is the "one" countable "meaning of life," Lacan's intention is not so much to make a new assertion answering the perennial question of the "meaning of life," which would make of Lacan's ethics of psychoanalysis only the continuation of the philosophical traditions of ethics, yet another avatar, yet another modality of a very traditional way of talking about ethics. Rather, perhaps the agenda in *Seminar VII* is to recast and upset that entire tradition by taking the question of the "meaning of life" to a point where it no longer makes any sense, where "meaning" touches upon its own death, its own destitution. Lacan probably sees the traditional philosophical perspectives on ethics as framed and trapped in the theater of a philosophical mirror stage wherein the human, ethical subject is conceived as born prematurely, a fragile, helpless and fragmented body confronting and recognizing its wholeness in the other of the mirror image before it and longing to be that wholeness. Is Lacan's psychoanalytic ethic not first and essentially the critical attempt to move beyond this ethical mirror stage, to move beyond the search for the anticipated wholeness of a "meaning of life"?

Before Hegel's *Phenomenology* made it philosophy's most challenging and dramatic task to confront the rending negativity of death and to take it up—to take up the power of this negativity—into the very architecture of Truth and to make death the productive labor and the keystone producing that architecture—before all of this, philosophy could never transform the diremptive stench of death into the glow of an imaginary meaning and wholeness of life. Meaning had to exclude death. It had to consist not in the dissolving power of negativity and death but rather in the unity of a Truth beyond the reach of death. This is why Hegel is so important for Lacan, because Hegel, too, made desire-borne death the "one meaning" of life insofar as the philosophical confrontation with death was the key to philosophy's desire for Truth ultimately realizing itself in and as Wisdom. Moreover, Hegel made the confrontation with death into a memorable scene in his *Phenomenology*—the "life-death-struggle" in the master-slave dialectic. So, to say that "desire borne by death" is the "one meaning" in human life is in many ways a very Hegelian formulation.

But it is a formulation also ultimately turned against Hegel. It must be heard as a formulation that Lacan might well intend to subvert both in the course of his seminars and in the course of his psychoanalytic practice. If the Lacanian ethics in this regard is an ethics of speech, if, contrary to the early Wittgenstein, ethics for Lacan is not among what cannot be said but only "shown," then the ethical, psychoanalytical Truth that arises in the psychoanalytic brushes with death would not wish to install or monumentalize Truth or Death itself as the ultimate and hidden meaning in life. Its pronouncements would not articulate either a timeless Truth or a terrifying Death as the "one" meaning of life, for this might make psychoanalysis a type of hermeneutics, and "death" would then be something, a "meaning," that, given the proper methodology, the proper hermeneutic, could somehow be brought from the depths to the surface of language and stated—phenomenalized, made to appear—perhaps in the form of a proposition, or in a form of life, as the statement of a Truth that would guarantee that life is not "for nothing." In Lacan's work, the relationship between language and death is completely different than this familiar scheme. The Lacanian ethics of psychoanalysis is therefore first a disruption of this hermeneutical scheme, a form of resistance to the systematic statement of a philosophical meaning of life taken as the key element and link in the triumvirate of the True, the Good, and the Beautiful. Must the Lacanian ethic not first and fundamentally be a resistance to the Hegelian way of taking up death, whereby death, "desire borne by death," is made into an effective and essential element—that of the "labor of the Negative"—in the system of Truth? By saying, in the form of a proposition, that "desire borne by death" is the "one meaning" of life, is the Lacanian ethic not undermining the very meaning of "one-ness" and "meaning" in life? Is the "one meaning" always going to be "not one"? Is Lacan's statement not the instauration of the ethical necessity of confronting the disruption and the destitution of life that abides in every such statement, a death that takes place in language, that is to say, in desire? Disruption rather than salvation in and through the systematic statement of the ultimately religious *telos* of Truth and Oneness: is this not Lacan's desire, a desire borne by the death of philosophy?

In summation and in terms of the way ethical thinking and practice is perceived from the standpoint of psychoanalysis, where one might expect to find psychoanalysis to be entangled in the basic values of the philosophical tradition of the "care of the soul/self" (and one might even find Hegel's *Phenomenology* still entangled in this tradition), entangled in the "humanistic" values of "meaning," "Truth," "Oneness," and so on, does Lacan not likewise wish to disentangle the ethics of psychoanalysis from this tradition, and in doing so, to create new values where those of the tradition of the "care of the soul" have been devalued, and so to move beyond the limits of any conception of ethical thinking constituted as a *search* for meaning in life, a search organized around and focused upon the captivating images of an ultimately attainable self-knowledge, the *telos* of "happiness" and the Good of life? What is the status of such highest goods and values for Lacan? Does he not participate in their "devalua-tion"? In the end, do they not prove to be little more than images of a lost wholeness and resolution of life's tragic dimensions, a never again to be realized healing and suturing of the wound at the heart of human existence? Are these not symbolic images that would no doubt seek to answer a fundamental yearning, an immemorial human demand for some-thing, a measure, beyond life's fragmentation, torment, and finitude, a hallucinated "refound" object of desire, which, if attained, would bring desire to its completion? And does not psychoanalytic practice show us that this yearning, as matters turn out, in aiming for the whole of truth is also always and already aiming for something buried within the very ex-istence of our being, something unspeakable? Does not Lacanian psychoanalysis show us that any such insistence is evidence of the death drive? Does it not show us that the highest values of the Good, the True, and the Beautiful, are in some ways effects, outgrowths, and values offered up by the very insistence of the death drive, that they are both the lures and barriers to the Thing and to the real buried—but not like a hidden oneness of a "meaning"—within the very ex-istence of our being?

In pursuing these questions, we shall see how Lacan thinks both with and against this kind of thinking, especially with and against that tradition of ethical, philosophical thought in which death and desire are confronted and brought to thinking, that is to say, brought to presence and appearing in their absence as forms of finitude and negativity and so productively put to work in the realization of Absolute Self-Knowledge. Does Lacan not operate a demystification of this complex of traditional categories? How is Lacan's teaching, the teaching of *Seminar VII*, thus an ethical thinking, one that beginning with Freud and Hegel and from there into the tragic poetry of Shakespeare, Sophocles, and Claudel digs a little deeper into the paradoxes and knots of desire, truth, and death, and so calls profoundly into question the European heritage of the "care of the soul"? How is this a thinking that attempts to break the hold that a certain tradition of thought has had on the way we conceive the human situation, its goals, ends, and purposes, its duties, its obligations, and its barriers and limits? How is *Seminar VII* an attempt to move toward something new, a new way of thinking truth, death, and desire, and all else that is constitutive to human subjectivity and its chances for "happiness" and well-being?

THE SPLENDOR OF DEATH IN HEGEL'S PHENOMENOLOGY

For much of modern philosophy, for Heidegger, or Hegel, death is a mark of finitude and the question is to think the essence of human experience in relation to finitude. But, for Lacan, insofar as death is a mark of finitude, death (*la mort*) is nothing in psychoanalysis. Finitude—death—like desire, is said to be "lack." Insofar as death makes an appearance, death is lack in being. Death, as has been said of Lacanian psychoanalysis, counts only insofar as it is a "mark of the in(-)finite."[6] This means that the Lacanian ethic will not be an ethics of finitude, as one finds in the modern existential ethics of authenticity, or, perhaps, as in the Platonic-Socratic ethic of the "care of the soul," which can also be described as a technique in the philosophical task of "preparation for death." The Lacanian ethics of psychoanalysis will commence with the thought of man as a finite being only in the sense of being an infinite lack at the heart of being: not a being unto or toward death, but rather as a *desiring* being, where desire, as lack, is rooted in a death *drive* (*Trieb, pulsion*). This makes all the difference.

The pathway for this thinking commences for Lacan not only in Freud and in "the return to Freud," and not only in Heidegger, but also and importantly in Hegel's *Phenomenology of Spirit*, especially as read through Kojève's seminar in the 1930s. For Lacan, Hegel's is a "master" discourse of absolute knowledge, and death, which stalks the *Phenomenology* practically from one end to the other, is, in Lacan's words, the "absolute master." No philosophical system before Hegel's had confronted death and the death drive in quite the powerful way that Hegel did in his *Phenomenology*.

Kojève's reading of Hegel begins rather intriguingly with the dialectic of self-consciousness, a consciousness that has as its object not an inert thing, but rather the active freedom of another consciousness.

Self-consciousness, Hegel says, is desire (*Begierde*) in general. It becomes a desire for pure prestige, a desire for recognition, a desire for the other's desire. Kojève's reading strongly emphasized the fight to the death for prestige in which each seeks the recognition of the other. It emphasized how, in Hegel's *Phenomenology*, human and animal society—a phrase Lacan also uses in his second seminar—differ in that the former, human society, confronts death and so, as a desiring being, a human desiring being, "goes beyond the given reality." Human reality is thus a reality defined by self-differencing, always perpetually negating itself as reality. This is desire; this is the death that lives a human life. Death makes its debut appearance in Hegel's *Phenomenology of Spirit* in and as the life-death struggle between two self-consciousnesses. This struggle is mythic and never "really happened" at some time in the past. It is an imaginary scenario constructed retroactively and knowable only in its effects. What emerges from the life-death struggle is a dialectic of mastery and servitude, the fact that there is work and regular hours, and that a certain now unnamable *jouissance* has indeed been given up, cut off, and foreclosed in order to make work, knowledge, and life in the symbolic order possible.

It is Hegel's genius, then, to make death so appear in the life-death struggle and in the slave's trembling encounter with his own death, and so to put death to work in the *Parousia* of Being as the heart and soul of the labor of the negative through which Absolute Knowledge will be realized and the ultimate triumph of life over death secured.

Especially three general points are essential to Lacan's reading of Hegel.

First, Hegel's dialectic formulated in the life-death struggle for recognition, especially as portrayed in Kojève's reading of Hegel, the idea that desire is not just desire for an object but it is desire of the other's desire. Human desire is desire *of* desire, desire *as* desire, empty desire, desire without object, an unsatisfied desire, a "revealed nothingness," in Kojève's phrasing, "an unreal emptiness . . . the revelation of an emptiness, the presence of an absence of a reality . . . something other than a thing . . ."[7] Kojève asked, how could desire, revealed nothingness, reveal itself if not by negating everything that could present it and incarnate it, realize it and satisfy it? Lacan saw something similar in the logic of the Freudian *Verneinung*, "negation," whereby death is present in its absence, in its very negation.

Second, Hegel's *Phenomenology* situated death not just at the biological level, but at the level of the imaginary and the symbolic, as well. Death, abyssal death, the death life brings, never appears and so is always outside the phenomenology of absolute knowledge and so beyond the limits of the possible, beyond what Lacan would call the symbolic order. For it to appear, for death *to be*, it must be included within the symbolic order, it must be symbolized in a primordial act of affirmation Lacan refers to as the *Bejahung*, a term found in Freud's essay "Negation" (1925). This is what Lacan calls the "mythical moment" of an affirmation logically prior to any negation, an affirmation, prior to any judgment of existence, that concerns the relation between the subject and being and not the relation between the subject and the world. The *Bejahung* that Freud posits and that Lacan emphasizes is "the primordial condition for something from the real to come to offer itself up to the revelation of being, or, to be 'let be,' as in Heidegger's terminology."[8] It is the "primordial act of symbolization," the "primordial inclusion of something in the symbolic."[9] As so affirmed, death attains a kind of splendor. It plays a role as the terrifying, all-shattering "other" of life. This is the splendor of death in Hegel that is something of a counter-image to that even greater splendor we shall encounter in the image of Antigone as she steps alive into her tomb.

So, death makes its appearance in the confrontation—the "tragic drama," one might say—of the fight to the death that comes as each of two self-consciousnesses seeks recognition from the other. As Lacan reads Hegel, where the life-death struggle begins in the face-to-face confrontation in a way reminiscent of the imaginary order, it is thus quickly brought into the symbolic order.

Hence, Lacan also sees the desire for recognition as initially obtaining not just at the imaginary level of images and ego identifications, as in the face-to-face encounter of the fight to the death, but even more so at the level of *imaginary discourse* that obtains at the level of the symbolic order, wherein language is tied not so much to its communicational functions, the transmission of meaning or of signified content, as it is to its most basic function as the medium of mutual recognition between speakers, what Žižek has termed, in a reference to Lacan, *the mot-de-passage*, the password. Unlike full speech, speech filled with the subject of the enunciation, the password is empty, it is "a nullity of enunciated, signified content," and so functions only as a "gesture of recognition," facilitating entry into the space of the symbolic order. Its very emptiness "creates the space for 'full speech,' for speech in which the subject can articulate his/her position of enunciation."[10]

Not only are the "master" and the "slave" positions within the symbolic network, but also work itself is defined by the symbolic order as a regime whereby desire—and death "itself"—is disciplined. In the life-death struggle, the subjectivity destined to become the "slave" becomes so by giving up *jouissance*. Lacan writes, "when you go to work, there are rules, hours—we enter into the domain of the symbolic" (S2: 223). But the relation between the imaginary order—the order of the face-to-face confrontation between the two consciousnesses—and the symbolic order—the order of language, of signifiers, of rules and hours to keep—is not one of simple succession. So, it is not just death itself that is important here, but above all the relationship between death and the signifier, death and the "symbolic order," as Lacan phrases it. Hence, in his second seminar, Lacan referred to Hegel's master-slave dialectic as a "limit-experience," one marked at the border between the imaginary and the symbolic dimensions. In the master discourse of Absolute Knowledge, death is the "master signifier"; not just the abstract negation of life and of discourse, then, it is what introduces negation into discourse, the infinite discourse of absolute knowledge. Lacan maintains that the death drive is, thus, not natural, not just a biological pulsion, but is cultural, and is identified—at least in Lacan's work from late 1950s and early 1960s—with the symbolic order. There is no drive that is not always and already represented in and as signifiers, as in Freud's *Vorstellungsrepräsentanten*. This essential, defining link between death and the symbolic order is not only Freudian, but is also a Hegelian influenced notion active in Lacan's seminars.

As a determinate negation, Hegel brings death to appearing (phenomenality) and so to existence. This means that prior to its presentation in the systematic discourse of absolute knowledge, prior to its symbolization, one could equally say that death has no existence at all, that its signification is retroactively constituted from its being a signifier. One of the upshots from this is that Lacan thus minimizes the "biological panic" (S2: 223) of the slave in the life-death struggle for recognition. "Death," Lacan writes, "is never experienced as such . . . it is never real. Man is only ever afraid of an imaginary fear. . . . in the Hegelian myth (of the Master-slave dialectic), death is not even structured like a fear, it is structured like a risk . . . like a stake. From the beginning, between the master and the slave, there's a rule of the game" (S2: 223).

In Lacanian terms, where the term "Other" designates the symbolic order, by being included in the dialectic of Absolute Knowledge, death is thus born to life, a human life, no longer the other, the mere opposite of life, but now within the Other, the symbolic order, as a signifier, both the death of the thing and the life of the signifier. The signifier "kills" the thing, but the life, the "being of language *is* the non-being of objects."[11] This is the life that death brings.[12] Primordial symbolization thus owes something to death, something that brings us to the intersection of the real and the symbolic.[13]

But, for Lacan, the core issue seems to lie not in death conceived as mere biological finitude but as the death drive. The death drive, as was said before, is not just an organic function. It "inhabits" that function, Lacan writes, but is not identified with it. Rather, the death drive is first defined as what obtains at the level of the symbolic. As a drive, it is defined as "*what becomes of demand when the subject vanishes from it.*"[14] Demand, as distinguished from need due to its belonging to the symbolic domain, also disappears. The drive, thus, has no subject; hence, it is somehow both inside and outside the symbolic. Yet, the "signifying cut," that wound, that inscribed lack that determines and defines the subject, remains. The death drive, albeit a drive without subject, is thus said to exhibit a minimal "grammatical artifice . . . manifest in the reversals of its articulation with respect to both source and object." This grammatical structure thus distinguishes the death-drive from the organic function "it inhabits." The death drive delineates not only a grammatical artifice; Lacan also calls it an "erogenous zone" independent from metabolic functions.[15] So, the death drive escapes, or is situated at the limit of Hegel's *Phenomenology of Spirit*, where death plays an essential productive and articulate role clearly only *within* the symbolic domain, in the labor of the negative by which absolute knowledge is finally realized precisely by taking up death as an appearing within the dialectic of appearings. For, Lacan, the drive, while not organic, is neither inside nor outside the symbolic and the discourse of the Other, and so neither inside nor outside the dialectic of subjectivity, the dialectic of the subject qua absolute subject of knowledge. The death drive is the "subversion of the subject." Like the *mammilla*, the feces, the phallus, and the urinary flow, like the gaze and the voice, so death, "the nothing," has no "*specular image*," no "alterity."[16] It is rather, the "lining," the "stuff" "of the very subject people take to be the subject of consciousness."[17]

Thus, within the Other, death is also the *extimacy* of the Other, the "rim," the lining, an intimate exteriority, its opening toward what Lacan would call, at least in the late 1950s, "the Other of the Other," the Thing, *das Ding*, or the "Real."[18] It should be noted—and not just in passing— that in this same 1950s period, when the shadow of Hegel's influence was so strong, Heidegger's "being-toward-death" (the *Sein-zum-Tode*) was also influential on Lacan's conception of death qua death drive, as the inherent and ultimate limit of the symbolic order, without, however, that influence being definitive.

So, by giving death a role to play, not just as biological force, but as a signifier, a master signifier in the rule-bound play of signifiers, Lacan also read Hegel's "making death appear" as an attempt not only to open the gap, the wound, the signifying cut in and by which both death and desire come to be, but also to plug the very gap it opens, to fill the abyssal lack and void that opens from within desire and that is intimate to the symbolic order and to the desire for recognition that obtains within it. In Lacan's reading, death, qua "master signifier," becomes thereby restricted to the symbolic order and is reduced to being the signifier around which the whole labor of the negative that unfolds at the symbolic level is organized. Its destructive dimensions are lost. Lacan thus saw the Hegelian dialectic as always attempting to foreclose the disruptive force—not just of "death" as such, plain old ordinary death, or even death qua master signifier, but death as the "death drive"—precisely by bringing to appearance the excess of appearing, and by thus lifting and retaining its liquidifying force through the *Aufhebung* into a new, higher configuration, lifting it into a higher "peace" in which two self-consciousnesses of the life-death struggle, for example, the two warring consciousnesses, can assume their positions in the Hegelian symbolic order: one, as the Master, who is recognized, and the other, as a Slave, a recognizing consciousness, both now working, each in their own way as figures in the totalizing dialectic of absolute knowledge, one to consume, the other to produce. Death is thus carried over into a dialectic of labor and utility whereby the diremptive power of the death drive as well as the related disruptions and excesses of *jouissance*, a kind of pleasure, like the death drive, in excess of the symbolic order and of the "pleasure principle," are excluded as useless unrepresentable expenditures.

But, in his *Écrits*, Lacan marked a double torsion opening from within the symbolic.[19] The articulation of death is the very thing that makes both death and desire ultimately *inarticulable*. Like death, desire can never be said; it remains both said and unsaid. Death is the great "(un)said." This points out the gap that will become important for *Seminar VII*, the gap between language, between the symbolic, and what Lacan calls the real, which is somehow both within and in excess of the symbolic. Lacan's *Seminar VII* will conceive this gap between the symbolic and the real as a gap between the symbolic and *jouissance*. Lacan's insight is to show how this gap affects the symbolic order itself and how it functions as the inherent limitation of this order.[20]

Thus, the third point of importance: as in his critical review of Hegel's reading of the drama *Antigone*, so here too, in his reading of the master-slave dialectic, Lacan will stress not only the power and systematicity of the dialectic, but also the way that dialectic must open beyond itself from within itself, how desire and death resist foreclosure or delimitation by the higher, peaceful reconciliations envisioned by the dialectic. Hegel's dialectic is one of the dialectical transgressions of limits whereby transgression is always productively employed. But for Lacan, on the other hand, there is also the question of how transgression, especially in and as *jouissance*, is also a transgression of the limits of the symbolic order itself, and of the dialectic of Absolute Knowledge sustained within it.

Lacan read Hegel as thus having brought the philosophical conceptions of death and desire to a higher level, not merely excluding them, or reducing them to useless negativities poised outside the limits of reason, but by including them within the dialectical circle of Absolute Knowledge. By making death appear as an essential shape or configuration (*Gestaltung*) within the dialectic of absolute knowledge, death, qua negativity, is no longer excluded from absolute knowledge but made to appear within it and so put to work as a productive negativity. It is by and through Spirit's intimacy with death, an intimacy achieved when making death appear within the dialectic of absolute knowledge, that

Spirit objectifies itself, opens itself beyond itself and thereby returns and appears to itself. It becomes then a kind of intimacy within it; but it is also an intimacy that opens the dialectic of absolute knowledge beyond itself, an intimacy that is also an extimacy of the circularity of the dialectic of Absolute Knowledge.

We can witness a related early formulation of this in Lacan's 1953 Rome address.[21] Apropos the death drive, or death "instinct," Lacan writes that the very meaning of the "notion" of the death drive contains a "conjunction of opposing terms," namely, "instinct," "which," as Lacan writes, "in its broadest acceptation, is the law that regulates the successive states of a behavior cycle in order to accomplish a life function," and "death," which is the "destruction of life." Destruction and life come together in the death drive "in a relation of polar opposites" that necessarily remains open, without dialectical closure. This unity of polar opposites is also found in the repetition and automatism Freud discusses in *Beyond the Pleasure Principle*, the repeated "Fort! Da!" exclamations of a child Freud observed, who used the expressions as ways to deal with the successive presence and absence of his mother, the words seemingly both sending her away and recalling her to presence. Freud thereby linked the death drive to repetition, and Lacan carried this further by linking it not only with the theme of desire as desire of the other, but also with the child's birth into language, his ascension to the symbolic order. Far from canceling desire, this birth "humanizes desire" by raising it to a "second power," for it "destroys the object that it causes to appear and disappear by bringing about its absence and presence in advance."[22] The link between the death drive and the symbolic order is also evident, for example, in the "death wish" that a subject may express, or even in the solitude of the suicide who denies the master his victory in the life-death struggle. In all of these there is an affirmation of life. They are not really about death at all, but about life, in the sense that in its purest form, the death instinct is not only identified with destruction but is also and equally "an affirmation of life." Conceived symbolically, the word is "the killing of the thing," and this death "results in the endless perpetuation of the subject's desire" in the symbolic order. The life and birth of symbols is then linked with death, and the regulation of life linked with destruction of life. We will encounter this again in the tragedy of *Antigone*.

Yet, there is always a moment, a muteness, a "mortal meaning," a lack or a void, a center both intimate to the system and yet also outside it, outside language, and outside the discourse of Absolute Knowledge. In these pages,[23] Lacan says if he wanted to give "an intuitive representation" of "the endless circularity of the dialectical process that occurs when the subject achieves," what Lacan calls "his solitude in the full assumption of his being-toward-death," he could have resorted to the figure of a two-dimensional ring, but it would be better to use the three-dimensional torus, the center of gravity of which is death, is desire, is a void, a lack, an absence, in other words, only for the form that encloses it. The torus is a topological figure in which "the peripheral exteriority and the central exteriority constitutes but one single region."[24] The torus is thus the topological figure of extimacy. It problematizes the relation of inside and outside by installing the opening to the outside in the very intimacy of the dialectical circularity, not only of language, but also of the circular system of Absolute Knowledge itself, which has its end in its beginnings. The outside and the inside, the limit and the center thus form one, single continuous surface. To follow the curve of one is to trace the topological profile of the Other and the opening from within the dialectic of Absolute Knowledge to its impossible outside.

While these themes are of importance to Lacan's development in the 1950s of his notions of the Imaginary (the register of images and illusory identifications with "the other"), the Symbolic (the radical alterity of language, discourse, and the law, all that cannot be assimilated through imaginary identifications), and the Real (beyond the symbolic and the imaginary, the process of signification that introduces a "cut" into the real), they also show how it is indeed highly problematic to simplify Lacan's relation to philosophy, in this case to Hegel's dialectic, as purely and simply "anti-philosophical." Rather than opposing philosophy and Hegel, the philosopher par excellence from the outside, Lacan locates from within Hegel's discourse, in its moments of greatest intimacy and intensity, the surface of an uncontainable extimacy of the symbolic and the discourse of absolute Knowledge.

But there is something else that must be mentioned here, in conclusion: Lacan also sought a way out from the ethics of finitude, a way out of the existential confrontation with death and the philosophy of authenticity in the face of death that had so dominated his own intellectual era. The ethic of psychoanalysis is not organized around death in the way much of the rest of twentieth-century European philosophy was, and not just the ontological, biological, and existential fact of death, but death as a master signifier, death as the organizing, signifying force for a modernist ethics of finitude. Perhaps Lacan saw the ethics of finitude not as an overturning of the Platonic "preparation for death," as it may have claimed to be, but rather as its continuation in another register, one stripped of the promises of eternal truth and immortal life. Perhaps, as with Bataille, for Lacan, death was but an "imposture." While it could be said that the ethics of psychoanalysis seems to be seeking a way to infinitize the finite, it is also seeking the way toward an ethic of the in-finite, of the in-finite as the extimacy of finitude, whereby the traditional philosophical opposition of the finite and the infinite is no longer in play; indeed, it is an opposition that finds in the ethic of psychoanalysis its own death. This is a theme and a question to which I shall return in the other essays in this collection.

3

THE "TRUTH ABOUT TRUTH"

At the level of the unconscious, the subject lies. And this is his way of telling the truth of the matter. The *orthos logos* of the unconscious . . . is expressed as the *proton pseudos*, the first lie.

—Jacques Lacan, *The Ethics of Psychoanalysis*

Il n'y a pas d'Autre de l'Autre, il n'y a pas de vrai sur le vrai.
Je me suis amusé un jour à faire parler le vérité. Que peut-il y avoir de plus vrai que l'énonciation 'Je mens'?

—Jacques Lacan, *D'un discourse qui ne serait pas du semblant*

The following pages explore the relationship given voice in these startling passages: the relation of identity between the *orthos* and the *pseudos*, between the "straightness" (*orthos*) of the truth and the necessary refractions of the lie, which is a signifying relation that follows from the thesis, "the unconscious is structured like a language." Insofar as truth is not just objective truth, but also truth as something said by a speaking being, my study of truth will also necessitate an investigation into the engendering of the subject as a speaking being through the double relation of alienation and separation.

PRELIMINARY REMARKS

In his concern for truth, in the many ways he posed the question and the questioning of truth, Lacan was perhaps the one psychoanalyst and structuralist closest to philosophy. Certainly more so than Lévi-Strauss or Roland Barthes, Lacan's conceptualization of the analytic situation was much more "philosophical," and not only in its explicit engagement with philosophical texts by the likes of Plato, Hegel, and Kant, but especially in his questioning of and concern for the question of truth. His seminars made truth not so much a Copernican center of their conceptual universe as they made of truth a problem, an elliptical fissure traversing both the scientific and philosophical traditions that placed reflection and research into the essence of human experience at the forefront of their endeavors. Yet, there is always something provisional and even hesitant about Lacan's seminars on truth. A questioning, even provisional mood of thought was never supplanted by dogmatism. Truth, for him, the truth of his teachings, was never empowered by a certitude held beyond all questioning and reservation. There thus remains a strongly Socratic element in his search for truth. Lacan's ways of telling the truth about truth are, thus, knotted into the philosophical tradition's ways of thinking truth, and yet, it must be said in the same breath, they mark a certain limit and a point of breaking with that tradition.

Over the years, Lacan formulated his conception of truth in several different ways. Let us take a quick preview of those that seem most prominent and provocative.

No doubt, the first truth for Lacan is Freud's truth: the truth of the unconscious. This is an unsurpassed truth, something that Lacan never calls into question. It is the fundamental starting point for all of Lacan's various ways of thinking about and talking about truth. Everything follows from this. Among the ways Lacan talks about truth, the many ways in which truth is said in the Lacanian seminars, let us list these:

First, he rejects the philosophical, propositional definition of truth, whereby truth is a value assigned to a proposition, a truth-value. He finds such a definition of truth in Wittgenstein's *Tractatus Logico-Philosophicus* (S17: 59/67). This is also a philosophical truth insofar as it is a truth located at the level of the "ideal I," "the I that masters," and that is identical with itself (S17: 63/71). Lacan's overall orientations come not from philosophy, therefore, but from Freud, for whom the I-qua-ego is an illusory formation. Obviously, Freud's "truth," the truth of Freud's discovery of the unconscious, is most fundamental in Lacan's teachings. That there is a truth of the unconscious is verified through clinical experience. Thus, for Lacan, the subject is always a divided subject, divided between a thinking that obtains at the level of the unconscious, and its being, the "I am" that is established in and through the symbolic order.

Second, and emerging from this, is the definition of truth as the truth of desire. This is the truth that pertains to the symbolic domain, a truth masked or blocked by the imaginary registers of the ego formations, those of self-knowledge and self-mastery, the subject as one who knows or who is "supposed to know" (in the sense of *connaissance*), the register, in other words, of misrecognition (*méconnaissance*). Access to this truth is one of the targets of psychoanalysis. Moreover, where desire and being are defined chiefly in terms of lack, so truth—like death and desire—shall likewise be thought in terms of lack. Truth is lack in being (*manque à être*). For Lacan, being is nothing other than forgetting in the sense that truth hides this lack, which Lacan also identifies with a "weakness," namely, with castration. This is the lack at issue that must always be covered over and that is nonetheless still there in the register of its effects. Thus, as Lacan goes on to argue, the "love of truth" is the love of this weakness (see S17: 52/58). Now the lack, the weakness that truth "loves," the signifying ordeal of castration, is located at the level of the unconscious and pertains directly to the ascension of the subject through castration into the symbolic order, which is its proper domain. In anticipation of the seventh and concluding essay in this volume, it could be added that the "love of truth" is something Lacan identifies with philosophy. Philosophy is a love of truth. As we shall see in connection with the "triplet" of truth–knowledge–and "the real," it may be that philosophy's love of truth is essentially linked to a "lack" that it "forgets," that it must forget. Insofar as philosophy identifies truth, at least in Lacan's reading of it, with being as sense, with being as the plenitude of meaning, philosophy typically does not conceive of being as lack. This, philosophy forgets by covering it over or filling it in with an illusory love of truth qua meaning and sense of being.

This brings us to a third direction of Lacan's phrasing of truth, one that indebts his discourse to Heidegger's articulation of truth as *aletheia*, the giving and withdrawal of Being. The Heideggerian reformulation of truth as *aletheia*, as both the giving and withdrawal of being, helped Lacan to redefine and escape the philosophical definitions of truth. Through Freud, Lacan situates truth in relation to lack qua castration. Castration, then, is a kind of "withdrawal," allowing the subject to come into presence in the symbolic order, which is its domain, its "dwelling" place.

Fourth, truth, Lacan says, is "inseparable from the effects of language" (S17: 62/70). Truth is always something said. But, in accordance with the aforementioned "third direction of truth," truth is something only half-said; truth is *mi-dire*. This is the formulation of truth that Lacan adapts in the 1960s and that he maintains in his seminars all through the early 1970s. While something like this formulation may be foreshadowed in the earlier seminars, it becomes the most fundamental way of phrasing truth especially in Lacan's later seminars. Again, this shows how Lacan's ethic is an ethic of speaking, speaking the truth.

Finally, in light of this formulation of truth as *mi-dire*, truth is linked with semblance, with error and lying. Truth is a lie in the sense of being a "deceitful transformation" (*transformation mensongère*) (S7: 74/90).

Regarding the identification of truth and the lie, it must be said that there is no moral fault in this. The telling of a lie in this context is not a moral failing because when I lie, when I forget or cover up, I do not know that I am lying; I do not know what I am saying. Here, in this psychoanalytic context, the lie is told at the level of the unconscious (S7: 73). This follows from the thesis asserting the truth, Freud's truth, of the unconscious, whereby the first truth is also the *proton pseudos* operational in the first signifiers installed at the level of the unconscious. The lie is a way of saying the truth as *mi-dire*. That is to say, it is a way of speaking the lack, the lack introduced by castration, that defines desire and so, the speaking subject.

Actually, the *quaesitum*, the "why" for all of this lies in the human modalities of defense. Defense against what? Against the lack? Yes, but also, against the "extreme good that *das Ding*, the Thing, may bring." I shall be returning to this rather strange and rather compelling notion of "the Thing" in my reading of Lacan's meditations on Sophocles' *Antigone*, where the Thing (*das Ding*) is articulated as a dimension of both attraction and repulsion, both a lure and barrier. So, it might well be that against which a defense must be erected. This is the direction of Lacan's thought in *Seminar VII* (S7: 73).

Lacan notes on those pages how human modalities of defense differ from those of animals, which he likens to "the way a crab gives up its claw" (S7: 73). Human defense, rooted in repression and the unconscious, has its own human modes of self-mutilation. Yet, comparable to an animal's modalities of defense, the human mode of defense also involves giving something up. The human defense, the human way of self-mutilation, Lacan calls "castration" and "alienation." But this, too, as we shall see, is a mutilation that occurs only at the level and the limit of the symbolic order, the order of the signifier, the level of the inscription of the subject into the symbolic order. Unlike that of animals, the human defense involves something more than motor responses. The human defense works through the symbolic order, in the systems of relations that define metaphor and metonymy by which Lacan articulates at this stage of his thought the structure of desire, and which, from the point of view of psychoanalysis, are also ways of "displacement" and "substitution," whereby repressed material is represented by signifiers, with the result being that a certain level of potentially destructive energy, a certain pressure brought on by the mechanisms of repression, is effectively reduced. Human defense works through all the sublimations and symptoms, all the compromise formations, for example, by which a desire for the extremes of good and evil, as the desire for the Thing, is made livable through an overall reduction of intensity. Hence, the human defense also involves "lying about evil" (S7: 73). Hardly an act of treachery, telling the truth by lying, especially lying about evil, is but another and no doubt essentially human way of defense: defense against the extremes of both good and evil, something Lacan approaches in terms of *jouissance*. It is the way, he says, that we reluctantly give it up, our discreet little unavowable *jouissance*, like a crab gives up its claw.

Returning now to the essential binding of truth to language, it must be added that insofar as truth is something said, insofar as truth may be said to be a "signification," truth is not apprehended at the beginning of an enunciation, but only retroactively (*après coup*), at the end of the saying, or at the end of the sentence (S7: 74/90). This is the diachronic dimension of truth, and the function of the punctuating "button tie" (*point de capiton*) that brings the sliding of signification to a halt; signification—truth—if it comes at all in this case, comes only with the last term of the enunciation, at the halting of the sliding of the signification. Thus, there is a deferral of truth. It is never given as something whole and complete in itself but only as something worked through across the spacings and deferrals of signifying differences (the signifier being defined as a system of differences). Truth is spaced and temporally played out across the relations of signifiers. This is also an important dimension to understanding how truth is always *mi-dire*: one must wait for the end, but one must wait for an end that never comes. Truth is always something yet to come and not something ever finished or given from the beginning as a unified presence. Truth as lack, as traumatic lack, is, thus, always deferred and delayed through the *proton pseudos*, through the "*défilés* of the signifier," as Lacan phrases it, and never achieves full presence. This also ties in with Freud's concept of the *Nachträglichkeit*, "deferred action," which describes the way the present reworks the memories of the past, the way memory is altered and reshuffled in and by the present. In the psychoanalytic account of this, it is usually a question of something, a traumatic experience, for example, something that at first could not possibly be incorporated fully into a meaningful context, that undergoes such deferred action. But a possible political dimension is also suggested: does this not describe a Stalinistic way of rewriting history, whereby the past, whereby what counts as the truth of what happened, is altered to suit the needs of the present?[1] As something said, even "half-said," truth is looped through the machinery, through the defilements of the big Other, the symbolic order, and comes back to "me," the speaking subject, as a message seemingly from my-self (*moi-même*); in the speaking of "my truth" and the "speaking of my mind," *défiler son chapelet*, as a French expression says, I speak the lack in the Other. This "loop" is the loop of difference, the loop of the lack constitutive of the speaking subject.

It is formulations such as these that mark the separation of Lacan's discourses on truth from the philosophical discourses on truth and that also sutures them to it. Accordingly, Lacan's hypotheses about truth shall be shown as maintaining, or "putting up with," such disjunctive links with the discourses on the therapy and care of the soul or self, as in the Socratic and Aristotelian ethical traditions, for example, and also with Heidegger's meditation on truth as *aletheia*, as *ereignis*.[2] This is the truth about truth that shall always be lacking in Lacan's seminar:[3] Lack is the ultimately unspeakable place of truth in the speaking subject.

It is this "lack" that distinguishes Lacan's seminars and singles them out as crucially important to the heritage of modern philosophy insofar as it still shelters both a care for truth and a related care for the ethical welfare and condition of the human soul/self. They are important to an epochal questioning of the limits of the significations and of the concept of truth active and predominant in that heritage. As Jean-Luc Nancy expressed it, Lacan helps to define our modern epoch as the "epoch of a . . . passage to the limit of all possible signification," a passage to the limit of significations annulled or imported that can yet be pronounced or announced under the headings of "Europe," or "the third world," "communism," or "art," or yet as "philosophy," or "psychoanalysis."[4]

THE TRUTH OF THE UNCONSCIOUS

In *Seminar VII*, Lacan refers to a time when he was asked by one of the participants why he never told them the truth about truth. To which Lacan protested that there is no such "truth about truth," there is no metalanguage of truth. Such a metalanguage is a kind of "metaphysical knavery" (S7: 184). Such a remark places Lacan's reflections at the vanguard of late twentieth-century philosophical thought, which tended strongly toward the critical questioning of any notion of a transcendent or transcendental dimension of truth. Lacan is well within the mainstream of twentieth-century critical thought when he denies that truth is something eternal, a transcendental dimension beyond time as in the classical Greek triumvirate of the True, the Good, and the Beautiful, just as he also recoils from the reduction of truth to the status of being but a "value" conditioned by the adequation of a statement to an observable "fact" somehow transcendent to that statement. Hence, this question: when Lacan asserts the truth of the unconscious, if not a transcendental dimension or the correspondence of a statement and a transcendent fact, what is the status of this truth? The short answer is that Lacan defines both the unconscious and its truth in relation to language, and this is something else he shares with other late twentieth-century philosophers for whom the question of truth was also increasingly posed in terms of truth's provisional, always deferred character, and truth's immersion in the temporal, historical, and spatial structures and byways of language. Lacan has something in common with such perspectives. Yet, Lacan's constant return to the questioning of truth makes something else stand out in his teachings: there is truth, he says, the truth of the unconscious taken as both a Freudian discovery and a dimension of human experience that, while it cannot be denied, cannot be reduced to the status of an empirical entity. This truth is not *just* an illusion, not just a play, not an irony, not a lie that has yet to be found out. Perhaps this truth is precisely what both the analyst and the analytic patient are seeking: the truth of desire, the truth that is somehow the key to suffering.

Hence, where so much of his seminar work is concerned with a critical inquiry into truth, Lacan's often fulsome attacks on philosophy, his ostensible breaks with philosophy, only serve to engage him more deeply in a dialogue with philosophy. Yet, it is not just an abstract philosophical search for truth that is undertaken in his seminars, for once again Lacan's chief concern is for truth as encountered in his work as a practicing psychoanalyst, and it is this that especially caused him to deeply question the way the European philosophical tradition conceived of truth beginning with the ancient Greeks. What emerges from this is perhaps the most singular and prominent way Lacan breaks with that tradition: his refusal of an axiom essential to it, namely, the axiom asserting the identity, the belonging together, of truth and being, of thinking and the plenitude of being. As found in Parmenides, the axiom states: That which can be thought must also be. Moreover, insofar as truth is what is thought in and by thinking, and if thinking, according to the Parmenidean axiom, is identified with being, then truth, for the classical heritage of philosophy, and for the Socratic care of the self, truth is the truth of being, or being as truth. In this case, truth is identified not with lack, or the void, but with plenitude, with being as "what is." This Lacan contests by casting the whole problem in a strikingly new way.

The thesis, affirming the identity of thought and being, has been carried forth into modern philosophy in the form of the famous Cartesian assertion, "I think, therefore I am." In its Lacanian reformulation, which comes somewhat to a head in his rightly famous eleventh seminar (1964), it undergoes a severe but coherent deformation. In Lacan's seminars, the Parmenidean/Cartesian axiom form is now written as a Cartesian disjunctive proposition, or *vel*: "Either I think *or* I am," or, in other Lacanian words, "where I think, I am not, and where I am, I do not think." What are the consequences of this *vel* for the ethical and political dimensions of Lacanian psychoanalysis, especially in relation to the European heritage of the care of the soul/self?

As we take up these questions, let us recall Lacan's theses on truth just previewed.

First, Lacan sees himself as operating a return to *Freud's truth*, a truth of the discovery of the unconscious. This is a truth that has been lost, forgotten, or mangled by the institutions and practices whereby it was formed into knowledge. One of the essential dimensions of Lacan's "return to Freud" concerns the way Freud's discovery of the unconscious affects truth, puts the conventional ideas about truth into critical questioning. Lacan is thus eager to restore this Freudian "truth" of the unconscious and to hurl it against the neglect of this truth that has developed in the rapid internationalization of psychoanalysis. These points are underscored in a short text from Lacan's 1955 lecture "The Freudian Thing":[5] "The meaning of the return to Freud is a return to Freud's meaning. And the meaning of what Freud said may be conveyed to anyone because, while addressed to everyone, it concerns each person. One word suffices to make this point: Freud's discovery calls truth into question, and there is no one who is not personally concerned by truth."

Second, while truth is the truth of desire, the truth of the subject's desire, or of the subject staged as one who both knows and yet also cannot know the truth, and who yet must speak (*mi-dire*) the truth of his desire, this is yet a truth attained through the other (*par les autres*). How is truth said through the Other qua "other" (small "o"), namely, other persons (*par les autres*), and in what forms? The classical model for this is in Aristotle's account of friendship in which one attains self-knowledge, comes to know in some sense the truth about what one is, only through the friend, the other. But for Lacan, this dialectic works in threes, not in twos. The scene is Oedipal: there is the Father, the

Mother, and the Child, trapped in their private hell. The relationship is structured on something that is missing: the phallus, the "privileged signifier," "the signifier of the Other's desire."[6] None of them have it, yet it must be taken into account as a privileged signifier in order that each successfully calculates his/her true respective position by which they become the Father, the Mother, and the Child. If the Father commits an error and thinks he is *The Father*, or if the Mother thinks she is *the Mother who has the phallus*, or the Child thinks it *is the phallus*, the object of the Mother's desire, then each gets stuck in the calculation of the truth of their position and of their interrelationships. "No one will find a way out. They will be stuck in eternal repetition."[7] Truth is here attained intersubjectively. As Éric Laurent has shown well, this same scene is also worked out in Lacan's example of the three prisoners, each trying to figure out the color of the disk attached to his back, and in Sartre's play *No Exit*: "The structure of the three condemned people trapped in a room, each is guilty of a crime, each can see the torment of guilt written on the faces of the other two, but none can know in what sense he is guilty except through the two others."[8] The locus of truth is not only within the subject, within its hidden interior, its "intra-said," nor within the other (person), but also pertains to the "inter-said" of the Other as discourse and as "intersubjective game." Moreover, this is a retroactively apprehended truth, one that only comes at the end of, or across the "inter-said," not as something given in its beginnings. This "intersubjective" and retroactive locus of truth is that of the subject as both the topological locus of the signifier and as exceeded by the process of signification. Signification, originally introduced as internal to the subject, takes place outside of it, through the Other, as "something quite other," and "between the lines."[9]

Third, Lacan thus plays on the phrase *par les autres* to suggest that truth is *parlé*, spoken, and so, again, retroactively apprehended, but, only as half-spoken. "Truth draws its guarantee from somewhere other than the Reality it concerns: it draws it from Speech. Just as it is from Speech that Truth receives the mark that instates it in a fictional structure."[10] Due to its retroactive dimension, truth is thus inescapably temporal, yet without being chronological. This is an ontological truth, the truth of the being, the kernel of being, of the subject as the "I am" that is attained only in and through the Other. But there is also a mathematical sense to this: time is the "intersubjective time that structures human action," in the sense of being the time of strategies and game theory, the time of tensions between waiting and haste, hesitation and urgency, what Lacan also calls "logical time."[11] There is thus a temporality of truth that follows from truth being retroactively "inter-said," and "half-said."

Fourth, in light of Freud's discovery of the unconscious, Lacan emphasizes the peculiar ways in which truth is hidden, masked, concealed, disguised. It is not that truth is the object of censorship, or that truth is censored. Rather, the truth of the matter is, truth actively censors itself. Truth requires censorship, as it requires error. In the words of Nancy and Lacoue-Labarthe, truth not only does not give itself, but as it refuses itself, as it hides, or is forbidden, it is yet powerful in its withdrawal: it "forces the inscription of its very refusal."[12] But this disguising and this withdrawal do not disguise truth. Truth is not what is disguised, for one cannot disguise what cannot be defined. There is no pure interior truth to mask or disguise. Rather, truth disguises and conceals nothing. Truth is rather identified with disguises and false appearances. Insofar as it is something shared, insofar as language (*langue*) is something shared with other subjects, insofar as language exists, what the signifying chain discloses is that language can do something other than report the facts. There is "the possibility I have . . . to use it to signify *something altogether different*, something "quite other." The truth is conveyed, despite all the censors, "between the lines"; it can be evident only to the "trained eye," or, depending on the intention, understood by the many or the few. This obtains in the metaphoric and metonymic structure of desire and speech, for which Lacan's examples are those of the French locution *grimper à l'arbre* ("to be fooled") and the usage of "thirty sails," where the signifier "sails" takes the place of the signifier "boats." The play of metonymy, "displacement," and metaphor, "condensation" is, thus, the inscription of the withdrawal that truth forces and obtains in language.

Recall the fundamental thesis of Lacanian psychoanalysis: there is an unconscious; this was the Freudian discovery and the Freudian truth. Lacan calls the unconscious Freud's discovery because, before Freud, the unconscious was not something that simply went by another name. Rather, before Freud, the unconscious, purely and simply did not exist, "it names nothing (prior to Freud) that counts any more as an object."[13] But this is not a truth that Lacan simply takes unaltered from Freud's texts. "The unconscious is what I say it is," Lacan writes, "assuming we are willing to hear what Freud puts forward in his theses."[14] There is always a note of resistance in the Lacanian teachings on the unconscious, resistance to what "psychology," mass marketing, and academic stagnation have made of the Freudian discovery such that the unconscious is only given enough profile, enough definition in order to argue against it dismissively.

On the basis of Freud's discovery of the unconscious, Lacan asserts the radical split between thinking and being. From this truth of the unconscious, Freud's truth, from this "discovery," Lacan also finds the grounds for his new topology of the subject, developed in terms of the "alienation" and "separation" of the subject, distinguishing thereby the subject of the statement "I am" from the subject qua subject of the enunciation, the subject of the unconscious, the level of the "I think," and the subject of the imagination, the ego, from the subject as defined by symbolic order, and beyond this, the subject of *jouissance*. This topology shall play a significant role in Lacan's characterization of truth as lack and as *mi-dire*.

Lacan phrases this as a disjunctive, a *vel*: I must choose to be, choose to be as *ego cogito*, or I must choose to think. Lacan does not assume their identity, but rather asserts their disjunctive diremption. It is Lacan's argument that in choosing to be, I, qua ego, separate myself from the unconscious, separate myself from the subject of the unconscious, separate myself from thinking insofar as it is the unconscious that thinks. It must be said that the "being" named in choosing "to be" is not simply being as such, but being transformed by language. It is being as registered in the "defiles" of the signifier.

This, then, is Lacan's most striking thesis: There is either thinking or being, and where there is thinking, in the terms of psychoanalysis, it is the unconscious that thinks. This receives emphasis, especially in Lacan's eleventh seminar, and its articulation of the so-called disjunctive *vel* of being and meaning.[15]

The disjunctive and subjectivizing *vel* proposes an impossible choice: "to think or to be." As such, it clearly resembles another *vel* we are sometimes unlucky enough to encounter, namely, "your money or your life." Lacan points out how this *vel* appears in Hegel's master-slave dialectic: "your freedom or your life." If you choose freedom, you lose both (S11: 212).

What these *vel*s have in common, of course, is that they all pose false choices. There really is no choice here; one cannot choose to give up one's life in order to save one's money. Both would be lost. So, in the Cartesian *vel*, one cannot give up one's "being," one's existence as a subject represented by a signifier for another signifier, for "thinking." For Lacan, this *vel* thus marks the gap of the unconscious. We do not make existential choices here. We live this impossible dilemma.

So, where truth is identified with the unconscious as the truth of the unconscious, and so identified with thinking, where thinking is the scene (the "Other scene") of truth, and where it is the unconscious that "thinks" and so excludes being, namely, *the* being asserted in the enunciation "I am," it must be that, according to the Lacanian teaching, truth "is not," truth is always lack *in* being. The truth of the "I am" is that it is a lack in being.

But why does Lacan insist that the unconscious "thinks"? One general way of describing the identity of the unconscious and "thinking" can be found in Lacan's famous assertion "the unconscious is structured like a language." This does not say that the unconscious *is* a language, but that it is structured *like* a language. That is to say, it is structured according to the structure of the binary signifier. Conversely, the unconscious is the effect of the constitution of the subject by the signifier. By identifying the unconscious with a thinking and as an intersubjective symbolic domain, at least one thing becomes clear: The unconscious cannot be described as a mysterious, interior reservoir of archaic and amorphous energetics, a closed room full of hidden, repressed instincts and desires, or pulsions, a secret held behind locked doors. Rather, it is a structure—a "thinking" structure—not a container.

Whereas it might seem preferable to regard the unconscious process as the "unthinking" condition for thinking, *Seminar VII* gives us two further related reasons for identifying the unconscious and elementary "thinking": First, whereas the unconscious is demarcated as a result of repression, *Verdrängung*, such repression "operates on nothing other than signifiers" (S7: 44). This means that repression and the unconscious do not bear upon raw organic instincts as such, but on signifiers, which are the representatives of the instincts. Hence the formula: The unconscious is structured like a language. Even though Lacan distinguishes truth and knowledge, the unconscious is said to harbor a certain level of "knowledge" unbeknown to the subject. The unconscious is a domain of signifiers and as such is structured by signifiers. This is the *Sachvorstellung*, the "representation of things," at the level of the unconscious, and it is linked in Lacan's reading of Freud to "words as representations," *Wortvorstellungen*, whereby things are to words as "straw" is to "grain." *Sache*, the thing "as a product of industry and of human action as governed by language," and *Wort*, word, are closely linked, and so, in Lacan's reading, and somewhat against the grain of the usual reading of Freud, "they form a couple." Meanwhile, beyond the *Sache*, linked and bound with words and language, that other Thing, that radically Other Thing, *das Ding*, as Freud called it, is found "somewhere else" (see S7: 44–45/55–58).

Thus, the human world, even at the level of the unconscious, is distinguished from the animal world in that the human world is a universe structured by words, by a symbolic process; "man is caught up in a symbolic process" at the deepest levels of human existence. Second, the unconscious is a level of "deep subjectivization of the outside world," such that it performs a sifting (*trie*), a selecting process whereby "reality is only perceived by man as radically selected" (*profondément choisie*). "Man deals with selected bits of reality" (*L'homme a affaire à des morceaux choisis de réalité*) (S7: 47/59). So, "thinking" does not mean conceptualization as such, but rather refers to this deep level of subjectivization that is defined by the register of the symbolic order that defines the unconscious and defines the human relationship with the external world. In his seventeenth seminar, where Lacan develops his theory of the "four discourses," he diagrammed this position of the subject of the truth of unconscious as the position marked as the "S barred" ($) (S17: 93). The S barred is the position identified in Lacan's schema of the master's discourse, the first among the four discourses, as occupying the position of truth.[16] As such, it is below the line, under the position of desire and the "master signifier," marked as "S_1," and so cut off from the subject as a speaking being. The subject shall always thus "lack" this truth (see S17: 92–93/105, 106).

And where I am, where I am as cogito, the speaking subject, the subject as having undergone the signifying cut (that cut of castration that marks the emergence of the subject as represented by a signifier to another signifier), the subject as now marked in and by the position of the unary signifier, S_1, there, where "I am," I am not thinking, and where I am thinking, qua subject of the unconscious, I am not, qua *ego cogito*. Here, at this level, is where we find the truth as a lack in the subject, at the level of the subject as a speaking and desiring being defined by castration, "the signifying cut" of castration, that "cut" whereby the subject comes to be in and as a "subject" only through language.

Again, the Lacanian teaching is that truth must be taken as lack in being, a lack at the heart of the subject qua "I am." This is truth as the truth of the unconscious, the unconscious as the "I think," where "I am" not. Thus, the truth of the "I am," the truth of the cogito, is the "I think"; it is the thinking "I" of the unconscious that cannot, however, think-and-be at the same time. This is truth at the level of the subject of the unconscious, the subject of the enunciation of truth, as distinguished from the truth at the level of the subject of the statement (the subject of the *énoncé*), whereby the subject is defined as nothing but a signifier, in other words, a subject represented by a signifier to yet another signifier ($S_1 \rightarrow S_2$). There are two levels of the subject and two levels of truth at work here. Psychoanalytic practice brings out their troublesome interaction.

Phrased otherwise, the absolute "un-truth" of the subject is the subject that says "I am" and that sees itself in this saying as an absolute truth, something unified, a completely self-present whole existing independently of language. For, in truth, the subject is defined not by such self-presence but by a lack in being, a lack marked by language and by the "where-I-am-not" of the unconscious. Insofar as thinking is the thinking that takes truth as its object, its goal and its telos, thinking is actually taking the nullity at the heart of thinking as its goal. Lacan's assertion of a disjunctive relation between being and truth has practical consequences. In the analytic situation, when the patient says that what he/she says is true, this is truth as "not being" in the sense that the speaker may not know what he/she is saying. The disjunct of being and thinking thus marks a moment in Lacan's discourse that is at once most philosophical in that it poses a philosophical question about the relation of truth and being, and at the same time is most anti-philosophical in its attempt to cut the very ground from under traditional philosophical thinking.

THE COMING INTO BEING OF THE SUBJECT: ALIENATION AND SEPARATION

From the thesis "the unconscious is structured *like* a language," *Seminar XI* deduces a topology of the subject, showing the constitution of the subject in and through the Cartesian *vel*. This surprising "deduction" marks new stage of thought, new at least in Lacan's eleventh seminar, when the structuralist, literary terminology of metaphor and metonymy, used to great effect in the earlier seminars, is, in the eleventh seminar dropped and replaced by the introduction of the terms "alienation" and "separation."

Lacan uses these terms in new ways; they do not so much name or account for the phenomenological-existential situation of the subject, the alienation between men, or the alienation of the individual from his/her work or society as in the philosophical language of existentialism in the late 1950s and early 1960s. Rather, in Lacan's eleventh seminar, these terms show, in light of Freud's discovery of the unconscious, that alienation and separation are not the consequences or outgrowths of an imaginary "human condition" but the very first-order constituents necessary in order to become a human being in the first place, a being living in a human world, which is a world of language. They name the ontological constitution of the subject, the "advent of the subject to his own

being in the relation to the Other" (S11: 205), in the topological circle
of "meaning" (see S11: 211).

In his 1960–1964 essay "Position of the Unconscious," Lacan elabo-
rates a bit on his new usage of the word "alienation." "Alienation," he
writes, "resides in the subject's division."[17] The subject cannot be the
cause of its own being. In the sense that it cannot be its own cause,
it is alienated from itself. It comes to be in the locus of the Other. As
Lacan says, the signifier "brings forth a subject from a being that cannot
speak." The Other is, thus, the signifying cause of the subject. And as
the subject comes to be, something in it, something "that cannot speak,"
is cut away, lost, thrown down, sacrificed as the subject comes to be in
the locus of the Other. This is the "disappearance" of the subject; the
aphanisis of the subject, its "fading," in other words. Lacan's essay "The
Subversion of the Subject and the Dialectic of Desire" characterizes this
"fading" as a moment of "eclipse of the subject." It occurs in the splitting, or *Spaltung*, of the subject brought on by its subordination to the
signifier, a splitting that results in the engendering of the subject insofar
as this splitting results in a transfer of the permanence of desire to an
ego (the "I") that "is nevertheless intermittent," and in which the subject inversely protects itself from its desire by attributing it to the very
intermittence of the ego.[18]

"Alienation" and "separation" thus name two distinct levels, two
operations of the inscription of the subject into the signifying, symbolic
order. What is "the symbolic order"? Lacan refers to the symbolic order
as the Other, the so-called big Other. Each and every subject finds its
being, its identity not in itself but in the place assigned to it in the big
Other of the symbolic order. This is "alienation." The symbolic order
names every subject; it designates and defines each and every subject
by assigning each and every subject a defining place and a role in the
symbolic order. Most importantly, this occurs with regard to the way
each and every subject must be identified as a "he" or a "she," and, in
accordance with this assignation, the subject thus assumes its place as
defined by the social system of gender relations and the laws of sexual
difference that constitute the social fabric. This is the topology of sexual
difference that is a direct consequence of Lacan's thesis whereby the
unconscious is structured like a language for the structure at work there
is that of the symbolic order.

The beauty of this is in its economy of principles. The topology of
the subject, the account of the formations of the unconscious, the dreams,
slips of the tongue, the whole matter of truth and error (to which we

shall return shortly), the primary thesis of the split between thought and being, all of this is understood on the basis of a single definition: The subject is defined as a subject insofar as it is represented by a signifier for another signifier.[19] This, for Lacan, is the "subject": a "soul-less" lack in being. The subject is but a nullity, a position in a signifying chain, the nullity of a representation of a signifier, as represented to another signifier.

What about "separation"? Compared to alienation, separation is given much less discussion time in *Seminar XI*, yet, it is perhaps the most interesting dimension of the two. Lacan develops his definition of this by way of some word play: "Separation" (*separare*) by way of a separation of the reflexive prefix *se* from the cognate *parere*, and with the function of the *pars*, becomes *se parere*, "engendering oneself," meaning "to attribute to himself (*se parer*) the signifier to which he succumbs."[20]

Emphasis must for the moment fall on the term "succumbs," for this is precisely what happens. Something goes under. Something dies in the movement toward "life," where "life" is defined as life in the symbolic order. Separation, *se parer*: The subject is "engendered" in and through its ascension to the symbolic order, and, one must also say, into the order of sexuality and sexual difference. The birth into the locus of the signifier, upon which birth the subject says "I am," is a birth in which something without memory, something comparable to the gliding, soft membranes of a mute organism, something unnamable and lost in the swift cut of the signifier is cut away, left behind, as though to die. Lacan calls this the "lamella," this deathless, immortal and lost part that appears as it disappears in the engendering. If the engendering is the interpolation of the subject into the symbolic order, into the structure and into the locus of the desire of the big Other, then there is also something else, something in excess of structure, something that is there and not there that Lacan describes as being "organic," an "organ," namely, the "drives," the organ of the drives, the organ of the libido, in other words, the "lamella." A Lacanian play on words perhaps says it best: "The Man" (*l'Homme*) thus born is born broken, like an egg whose membranes are torn when the egg is cracked, born thus a "Manlet" (*l'Hommelette*)."[21]

In the engendering of the subject, something of the subject dies, or is sloughed off like dead skin. Death, in a manner of speaking, is the afterbirth of the coming into life of the subject. Not its biological life, but its life in and as a being represented by a signifier to another signifier. Now inscribed into the locus of the Other, the subject makes its death "the object of the Other's desire." Engendering and death are here coupled irrevocably. Lacan says so himself in his essay "Position of

the Unconscious": "The signifier as such, whose first purpose is to bar
the subject (qua 'S barred') has brought him into the meaning of death.
(The letter kills, but we learn this from the letter itself.) This is why
every drive is virtually a death drive."[22] This, then, is the upshot of the
separation of thinking and being, namely, the engendering of the subject
by and through the operation of the signifier, the so-called signifying cut,
and the introduction of the subject into the realms of sexuality and death.

Engendering itself, the subject "attack(s) the chain of signifiers. By
way of the fantasy ("S barred in relation to object a") produced in and
through this engenderment, the subject deals with the loss, deals with the
death it undergoes in such a way as to restore to him/herself this "earliest
loss."[23] The role of fantasy ("the barred subject in relation to object a"),
is to plug the nullity in being of the divided subject engendered in and
through initial alienation.

Separation, once again, is the way of return of the *vel* of alienation.
Alienation comes full circle, so to speak, in and through the operation of
separation. Here, at the level of or in terms of the operations of separation, "the subject works with his/her own loss and so brings him/herself
back to the point of departure."[24] It is in separation, and in terms of
the structure of the fantasy ("S barred in relation to object a"), that the
subject's return operates by answering, through the positing of the object
a of fantasy, the question posed by the "big Other," namely, "What does
it, the big Other, want?" The subject's desire is the desire of the Other,
and separation is the subject's encounter with that desire, a desire the
subject marks as being a lack of something, something that the subject
would like to provide or fill and so answer the desire of the Other. Desire,
Lacan asserted, is always desire of the Other. The subject's response to the
question it, the subject, always poses for itself, namely, "What does the
Other want of me?" finds its response in the fantasy that structures the
subject's desire. Thus, it is here, in the Other's desire, that we encounter
the gaze and the voice of the Other as modes of "object a," an "object"
that kick-starts desire and sets it into motion.

Separation's operation thus puts S barred, the divided subject represented by S_1, in relation to the signifying chain only on condition of
the position of object a, which is not only the motivating object of the
fantasy, but is also the condition of lack (S11: 209), the level of truth as
lack, the truth that *Seminar XX* will characterize as "sister to *jouissance*."

"Alienation," meanwhile is the unconscious operation by which S_1,
the master signifier or "unary trait," represents the subject for another
signifier such that the subject is named or characterized and so inscribed

in the symbolic order, and so is in relation to S_2, the signifying chain, or "Meaning." Alienation, Lacan says, thus constitutes the subject "as such."[25] The subject "as such" is the subject as what must withstand the necessary aphanisis, or "fading" of the subject before the unary signifier (S_1). The subject "as such" is thus what emerges from the "disappearance" and subsumption of the subject. The subject emerges as submitted to the governance of a rule. The subject lives only as what has already "succumbed" beneath the sway of a unary signifier, which Lacan says "represents the subject for another signifier," and by which the subject appears somewhere as having a meaning.

This unary signifier, Lacan continues, constitutes the central point of the *Urverdrängung*, of repression, and as such also marks the point of attraction (*Anziehung*) through which all the other repressions will be possible.

Furthermore, it is the meaning of the Freudian term *Vorstellungsrepräsentanz*, the "representative of the representation," as Lacan translates it, that "enables us to conceive that the subject appears first in the Other insofar as the first signifier or unary signifier emerges in the field (or locus) of the Other and so represents the subject for another signifier." It comprises the unary signifier of the unconscious and thus constitutes the unconscious as a language based on the binary signifier, the language of desire as the representative of need (see S11: 218).

Again, separation is the way of return of the *vel* of alienation (S11: 218), the closing of the rim, and the *situ* of the erotic. It is here that the analytic moment of transference takes place, whereby the analysand, the patient, seems to transfer onto the analyst all of his/her loves and desire. Transference is also the scene of deception, where truth presents itself in and as the lie of deception. Here, the Other is the symbolic order, the field of knowledge that *Seminar XX* will also characterize as a "means of *jouissance*."

Separation and alienation form something like a circle completing the subject's ascendance, its interpolation, in other words, into the symbolic order. This circle is given a form in the schemas for alienation and separation. At this linking point of nullity, or of non-being, between the Subject in being and the Other, or Meaning, Lacan locates what he calls the "punch," or the *losange*, which, as produced in its visual, legible configuration, appears as a useful artifice, whereby each *vel*, that of separation and alienation, is marked by a "V," thus comprising the combination of the two levels of alienation and separation, of thought and being, one above the other, so as to form a diamond shape. The resulting *losange*, or "punch," traces, marks, or even symbolizes the pulsating rim of the unconscious (see S11: 209).[26]

This marking of the "rim" situates the unconscious as obtaining between the Subject and the Other; it is their mode of conjunction, the "circular, albeit nonreciprocal articulation" between the two domains. In Lacan's terminology, it is "their cut in action," the "action" being the opening and closing of the unconscious, or the unconscious as closure and entry.[27]

"Engendering" is also "gendering," as was suggested before. In the engendering, in the coming to be in and as a signifier, the subject also withstands a passage through the "straits" of sexual gender, a passage in which something of the living being is lost.[28] Sexuality, sexual difference, Lacan remarks, is then distributed on one side or the other of the rim as the threshold of the unconscious. Lacan sees this as happening in the following way: "On the side of the living being," which becomes the subject insofar as it becomes a speaking being, the subject never quite successfully comes "altogether in speech." The subject is always a bit "shy" of the threshold, neither inside nor outside. Access to the "opposite sex as Other" is possible only via the so-called partial drives where what the subject seeks, whether it is the breast, the feces, and so on, the subject seeks as something, some part, that can take the place of, or fill in the hole left by, the loss of life the subject sustained due to the fact that the subject is a sexed subject.[29]

On the other side, on the side of the Other, we thus find the other sex as well as the economy of the exchange of signifiers, plus the realms of the political and ethical ideals, the elementary structures of kinship, and, most importantly, the "metaphor of the father" and what Lacan calls the "phallic function," considered as a principle of separation, and "the ever reopened division in the subject owing to his initial alienation." It is here, in the field of the Other, that the subject learns what it must do insofar as it is a woman or a man.[30]

Through the operations of alienation and separation, through the "castration" that marks the subject's coming into being as a being represented by a signifier for another signifier, the subject is marked both as a "sexed being," a being inscribed in the structure of sexual differences, and as a finite being. As a sexed being, not in the biological sense but in the sense of being inscribed as a sexed "I am," the subject "is no longer immortal" (S11: 205). As in every castration, something is lopped off. Not only is the subject's immortality lost, there's also that "pound of flesh," as Lacan put it, that "must be paid" for this inscription of the subject into the chains of the signifier, and so into the domain of sexual desire. This becomes thought at the level of separation and experienced as the "lost object," the object of a transgressive *jouissance* in excess of the pleasure principle, identified in the Lacanian topology as contact with the real, and called, in *Seminar VII*, "the Thing" (*das Ding*), or in *Seminar XI*'s account of structure of the fantasy, as "object *a*," and as the "lamella," the "myth" of the deathless lamella, all of which Lacan will speak of in connection with the drives, including the death drive, that lethal "portion of death in the sexed living being" (S11: 205).

Thus, sexuality and gender, like death and finitude, come to be as a result of inscription into the symbolic order, not as a result of organic conditions or differences. Sexual difference, as Lacan shows in his later seminars, is determined by the different ways of being inscribed in the symbolic orders relative to the position and function of the phallus, which itself has a symbolic rather than organic function. The organic enters into this only in terms of the "lost part," the speechless, voiceless lamella, the organ of the libido and the drives.

This is the true significance of Lacan's claim that the inscription of the subject in the symbolic order comes about through a necessary "castration," "the function of the cut" (S11: 206), which institutes the reigns of sexuality and death. With castration, with the entry into the realms of sexuality and death, the subject now "exists," the subject "is," as having a position in the domain of language; it says, "I am," whose truth and certainty is as an "I think," where I am not. This is the lack at the heart of the subject designated by the barred S, and it is this lack that engenders the subject not only as a conscious cogito, but also as a desiring being, a being riding the crests of the drives.

Lacan further demonstrates these relationships by using a two-circle Venn diagram, as used in simple logic, having three areas: one for Being (again, being transformed by language, being transformed into a subject by the Other of language), one for Meaning or the Other, and the third being the overlap of the two circles, which is that of non-being, or lack, that area marked by the rim of the unconscious.

At the level of alienation, the subject, marked as "barred S" is shown as being within the circle of the field of Being. This subject is alienated from the other circle, which would be the circle of "meaning," marked as S2. The lack is located in the overlap of the two circles, a zone marked as S_1, which designates the "unary signifier." In Lacan's later *Seminar XVII*, S_1 is said to be the "master signifier," the signifier which represents the subject, barred S, for another signifier (S_2). Hence, the lack at this level is the fact that the subject cannot be wholly represented in the Other, in the field of meaning. The Other, defined by Lacan as "the locus in which is situated the chain of the signifier that governs whatever may be made present of the subject—it is that field of the living being in which the subject has to appear . . . the subject depends on the signifier and the signifier is first of all in the field of the Other" (S11: 203–205). And this field of the Other, within which the subject is thus alienated, implies that there is always a remainder, something left out or left behind, which Lacan says is the subject's sexually defined being. The level of alienation is also the level of the analytic transfers, and so, a level of deceptions and uncertainty. According to Lacan, once again using the language of the Cartesian philosophy, the unconscious that "thinks," that is the lack, the non-being, at the heart of subjectivity, is the locus of the only certainty the subject shall ever have.[31]

Commentators have remarked that the introduction of "separation" is one of the true innovations of *Seminar XI*,[32] although Lacan himself traces it to Freud's notion of the *Ichspaltung*, "the splitting of the subject."[33] Lacan did not diagram the level of separation, but, following Jacques-Alain Miller, Éric Laurent has provided one which, again using the two-circle Venn diagram, has barred S in the far left area of the first circle, separated from the signifying chain S_1—S_2 (meaning that it takes at least two signifiers to designate the structure of the Other), with "object *a*" in the overlap of the two circles, the area of "non-being."[34] Lacan calls this a logical operation of "intersection": "it is the product formulated by a belonging *to* ____ and *to* ___. The function is modified here by a part taken from a lack (that of the desire of the subject) situated within another lack (the lack in/of the Other)."[35]

It is at the level of separation that Lacan introduced the *velle*, from the French *vouloir*, that is to say, a "want to be," a want to get out, to pull oneself free, to know what is "beyond the Other."[36] At the level of separation, the Other is, thus, not quite the same Other as that at the level of alienation, where the Other was the Other as the treasury of signifiers. The Other at the level of separation is an Other in which something is lacking, the Other as lack, written as a "barred A," where the capital A means *Autre*, Other.[37] The lack at the heart of the Other is desire. The question the subject continually asks of the Other is "What does he/she (qua Other) want?" ("*Chè vuoi?*" as Lacan phrases it.)[38] Separation thus marks the encounter with the lack, the desire of the Other, the encounter with desire's lack.[39] Now, since the subject at the level of separation is thus a subject that lacks in being, it is a subject that wants to be. Thus, as Lacan writes in his essay "Position of the Unconscious" (1960, rewritten in 1964), "*Separare*, separating, ends here in *se parere*, engendering oneself" in view of the lack in the Other. Separation is the level at which the subject's "causation closes."

Here is where we find the elements fundamental to Lacan's conception of truth as lack, for there are thus two overlapping lacks active here. The first is that marked in the operation of "alienation" as S_1, the dependence of the subject on the signifier qua "field of the Other" (level of alienation). Then, there is the "real lack" marked in the operation of separation as "object a," a lack that comes with castration, that comes with "the function of the cut," and so, with the "function of the rim," for, with every cut there is a rim, a living edge, a gap that was not there before (S11: 206), and this gap names the unconscious as situated in the locus of the Other. As Lacan writes, his thesis enunciates "the presence of the unconscious, being situated in the locus of the Other can be found in every discourse, in its enunciation."[40] This is the way and the topos of the unconscious: to be the lack of being in the locus of the Other.

The "real lack," the lack in the real, to use the language of the Lacanian topology of the imaginary, the symbolic and the real, is the price to be paid for this advent of the subject into the signifying chain, the symbolic order. In terms of alienation and separation, Lacan continues to mark the disjunction of thinking and being. These two operations moreover provide his doctrine with the "dynamics" it was seeking. He calls this the topology of the subject in a "logical dynamics" (S11: 203), a dynamics of the structure of the subject defined not in terms of unity, coherence, self-presence, and transparency, but in terms of the shadow plays of language and desire, identifications and fantasies.

At the level marked by the structure of separation, where transgression, *jouissance*, and the real are encountered as either "the Thing," or as "object a," we also have the special ethical domain that was the focus of the ethical concern at the heart of Lacan's psychoanalysis. For Lacan, the ethical question obtains not only, as in Levinas, in the face-to-face encounter with the other, and not only at the level of the imaginary and the transference, but more fundamentally at the level of the symbolic, which Lacan will show as a vector directed toward the faceless encounter with the "real" (see also essay 7 in this volume). These ethical dimensions of the analytic situation will especially pertain not to the subject as patient, but especially to the desire of the analyst, which must be the position of non-being marked in the "discourse of analysis" as "object *a* in relation to S barred (\$)" (see S17; on "The production of the four discourses," also discussed in essay 6 in this volume).

This "topology of the subject," deduced from the primary thesis "the unconscious is structured like a language," thus distributes the ways and manifestations of truth according to the two levels marked as separation and alienation. But there is more at stake than this: By this use of topology, set theory, and the other *mathèmes*, by this overall formalism and abandonment of assurances from intuitions, Lacan says on these pages from *Seminar XI* that he hopes to show the scientific basis for a psychoanalysis now recognizable as the "science of the unconscious" (S11: 203). An inquiry into the scientific basis for Lacanian psychoanalysis cannot be broached here, but what should be emphasized is that Lacan's science of the unconscious was based not only on rather static structures and formal, mathematical and logical relations, but that he was also insisting on a "dynamics." In other words, his concern throughout these pages from *Seminar XI* was for dynamics, for something in excess of structure and yet constitutive of it. Particularly this last point shall be of interest to any inquiry into the ethics and politics of Lacanian psychoanalysis, for it offers the possibility of placing at the heart of that ethic the dynamics of the act, the dynamics of truth, of *jouissance*, and the death drive, the dynamics of the joys and hells, both private and public, unleashed in the two operations of alienation and separation that drive the constitution of the subject in its subjection within the symbolic order.

CAN THE TRUTH BE SAID?
TRUTH AIMS AT THE REAL

It was shown earlier that it is insofar as it is structured like a language that the unconscious is said by Lacan to think. We are now in a position to develop this idea and carry it further. What Lacan is referring to here as "thinking" is in fact a functioning governed by a principle first isolated and described by Freud as the pleasure principle, whose job it is to maintain a low, steady state of balanced excitations. There is an opening and closing of the unconscious that determines the border of inclusions and exclusions, of acceptance and rejection in accordance with the governance of the pleasure principle. Here, thinking is this structural opening and closing of the "rim of the unconscious."[41] This pulsation, which is the temporality of this opening and closing of the unconscious, also comprises the dynamics of truth in the analytic experience. Moreover, this dynamic of the opening and closing of the unconscious is one of the important reasons why, in that experience, truth remains but a half-saying (*mi-dire*). It is to this that we now turn.

It is especially Lacan's seventeenth seminar that characterizes truth at this level of the pulsations of the unconscious that emerge in the analytic experience as *mi-dire*, a half-saying, or as half-said. This is the key property of truth in Lacan's teaching. "If there is one thing that our entire approach delimits, and that has surely been renewed by analytic experience, it is that the only way in which to evoke the truth is by indicating that it is only accessible through a half-saying (*mi-dire*), that it cannot be said completely, for the reason that beyond this half there is nothing to say. That is all that can be said. Here, consequently, discourse is abolished" (S17: 51/58).

Hence, while truth is thus folded and doubled in Lacan's teachings—there is the truth of the unconscious, the truth of the subject of the enunciation, and the truth of the subject named as the subject of the statement, the *énoncé*, the subject as inscribed in the chain of signifiers ($S_1 \rightarrow S_2$)—the essential point is this: whether at the level of the *énoncé*, that is to say, at the level of truth in the field of knowledge, which, in Lacan's seventeenth seminar is identified by the algebraic symbols $S_1 \rightarrow S_2$, or at the level of the master signifiers and their relations to the fields of knowledge, whether at the level of the analytic experience, or at the level of the subjective enunciation, truth is essentially and always delimited as lack and *mi-dire*.

There is something more. Considered as a presentation, as manifestation, whether at the level of the unconscious or of the chain of signifiers, truth, thought in terms of lack, is not the manifestation of lack. Truth is manifestation *as lack*, just as death, as radical finitude in its manifestation, was brought to life in and as the signifier. So, manifestation as lack is the simultaneous evental giving of truth and the withdrawal of truth in the real. Truth bores a hole in the real. As manifestation, like Beauty and the Good, so Truth, too, is also withdrawal into concealment, but this is phrased as the "half-said" of truth. In its links with desire, in being the truth of desire that every analysand must confront, and in its essential links with language, in the constant postponement and metonymic deferrals of language and desire, in truth's links with censorship, with error and lies, truth is lack, having *mi-dire*, the "half-said," as its essential property. Truth as lack is thus not just a lack of truth, or as a lack in truth, but truth *as* lack. Truth is thus taken as manifestation, as the lack at the heart of manifestation. This is truth as *manque à être* evoked earlier, truth as lack in being, which, as we have said, links truth to the unconscious insofar as it, like the unconscious, is a lack of forgetting, which is to be understood in terms of the indestructible desires and unconscious "wishes" and "processes" Freud speaks of at the end of his *Traumdeutung*. But truth is here also linked to the lack brought about through castration, which truth as semblance likes to cover up (S17: 52/58).[42] Lacan has shown that truth is the lack in being (*manque à être*), but Jean-Luc Nancy writes that truth, as lack, is "the lack of nothing" (*manque de rien*).[43] The *de* has a double significance, both objective and genitive, as in Lacan's thesis, "desire is always desire *of* the Other." Thus, truth lacks nothing, and, at the same time, truth is nothing's lack, so to speak, nothing's lack in being. Lack, in its doubling, its strange multiplying, is always presented as having a positive, constitutional role to play vis-à-vis the subject, which is most decisively evident in castration whereby the subject is subjected to the symbolic order. Lack, truth, is constitutive of the subject, which arises in and through castration. The subject is thus written as "S barred," as we have seen in connection with the levels of alienation and separation. The bar is the decisive, inaugural mark of the "unary trait," that mark by which the subject is marked, named, and given a place in the symbolic order.

This is a more primal orientation on truth than that achieved in the philosophical conception of truth as adequation, whereby truth is the discursively noted link or measure between thought and being, whereby being is not thought as manifestation itself, but as an object-qua-entity of thought. This philosophical conception of truth as the adequation between objects, or "states of affairs," and propositions sees truth as a building block for a true system of knowledge. The psychoanalytic conceptions of truth as "lack in being," as "inseparable from the effects of language," as *mi-dire*, all link truth not with objects and propositions, but with the nullity of the "real," and so with *jouissance*. In Lacan's seminar, truth is the "sister of *jouissance*." Whereas the philosophical conception of truth as a "truth value" may be important for the building of a true knowledge, truth as "the sister of *jouissance*," as Lacan phrased it in his seminars from the early 1970s, is a truth for an ethics of the real, and for a real ethics of truth. The concluding essay in this collection shall approach this in terms of an "ethics Well-spoken."

At the same time, in and as the truth of both the field of knowledge and that of the unconscious, truth is both an approach to and a barrier posed, in its very lack, against the real, which is also described in the Lacanian discourse as certainty, as what lacks nothing, as what always returns to the same place. Truth, and for Lacan this is essentially and most importantly the truth of the unconscious, is both a lure, an object of desire, and a barrier to the *jouissance* that exceeds language and the pleasure principle.

As a network, a chain of signifiers, language is also a "net" seemingly cast over the totality of the real. "It inscribes on the plane of the real this other plane, which we here call the plane of the symbolic" (S1: 262). So, what is the relation between the symbolic network of language and what Lacan calls the "real"? Lacan says that at this point, we encounter an enigma, the enigma of truth itself. The network of signifiers does not just more or less adequately name or reflect the real, but is an *effect* of the real. Truth, as lack, carves out a hollow in the real, attempts to bore a hole through the real. Thus, another key link between psychoanalysis and philosophy is the question concerning the relation of truth and the real, where "the real"—at least as Lacan conceptualized it in *Seminar VII*— names all that is outside, in excess of language and the symbolic domain. This definition, which obtains in *Seminar VII*, also effectively places "man" in the "mediating function between the real and the signifier" (S7: 129/155).

The dark, insistent, and unspeakable *jouissance* of the real, the real as impossible object in desire, is, if you will, the other side of the splendor of philosophical truth, truth as the Platonic light in which all existent beings are brought to light. Like the Good and like Beauty, Truth has a double role as both lure and barrier to the real, to the Thing and to *jouissance*. And, it is precisely because of this essential and positive role that the "truth about truth" cannot be said, or that is, at best, truth half-said.

Freud and Lacan thus recast truth in its relation to the real, the unknowable real, which, insofar as it is beyond the imaginary and the symbolic domains, is also beyond all contradiction and self-differencing. "Truth hollows its way into the real thanks to the dimension of speech" (S1: 228). When truth hollows its way into the real, when it speaks *of*, or, impossibly *from* the real in this sense, it is here that one also encounters the gamut of errors and mistakes, cracks and breaks and slips of the tongue that Freud so aptly termed the "psychopathologies of everyday life," for this is where speech breaks down, where truth "slips away as soon as she appears." Again, we encounter Lacan's theses of truth as lack and *mi-dire*: The whole of truth can never be said, but only "half-said" (*mi-dire*) (S20: 92). And so, as Lacan will say in 1973, *jouissance* is such a limit to truth, one that can only be "questioned, evoked, tracked, and elaborated on the basis of semblance" (S20: 92).

In support of this, it is also helpful to recall how, in his eleventh seminar, Lacan thus described the real as the "obstacle to the pleasure principle." Hence, insofar as the unconscious "thinks," as was said before, and does so in accordance with the pleasure principle, then what Lacan calls the real as an obstacle to the pleasure principle, is an obstacle therefore to thinking, and as such, it is that impediment, that opacity against which thinking and truth "run aground." Lacan adds, "The real is the impact with the obstacle; it is the fact that things do not turn out all right straight away, as the hand that is held out to external objects wishes" (S11: 167).

This is important for Lacan's ethics, which, as was said before, could be called an "ethics of the real." As such, it is an ethics that takes up all those situations and instances within a situation where "things do not turn out alright." It is this Lacanian emphasis on the gap, on the "lack in being," on the "impact of the real," encountered in "death" and "truth" that marks the "blind spots," that marks the real as the opacity in the watchful eye and the discourse of the "care of the soul." In the European tradition of the care of the soul that commenced in Pythagoras and Socrates, there was always a privileging of proximity to self and mastery of self through truth. The infinite inner conversation was always a way of keeping the soul in the light of truth. Proximity was essential for purification of the soul, which was the objective of care, the purification of the pathological and all else that would keep the soul from its rendezvous with the divine. The Lacanian perspective has another direction. Truth, in the analytic situation, is linked not with purity but with "error," with what "fails," runs aground on the impact of the real. Truth may never seal its lips; yet, can never say all. Truth is never whole and never wholly said. For Lacan, truth as *mi-dire* is lack, always the infinite lack of something in everything said. What Lacan calls the real or the Thing (Freud's *das Ding*) thus maintains for Lacan a point of rupture and opacity that ultimately shipwrecks the philosophical project of complete self-knowledge that defines the tradition of the care of the soul. The truth is always and only *mi-dire*. There is always that impact of the real that tears a hole in the transparency of the immortal soul.

Now, if all of this is indeed the case, then it certainly follows that the real is something that must be kept at a distance from the subject, and in that sense, can even be identified with the sovereign Good of the subject, compared in Plato's *Republic* with the sun and so characterized by Plato as a solar burst in excess of the powers of the finite capacities of human thought, and so as the destruction of the subject. Hence, the Good, in all its destructive, overwhelming powers, could even be experienced as a great suffering and evil. Hence, somewhat like truth, and the truth about truth, what Lacan called "the Thing," as what names the *jouissance* in excess of the pleasure principle, and as the encounter and impact of the real, must be maintained by the pleasure principle at a distance, kept apart, as something inaccessible, forbidden, and unspeakable. If Lacan's analytic theory is indeed an "object theory," then the Thing, or the real, are objects that must be kept at a distance, and the ethical task of analysis is to maintain this gap, this distance.

This might be termed the Lacanian "care of the self": care maintains the gap between the subject and the real, or, in other words, between the subject and the Thing (*das Ding*). It is this gap that is taken up and described in Lacan's seventh seminar, *The Ethics of Psychoanalysis*. In that context, this gap between the subject and the Thing was very strikingly connected with something Lacan considered to be a chief ethical problem often encountered in analysis, namely, the attraction of transgression and the will to transgress.

Here, then, is the ethical function of truth as lack: to be both the scene or the screen by which the Thing and *jouissance* are there and not there; its role is to keep transgressive *jouissance* of the Thing at a distance; to take aim at the real outside of the symbolic and imaginary orders so as to keep it at a distance. We shall be returning to this theme further on.

Badiou's reading of Lacan as anti-philosopher also casts the Lacanian determination of truth in terms of the ethical situation rather than as a purely theoretical one; likewise, the real is also cast as the relation between truth and lack, or "void," as he calls it, where "the void," like the real, is the "nexus" for truth.

In Badiou's reading of Lacan, where the philosophical axiom is that "Thought must be understood on the basis of Being," the psychoanalytic axiom is that "there is unconscious thought and an unconscious truth." Badiou provides a quote from Lacan's seminar in support of this in this: "Truth aims at the real" (S20: 91, seminar of April 1973). So, "what is truth such that it only concerns the real"[44] and how do philosophy and psychoanalysis differ in their determinations of the relation of truth and the real?

Well, Lacan completes the idea of truth aiming at the real by saying that "wherever truth presents itself, asserts itself as if it were an ideal that could be based on speech," its connections with the real proves that this idealization of truth, this "pretension to truth," "is not so easily attained" (S20: 91/84). The key phrase that should be emphasized here reads, "wherever truth *presents* itself;" wherever truth presents itself, (and here, too, is the profound investment of truth in death, as the death drive), it presents itself in and through language, through speech. Thus, "I, truth, speak," as Lacan writes in his 1955 essay, "The Freudian Thing" (*Écrits*: 340/409). Speech, Lacan tells us, speech deposited, *déposée*, 'registered' or 'deposed' in the Other, in the "hole" of the Other, founds truth, and with truth, it also founds the "pact that makes up for," or, as one might say, it 'supplements' "the non-existence of the sexual relationship" (S20: 114/103). That there is no sexual relationship is one of Lacan's primary theses. This thesis must in turn be thought on the basis of the trium-virate of truth, the subject as a speaking subject, and the indefatigable real. Truth is founded on language, on speech, deposited in the hole of the Other. So, in thinking truth and its relation to the real, one must think of truth in its relation to language where it always presents itself as lack, a lack similar to the real, an in-finite lack. Again, in this way, truth is an effect of the real. Recall that truth, for Lacan, can thus never be the correspondence, or the adequation of thought, language, and being. Badiou says that this is something contemporary philosophy and Laca-nian psychoanalysis have in common.[45] There is no relation of adequation between speech and the real. Thought, language, and speech are always separated from the real. The relation of the symbolic order with the real is always mediated by "semblance" (See the diagram, S20: 90). Yet, Lacan also maintains that "discourse cannot be reduced to beginning solely from semblance" (S20: 114/103). So, like the real, truth and speech are also defined in terms of lack, or of a void. Truth takes aim at the real, but can never attain it. This "taking aim" and this failure thus become intrinsic and essential components of truth. Truth has a direction, an "aim," but it must always fail. Truth as "failure" is truth as lack. The failure of truth, its running aground on the edge of the real, is the "knowledge about truth that psychoanalysis can constitute on the basis of its experience" (S20: 91/84). Truth, as lack, as what always fails, runs aground on the real, yet it is also confounded, is confused with the real. But its similarity with the real obtains only in its conjoint failure to attain the real and its taking aim at the real. As one commentator phrases it, Lacan shows that "truth is similar to the real; it is impossible to articulate the whole of truth," and, quoting Lacan, he concludes, "[p]recisely because of this impossibility, truth aspires to the real."[46]

Where philosophy and psychoanalysis both elaborate the question of truth and the thinkable relationship between truth and the lack/void, they differ in the way each locates it, and so the nexus of truth. For Lacan, with his emphasis on the death drive and on the Other as the hole, as the lack, where speech, through being deposited, founds truth,[47] the void is thereby localized not on the side of Being but on the side of the subject, the subject as the lack, as the hole, the gap, the pure difference that is "myself," *moi-même*, as *meme*, making it a difference that is "self" and "sameness." As Lacan writes in *Seminar VII*, "that which is most myself in myself, that which is the heart of myself, and beyond me, insofar as the self stops at the level of those walls to which one can apply a label, what in French at least serves to designate the notion of self or same, then, is this interior or emptiness [which Lacan refers to as the *metipsemus—meme*], and I don't know if it belongs to me or to nobody" (S7: 198).

What is more, in his "Seminar on *The Purloined Letter*," Lacan locates truth as lack "at the very foundation of intersubjectivity." Thus, it is situated where the subject can grasp nothing but the very subjectivity that constitutes an Other as an absolute."[48] But, here, too the Other is also marked by infinite lack.

Continuing with Badiou, philosophy locates this void, as in the instance of the Heideggerian concept of truth as *aletheia*, the "clearing of Being," on the side of Being. In Heideggerian terms, Being appropriates "Man," *Dasein*, to his nature, which is to be "released" (*Gelassenheit*), or open to Being, and man's proper nature or essence is to attend to Being. Care is a tending to one's appropriation by Being. Badiou continues, "Philosophy and psychoanalysis agree that truth is separation, that the real is irreducible or, as Lacan says, unsymbolizable, that truth is different from knowledge, and that truth thus only occurs under condition of the void . . . but philosophy localizes the void—or "lack"—as a condition of truth on the side of being *qua* being."[49]

But for Badiou, situating the void, or lack, on the side of being would have, for Lacan's discourse, the consequence of also situating thought on the side of being. To the contrary, it must be recalled that truth as lack is situated on the side of thought as separated from being.

By taking truth as lack, Lacan rejects this identification of Being and thinking. It is the unconscious that breaks the Parmenidean axiom identifying Being and Thought. Here lies the basis for what Badiou, too, sees as Lacan's opposition to philosophy, and, to the discourses on the care of the soul, for which all action and desire aim at some good, especially the highest Good, "happiness" (*eudaimonia*), and so aims at the Beautiful and at Truth as plenitude of Being, aims at God, the Other as the locus of truth, and so identified with Being. Lacan's question to the discourses on the care of the soul, at least on these points, might be: Are these modes of care of the soul not also modes of defense, barriers raised against the lack, the cut, the division at the heart of the subject, just as they are defenses, barriers raised against the *jouissance* of the Thing and the real?

Now, the Freudian truth Lacan brings to light is a truth other than either the truths confirmed by referential observations or the truth of St. Augustine's inner light. It is a truth radically and, for that Greek and Augustinian tradition, unthinkably Other. The truth of the unconscious that Freud discovered behind speech (*la parole*) is not an inner light, nor does it recognize the laws of contradiction. Lacan: "Absolute knowledge is this moment in which the totality of discourse closes in on itself in a perfect noncontradiction up to and including the fact that it posits, explains, and justifies itself. *We are some way yet from this ideal.*" (S1: 264, emphasis mine). The errancy of truth, truth as *mi-dire*, will have the last word.

TRUTH, SEMBLANCE, AND ERROR

Lacan thus situates Freud's concepts of truth and error not only in the subject of knowledge and science, and certainly not in terms of the "truth value" of a proposition, but also in the subject of desire. This puts the domain of truth not in the field of the proposition and its relation to an object, but in terms of desire and the objects of desire. Thus, there is a further emphasis in Lacan's teaching on the interplay of truth and semblance. In the philosophical, and especially the scientific traditions dating from Plato and the Greeks, truth, the light of truth, is the light that reveals things as they are in their essence, as opposed to things as they only appear to be. The old philosophical distinction between a True World and an Appearing World arises from this. The philosopher-scientist must escape the allure of false appearances (S7: 310). As one learns from reading Descartes' *Meditations*, scientific and philosophical certainty can only be purchased on the basis of the demonstrated assertion of a God that does not deceive. The doubt that attaches itself to every piece of sense data and to every perception of the senses must be overcome by a certainty ultimately founded on a truthful God. But, for Lacan, the distinction between a True World and a World of Appearances is cancelled. Truth is related to semblance, as in the most prominent example of sexual play where there is an irreducible play of semblance, or of masquerade. In this sense, truth becomes identified with "Woman," a word quoted and erased in Lacan's seminars, under the slogan "truth is a Woman," but especially and more accurately, with feminine sexuality.

This is most evident in the case of animal mimicry, which is found in the animal dance of sexual partners, whereby the being of the animal "breaks up," as Lacan said in *Seminar XI, The Four Fundamental Concepts of Psychoanalysis*, into "itself," and that "paper tiger it shows to the other" (S11: 113). Similarly, love is always addressed to a semblance, Lacan says in *Encore* (S20: 85). One erects a semblance of one's being, based, no doubt, on one's ego ideals, in the play of desire and in the sexual relations with the body of the Other. In his seminars from the early 1970s, semblance is generalized such that it even comes to characterize the symbolic order itself and its relations to the imaginary order and with the real. "Every act of speech . . . introduces the dimension of truth into the real," and with this comes deception, the necessity of deception. Speech deceives, Lacan taught in his first seminar, *Freud's Papers on Technique* (1953–1954), but in order to do so, it must affirm itself as true (S1: 263).Thus, the old philosophical distinction between essence, or truth, and false appearance, begins to breakdown in Lacan's seminars. Truth becomes more and more identified with what is said, with the deceptive saying of truth, a saying that is, thus, said to be *mi-dire* and so continuous with error. Truth and error, truth and the lie, are thus no longer opposed, but become the two sides of a Möbius strip.[50]

This is especially the case in the interplay between what slips through the barriers of censorship and what remains repressed in the unconscious, the barrier of discourse where condensation and displacement come into play. In Lacanian terms, "Our abortive actions are actions that succeed . . . these acts, these words reveal a truth from behind . . . if Freud's discovery has any meaning, it is that truth grabs error (what we call free associations, dream images, symptoms, a word whereby truth is revealed) by the scruff of the neck in the mistake" (S1: 265). Further on, citing Freud, Lacan calls this "the revelation, within the phenomenon, of subjective moments in which speech goes beyond the discoursing subject" (S1: 265).

Now, with truth defined as lack and as *mi-dire*, and as further linked with error and the field of the mistaken, the symbolic order, the order of the signifying chains that comprise the structure and the law for the ethical and political functioning of the subject, must play a role as witness and guarantor of truth. The lack requires its guarantor insofar as truth has a function in the symbolic order.

Speech springs not from the ego, nor even from the subject, understood in a psychological sense of the word, but from another place outside of consciousness, in the unconscious, the "discourse of the Other."[51]

Moreover, speech is always founded in the existence of the Other qua "witness to truth," the other who is the Other that even my lie invokes as a guarantor of the truth, and which my lie must ironically sustain.[52] Where there is language, there is truth as error, forgetting, and lies. But, the Other (capital O), the big Other, the symbolic order, is, for Lacan, first of all not only what precedes the subject, but what is also the locus in which the subject's speech is constituted as the guarantor of its truth. Its rules will determine the place of the subject and guarantee the truth of its speech—even if false.[53] As lure and barrier before the real, truth is not just deception, but also error. Either way, it requires this guarantor found in the Other in order that deception succeed or that error be recognizable as such.

Thus, Lacan distinguishes error, qua pathway, and manifestation qua *mi-dire* of truth from deception (S1: 263). Deception is always cast against a background of truth and requires, in the case of a conventional lie, a good memory. "You have to know a hell of a lot of things to sustain a lie" (S1: 263). But error is "the incarnation of truth" (S1: 263), not just a background or implication.

Hence, Lacan's usage of the term "error" must also be distinguished from "erroneous," with the resulting dividend being a more proper understanding of the analytic relation of error and truth. Lacan does not say, "without error there would be no truth," but rather, "to be entirely rigorous," he says, "we would say in all probability that, as long as the truth isn't entirely revealed, that is to say in all probability until the end of time, its nature will be to propagate itself in the form of error" (S1: 263). Not the contradictory of truth, error is the proper form of truth. This binding relationship is, Lacan writes, "a structure constitutive of being." And when Lacan speaks of being, in connection with truth, he speaks of desire in its ceaseless metonymy. His account of truth and error can only be understood in relation to desire, desire as lack, and to the ways in which language, the symbolic order, is linked in this ceaseless metonymy of being to the double play of lure and barrier to the Thing and to *jouissance* in the real. The signifier, the master signifier, for example, the phallus, can be seen as the form in which formless lack, death, and the void are all "propagated" and annihilated precisely in being given signifying form.

The upshot of this is that where truth and error are each the proper form of the other, where, as Lacan says, "there is no error which does not present and promulgate itself as truth," and where "error is the habitual incarnation of truth" (S1: 263), then there is no way to distinguish truth from error, which would entail that the laws of thought and of noncontradiction be forfeited. And this is in fact the case where it comes to the logic of the unconscious. Nothing, nothing but the nothingness of death, the absolute master, could ever oppose error.[54] Since error can only be discerned through "recourse either to the test of experience entailing confirming and referential observations, or by the light of an inner truth, which is the aim of the Augustinian dialectic" (S1: "Truth Emerges from the Mistake": 263–264), this error identified with truth, is more than just a mistake. It is error, the error and errancy of the lack of being.

TELLING THE TRUTH: TRUTH AND THE VOICE

The meditations on error and the relation between truth and the field of the mistaken, points to important consequence of the *mi-dire* property of truth: namely, that truth *speaks*, that the abode of truth is not "light," as in Plato's *Republic*, but speech as the field of the mistaken and *mi-dire*. If truth speaks, it must not only do so indirectly, in breaks, and disruptions, but also in lies and errors. Thus, the pathways of truth are pathways of *error* as the many ways in which speech is disrupted, half-spoken in and by the breakages in speech, the slips, and errancies of the voice. Truth is *mi-dire*: one is never able to say the whole truth.[55] The Lacanian subject is, thus, unable to know or to pronounce the truth of the unconscious at the core of his being. The subject fundamentally remains a subject deprived of self-knowledge as well as a subject whose speech will also be haunted by error.

Paradoxically, then, this subject of truth, the truth of the subject marked as the barred S, would be a subject who must both speak the truth about his/her desire, yet cannot know it, for it is a truth anterior or exterior to all knowing. Because of the identification of truth with speech, qua *mi-dire*, and so with error, this is a truth without any ultimate objective reference in the sense that, for the Lacanian psychoanalytic discourse on truth, there is no metalanguage on or about truth: there is no truth to tell about truth, there is no meaning of meaning.[56]

The importance of speech and the voice for Lacan's formulations of truth as lack and as *mi-dire* essentially springs thus from his clinical experience, from the analytic transference, for example, where deception, error, the *mi-dire* of truth obtains. In the analytic situation, the analyst must play a double role: both the "imaginary" (in the sense of Lacan's use of the word "imaginary") other person in the room, and as the Other, the one who knows that answers to the patient's sufferings. Here, is the crux of the ethical domain and problem for Lacanian psychoanalysis, in this interrelationship between analyst and analysand that is sustained in the voice, in talking. Analysis is a "talking cure." Analysis is first and foremost a "technique of speech" (S2: 261). Speech, the voice, is the "engine" and milieu of analysis. It is the "third term" between analyst and analysand and, as such, cannot be reduced to being just a means for the communication of signified contents. Thus, from the outset, there is a privileging of speech (*la parole*) and of the voice. Scientific discourse, by contrast, tends toward the development of a language deprived of all reference to the voice. So, it is the Freudian discovery that institutes a strikingly new role for the voice.

For Lacan, the scene of truth is in the speech of the Other as deferred desire. I must tell the truth about my desire in speech as though it were a "revelation," but, this is also a speech that conceals. It is a speech that is both full and empty. The demand remains and its topos is the Other qua "locus in which is constituted the I who speaks along with that second 'other' [small "o"], the other who hears."[57] The truth of desire and of the unconscious is a truth manifest in the speech—both full and empty—of the subject who must tell the truth ("I, the truth, speak"). From which it would follow that the conscious subject is one who both speaks and does not speak this truth. It really isn't the subject "who" speaks, but rather, an "it" that speaks in the Other, that speaks "in man and through man."[58]

So, everything obtains in the cross-current, at a point of resistance, between what Lacan in an early 1953 formulation called "mediational" discourses, the prosaic address of one subject to another, and the discourse of "revelation," that "other side of speech" in which the unconscious both reveals itself and hides in deformations, in the "smoke of dreams," in distortion and transportation. "Revelation is the ultimate source," Lacan said in one of his early seminars, "of what we are searching for in the analytic experience" (S1: 49). The aforementioned resistance obtains "at the moment when the speech is not said, when the revelation of the truth of the subject cannot be said, and when speech must function instead as mediation. This means that there is a pivotal point at which something is pressed away as unspeakable within the subject, something that nonetheless seeks to attain arrival ("revelation"), but that finds such arrival impossible. Speech thus "seesaws over into its initial aspect as it is reduced to its function of relationship to the other." In other words, it reverts to "mediation" with the other as a recourse at this pivotal moment of the failure of revelation, in which case there are moments when the smooth, operational flow of discourse falters due to forgotten words, bungled syntax, and the double play at work between things that are somehow "on one's mind" and what one actually says to the other.

The classic example of this, discussed at some length by Lacan,[59] is Freud's forgetting of the name of the painter Signorelli while making polite conversation with a doctor he was traveling with on a train to Herzegovina.[60] Freud had been thinking to himself of how the Bosnian Muslim Turks seem to take both a fatalistic attitude toward death and yet at the same time greatly fear the loss of sexual potency, and also how he had learned at Trafoi about the suicide of one of his patients and of a doctor's responsibilities in such cases. These topics deeply touching on sex and death seemed too delicate for Freud to discuss in polite company, so he kept his thoughts to himself. But, when in the course of the conversation, which was taking an altogether different direction, the discussion veered toward the famous frescoes by Signorelli at Orvieto, Freud, in describing them, could not remember the name of the artist who painted them, but, in error, attributed them to Botticelli or to Boltraffio. Because the frescoes in question have as part of their theme images of death and the Apocalypse and so were linked with his troubled thoughts on death, Freud stumbled and could not recall the name of the artist and listed other names instead, fragments of names: Botticelli, Boltraffio. Perhaps, as he stumbled in the midst of trying to maintain this polite conversation and keep to himself the unapproachable topics of sex and death, Freud had hoped that his interlocutor could "bear witness," as Lacan phrases it, and help him to bring the hidden, repressed, forgotten, broken word to memory. The proper name Signorelli, contains *signor*, master, as Herzegovina suggests *Herr*, also meaning master. These signifiers, which Freud might also think of as *Vorstellungrepräsentanten*, representations, thoughts attached to an unconscious desire, were subjected to repression, as Freud's self-analysis shows, because they referred to the resisted, hidden thoughts of death. Perhaps there was even an unconscious "wish" (*Wunsch*) for death, death being the absolute master signifier here, the "absolute master," as Lacan phrases it, both veiled and unveiled in the *signor* and *Herr* of the *parole*, speech. Thus, they were replaced, in an error, when the name Botticelli, for example, or Boltraffio (containing a fragment of Trafio), took their place and appeared in their stead. Lacan calls these fragments, the *signor* of the name Signorelli, the *Herr* of Herzegovina, the "broken tip of the memory's sword." Broken "because *signor*, along with *Herr*, the absolute Master, is aspirated and repressed by the apocalyptic breeze that blows in

Freud's unconscious in the echoes of the conversation he is in the process of carrying on: It is the disturbance, as he insists, there, of a theme which has just emerged, by the preceding theme—which is, in fact, that of death for which one has assumed responsibility."[61] Freud, to use the terms of *Seminar VII*, had thus "given way" on his desire. He had retreated, in a sense, back into polite conversation rather than name what it was that he had to say but could not bring himself to say. In his second published seminar, Lacan speaks of this as one of the aims of psychoanalysis, and the passage is worth quoting at length:

> What is important is to teach the subject to name, to articulate, to bring [his/her] desire into existence, this desire, which quite literally, is on this side of existence, which is why it insists. If desire doesn't dare to speak its name, it's because the subject hasn't yet caused this name to come forth. That the subject should come to recognize and to name his desire is the efficacious action of analysis. But, it isn't a question of recognizing something that could be entirely given, ready to be put to use. In naming it, the subject creates, brings forth [reveals] a new presence in the world. He introduces presence as such, and by the same token, hollows out absence as such. It is only at this level that one can conceive of the action of interpretation. (S2: 228–229)

Lacan veers quite close to saying and thinking here that truth is an "occurrence." Not a thing, value, concept, convention, or "correspondence," truth is an event in which something is both given and withdrawn. As such, truth, in this almost Heideggerian sense of being an occurrence, always requires a place, a locus, an abode, an opening in which truth can occur. For Lacan speech and the voice are the topos of truth, "in which is constituted the I who speaks along with he who hears," a locus that "extends as far into the subject as the laws of speech reign there, that is, well beyond the discourse that takes its watchwords from the ego."[62] The locus, the scene of truth, is the Other scene in Freud's sense, the scene of the Other and of the unconscious, the scene of the real, of the staging of the Thing as outside or beyond what can be spoken. And so, just to remind ourselves, when we speak of just how far this locus of the laws of speech extends into the subject, we would have to say it goes all the way down, all the way to the "true subject" of the unconscious. For Freud, the unconscious is thus the scene of the laws regulating not only speech, but especially and first of all sexuality; they are the structural laws regulating the permissible and the forbidden in sexual alliances and relations. Thus, the link between truth, law, and desire obtains for Freud and for Lacan at a level where "it" speaks, the "it" from which "I" must come to be and to speak. (*"Wo es war, soll Ich werden."*)

Let us hear this by returning for a moment to something briefly alluded to earlier: the link between truth, the voice, and woman. Lacan's seminars develop this connection between truth and the voice in a variety of ways. As *mi-dire*, as the lack that lacks nothing, truth "speaks for itself," as in Lacan's 1955 "The Freudian Thing," its voice is a woman's voice, like Socrates' Diotima. The truth that holds and embraces us is "truth as a woman":

> "To you [men, and philosophers] I am . . . the enigma of she who slips away as soon as she appears, you men who try so hard to hide me under the tawdry finery of your proprieties. . . . Will I perhaps tell you someday? But so that you will find me where I am, I will teach you by what sign you can recognize me. Men, listen, I am telling you the secret. I truth, speak."[63]

Truth as "lack" speaks as a woman. This is a familiar metaphor of truth: truth as a woman. But in Lacan, the metaphor of truth as a woman could be read as the veiling and unveiling of castration, castration being one of the forms of a "lack of object." Derrida pursues this in his reading of Lacan's seminar on Poe's *The Purloined Letter*.[64] Barbara Johnson has reminded us that the word "castration" does not even appear in Lacan's seminar, although it is strongly suggested, so Derrida is filling in what Lacan left blank.[65] Moreover, woman is not just an image of castration, but more properly an image of what Lacan calls "privation," the real lack of a symbolic object (see S4: 219). In any case, truth-woman-castration would not be an image of fragmentation and loss, but precisely the opposite: it is that by which the phallus can fill its role as the signifier of a lack, it is that which brings the phallus, the phallus as a lack which must not be missing from its place, back to its place. As Derrida writes, "The phallus, thanks to castration, always remains in its place, in the transcendental topology, . . . the phallus is indivisible, and therefore indestructible, like the letter which *takes its place*."[66]

But doesn't Lacan also pursue this in a slightly different direction when he compares truth to the virgin goddess Diana (Artemis) and places

Freud in the role of Acteon, the hunter pursuing truth, no doubt on the promise of seeing what no mortal should see, seeing truth unveiled, seeing her, naked in her abode, in her dark and moist grotto, seeing her, and in the moment of seeing her also reaching out to touch her, and at that moment of truth, he is both denied by the goddess and then devoured by his hounds precisely for attempting to see and to touch what is forbidden to see or to touch.[67] Isn't this a simulacrum of truth—not just a metaphor but an image of truth—as both lure and barrier? Truth is, in this scenario, the object of a fantasy.

But because of the way truth, hidden and demur, like a woman, because of the way this truth must be dressed in the "tawdry finery of proprieties," Lacan says it has become something "of almost ill repute, a word banished from polite society" and he apologizes to his audience for throwing this philosophically inclined word into their faces.[68] Against any such politely received, transcendental and universal conception of truth, Lacan argues that truth is always singular, yet attained through the Other. He writes, "This truth that we are seeking in a concrete experience is not that of a superior law. If the truth that we are seeking is a truth that frees, it is a truth that we will look for in a hiding place in our subject. It is a particular truth" (S7: 24). For Lacan, truth is "inscribed in the very heart of analytic practice, since this practice is constantly rediscovering the power of truth in us and in our very flesh."[69]

Hence, for Lacan, truth is a truth "founded by the fact that it speaks." As such, and not surprisingly, the Lacanian concept of truth as lack has nothing in common with the Kantian noumenon that, "for as long as pure reason can remember, has always kept its mouth shut."[70] Insofar as truth is something said, its locus is not in the noumenal but, as was said earlier, in the Other, the Other of the unconscious, where the "unconscious is the Other's discourse in which the subject receives his own forgotten message in the inverted form suitable for promises."[71] The Other as discourse is also the locus of truth qua remembering and forgetting and so, too, the locus of the promise.

In speaking, truth holds itself in the hole of the signifying structure, a pathway that does not, as in a philosophical "search for truth and a search for self-knowledge" so much "target" the Thing, the unspeakable "core of our being" (Freud's *Kern unseres Wesen*), as it does circle around it. As Lacan writes in "The Instance of the Letter in the Unconscious," a psychoanalytic "search for self-knowledge" would not so much target this *Kern*, this "core of our being," as though it were a hidden, noumenal meaning, because this core of our being is not a hidden meaning at all but rather what Lacan calls "ex-istence." It is radical alterity, the ex-centricity, the gap, the division, the lack in being at the core of our being. In his early seminars, Lacan thus spoke of the unconscious not only as being structured like a language, but it is a language that, at certain moments, unexpected moments, moments of error and errancy, breaks through in analysis, is revealed in the gaps, disruptions, and derailments of spoken discourse. These are spoken moments when the subject approaches the Thing, the real, and when the gap is closing. Such moments Lacan calls "*la parole*," speech, "full speech" (*parole pleine*), the speech of revelation, where the "fullness" in the revelation of the truth of desire manifests a paradoxical plenitude of *lack* in being. In moments of error, this lack becomes eloquent. The "other side" of the speech, when the real is both there and not there, is here, in error, manifested as lack. The language of everyday life, the imaginary discourse in which there is always and necessarily a *méconnaissance* of desire, a misunderstanding or a misrecognition of desire's lack that also yet implies a recognition of desire (S1: 167), here runs aground on the groundless ground of its truth.

But, it is important that these considerations of the interplay of truth, speech, and the role and presence of the voice—even at this early date in Lacan's *oeuvre*—withhold Lacan's thought from being too quickly and summarily reduced to being yet another epiphany of "phonocentrism" and the "metaphysics of presence," where the voice is identified purely with consciousness and "auto-affection." Freud's 1923 *The Ego and the Id* introduces other perspectives when it traces the origins of the super-ego to "word-presentations" (*Wortvorstellungen*) and the "verbal residues" of especially familial authority figures.[72] The voice becomes the acoustic surface of truth and the law. A voice hammers somewhere in one's head, inculcating a sense of guilt and shame ultimately linked to the Oedi-pal complexes, which although rooted in the unconscious are brought to consciousness via the word-presentations. It is the morality of the neurotic, Lacan adds in 1953, the morality of the imperative law that becomes senseless, oppressive, and destructive, "a simple tyranny." While the superego is identified with the law, and so with the whole system of language, it is also a failure to recognize (*méconnaissance*) the law and so is the destruction of the law. He locates the "constraining" superego, which he thus formulates as being both the law and its destruction, "within the symbolic plane of speech," in contrast to the "exalting" ego ideal, which is located at the level of the imaginary (S1: 102). Moreover, this will pos-sibly relate and at the same time distance Lacan's thinking of the voice from Heidegger's notion of the voice in *Being and Time* as the "call to conscience," and even further relate it to the problematic of the "who" or the "what" that speaks in Kant's categorical imperative, to wit: "Act only on that principle . . ." We will be hearing echoes of these voices in the very ethical imperatives Lacan hears in Sade, especially in his *Philosophy in the Bedroom*—"Let us take as the universal maxim of our conduct the right to enjoy any other person whatsoever as the instrument of our pleasure" (S7: 79)—and also in that maxim given voice in *Seminar VII,* Lacan's own: "Do not give way on your desire." Who or what speaks in such voiced imperatives? Are these also rationalized echoes of the super-ego? It cannot be the voice of consciousness or of the conscious subject. Rather, it addresses us both individually and universally, at least in the case of Kant, from a place beyond consciousness, a place both inaccessible and yet essential to the subject for it is the locus of autonomy. It is a place Kant would identify with reason. For Lacan, on the other hand, this voice might speak from the overlap of the subject and the Other, in the topos of unconscious desire, which turns an unconditional demand into an absolute condition, it calls for "an incommensurable measure, an infinite measure," one by which every object falls short, a measure and a force usually reserved for moral law itself (S7: 316). In any case, it is a place unattainable for the subject qua ego, although it is the very locus of the subject's autonomy and the kernel of its being.

Alternatively, in Plato and Aristotle's ethics and politics, it is the master's voice that speaks. Theirs is an ethic of the "well-said" (*bien dire*). The master's voice speaks and counsels what must be done in well-said argumentation. It speaks the truth rather than what is merely persuasive. But in Lacanian psychoanalysis, there is a confrontation with the unconscious and with castration in which there is an effacement of such mastery. Mastery is effaced, silenced in the pulsions of anxiety and *jouissance* that punctuate the ethical act. In this way, Lacan goes beyond mastery toward an essential relation with the Other (the trans-individual unconscious, "the Other who is within me"), which is neither ideal nor ascribable. What speaks in the ethic of psychoanalysis is a voiceless voice, the subject of an enunciation that pronounces from truth defined as the hole, the tear in the fabric of discourse.

As such, this is a truth addressed to the ends and goals of psychoanalysis, which are heard in Freud's *"Wo es war, soll Ich werden,"* which Lacan translates as "Where 'it' was, *must* I there come to be as a subject," a signifying being. Lacan here accentuates the "must": I *must* become a subject, I *must* speak the truth of my desire, I *must* affirm the truth of my desire, or of the desire that has me and that uses me, and "not give way on this desire." In naming this desire, in allowing its truth to speak, desire comes to be and so the subject "I," what must become, comes to be. Hence, "I" come to be what "I" am.

Thus, Lacan's taking of the measure of truth, the way he thinks again about the "construction" and the being of truth, shows that Lacanian psychoanalysis is concerned with more than the removal of neurotic symptoms and the collateral production of "normal subjective structure," as Badiou has accused it of doing. Rather, Lacan's emphasis is not on the reduction of symptoms at all, but on the clinical structure of the patient, and while Lacanian psychoanalysis does begin with the suffering subject who wants to understand "why" he/she suffers, the emphasis is on structure, for which language is paradigmatic. The symptom itself is conceived in terms of metaphor and message, not so much as a surface, organic phenomenon indicating a deeper disturbance hidden in the psychological-physiological depths of the patient. Lacan's thinking of truth does not pursue a way of normalizing neurotic patients, but is rather a way of effecting a radical change in the subject, a radical changing or reconstructing of his/her relation to the truth of their desire.

Lacan, thus, calls into question what counts for truth in psychoanalysis, especially for a psychoanalysis that seems to have forgotten the import and depth of the Freudian discovery. Lacan's meditation on truth not only provides a way for patients to achieve a healing insight into the stupidities and suffocating patterns that are destroying their lives, it also invents new possibilities and concepts concerning truth that are of value for anyone trying to think against the prevailing norms of a modern Western society. It addresses thereby the discontents of modern civilization as such.

Before the new formulations on truth found in *Seminar XI*, wherein truth was studied in terms of the rubrics of alienation and separation, Lacan's early meditations on the voice and truth explored the synchronic, discursive dimensions of truth: truth's presentation takes time; truth comes, like signification, at the end of the statement, in what Lacan called "the backward movement (*recul*) of enunciation in which metaphorical and metonymical effects are constituted," as the "very mechanisms of the unconscious."[73]

So, desire, constrained by inaccessible truth, thus follows a "metonymical procession and indefinitely defers itself or indefinitely defers its 'end.'" In speech, meaning always *insists*, but never *consists* in the signification that a chain of signifiers provides.[74] The signified is always sliding, necessitating Lacan's recourse to the so-called "button ties" (the *points de caption*) that will tie signifier and signified and bring this sliding to a temporary halt. The signifier thus also always anticipates its meaning, deploying it before it. This is evident in those instances when a sentence is interrupted, as in "I'll never . . ." and "The fact remains . . ." Or, as in the postponement of the "but."[75] Moreover, in his "The Instance of the Letter in the Unconscious," Lacan repeats the adage that desire must be taken literally, "to the letter." There is a relation between truth and the letter. The truth of desire is precisely in the letter that materializes the agency of death. The letter kills. Thus, the truth is that desire is "dead desire," an instance of truth identified not only with Saussure's linguistics but especially with Freud's discovery, Freud's truth, of the unconscious.[76] This relates to Lacan's idea that truth, at least at the level of the signifying chain, truth in the fields of knowledge, can be seen as structured like a *construct*, what Freud called a *Konvention*, which is not quite a myth, the truth of the drive is not a myth, for Lacan, but rather is closer to being a "fiction" (S11: 1978: 163). This is another way of encountering the *mi-dire* of truth.

Again, there is no transcendental, sustained, and secret truth, no pure presence of truth, apart from speech. "Before speech, nothing either is or isn't (*rien n'est, ni est pas*)" (S1: 228). There is no "truth of truth" apart from the disguises, errors, and parapraxis in which it is voiced. Truth is inaccessible only in being a truth not only of the "flesh," but of the unconscious and the "core of our being," and as such, inaccessible as an object of knowledge for the subject, like death, or like the freedom that is the core of ethical being and the moral imperative. And insofar as the unconscious is also characterized as being in the locus of the Other, the discourse of the Other, neither the unconscious nor truth is anything interior. As the discourse of the Other, the unconscious is trans-individual, outside, "ex-timate" as much as inside. In the words of *Seminar XI*, the unconscious is the effect of speech on the subject. This is thus a truth that has its effects insofar as repressed signifiers return in the opening and closing of the unconscious in the form of symptoms, jokes, slips of the tongue, and parapraxis.

What emerges from these meditations on the truth as lack and as *mi-dire* is that it is not we who hold the truth in the grasp of concepts. Rather, it is the truth that appropriates us, that holds us. The subject, in truth, is a subject as the retroactive effect of speech; the subject is in being nothing but the desire of the Other; it is sub-jected to the signifier; it disappears beneath the signifier.[77] This, as was discussed earlier, is the operation of alienation. The second "subordination," separation, closes this "gap," this "split" by "projecting the topology of the subject into fantasy," and this "seals it," this conceals it from the subject of desire that he/she is an effect of speech, that he/she is in being but the Other's desire.[78]

Telling the truth in the analytic situation can be thought of as a moment of power, Lacan says,[79] the power to speak the truth about one's desire, the power of the moment of truth in the speech of revelation (Lacan strongly resists the term "expression" in this context), where, at a pivotal point, perhaps where power and the surrendering of power coincide, speech speaks the truth as lack and thus and at the same time, it must always and also tell a lie. It is thusly that we are within the grasp of the Other, precisely at that moment wherein one believes to have seized truth, when one believes one's self to have awakened, so as not to continue dreaming.

"The man who breaks the bread of truth with his *semblable* in the act of speech shares a lie," Lacan wrote.[80] If so, it is in the healing lie spoken in the presence of the neighbor, the *semblable*, that the split speaks, that the truth is as the hidden, disguised, and withdrawn splendor of lack.

THE TRUTH OF ETHICS AND
THE ETHICS OF TRUTH

Lacan's varying formulations of the question and the problem of truth thus constitute what may be termed, and in quite a philosophical sense, as well, as *a way of thinking through an interpretation*. Not in a metaphysical, hermeneutical way thinking, in the simplistic sense of being the bringing to light of a hidden meaning, but a philosophical, political, and ethical thinking that always takes its start from the situation of a human subject who suffers and who wants to know why. It is a thinking that addresses the madness of the world as much as it does the torment and suffering of the individual human subject.

But it isn't only the truth of ethics that is the issue here, but also an ethics of truth. When Lacan brings truth to thought, he does in terms of negative or ambiguous categories: truth is error, ultimately undecideable, unknowable, and indiscernible. This suggests that Lacan is presenting a new ethic of truth, perhaps in a sense suggested by Badiou, an ethic of truth that would reside entirely in the measure taken of the negative, of hesitations, deferrals, error, and lies in their structural relation with truth. In other words, it is an ethic of the limitation(s) placed on the potency of truth by the hazards of its construction.[81] The potency of truth for Lacan is truth's potency to impose its form on desire and to have an effect on desire and on the real. That effect is not only in the ways it structures and sustains desire, but also in the way it is both lure and barrier to the real and to the ultimate, forbidden objects of desire.

Insofar as Lacan's thinking of truth bears especially on the "inter-subjective game by which truth enters reality (*réel*),"[82] it is a practical truth, an ethic of truth, where the "of" has both objective and subjective possessive senses, that seeks and finds the measure, the *logos* of truth in language and desire. Where desire is defined in terms of lack, so truth is lack and the density of the lack, the density of truth's function as object *a*, and as a lure and barrier to the Thing and to *jouissance* in the real. It is this truth, this half-spoken truth, that is both lack and the density of lack, that is the impossible object of the Lacanian thinking as interpretation of the lack in being.

Finally, an important question concerning the ethical-political dimensions of Lacan's teaching on truth: Lacan always takes the subject as a subject not only divided but also as "subjected." The subject is a subject of domination. While Badiou would deny it of Lacan, could it not be shown along these lines that Lacan's theory and practice are more invested in a mode of resistance to domination than in providing normalization schemes? Moreover, wouldn't Lacan be the one to recognize that having the badges of conventional normality, described in terms of happiness, bourgeois success, and genital satisfactions, as guidelines, ends, and ideals for determining the promise of psychoanalysis might indeed be to make its patients truly and deeply ill, but now at a level at once social and individual? It was Adorno's claim that "no science has yet explored the inferno in which were forged the deformations that later emerge to daylight as cheerfulness, openness, sociability, successful adaptation to the inevitable, an equable, practical frame of mind."[83] Far from holding out the promise that a higher normalization shall emerge from the infernos within, Lacan's thinking on the death drive and on truth shows his to be among the first of the "sciences" to confront the irreducibility of the hells that burn in every religious, philosophical, and scientific attempt to promise "normality" in today's damaged world.

As with political thinking, psychoanalytic thought, too, attempts to "search within a situation for a possibility that the dominant state of things does not allow to be seen."[84] Lacan's thought would then be situated, in Badiou's terms, in the "faults and impasses of a situation's structure,"[85] again making Lacan's teaching a thinking, a way of questioning truth, not as a metaphysical thinking, linked with the forgetting of the being of the subject, but with an ethical and a political thinking that makes interventions and changes the way we think about truth and its relation to death and desire.

4

THE KNOTS OF MORAL LAW
AND DESIRE

Ethics begins at the moment when the subject poses the question
of that good he had unconsciously sought in the social structures.
And it is at that moment, too, that he is led to discover the deep
relationship as a result of which that which presents itself as law is
closely tied to the structure of desire.

—Lacan, *The Ethics of Psychoanalysis*

The law makes its nest in the peel of desire.

—Hélène Cixous, "Attacks of the Castle"

Lacan's *Seminar VII* can be situated apropos the European Enlightenments, first that of classical Greece, the tradition that culminates in Plato
and Aristotle, and second, that of the eighteenth-century, the tradition
that culminates in Kant and Sade. But, it is also Lacan himself who makes
this connection. Not that he considers his work to be a continuation of
the Enlightenment, yet another attempt to engage in its "unfinished project." Rather, Lacan turns the critical, demystifying thrust of the Enlightenment against itself. He enacts a revaluation of the moral-ethical values
of these two European Enlightenments. If the European Enlightenments
had sought to demythologize and to liberate, this is what Lacan attempts
to do with regard to the very ethical traditions that emerged from those
Enlightenments: he seeks to subvert them, to "demystify" them (S7: 282).
He attempts, as he says, a "small step outside ethics," a step that will not
be just "another development of ethical reflection" (S7: 19). He risks a
new critical reflection on the role and place of moral law and a revaluation of the ethical values of the Good, the True, and the Beautiful. This
is the oddly liberating, "enlightening" effect of Lacan's teaching, the way
it not only enables us to think in new ways, but, also teaches us how a

self-imposed tyranny and malignant cruelty comes to be established from within, precisely in and by the very ethical voice that commands respect for moral law, or counsels us as to the prudential routes conducive to the Good and the realization of human hopes for happiness. Over the course of his seminars, Lacan puts into effect a revaluation of the ethical values that are the heritage of the European Enlightenments, for it is precisely these values that have brought with them a largesse of guilt. Guilt, the kind of guilt Lacan encountered over and over again in his clinic, a crushing, deforming burden of guilt, guilt before the terrifying, punishing fathers, guilt for the past, guilt for all the ways in which life turned against itself and defeated itself, is all too often the legacy of the imposition of moral law. Guilt is the price one pays for the necessary submission to the reign of moral law that each and every human being must undergo. Whence this burden of guilt? What are its sources, if not in the very knot of moral law and desire? It is this knot that the Lacanian revaluation brings into view.

A PSYCHOANALYTIC REVALUATION
OF ALL VALUES

Primarily these aspects of the Lacanian revaluation shall be considered:

First, the subject: the subject as a capital, defining moment in philosophical modernity. Lacan is unique in the brief history of psychoanalytic theory in that he both insists upon the pivotal role of the subject and yet operates a subversion of the subject, at least as it had been defined by the philosophers following Descartes. One of the oft-repeated mantras of Lacan's seminars is a quotation from Freud: *"Wo es war, soll Ich werden,"* Where "it" was, there "I" shall come to be as a subject.[1] This "I," as a "subject" that comes to be where "it" was, is where Lacan seeks the root of desire. The Cartesian revolution had made the subject into a thinking, knowing subject, identified with consciousness and made the foundation and the condition for truth and certainty. The Lacanian psychoanalytic turn pulls this venerable tradition inside out, like an old glove, and shows it to be but a construct, something imaginary, having its lining, its *envers*, its other side in language, desire, and the structure of fantasy. Not the privileged experience of self-presence, the Lacanian subject is "split," divided; it is the subject of the unconscious, a subject "supposed," a subject defined in its relation to a new level of truth, the truth of desire.

Second, and in direct relation to this is desire, which in its moral and ethical life since the Greek Enlightenment was taken to be a desire for the Good, defined as happiness (*eudaimonia*). But the psychoanalytic encounters with transgression and *jouissance* force a crucial step beyond this romance of the desire for the Good, which culminates in the Kantian transformation of desire into a Good Will.

Third, there are the ethical dimensions of the psychoanalytic theory of the subject and desire to consider. The Lacanian subversion is not imposed from the outside, but works from within the moral discourses. Where the Kantian morality had made the subject in its freedom and autonomy to be the legislator of moral law, and where Kant had likewise defined the good as the good will, and purified desire to the point where it shed all its affiliations with a desire for happiness in order to become but an absolute respect for moral law, the Lacanian subversion shows us how this absolute choice of the good can also be identified with transgression and evil, and the Kantian legislator, therefore, the good neighbor of the Sadean rake. Purged of all a posteriori and pathological dimensions, Lacan shows the Kantian morality to be equally capable of a pure choice of evil. The Kantian universal moral law is thus situated in close proximity to radical evil. Whether it comes from the hand of Kant or Sade is no matter, alongside the guillotine, radical evil is one of the more intriguing inventions of the Enlightenment, the flower of its theory of the subject purified of all feelings, quickened only by a taste for *a priori* categorical moral imperatives. Although the Lacanian subversion is a revaluation of such classical moral-ethical values as that of "the good" and "happiness," it must not be taken to be only a nihilistic devaluation of all values, for, and perhaps not in spite of its own best intentions, it is also a creator of new values. Along the shimmering contours of a *jouissance* the Lacan of the early 1970s calls a "feminine *jouissance*," a new, "higher value" is brought to presence, a "good" in excess of "happiness" and the exchange and the economies of the circulation of goods, something immeasurable, infinite, not beyond, but in excess of the moral and metaphysical opposition of good and evil. Let us now follow these steps in the Lacanian subversion of the subject and its demystification of the moral dimensions of the European Enlightenment.

ON THE SUBJECT OF THE SUBJECT

We begin with the Lacan's subversion of the subject.

In his seminar of January 16, 1973, Lacan said that "the Subject is nothing other than what slides in a chain of signifiers, whether he knows which signifier he is the effect of or not" (S20: 50/48). The quotation suggests just how much Lacan had departed from the long European tradition of the moral-ethical subject, where, as in Aristotle, the ethical subject was first defined as a human soul teleologically directed toward its *eudaimonia*, its Good, and then in the Kantian tradition, where it was defined as a rational will, a subject that legislates the very moral law to which in turn it will subject itself—making itself, therefore, both the subject and the object of moral law, both its condition and its objective. For this tradition, the subject was always something primary, fundamental, and originating. For Lacan, on the other hand, it was something secondary, something of an achievement or an accomplishment that could just as easily be undone or come unraveled.

Working from a particularly French textual milieu of Freud, Heidegger, Saussure, and Lévi-Strauss, one of the striking features of Lacan's work in the field of psychoanalysis is his insistence on "the subject," which is not found in Freud and which may, in fact, betray something of a specifically French, philosophical dimension in Lacan's work. But, across its historical development in Lacan's work beginning in the 1930s, Lacan's notion of the subject acquires a polyvalence that situates it as both a philosophical and an anti-philosophical notion. We could summarize Lacan's position by also quoting *Seminar XXIII*, where he says, "the subject is never more than supposed."[2]

The primary reference for this critical remark—as is the case for much of the modern French philosophical tradition—is Descartes. Thus, I return to a question, taken up in an earlier essay: What is the difference between the Lacanian, psychoanalytic conception of the subject and the specifically Cartesian philosophical notion of the subject?

Chiefly this: for the Cartesian tradition, culminating in Kant, Hegel, and phenomenology—and this would be the immediate philosophical context for Lacan—there is a fusion of subject and consciousness, which Lacan calls "misleading" and a philosophical "error." It is also a philosophical moment both "privileged" and "misleading."[3] But, even before that, in the Aristotelian tradition, there is a homologous identification of thinking and the human soul. For Lacan, "man does not think with his soul. . . . Thought is in disharmony with the soul." Rather, "man" thinks because a structure, language, "carves up his body, a structure that has nothing to do with anatomy."[4]

As for the fusion of consciousness and the subject in and as the Cartesian cogito (the "I think"), Lacan marks in the very moment of this coincidence of thinking and existence, of thought and being—a moment Descartes grasped in and by a philosophical intuition—the site of a rift, a split (*refente*), that of castration and the "signifying cut," wherein the "psychoanalytic experience makes its entrance." Lacan says, "That rift or split (*refente*) is precisely that whereof psychoanalysis affords us a daily experience. I have castration anxiety at the same time as I regard it as impossible."[5] Thus, "the subject of the 'I think' reveals what it is: the being of a fall,"[6] a being divided, barred, "castrated." As Lacan puts it, in the Cartesian statement, "I think, therefore I am," the "therefore" is this "causal stroke . . . inaugurally" dividing the "I am" of existence" from the "I am" of meaning.[7] But, it is a stroke both affirmed and, at the same time, bracketed off, excised, "foreclosed," as Lacan translates the Freudian term *Verwerfung*, a term used in connection with castration. For Descartes, the "therefore" was meant to seal the identity of thought and being, meaning and existence, but for Lacan, the "therefore" is the cut that distinguishes them. For him, the situation is something like a *vel*, as in, "your money or your life." This *vel* between meaning and not just "existence," but "ex-istence"—a word Lacan invents to express the extimacy at the heart of our being, the extimate "kernel of our being" (*Kern unseres Wesen*), whereby our being is being radically Other, strange, not only intimate but also outside—is crucial for Lacan's account of the subject.[8] It is the *vel*, the difference between existence in the symbolic and ex-istence in the real. Castration, then, is the cut between these two, the castration in which the subject gives up *jouissance*, gives up either *having* or *being* the phallus, and so becomes a *subject*, inscribed in the symbolic domain as lack, as void, as desire. Castration—and there is obviously nothing organic about this—is, thus, the *vel* between meaning and "ex-istence," between the symbolic and the real. Žižek sums it up nicely: "We could say that we are always caught in a certain *vel*, that we are always forced to choose between meaning and ex-istence: the price that we have to pay for access to meaning is the exclusion of ex-istence, existence in the real, existence in the Thing, the beyond-the-symbolic real of a *jouissance* necessarily set aside, castrated, necessarily impossible and so opening the ascension from ex-istence in the real to existence in the symbolic."[9] The subject is thus a "discontinuity in the real." Lacan's thesis is that the subject is structured by a "signifying cut," by which the subject not only enters the symbolic order, but also excavates a hole in the real.[10] The philosophical fusion of subjectivity and consciousness, according to Lacan, thus has "no other function than to *suture* that cleavage of the subject" and "to bolt shut the door of truth."[11] It is this suture and this shut door of truth that Lacan opens in and by his return to Freud and to the discovery of the unconscious.

Split, the subject, for Lacan (S2: 188), is thus, a subject "subjected to the field of the Other," that is to say, to the field of the law, of discourse, language, and the phallus. Hence, Lacan's formulation: A subject desires in and only as an Other. The subject is "split" (*refente*), divided, and barred, without hope of closure, synthesis, or self-knowledge. Ever failing perfect self-consciousness, the Lacanian subject is always cut-off from self-knowledge, like an Oedipus who never reaches his Colonus, due to the very act of speaking, the very fact that man speaks, that he has speech, that he is divided, a castrated being, cut-off, as it were, from either *having* or *being* the phallus. Thus, Lacan's related distinction between the subject of an enunciation (*sujet de l'énonciation*) and the subject of a statement (*sujet de l'énoncé*)[12] is also a distinction between the unconscious and the conscious dimensions. The source of speech, the subject of the enunciation, is, here, not the ego, or consciousness, but the unconscious. *Es*, "S," qua "subject of the unconscious," *it* speaks in the word, *parole*, of revelation. This *Es*, as was said earlier, is the "lining" or the "stuff," "of the very subject people take to be the subject of consciousness."[13] So, again, what is misleading and perhaps doomed to fail in the philosophical, Cartesian notion of the subject is its very foundation in the moment of philosophical reflection wherein subjectivity and consciousness, existence in meaning—possible only at the symbolic register—and ex-istence in the real—impossible existence in "the real of the Thing embodying *jouissance*, impossible enjoyment," are said to coincide.[14] This unity of thought and being, perfect presence of thought to itself in and as conscious subjectivity, this which comprises the very foundation, the *sub-stratum* and *sub-jectum* of Descartes' project of a philosophical science of nature, this is "misleading"[15] and it is therefore what Lacan resists in each and every attempt he makes to articulate the structure of subjectivity in its connection with castration and the "symbolic cut."

For *Seminar VII*, the "subject," beginning as a philosophical term bearing a philosophical, distinctly Cartesian pedigree, thus undergoes a transformation or "de-formation." Unlike the Cartesian subject, the *ego cogito*, which is a subject of consciousness, the Lacanian subject is a subject of the unconscious, not so much an agent, which would only be an illusion produced by the ego, but "a *true* subject of the unconscious, constituted in its nucleus by a series of alienating identifications."[16] Moreover, where the Cartesian subject was the "original subject," the ultimate rational completely self-present foundation for the possibility of a new science of nature, Lacan says he has a "completely new formula" for (it): a subject that "can forget"; "the subject is literally at its beginning the elision of a signifier as such, the missing signifier in the chain of signifiers" (S7: 224). So, not only is the subject essentially inscribed at an unconscious symbolic level, but it is also inscribed at a level inaccessible to empirical science, a level that subverts rather than secures rationality. Yet, the unconscious is not just a pre-linguistic, repressed reservoir of the instincts. It has a structure, a linguistic structure. This is where Lacan situates his notion of a "subject of the unconscious."

One more point before we move on: Whereas Freud claimed that there are only "thing presentations" in the unconscious, and whereas this might seem to militate against what Lacan said about the unconscious being "structured like a language," Lacan reads Freud as calling these "thing presentations" *Sachvorstellungen*. "*Sache* is the thing that is "juridically questioned, or . . . the transition to the symbolic order of a conflict between men" (S7: 44). So, the *Sachvorstellungen* are not opposed to *Wortvorstellungen*. *Both* obtain at the symbolic level. This is the language of the unconscious. But beyond this, beyond all meaning, there is the Thing, not the thing as *die Sache*, but as *das Ding*, the "dumb" ex-istence in the real, the "beyond-of-the-signified" (see S7: 44–45, 57, and 62–63). So, Lacan here plays on two German words for "the thing": both *die Sache* and *das Ding*.

Strengthening his reading of Freud, Lacan points out on these pages (S7: 44–45, *Le Seminaire, Livre VII*: 57) how, despite the nascent state of linguistics in Freud's time, Freud was nonetheless able to distinguish between *language as a function*, playing an essential role in the preconscious, and *language as a structure*, "as a result of which the elements put into play in the unconscious are organized." The connecting links between these two are the "coordinations," the "*mise-en-chaîne*," as Lacan translates Freud's term, *die Bahnungen*, or "facilitations" (*frayage*).

Even before *Seminar VII*, Lacan considered the unconscious to be structured "like a language" (see S3: 63), structured as a synchronic system of signifiers. While the unconscious, for Lacan, is cut off from the access of consciousness—*Seminar VII* considers it to be a "field of non-knowledge" (236–237)—it is nonetheless not merely identified with the "repressed" (*die Verdrängung*), especially if the latter is taken as some kind of pre-linguistic feeling or instinct. Again, *Seminar VII* emphasizes this linguistic conception of the unconscious: "what we know of the unconscious *reaches us*," reaches consciousness, "as a function of words" (S7: 32). Thus, the "cry" of pain, for example, by which a hostile object is acknowledged at the level of consciousness, this cry is the bridge "whereby something of what is happening may be seized and identified in the consciousness of the subject." The cry gives "this something," this disturbance, for example, "its own weight, presence, structure. It gives it as well a potentiality due to the fact that the important objects for a human subject are speaking objects, which will allow him to see revealed in the discourse of others the processes that, in fact, inhabit his own unconscious" (S7: 32).

Likewise, noting how the schizophrenic's attitude posed for Freud the "manifestly extraordinary prevalence of affinities between words," Lacan continues by concluding that the "repressed" (*Verdrängung*) operates "on nothing other than signifiers" (S7: 44). So, for Lacan, the unconscious is primarily a linguistic structure; it is the "discourse of the Other."[17] As such, not only is it separated from consciousness, but it makes itself known or felt only indirectly by "passing into words" (S7: 32), in certain functions, formations, and phenomena of speech. In this sense, the unconscious marks the effect of the signifier, the effect of "speech" (S11: 126) on the subject. It is the signifier that has been repressed and that makes itself felt through ruptures and discordances in discourse.[18] Again, as *Seminar VII* insists, the thought processes of the unconscious are available to consciousness only to the extent that they are verbalized in some manner (S7: 48).[19]

One important consequence of this is that the unconscious is not a private, interior dimension of the subject but, insofar as it is essentially linguistic, it is also intersubjective, an intimacy that exteriorizes the subject, an ex-timacy, in other words. There is no private language of the unconscious, but at the level of the unconscious, the subject is already determined or inscribed in the symbolic order itself. Yet, the unconscious remains irreducible. Analysis cannot bring it totally to consciousness.

The subject comes to be through the signifying cut that marks the acquisition of language. Insofar as the unconscious is "structured like a language," and language is the domain of the subject situated at the symbolic level, the subject is the subject of the unconscious. Phrased otherwise, the subject is "that represented by a signifier to another signifier."[20] The subject is never but represented. Hence, it is never present as such. The *mathème* for the subject is, thus, the barred S ($). Only with the inscription of the signifier does the subject come into being precisely as desire, as lack-of-being.

Here, then, is another point of rupture with the Cartesian tradition: as desire, the subject is not a Cartesian interiority. Rather, in desire, in the death drive, the Lacanian subject of the late 1950s is always projected beyond itself, albeit this is thought in terms of the structure of metonymy. Still, if anywhere, it is here, in desire conceived as lack, that one can locate something like the being of the subject. In the Heideg-gerian terms that were also influential on Lacan in the 1950s, a subject is, thus, not a substance but a transcendence, a projection, a being thrown into the world. Jacques-Alain Miller uses Lacan's term "ex-sistence" in this regard as meaning a "staring outside." He writes, "Heidegger invented the distinction between ex-sistence and insistence. Having no interiority, one projects outside, and this repeats itself. Lacan's wordplay on '*L'instance de la lettre*' (*l'instance*, meaning 'agency' or 'insistence' of the letter) stems in reality from Heidegger."[21]

"Hence," Lacan writes in his essay "The Subversion of the Subject and the Dialectic of Desire,"[22] the place of the "inter-said (*inter-dit*), con-stituted by the intra-said (*intra-dit*), the between-two-subjects, is the very place at which the transparency of the classical subject divides, undergo-ing, as it does, the effects of fading that specify the Freudian subject due to its occultation by an ever purer signifier."[23]

So, in the return to Freud, by which Lacan contested the Cartesian and Aristotelian traditions of the subject and the soul, Lacan retained much of the Freudian terminology and its distinction between conscious-ness and the unconscious, yet he transformed its topology by introducing the registers of the imaginary, the symbolic, and the real. In this Freudian register, the use of the term "subject" in Lacan's work must furthermore be distinguished from the psychological ego, and so from ego analysis. In other words, the ego belongs to the imaginary order, the "subject" to the symbolic.

Here, the emphasis on the symbolic domain meant that for Lacan, the ontological and phenomenological conceptions of subjectivity were strongly complemented by structuralism, particularly that of Lévi-Strauss, whose influence had greater weight for Lacan than that of Heidegger. Structurally determined by the symbolic order, defined by the presence of the signifier within it, "the subject is thus subjected to the Other, sub-jected to the field of the Other" (S2: 188). As a consequence, the subject is a subject "reconstituted by alienation,"[24] for which transgression and the death drive are more constitutive and fundamental than 'restoration' and healing. This has implications for the so-called ends of psychoanaly-sis. Thus, while one might expect to find in Lacan's quasi-structuralist account of the subject nothing but a cold-blooded rationalism, there remains an essential place for a meditation on what might seem the more "existentialist" domains of radical finitude and evil, transgression and *jouissance*. However predominant the influence of structural linguis-tics was for Lacan, it is important to point out that Lacan's subject is

not reducible to the impersonal status of being a mere grammatical subject, the first-person pronoun, the linguistic shifter, "I." Lacan does not
reduce the subject to being situated in a system of reciprocal exchanges
and equivalences (as named in the "assertions about oneself"). Rather, as
Lacan says in another, rather early formulation, the subject, at least at the
level of the imaginary, the subject as the "ego," is also personal and unique
in that it claims itself in an act of self-assertion or self-affirmation.[25] This
can also be seen in Lacan's reading of Sophocles' *Antigone* in particular.
But, Lacan's teaching more generally always focuses on this personal and
unique dimension of the subject.[26]

Finally, however impossible the Lacanian subject may be—it is a
gap (*écart*), something torn apart at its center—and however unassignable
its locus may be, it still has a determined and necessary role to play: the
impossible gap and the unassignable locus of the subject hollow out the
real and make possible the signifying order.[27]

Thus, however, as much as it is a subject split, hollowed, defined by
and as a gap, lack, hole in being, Lacan's subject is still a "subject" nonetheless, not as a substance but as process of "subjectivization" in which "I,"
the Freudian *Ich*, comes to be where "it" (*Es*), once was (*"Wo es war, soll
Ich werden"*). As translated by Lacan in 1965–1966, this reads, "Where
It—(*Es*)—was, there *must* 'I' (*Ich*) come to be as a subject." But, the fact
that the Lacanian symbol for the subject, the letter "S," sounds like the
Freudian *Es* further demonstrates how the Lacanian subject is situated
at the level of the unconscious.[28] This is a process of subjectivization that
is always in excess of the subject qua *Ich*, qua Cartesian *cogito*. There is
no final filling of the gap in this. There is no moment of completion,
of consummating "happiness" or *eudaimonia*. The wound remains open,
the tragedy inconclusive, its heroes and heroines, like statues, frozen as
it were "between two deaths."

Hence, beginning with a self-declared Cartesian determination of
the subject qua *cogito*, or with the Hegelian Subject determined in relation
to Absolute Knowledge, Lacan submits this to a subversion, a slippage,
a "de-suturing," in which the subject is emptied of its representational
content and structures, emptied of its relation to certainty, emptied of
any desire for the good or even for terrible beauty, but remains a subject
nonetheless, who, from the standpoint of the symbolic level, must become
the cause of his/her own desire, must become the subject of the enunciation. The subject becomes the one who chooses his or her own desire. This
is perhaps the freedom of Lacan's ethical subject that finds its parallel,
its homologue, and its heteronym in the fundamental *noumenal* freedom

of the Kantian legislating moral subject that chooses for the maxim of its subjective will an objective, universal moral law.

DESIRE

From Kojève, Lacan had heard such propositions as these: that "it is in Desire (Hegel's *Begierde*) that a conscious being is brought back to itself," that "desire is what transforms Being," and that "man is formed and revealed—to himself and to others—as an I, as the I that is essentially different from, and radically opposed to, the non-I," and most importantly, that "Desire taken as Desire—before its satisfaction—is but a revealed nothingness" ultimately, "directed toward another Desire."[29] Desire is not, therefore, reducible to a biological need and oriented toward an object, the attainment of which can bring about a state of satisfaction; desire is always *more* than an appetite surging according to the needs of the organism. Nor is desire to be confused with demand. Desire "begins to take shape in the margin in which demand rips away from need," this margin being that opened by demand in the guise of the gap need may give rise to, because there is no universal satisfaction.[30] As a child's needs become articulated, they take form as demand. Need subjected to demand comes back to the child in an alienated form, which is a consequence "of need being put into signifying form as such and of the fact that it is from the Other's locus (say, that of the mother with respect to the child) that the child's message is emitted.[31] While demand does articulate needs that can be satisfied, the child also takes the objects given to satisfy those needs as symbols of the love of a parent for the child, which the child then redoubles into an ever-increasing demand for love. The demand for love becomes insatiable and so is always in excess, always a surplus of the satisfaction of needs. Here is where desire arises. Compared to need, desire is scandalous in its being paradoxical, erratic and insatiable.[32] One of Lacan's definitions of desire reads, "Desire is neither the appetite for satisfaction, nor the demand for love, but the difference that results from the subtraction of the first from the second."[33] Desire is a surplus, something left over in the double function of demand as both the articulation of need and a demand for love, which is a demand "that bears on something other than the satisfactions it calls for. It is a demand for a presence or an absence."[34] That desire is irreducible to demand must be underscored, for it also prevents desire from being reduced to need. "To put it elliptically: it is precisely because desire is articulated that it is not articulable—by which I mean in the discourse that suits it, an ethical, not a psychological discourse."[35] Lacan had, in this way, wanted to answer those who see his teaching as just another instance of the dialectical, "logicizing" reduction at work, one ultimately indebted to Hegel. But, for Lacan as for Kojève's Hegel, desire is essentially desire for another desire and so not a desire for an object. This lesson also remained fundamental to Lacan's teaching. Desire is not primarily a relation to an object, but to a lack, as was discussed in an earlier essay. As we saw, the subject, defined as desire, is therefore, the "being of a non-being."[36] Now, the goal of analysis, according to *Seminars II* and *VII* is to bring the subject (the analysand) to the point where he/she can recognize and name his/her desire. But this is not to recognize or to name something that somehow pre-exists or already exists apart from the symbolic order. To name desire is to bring it into existence. Hence, the identification of desire and the signifier. Thus removed from the biological level of needs, even from demand, desire for Lacan is rather at the symbolic level of signifiers, at the interplay of metaphor and metonymy.

It is at the level of the signifier that desire realizes its full capacities as an irreconcilable, inconsolable force and uncompromising insistence. Desire bears no compromise with any particular object. It is always a desire for something else. Each object it encounters is always experienced as a "this is not yet it." This is the metonymic structure of desire, where metonymy, as defined by Lacan, is the way signifiers are combined or linked as to constitute a signifying chain, whereby the signifying function, the link between one signifier and another, is congruent with the maintenance of the bar between signifier and signified. The consequence of this is that signifying is never finished, never complete; no final signified is ever attained. Hence, the need for the punctuation mark, for what Lacan calls, the *point de capiton* (the upholstery button), which stops this sliding by knotting signified and signifier together. Metonymy, in short, is the diachronic movement from one signifier to another in a process of continual referral and deferral of meaning. So, we read in "The Instance of the Letter in the Unconscious," "the enigmas that desire—with its frenzy mimicking the gulf of the infinite and the secret collusion whereby it envelops the pleasure of knowing and of dominating in *jouissance*—poses for any sort of 'natural philosophy' are based on no other derangement of instinct than the fact that it is caught in the rails of metonymy, extending toward *the desire for something else*."[37] Lacan's thesis is that the movement of metonymy maintains a resistance to signification. In the movement from one signifier to another, the bar between signifier and signified is not crossed and no new signified is ever produced. But the greatest enigma is not in the nature of desire as such, but in its fundamental object-cause, namely, the Thing and the death drive, for these bring on the unsurpassable dislocation of the subject. Let us take a closer look at the knot tying desire not only to moral law, but also to the death drive and the Thing.

Essentially, each and all are knotted with the symbolic order. Both desire and the death drive belong to the order of the signifier. In both his 1953 essay "The Function and Field of Speech and Language in Psychoanalysis"[38] and the 1960 "Position of the Unconscious," Lacan asserted that the signifier, the symbol, is the death—"the killing"—of the thing, and that "this death results in the perpetuation of the subject's desire." The signifier takes the place of the thing—does away with it—and makes it present only in its absence. "The letter kills, but we learn this from the letter itself."[39] Thus, as was shown in an earlier essay in this collection, transposed from the biological to the symbolic order, desire becomes dead desire, desire as death, as the insistence of the letter that kills, and the death drive itself is, likewise, always and already a dead drive.

As was shown in an earlier essay, death stalks the symbolic order from end to end and is the key to desire, now defined in terms of the insatiable passing from one signifier to another according to the structure of metonymy. This circulation is regulated by the pleasure principle, which, as Freud understood it, is always intent upon maintaining the tensions of desire at a low point, a point of balance, *homeostasis*. Desire must be maintained within the symbolic order and never strive to go beyond it. *Jouissance* must be ever distanced, which of course only aggravates its appeal. Likewise the death drive, which is, after all, not really a separate drive, apart from all others, but is instead an aspect of every drive, every desire, is identified with a certain insistence of the letter active in the symbolic order, with a repetition that hammers away in the symbolic order. "Every drive is virtually a death drive," as Lacan concluded in 1960,[40] not because of this repetition by which Freud defined the death drive in his 1920 *Beyond the Pleasure Principle*, where the term first occurs, and not only because of the way the letter kills the thing, but also because of the way every drive seeks its own extinction and the way every drive attempts to surpass or go beyond the pleasure principle to attain *jouissance*. It is this repetition, this real of the drive, that characterizes finitude and the finite in Lacan and Freud, a movement by which life is always surpassing itself from within, to use Hegelian language, rather than merely coming up against its limit or its end as something external to it.

Both desire and the death drive have the Thing (which Lacan adapts from Freud's *das Ding*), as their object-cause. The Thing is at the center of a subjective world defined by the signifier already installed at the level of the unconscious. But the Thing is at the center of this subjective world and intimate to it only in the sense of being what is also excluded from it; the Thing is thus a "the prehistoric Other that is impossible to forget . . . something strange to me, although it is at the heart of me" (S7: 71). Ultimately, desire and the death drive are a desire for the attainment of the Thing, and so for the attainment of a *jouissance*, conceived not only as the true satisfaction of desire, but also as installed at the heart of the real and of the Thing. It is thus a *jouissance* exterior to or in excess of the symbolic order. This positioning of *jouissance* as exterior to the symbolic order completes and realizes a new stage in what Jacques-Alain Miller has termed Lacan's "*signifiantisation* of *jouissance*."[41]

From its position as exterior to the symbolic and the imaginary, as somehow on the far side of their limit, the Thing thus exerts a fascination that draws desire to its destruction. How so? Fascination is an effect of sublimation, which *Seminar VII* defines not in the Freudian way, as the redirecting of a brute and biological drive toward objects acceptable in polite company, but rather, as something essentially at work in the symbolic order and operating on drives that are themselves defined in terms of the symbolic order. Lacanian sublimation directs a "change of object in itself" (see S7: 293). An object is relocated, elevated, lifted up, in relation to the Thing. Lacan's formulation is: sublimation "raises an object to the dignity to the Thing" (S7: 112). But because all of this takes place in the symbolic order, the sublime, fascinating quality exerted by an object is not due to the inherent qualities of a thing understood as an object, but due to its position in the symbolic structure of fantasy. It is the position, not just the object that is now experienced and written as exerting a fascination, or as being somehow sublime. The position of the Thing is outside the symbolic order, outside the destructive reach of the signifier and so beyond the arm of the law. Yet, the remarkable effect of this fascination is to act not only as a lure toward the impossible Thing, but also ceaselessly to hurl up barriers and obstacles against it and this is what also occurs in sublimation, which operates from within the symbolic order.

It is precisely for this reason that Lacan takes up his confrontation with the philosophical tradition of ethical thought stretching from Aristotle to Kant and Sade. For, if *jouissance* is now established at this point in Lacan's seminars (from the late 1950s to the very early 1960s) as an excess or outside of the symbolic order, if it is identified with the paradoxical and painful attainment of the impossible to attain Thing, then it is precisely in defense against such *jouissance* that the moral law is erected. The symbolic order must always seek the obliteration of the Thing and of the *jouissance* identified with its attainment because the symbolic order, however it circles around the Thing in fascination with it, is also governed by the pleasure principle and so by a tendency toward homeostasis, the reduction of intensities. Hence, as Jacques-Alain Miller writes:

> at the level of the unconscious, the subject tells a lie about the Thing, [and] there is a sort of primal deceitfulness over *jouissance* that reflects, that is the comment on the fundamental severing disjunction between the signifier and *jouissance*. The actual clinical treatment is not developed in *The Ethics of Psychoanalysis*. However, the symptom, formerly ascribed to repression, is here ascribed to defense. . . . The symptom is the way in which the subject enunciates that *jouissance* is bad, that is, the symptom positions itself exactly on the barrier standing between the signifier and *jouissance* and reverberates *jouissance*'s radical disharmony vis-à-vis the subject.[42]

Thus, with sublimation, there is always the attempt to transpose the Thing and *jouissance* through substitution instances, through other signifiers that succeed in making *jouissance* present in its absence, obliterating it by entombing it in a sign. Sublimation thus becomes a creative force. In it, an object is effectively raised up, as in a movement of the Hegelian *Aufhebung*, to the status of the Thing in an act that one could only describe as poetic. But in this movement of sublimation, in this lifting up of an object to the status of the Thing, there is also a filling in of the fascinating hollow, the luring void of the Thing and the erecting of a barrier against it. Sublimation, in these terms, brings into view the complementary other side of the death drive: the death drive is linked not only to destruction, but also to creation *ex nihilo*, and therefore to artistic creativity. Hence, the temptation to read *Seminar VII* as an aesthetic of sublimation and to see Antigone as a figure of sublimation vis-à-vis the Thing.[43]

But we can also see at this juncture how Lacan submits the traditional and conventional notions of sublimation to a new articulation. Is there not a resistance in Lacan's seminars on tragedy especially to this Hegelian dimension of the prevailing *doxa* regarding sublimation, whereby sublimation amounts to a sort of *Aufhebung* of the real, and of the Thing, and so operates a kind of reduction of the real? In Hegel's dialectic, one sees a reduction of the real to the concept in the internal movement of the dialectic of Spirit whereby all differences and negativity, where finitude itself, play but mediating roles in the return of Spirit to itself in its freedom and truth. Sublimation, working in the economy of the "pleasure principle" ensuring a homeostasis, can be read in Hegelian terms as submitting itself to being but one aspect of the Hegelian "labor of the negative," necessary in the self-unfolding of Spirit, the repetitive return and reinvestment of alienated otherness back into sameness, a work of repetition that can be compared to the work of the death drive itself. One might call this a "restricted economy" of sublimation. What Lacan's teachings also pull out from within this finite sublimation, from within the play of repetition at work in sublimation, is a "*generalized* economy" of sublimation, one that would put itself in play in the play of semblances, masks and lures, all the screen figures of object *a*, all the masquerades of *jouissance* that mark the excess of the pleasure principle in every attempt to approach the real. This is the sublimation in play in the "passion for the real" that cannot be contained by the Hegelian dialectic, for it does not produce anything useful. It is a sublimation in excess of the limited economy of goods that comprises the very strings plucked, pulled, and tormented by the fingers of the pleasure principle.

Hence, Lacan's seminars seem to find both a limited and a general economy of sublimations, something he brings out in the exemplum of tragic drama of Antigone. For at one level the play no doubt provokes or induces a kind of Aristotelian catharsis, a great purging of emotions, which is to say, a purging that brings about a reduction of a certain level of intense energy to homeostasis, the stability and the reduction of intensities more in line with the good guidance of the pleasure principle. But in the splendor of Antigone, in her beauty, and in the "double death" of the tomb, there is something more, something brought to language and to imagery that cannot be returned or reinvested, a useless *jouissance*.

In connection with sublimation, one can see how the fascination of the Thing provokes the contestations and transgressions that Lacan takes up in his reading of Sade and Sophocles. *Jouissance* introduces a certain baleful empty space, a fragmentation of wholeness, characterized as expenditure and loss, as a hollowing out and an annulment of being that is coupled with a complementary filling up of the void of being, a filling of the lack that the Thing and *jouissance* introduce at the limit of the symbolic order and the center of the subjective world. This tension between the void and the filling up of the void is also creative and so at the heart of artistic creation, as shown in Lacan's January 1960 lecture (S7: 120–121) on Heidegger's vase, which Lacan treats not only as a work of art but also especially in its signifying function.

Lacan recalls how, between earth and sky, Heidegger situates the vase, a work of art, created as though *ex nihilo*. Taking earth, the potter bends the dark wet clay around a hollow, making the vase both a thing and yet a hollow, a thing having a void at its center. As a utensil for libations, it exemplifies a dual function, both lifted up to the sky to receive and to be filled, and also referring downward to the earth from which it was liberated in the creative act of the artisan and toward which it pours forth its libations. Thus, its signifying function creates the *nihil*, the void—the hollow of the vase—and thereby introduces the double possibilities of both filling and pouring forth. Emptiness and fullness are introduced into a world that by itself knows not of them. It is on the basis of this fabricated signifier that emptiness and fullness as such enter the world. Where the whole of ancient philosophy takes up the world, takes up nature as both closed and eternal, ancient philosophy could never imagine the world and interhuman relations within it as not enclosed in the suffocating plenitude of an eternal, essentially unchanging nature. But the signifying figure of the vase introduces the idea of a creative act in which the void, the emptiness at the heart of being, comes into existence. Lacan invites us to consider the vase as "an object made to represent the existence of the emptiness at the center of the real that is called the Thing" (S7: 121). *Jouissance*, the *jouissance* of transgression, will also be reduced to this emptiness, this depletion, as to a violent fragmentation of wholeness and plenitude of being. *Jouissance* is reduced to being an empty space that can be written, using Lacanian symbols, as equivalent to the divided subject, the barred S ($), the emptiness of which can be filled with a variety of ever-inadequate supplements.[44] This sometimes violent, sometimes delicate torsion—figured in Lacan's commentary on Heidegger's vase and on the figure itself of Antigone—comes to supplement sublimation's dialectical movement, so close to the Hegelian *Aufhebung*. Unlike the movement of the *Aufhebung*, however, this chiasmic tension of annulment and filling up always remains unfinished, open ended, a wound that never heals, a truth both said and unsaid. It is against this emptiness of the Thing and of *jouissance* that the barriers of moral law and aesthetic beauty are erected.

Lacan's meditation on Heidegger's vase helps to situate the Thing. Uncanny and unnamable, the Thing is really no thing at all, just a position, as was said before, a hollow that could be filled in with a variety of terms. The Thing stands for a true satisfaction of the drive, yet it is attainable only beyond the symbolic order and so at the very extinction of the drive, therefore, its attainment is forbidden. The Thing—a term Lacan takes more from Freud (especially the 1895 *Project for a Scientific Psychology* [SE I] and the 1915 essay on negation), and even in this case almost as a *Witz*, as Jacques-Alain Miller suggests, than he does from Kant or Heidegger (although these two are referred to, see S7: 65–66 and 120 for the texts on the latter)—is that Other, that emptiness, that void, which always returns to the same place and always sticks to the same place. The thing is that against which the whole of the symbolic and imaginary orders are opposed. Lacan thinks the opposition posed by the barrier not in terms of repression, which pertains to the symbolic order, but rather as *defense* against what is beyond that order. *Jouissance*, installed in the real and made absolute as the satisfaction sought and the object-cause of desire, must be constantly pushed back, according to the pleasure principle's strict maintenance of a low level of tensions.

The thinking of the limit, of the barrier, is a central question in *Seminar VII*. We find it anticipated in Sophocles' *Antigone* in its repeated use of the word *Atè*, doom or destruction brought on by the gods, and in its rightly famous choral ode on Man (lines 335—365), the one that begins, "many are the wonders in the world, but there is none more wondrous (*deinataton*) than man." The chorus says that while man is clever and uncanny in his ability to cross the sea, to capture the wild bird, to provide warmth for himself in the midst of a raging storm, in his ability to use language and to invent law, even though he is, in short, "all resourceful," yet, he is defenseless against death; "from Hades shall he apply no means of flight." The barrier of the imaginary and symbolic realms, the barriers manifest in the life and laws of the city, in the visions and imaginations of art and of the future, are erected against death, against the lure of the Thing, and yet, they may fall, and the walls of the tomb shall open.

This constitutes one of the core ideas of Lacan's 1959–1960 seminar. The barrier erected by the real against the symbolic and imaginary orders is the key to understanding Lacan's interpretation of the moral law and its relation to transgression. But it is also the key to seeing that ethical situation as the tragic dimension of *Seminar VII*, tragic not only in the way of tragic drama, but also as encountered in psychoanalysis itself and in the ethical situation of psychoanalysis. The tragic dimension, with its connotations of strife and struggle, and of a heroic tearing or sundering of the subject, provokes the very question of the ethics of psychoanalysis, just as the drive toward transgression is a definite and powerful experience encountered in the analytic situation, as Lacan himself points out in *Seminar VII*. This barrier, with the related thematic of transgression, and their connection with artistic creation and tragic drama, are at the heart of Lacan's thought over the course of *Seminar VII*.

So, whereas previous seminars had identified *jouissance* either with the imaginary or the symbolic, *Seminar VII* introduces a change by situating *jouissance* outside, beyond both the symbolic and the imaginary. Desire and the death drive both have—not as their object—but as their object-cause and their true satisfaction, the Thing, the "beyond-of-the-signified" (S7: 54), where all relation of word and reference breaks down.

Here we can situate both the moral law—that which says from within the symbolic order, "You must not," "it is forbidden," the law, in other words, of the father and of the master that arises from castration and that only succeeds in provoking further, greater transgressions—and the aesthetic, imaginary order of images, the order of signifying images such as Antigone. The latter, whose splendorous beauty is considered "unbearable" precisely in its being both lure toward and barrier against the Thing, is also a symbolic image of the transgression of that barrier and so an image of the true but impossible satisfaction of the drives. This will be the Antigone "between two deaths," between not just her biological death, but her symbolic death, as well. This is certainly a core idea of *Seminar VII* and is well summarized by Jacques-Alain Miller in his essay "Paradigms of *Jouissance*."[45]

Thus, it is in this barrier raised against both the Thing and *jouissance* by the symbolic and the imaginary orders that we can see the link between the ethical and the aesthetic, between the wonder of the moral law within, the *eudaimonia* of Aristotelian virtue, and beauty's splendor.

Yet, here, too, we again encounter Lacan's denial of the identity of truth and beauty: truth is not beautiful and will not be identified with beauty. Whence Aristotle's "beautiful gentleman" will be rendered in Lacan's eyes as something of a stick figure, a philosophical, ethical ideal constructed by the pleasure principle for which a low maintenance of tensions is always the guiding issue. Lacan's attention is turned toward what is in excess of that law, what is beyond the pleasure principle. His concern is for the way the law, the barrier, provokes its transgression and in doing so, exacts a penalty, a cost that must be paid.

Thus, the good, the price one pays for access to the truth of desire—its true satisfaction—will be counted in terms of totalized loss and expenditure without return. This is the kind of good Antigone names in her famous lament in which she lists all that she is giving up as the price she must pay in order to realize her desire, which, ostensibly, is to return her brother to the dead where he truly belongs. For this she must suffer: for her there will be no marriage, no conjugal bed, no children, no future life at all. She must herself step living into the tomb of the dead (see *Antigone*, lines 9–15: "And now he (Creon) leads me thus by the hands, without marriage, without bridal, having no share in wedlock or in the rearing of children, but thus deserted by my friends I come living, poor creature, to the caverns of the dead."). She will step between two deaths, not just the death of her particular biological life, but also the death of all that would have come from that life. As though from beyond the grave, her very being will be annihilated. Her whole place and role in the elementary structures of life, creation, and kinship will die, all her future children. She will die beyond death itself. What can be beyond death itself, except to die and yet to live a kind of everlasting death? What comes out of this is an ethic of fragmentation and expenditure, but a heroic ethic, an ethic of suffering pitched to heroic proportions.

To return to our theme, the barrier in question is, thus, not only a defense against the Thing, against the *jouissance* sought in desire and the death drive, but also a defense of life itself. The Aristotelian ethical virtues are in play here, on this side of the symbolic order, where the pleasure principle reigns supreme and *eudaimonic* homeostasis is held up as a highest good. Keeping sight on the realization of such goods and keeping to the pursuit of moderated pleasures, always guided as they must be by a rational principle and by the counsels of the master, *Phronesis*, prudence, embodied in the prudent man, the *phronismos, jouissance* is effectively kept at a distance and life becomes livable again. Alenka Zupančič calls this life "a *capacity* to be the support of a truth of desire,"[46] where that truth is the void, the emptiness, the lack by which desire always misses or does not attain final satisfaction, but is instead always driven, pushing on further toward the limits of desire. Indeed, how can one live a life overwhelmed by such desire? The moral law and the ethical goods delineated by the great philosophical traditions in ethics and morality make it possible for us to live with this insatiable desire seemingly intent upon its own destruction. They are ways of moderating and manifesting its intensity such that a certain practical functioning is possible, and so they are also a defense against what is beyond the imaginary and symbolic orders, the orders of desire, for a human life. Does not the central ethical problem then consist of how to respond to the unlivable demands of desire?

THE ETHICAL DIMENSIONS
OF THE PSYCHOANALYTIC SUBJECT

In this regard, what is the central ethical problem for Lacan in this knot of the law and desire? For the Enlightenment traditions, ethical experience is always linked to the experience of a moral demand and to the necessity that I approve of that demand. The demand for some end, law, or ideal, for example, must be perceived as good, and be affirmed or approved as the ethical good(s). But, for Lacan, as we have seen, not everything in ethics is simply related to obligation and its grammar of moral demand and approval. In both his clinical experience and in his studies of Kant and Sade, he found other problems in excess of that of obligation: transgression and the idea, the Enlightenment idea, of radical evil.

Let's begin with transgression. The Lacanian ethical subject, defined by desire, is not only what assents and approves of demand, but also what resists assent; as desire, it is what must always seek to unbind itself from such laws and to somehow become its own law. The problem here is not just the end(s) of analysis and a concern for determining just what it is that analysis can really do for the patient. There is something more, especially one "moral problem" that concerns him with regard to analysis: transgression, or better, "the attraction of transgression," transgression that seeks not just to violate the law so as to incur punishment, but the attraction of transgression itself.

This is the *jouissance* of transgression, a Pauline *jouissance* of transgression. As Lacan writes, "to trample law underfoot excites *jouissance*." The law is thereby not only a barrier, but also a means, a path, leading to the risk of *jouissance* (S7: 2–3).

Lacan began his seminar (S7: 2) with negative definitions of transgression: transgression is not the same thing as a patient "doing something in the hopes of being punished for it." This is transgression as *need* and must be distinguished from transgression as "crime" obtaining at the level of the symbolic and imaginary, especially the mythical "murder of the father" and even more so, from an even "more obscure and original transgression," namely, the death drive (S7: 2).

This places us on Pauline grounds, as in St. Paul's Epistle to the Romans, where he writes, "Sin needs the law, so that he [St. Paul] could become a greater sinner" (quoted in S7: 177). So, as we shall see in the case of Antigone, the moment the law speaks its decree condemning her, her *jouissance* arises all the more; the moment she is opposed is the moment the affirmation of her desire and her love are carried to their limits; commanded by the law, she must also die for the law and be dead before the law. No longer able to abide by the hollow talk of the chorus, the city elders, she is driven to her *Atè*, her destruction, not by hatred of the law but precisely by her love, her impossible desire. This "love beyond the law" is Lacan's Pauline ethic, according to Žižek.[47] In any case, this "knot of desire and the law" (Lacan S7) is the site, the situation, for both the ethical subject and ethical experience. It is here that we shall encounter Lacan's ethical imperative: do not give way on your desire (*ne pas céder sur son désir*), which would then conceivably link the choice of the good for desire and the choice of evil and crime.

The reference to transgression and crime also places us on Kantian and Sadean grounds. In this, we encounter the notion of "radical Evil," which stems not from Sade, but from Kant, as articulated in his *Religion within the Boundaries of Mere Reason*.[48] Evil is not just a particular evil or heinous act. For Kant, evil is radical in an *a priori* sense. It stands forth in the paradox of an evil act prompted by a maxim satisfying all the criteria for it to be taken as a moral law. So, consistent with his overall approach, as Kant conceives it, radical evil is not simply doing evil out of some pathological or prudential inclination. Rather, evil is "pure," in the Kantian sense of that word, meaning purified of the pathological and empirical contents. Evil thus has a purely *a priori* basis, so I can also say that I truly and freely choose or freely prefer evil over good without being persuaded to do so on account of my emotions or other pathological factors. In Kant's words, this is an evil that "cannot lie in any *object* determining the power of choice through *inclination*, nor in any *natural impulse*, but *only in a rule that the power of choice itself produces for the exercise of its freedom, i.e., in a maxim*."[49] Žižek and Jacques-Alain Miller have all commented on this theme. As Žižek outlines it, the real opposition Kant maintains between good and evil forms something like a "fantasmatic framework" for his moral thought. Where good and evil are conceived as opposing forces in a real opposition,[50] each out to destroy the other, "it becomes thinkable for one of the forces, evil, not only to oppose the other, endeavoring to annihilate it, but also to undermine it from within, by way of assuming the very form of its opposite."[51] So, this evil is *radical*, "since it corrupts the ground of all maxims."[52] Radical evil would thus undermine the demand of the good and all sense of obligation to do the good. Since it is both the opposite of the moral good and yet sharing in its maxim, it presents the danger that a disposition toward evil could be on par with a disposition toward the good, and so, from within the subjective structure of moral law it would corrupt the very grounds of the law.[53] Little wonder, then, that Kant recoiled before such "radical evil," because there is the danger that the corruption be irremediable. In this way, according to Kant, radical evil ironically prepares for a higher good: Homologous to the way the signifying cut opens the emergence of desire and the moral law, as for the whole subjective world, evil opens the space for the good,[54] but only in the sense of it opening the struggle to restore what Kant calls "the original predisposition to the good in us," which would consist not in the installation of new inclinations, but rather, in the restoration of "the purity of the moral law," "its holiness."[55] Every transgression of the law, every moment of *jouissance* would thus only reinforce the rule and purity of the law. But even here, holiness coincides with *jouissance*, the *jouissance* of moral law tangible in the pathological shiver of pain that accompanies its ever holier reign. Lacan saw this as a moral-ethical impasse, and something that had to be confronted.

When one thinks of pain and defilement, the name Sade always comes to mind. For Lacan, Sade supplies yet another paradigm of evil necessary for this conception of desire and the law in their relation to *jouissance*. If, as we have seen, *jouissance* and the Thing, the mute truth and object-cause of desire, are inaccessible except through a calamitous tearing of transgression, then it is necessary to think *jouissance* and its relation to law in terms of force. Hence, the gallery of heroes one finds in *Seminar VII*, not only Antigone, who forcefully transgresses the laws of the city, and whose splendorous beauty as we shall see, conducts her to the horror of the empty tomb—the counter-image to the Heideggerian vase discussed earlier—but also Sade's Juliette, who is practically identified with the violence and horror of a *jouissance* without limit or scruple.

Now it is Lacan's innovation to think of the torments of Sade not as apart from Kant, but as *with* Kant.[56] The filth and evil of Sade is here thought *with* Kant's purity. One might be tempted to say that Sadean "filth" is his form of "purity." The problematic "with" in "Kant with Sade," suggests an ambiguous reciprocity. Not only is Kant to be read with Sade, and not only is Sade used to read Kant and to bring out a truth hidden in Kant, that is to say, the truth of an evil that must always speak through the lie of the categorical imperative, but it also implies that Sade will be thought of as a companion, as one who accompanies Kant, as though Kant might say, *Sade, mon prochain*, My neighbor, Sade.[57] But, must there not also be an irreducible non-reciprocity between them, as there is in all intersubjective relations? How can we understand this reciprocity Lacan uncovers between Sade and Kant, both major figures, it should be remembered, of the European Enlightenment and its call for universal "rights of Man"?

This good neighborliness between Kant and Sade can initially be considered at the level of the moral laws that speak from their texts. Does not the categorical imperative, always associated with logical purity and consistency, allow the possibility that a rational agent could legislate a principle of evil fully in accord with this purity? Radical evil, as we have just said, is evil, occasioned not by some attachment to an empirical good such as money, or some empirical passion such as hatred, but from a pure principle of reason. It is the evil of rationality. An agent could be evil out of principle. This is an evil driven not by the Freudian pleasure principle, but by pure reason, and, so Lacan would argue, by the death drive, a severe and implacable fixation on the Thing, here refracted, as though in a mirror, as the unattainable absolute purity and holiness of the moral law. This helps to understand Lacan when he says that while the law is not the Thing, "I can," however, "only know of the Thing through the law" (S7: 83/101). We will return to this connection between the Thing and the moral law.

Moreover, does Kant's categorical imperative not also entail that its icy domain be installed at the cost of pain to the subject heeding its call to moral conscience? Is this not a Sadean moment or aspect to the categorical imperative, that the voice commanding obedience to the categorical imperative be the voice of the torture chamber, the voice of cruelty? And could Sade's commandment (from his *Philosophy in the Bedroom*, quoted in both "Kant with Sade," and S7)—the one that says, "I have the right to enjoy your body," so anyone can say to me, "and I will exercise the right without any limit to the capriciousness of the exactions I may wish to satiate with your body," or, as in its Lacanian articulation, "Let us take as the universal maxim of our conduct the right to enjoy any other person whatsoever as the instrument of our pleasure" (S7: 79)—could this maxim not be universalizable and so legislated from the perspective of Kant's categorical imperative? If so, then the supremely ethical position whereby all prudential and pathological concerns are set aside would also be the perspective at which evil and universal promiscuity become "live options." Again, the choice of the Good and the choice of Evil find themselves grounded on the same principle of transcendental universality. This is the radical evil that links Kant with Sade.

But what is more, under sway of a commandment fully universalizable under the terms of the categorical imperative, namely, "love thy neighbor as thyself"—according to Lacan, the only ethical commandment to still sound forth from the emptiness left by the death of God—a commandment that would attain its purely logical and rational form commanding respect for persons taken as ends, might Kant not also be commanded to love and respect Sade as himself? But how could Kant love Sade and not be overwhelmed and repulsed at the same time by the horror of evil that dwells within this neighbor who must yet be loved *as* himself? Is this not a love that would compel the recognition that Sade's evil must also be "in himself," in Kant, somehow not just outside, other, but also intimate to himself, an intimacy that is also an extimacy of being? (See S7: 186 and the lecture entitled, "Love of one's neighbor," from the section "The Paradox of *Jouissance*," April–May 1960.) Here the term "extimacy" designates "the intimate exteriority that is the Thing." This allows us to draw an important conclusion and to situate more precisely this "beyond" of the signified that Lacan marks as "the real," which is not the "Real as the Rational," as in Hegel, but the real as the Thing, the Other of the symbolic order, the "Other of the Other." The real, defined as what is beyond the symbolic order, is thus just as much inside as it is outside that order, its position being that of an insituable "beyond," a void, a lack at the heart of intimacy, the very extimacy of both the symbolic order and of the relation of good neighborliness defined and set forth within it. Thus, Lacan reads Sade, not in the conventional way as the polar opposite to the rational and composed Kant, the Kant always heeding in his way to the inner voice commanding both respect for moral law and the disdain of desire's pulsions, but as somehow the intimate truth of Kant and the truth of the Kantian moral law, the truth that could not be spoken, the truth hollowed out in the void of the Thing that is the extimacy of the Kantian moral order, both its interiority and its exteriority.

The reciprocity between Kant and Sade turns on the Thing. For Kant's symbolic *énoncé* of the moral law would seem the opposite and the annulment of *jouissance* and the Thing. Yet, in the absoluteness of the imperative announced, it can be paradoxically identical to it, such absoluteness being a hallmark trait of *jouissance* and the Thing, according to *Seminar VII*.[58] The moral law thus turns out to be the *jouissance* of desire, its absolute annulment in the paradoxical completion and attainment of *jouissance*.

But the non-reciprocal dimension of this relationship turns on the following theses: First, that the moral law is founded on a bipolarity, to wit, a voice commands and the rational will obeys. This bipolarity "is nothing but the split (*refente*) in the subject brought about by any and every intervention of the signifier: the split between the enunciating subject (*sujet de l'énonciation*) and the subject of the statement (*sujet de l'énoncé*)." Second, this split is masked in Kant and made explicit in Sade: "In coming out of the Other's mouth, Sade's maxim is more honest than Kant's appeal to the voice within, since it unmasks the split in the subject that is usually covered up."[59] With Kant, the voice that pronounces the categorical imperative seems to come from nowhere, or to be the voice of a pure auto-affection. There is no division between the voice and the ethical subject. The voice that commands is the rational subject's voice returning back upon itself. It speaks when all "pathological" contents have been set aside. It is a pure voice and perhaps senseless, but there is an undeniable reciprocity at work here. But with Sade, the voice that commands "I have the right to enjoy your body and you can say to me that you have the right to enjoy mine," is not a disembodied voice as though from nowhere; it is the voice that speaks as though from the Other, from the drives, the voice of a sadistic superego, which would imply that on one occasion I may be in the position of the master, taking my enjoyment, but on another occasion I might well find myself in the position of the slave, working to keep the master-Other happy. Sade's is a view Lacan confirms by considering the doctrine of human rights, which becomes the right to *jouissance*, "with which Sade himself establishes the reign of his principle." Lacan continues, "Thus, the discourse of the right to *jouissance* clearly posits the other qua free—the other's freedom—as its enunciating subject, in a way that does not differ from the *Tu es* (when spoken this could be taken as saying both 'you are' and 'kill!'), which is evoked out of the lethal depths of every imperative."[60] Hence, Sade's regime of the freedom of the other: The other is free to do whatever he/she wants with me. Again, the split between subject and other is clear here, where it isn't in Kant. The other is also in the position of the enunciating subject and not both the subject of the enunciation and the subject of the *énoncé* as in Kant.[61]

Finally, there is another turn to the Sadean role in *Seminar VII*, which brings us back to the central place of the death drive in *Seminar VII*. One could say, as Jacques-Alain Miller has pointed out, that the theme of "happiness in evil," cited by Lacan at the beginning of his "Kant with Sade," which could be phrased in Freudian terms as the taking pleasure in pain, is "the literary precursor to the death drive," for in the death drive "you have to conceive the possibility of finding satisfaction in aberration, in aberrant acts directed against yourself, a satisfaction in aggression for the sake of aggression. This is what the death drive and the Freudian superego are all about."[62] What is more, toward the end of the seminar, in a suite of lectures entitled "The Tragic Dimension of Psychoanalytic Experience," Lacan evokes what could at first be taken as the limit of transgression itself, but which in the end turns out to be something that only incites transgression to even further heights, something reminiscent of Sade's proclamation: "one more effort is required of you Frenchmen if you be Republicans." This is the impossibility of "crossing the limit of the second death," that death that was supposed to have represented the end of all our sufferings but which quickly becomes the scene of "a suffering beyond death," a *jouissance* beyond or in excess of *jouissance*, a *jouissance* without end. Certainly this would be both the actualization and completion of desire as desire's *jouissance* becomes itself the law of nature, and the summits, perhaps, of pleasure, but also at the same time, it would be the greatest nightmare of desire. Hence, the traditions of "hells," still present in Sade in the "idea he has of making the sufferings inflicted on a victim go on indefinitely," Sade, who, in Lacan's words, attributed a "refinement" to one of his heroes as he "tries to assure himself of the damnation of the person he sends out of life into death." It is Sade, then, Sade *avec* Kant, who opens up an "impasse, aberration, or aporia, in (the) domain of ethics," Sade, who becomes as much as Aristotle, Kant, or Freud a key figure in Lacan's map of the ethical situation he draws in his seminar, especially for the way Lacan makes transgression, not obligation, a fundamental component of that ethical situation. Nonetheless, it won't be Sade's Juliette who will be cast in the starring role in *Seminar VII*, but Sophocles' Antigone, the tragic heroine poised in her splendor "between two deaths." It is in her name and her image that Lacan shall see the death drive at its purest, prior to its reversal in and through sublimation.

Whatever the horrors unleashed in Sade, as far as Lacan is concerned the most horrific calamites of the contemporary moral and political situation do not stem from the drive for a Sadean *jouissance*, a "beyond of the pleasure principle," or from an encounter with the impossible Thing. Rather they stem from the moral frock coat of law, from the supreme rule of moral law, from the stern voice of the moral superego, so often enforced by the police, and especially it seems from the overweening rule of the desire for happiness as a desire for the True, the Beautiful, and the Good. All of this comes about in the supreme effort precisely to *avoid* the Thing, and to avoid confronting the undead beyond of any limit-experience. Moreover, this pulling back from every encounter with the Thing, a pulling back necessary for the procurement of human happiness, results in a certain nihilistic tendency in moral-ethical thought. Thus, Badiou phrases it, "The root of the problem is that, in a certain way, every definition of Man based on happiness is nihilistic."[63] In this regard, there seems to be a Nietzschean strain in Lacan's thought insofar as Lacan, too, undertakes a sort of "genealogy of morals" and an analysis of the nihilistic components of morality. Yet, it must be said, this Nietzschean dimension goes unremarked in *Seminar VII*.

In sum, Lacan shows in his reading of this paradoxical reciprocity between Kant and Sade how both must be seen as precursors to Freud. That is to say, Freud's precursors should be sought not only in Helmholtz and the newly emerging physics and laboratory scientists of the late nineteenth century, but also in figures such as Kant and Sade. They were necessary, Lacan shows, to open the path Freud would follow. Lacan: "If Freud was able to enunciate his pleasure principle without even having to worry about indicating what distinguishes it from the function of pleasure in traditional ethics . . . we can only credit this to the insinuating rise in the nineteenth century of the theme of 'delight in evil.' Sade represents . . . the first step of a subversion of which Kant, as piquant as this may seem in light of the coldness of the man himself, represents the turning point."[64] In fact, it seems that the moral-ethical reflections that came to occupy such a prominent place in the Enlightenment constitute a kind of preparation for science, a kind of rectification necessary for the advancement of science that occurred in Freud's time. As Jacques-Alain Miller phrases it, "you could say that in the Lacanian sequence, ethics precedes science," which is also something one can see well in the case of the ancient schools of ethics, the Platonic model of the *Republic*, for example, in which ethical training provides the basis for advanced studies in geometry, and the same occurs in the Epicureans, who certainly found refuge in their garden from the discontents of the civilization all around them and so found the peace of mind for their studies of a materialistic science. The example of Stoicism's studies of language and symbolic logic also comes to mind in this context. In between ethics and science, according to Miller, you have something like aesthetics or taste. "Kant and Sade constitute a rectification of ethics," Miller writes, and 'Kant with Sade' is devoted to what we might call the ethical break . . . with it a new world emerges in which psychoanalysis becomes possible."[65] Thus, Lacan's remark, "the status of the unconscious is fundamentally ethical." In their reflections on the wonder of the moral law within, Kant and Sade prepare the way for Freud's insights into the domineering and cruel reign of the superego, just as they bring to light the split (*refente*) that Lacan will see as definitive of the subject, the moral-ethical subject.

CONSIDERATIONS ON THE
MORAL GOOD AND MORAL LAW

Along these lines, then, Lacan brings into view a new status for the goods of traditional Aristotelian ethics, *Eudaimonia*, for example, and the Kantian good without qualification, the good will. The commanding, capital ethical goods of traditional philosophical ethics might be written using capital letters as "the Good." But for Lacan, they are not sovereign goods, not goods in the sense of being the end and highest *telos*, the *terminus ad quo* of all human desire. Rather, as Lacan sees them, they are goods circulating in a limited economy of goods, an economy of utility and/ or "means." In fact, the only "good" that Lacan will ultimately recognize will be, in the words of *Seminar VII*, "the price one pays for access to the truth of one's desire." Meanwhile, the ethical goods promoted by Aristotle and Kant can still command approval and respect, Lacan says, but only as possible ways by which a human life, defined by Lacan, as we shall see, in terms of a desire without satisfaction, can be made livable. But, making life livable might well entail the nihilistic humiliation of desire before a moral law, which Lacan defines as the "name of the Other's desire."[66] The moral law speaks "in me" as the law and voice of the Other. The ethical goods play a nurturing, healing, useful, and so illusory role for Lacan, illusory in the sense of being something like "fantasms." They are ways of approaching and putting out of play the unbearable depths of human experience in desire, especially the desire for what is impossible to attain, a desire for what cannot, should not, must not be desired, what Lacan calls the Thing (*das Ding*), that which resists all symbolization and which cannot be the signified for any signifier. In questioning the status of these goods, Lacan reinscribes the concept of desire, takes it from the psychobiological domain of needs and appetites, where Aristotle had situated it, and from the "pathological" category of mere empirical contents, where Kant had consigned it, and defines it in terms of the symbolic domain of the signifier. What, then, are the moral-ethical dimensions of this "split" and "divided subject," and for Lacan's reformulations of desire?

Chiefly this: the "bipolarity" brought about in the subject by the intervention of the signifier is the foundation for the moral law. "The moral law has no other principle," Lacan writes in his seventh seminar.

Lacan's clinical experience showed that the split, divided subject maintains a particularly Sadean perspective. The moral law is often linked with punishment, pain, and suffering. Pleasure is also found in pain. This is the *jouissance* of the law. Thus, there is a generally masochistic tendency that sheds important light on Lacan's theory of the subject, for it shows not only the impasse of the Sadean subject, but also the importance of Freud's notion of the superego and the importance of self-punishment for Lacan's theory of the subject. For example, during his tenure at St. Anne's Hospital, Lacan had the opportunity to observe a woman who had attacked a famous actress with a knife and whose delirium subsided once she was incarcerated. It struck Lacan that incarceration and punishment were the goals of her act, not the harm done to the actress. More generally, it seemed to him that at a certain level, the human subject does not want only what is good for him/her. Something drives a subject to transgress the barriers set up against desire and this transgression brings on punishment. Lacan notes in *Seminar VII* how he had seen this many times in his patients. Freud had thought of this in terms of the superego by which symptoms are organized, which means that for Freud, the "subject" is divided between agencies, that of the id, the ego, and the superego, that of consciousness, preconscious, and the unconscious and that one such agency can turn against the others, making conflict, self-conflict, definitive to the psychoanalytic subject. Thus, the superego is an internalized morbid voice of cruelty and punishment that sees to it that the self, the subject, attains not happiness, but guilt and unhappiness. Žižek is worth quoting at length here:

> Freud himself pointed out that the superego feeds on the forces of the id, which it suppresses and from it acquires its obscene, malevolent, sneering quality—as if the enjoyment of which the subject is deprived were accumulated in the very place from which the superego's prohibition is enunciated. The linguistic distinction between the subject of the statement and the subject of the enunciation finds here its perfect use: behind the statement of the moral law that imposes on us the renunciation of enjoyment, there is always hidden an obscene subject of enunciation, amassing the enjoyment it steals.[67]

For Kant, the moral law is purified of all pathological desire. Aristotle, while affirming that human beings are by nature desiring beings, also thought it necessary to shape and to educate desire, or at least to moderate it and make it virtuous so it would not be detrimental to the health of the soul. But, no matter what the purification of desire by moral law or by the virtues, desire nonetheless subverts the moral law. Lacan shows this in his December 23, 1959 lecture, where he discusses and formulates two instances of the moral law and its relations to desire: "Thou shalt not lie" and "Thou shalt not covet thy neighbor's wife" (S7: 80—84/97–102).

As for the first, Lacan takes desire to be unconscious desire and as what, in telling the truth about itself, must lie. Truth as error is the revealing and concealing of desire. So, the unconscious lies all the time. When it comes to telling the truth about truth, all men break the bread of the lie. Lacan: " 'Thou shalt not lie' as a negative precept has as its functioning to withdraw the subject of enunciation from that which is enunciated. There, at the locus of the divided subject, there where I repress . . . I, the liar speak" (S7: 82/99). The prohibition "Thou shalt not lie" includes within itself the "possibility of *the lie as the most fundamental desire*" (S7: 82/99, emphasis mine).

The second moral law taken into consideration addresses desire in terms of covetousness—what shall and shall not be coveted—with regard to the "neighbor's Thing" (S7: 83/101). The prohibition against coveting the neighbor's wife bears on the question of prohibiting access to something whose value lies not only in its being the property, and so the theft, of another man, but in "the fact that none of these objects (of value) exist without having the closest possible relationship to that in a human being . . . (which) is his good, the good in which he may find rest, namely the Thing." The knot of desire and the law ties the most intimate relationship with *das Ding*: "Is the law the Thing?" Lacan asks. "Certainly not. Yet I can only know the Thing by means of the law" (S7: 83/101). Hence the prohibition against coveting the neighbor's wife bespeaks this relationship between desire, the law, and the Thing. The Thing is not new; it was there from the beginning, from the very emergence of language and the symbolic order, yet it rises up, "flares up" in connection with the law. The coveted and resisted Thing, "without the law, the Thing is dead." This is Lacan's primary conclusion, drawn from St. Paul's Epistle to the Romans (Chapter 7, paragraph 7), that the law is the life of the Thing, that which is outside the law, appears only at the limit of the law. The death drive, the drive toward the Other, toward the Thing, is felt most tangibly in the law that prohibits it. Thus, the true function of the law is revealed in the very way it lies in the face of the Thing (S7: 82/100).

What is more, both of these forms of moral prohibitions provide the moral-ethical measure for our actions and relations with the other, in this sense of the word "other" meaning the "other subject." The prohibitions are directed at certain intersubjective relations and activities. Thus, Lacan promotes the telling of a lie to a moral right. The other's right to lie is what must be respected in him/her. It is in their exercise of their right to lie that they are ethical subjects and the bearer of rights and must be taken therefore as ends in themselves.

The ethical thread in the knot of desire and the law must furthermore be also followed in the Lacanian notion of fantasy. Are fantasy and the truth of desire that tells itself in a lie not both ultimately tied in the knots of desire and the moral law? Just as truth is not opposed to error and to the lie, in Lacan, so fantasy is not opposed to an unproblematic, objective reality. No more than we can dispel error and so reveal truth can we see fantasy as a screen hiding a deeper, true reality. Furthermore, fantasy, as something "fixed" and "reduced to an instantaneous state, somewhat like a frozen cinematic image, plays a protective role for Lacan, as a defense that veils castration and lack (see S4, January 1957: 119–120)[68] and so partakes of the veiling-unveiling structure of truth. What is more, the object fantasy, as image and pathos, takes the place of what the subject is symbolically deprived of. In Hamlet's case, it is the phallus. Thus, like truth, this imaginary object not *of* but *in* desire also condenses itself into the dimension of being a lure of being (*leurre de l'être*). So, Lacan calls Hamlet's Ophelia (the *O-phallos*) "that piece of bait."[69] But fantasy is also a way of responding to the enigmatic desire of the other; it is an answer to the question *Chè vuoi*, what does the Other want of me? This is "the best question" that "leads the subject to the path of his own desire."[70]

In any event, what must be kept in mind is that no matter the universality of desire, there is no such thing as a single truth of desire, there is no single, universal way in which each and every desire is oriented; there is *no one way* in which desire comes into being. For desire always comes into being in the emergence of language in any number of different ways as a relation to what Lacan calls the "fundamental fantasy," which he encountered, for example, in the Sadean fantasy of suffering. Fantasy is the object-cause of desire: "Desire . . . finds in the fantasy its reference, its substratum, its precise tuning in the imaginary register."[71] It is the end-term of desire, its orientation, what makes desire snap into focus. Which is to say that desire does not have an object as such, but only an "object-cause" posited not *before* desire but always retroactively. This retroactive dimension of desire upends the teleological conception of desire that is fundamental to the philosophical-ethical tradition. Thought in terms of lack obtaining in the symbolic order, rather than as the identity of thought and being or as the self-positing of a rational legislator, Lacan's *signifierisation* of desire thus exceeds both the physical positivity of desire as a biological force and the metaphysical positivity of desire as desire for the Good.

Such is the fantasm, the 'object *a*' (*objet petit a*) posited by desire. Such are the lures and barriers of *das Ding*. Such are the ethical and aesthetical ideals of the Good and the Beautiful, and the moral law itself. There is a similarity in structural organization in these functions in terms of the pleasure principle whereby desire seeks a way to sustain itself and to make itself a livable desire and so to mask, as it were, its truth in and as lack and the death drive.

This, at least, is Lacan's perspective in the late 1950s, when the moral law was conceived in terms of the way it forbids access to *jouissance*. Of course, the situation was different a decade later, when in the midst of a new permissiveness, in the midst of an age of shamelessness in which the only thing prohibited was prohibition itself, Lacan could say at the very end of his seventeenth seminar, in June of 1970, that what he has put forward to the majority of his hearers "makes them ashamed," as though the strange, Sadean purpose of psychoanalysis was to shame, humiliate, and shatter the fundamental fantasies by which different subjects are oriented in their symbolic worlds.

Yet, beyond this, the point seems rather to make us aware of the role of fantasy in structuring desire, and to enable the subject to reorient itself in relation to its fantasy such that it is no longer a source of suffering and self-mutilation, and perhaps even to learn to respect rather than to humiliate the other, the neighbor, by not intruding into or destroying the structure of their fantasy.[72] Thus, to respect the other's right to tell a lie might be essentially linked to the respect accorded to the other's right to his/her fantasy. So it would seem. But the job of the analyst is obviously to perform what could be taken as a violation of these rights insofar as it is the job of the analyst to intervene in and to participate in the restructuring of their patients' fundamental fantasies.

HAPPINESS, *JOUISSANCE*, AND MORAL LAW

While the connection between happiness and a certain nihilistic tendency in moral-ethical theory has already been noted, let us pursue this in a related direction by questioning the relation of happiness and *jouissance* to moral law. In his opening remarks to *Encore*, his twentieth seminar, Lacan says that this is what the law talks about—*jouissance*. Of course, when he said that, he was referring to political, conventional law, the kind of law that "veils" what we do in bed (see S20: 2–3/10), the law written in "small letters." No doubt there is a link between this kind of law, written in "small letters," and moral law, which might be written in "big letters." But the link Lacan especially tests and explores in his seminars, a link legible in these "letters" of the law, is the link between civil and moral law and human happiness.

This should be stated in its most rigorous form, as stated, for example, in Kant's writings on the *Groundwork of the Metaphysics of Morality* (the 1785 *Grundlegung zur Metaphysik der Sitte*): Along with respect for moral law comes an indeclinable moral duty to be happy. For, if one is not happy, one is less inclined to do one's moral duty. Happiness in this case seems to amount to no more than having a strong stomach. But, rather in light of this, how does Lacan question the relation between happiness, *jouissance* (*enjoyment*), and the law?

In the 1960 "The Subversion of the Subject and the Dialectic of Desire," Lacan remarks that *jouissance* is "prohibited (*interdite*) to whoever speaks." *Jouissance* "can only be said (*dite*) between the lines by whoever is a subject of the law, since the law is founded on that very prohibition."[73] But what about the commandment that rings in contemporary capitalist consumer culture, "Enjoy!" (*Jouis!*), "Thou shalt be happy!" to which the subject can only reply, "I hear" (*J'ouïs*), and *jouissance* is, thus, "no longer anything but understood."[74] In fact such a commandment is already installed as a constitutional right by certain countries: the right to happiness, which almost amounts to a "right to *jouissance.*" But a right is neither a command nor a duty. Nothing, Lacan says, "forces anyone to enjoy except the superego" (S20: 3/11), which was what Žižek was getting at in the quotation cited earlier.[75] As was said, such a command, duty, or right to happiness must be in the interest, must be for the enjoyment, the well-being, or happiness of some "superego" or other, a "*jouissance* of the Other" (*la jouissance de l'Autre*), in the sense of being "the Other's *jouissance,*" as Lacan called it (S20: 4/11), the enjoyment of a superego that is "in us" like an Other.

Analysis cannot remain at the level of the sort of "happiness" promised by the classical European ethical traditions, nor by that grim duty-bound happiness one finds in the moral traditions of the European Enlightenment, where happiness is actually underwritten by the letter of the law, and where happiness serves in turn to veil the nasty parts, the nomadic drifts of *jouissance*. Analysis follows the profile of that drift. *Jouissance* is always otherwise in relation to the law, whether moral or political-conventional. Such are the differences between happiness and *jouissance* in their relation to the law. In the 1960s, Lacan characterized *jouissance* as transgressive in its relation to the law, which might be perceived as barring the way, and as transgressive or in excess of the symbolic order itself. Transgressive *jouissance* would break through this bar of the law, break through this wall of language. It was access to the unspeakable Thing. But, in his 1960 address "The Subversion of the Subject and the Dialectic of Desire," Lacan makes an important clarification: it is really not the law that bars the subject's access to *jouissance*, rather it is the regulations of the pleasure principle, a regulation Freud discovered in the primary process.[76] Transgression is thus not just a wild act, enacted at the level of the imaginary, an act violent with respect to the law, but it involves the very self-transgression of the principle of pleasure itself, of pleasure's excess, its "beyond" in the drive, the one and only drive, the death drive.

Ten years later, in *Encore*, Lacan speaks of *jouissance* in other, newer terms as a "feminine *jouissance*," and of a new relation between *jouissance* and the law, a new relation between *jouissance* and the structural relations of exchange, and with language and the symbolic order.

In his seventeenth seminar, *The Other Side of Psychoanalysis*, and especially his twentieth seminar entitled *Encore, On Feminine Sexuality: The Limits of Love and Knowledge* (1972–1973), Lacan approaches this by delimiting "*jouissance feminine*" from "phallic *jouissance*." There is a kind of happiness linked with *jouissance*, a *jouissance* of the Other, whereby the Other is the big Other, the symbolic order, and a knowledge (*savoir*) as knowledge of the truth of desire. Lacan calls this phallic *jouissance* and the "happiness of the phallus." Although Lacan does say that phallic *jouissance* is sexual, that, "in other words, it is not related to the Other (the body of the Other) as such" (S20: 9/14), he also importantly characterizes it as an "enjoyment of speech." He calls this "another satisfaction" (S20: 64/61). In his earlier seminars, such as *The Ethics of Psychoanalysis*, happiness and the phallic *jouissance* are constituted by castration, alienation, and renunciation, and, while happiness was tamed, at least *jouissance* had to be to be put at a distance, forbidden, "forbidden to him who speaks as such," forbidden by the regime, by the domination of the pleasure principle and by the symbolic order. *Jouissance* "in its *infinitude*" thus begins by bearing the mark of its prohibition, and this mark is constituted by the "sacrifice" of castration and alienation, a "sacrifice implied in the same act as that of choosing its symbol, the phallus."[77] Thus, two registers become active here: the symbolic, which defines the sacrificial act, and the imaginary, which defines the image of the penis as the most powerful image of *jouissance*.

But forbidden *jouissance* becomes all the more attractive to the point of becoming something of a goal secretly, unavowably desired by all enjoyment. But, where happiness, or even *jouissance*, are set forth by an ethic as a goal, end, purpose, or eventually even as a right or duty, they begin to function as fantasms guiding desire. Ironically, such a goal would not release desire to a mythic, orgiastic state, but, to the contrary, actually contribute to disciplining it instead, and driving it ever onward in the service of the economy goods, which is an economy of utility, essentially. This is where duty colludes with discipline and with the sort *jouissance* of discipline touched upon in Žižek's quoted remark. It is the essential function of the Law (capitalized to signify the moral law), the function of language, the language of the law, of rights and duties inscribed and enounced in the domain of the big Other, to delimit that space—originally dominated and disciplined no doubt by the pleasure principle—where desire can be satisfied, and where the human Good can be realized in a human life. But, there is a secret delight, there is another satisfaction, and another pleasure in this.

Thus, phallic *jouissance* can become a *jouissance* of mastery, of domination, and death, insofar as death is the master signifier and *jouissance*, at least from the point of view of *The Ethics of Psychoanalysis*, is bound with pain and death. This is *jouissance* exercised not only through Nietzsche's "whip," that "whip" that one must take "when one goes to woman," but it also and chiefly finds its instrument and its thickness in the voice of command, in the interpolative *Jouis!*, and its call to the Kantian moral duty, "Be Happy!"

Now, where phallic *jouissance* and "the happiness of the phallus" is the happiness of castrated, alienated being, happiness comes to be essentially bound and tied not just by the principle of pleasure, but so also by moral-ethical law, and by political law, as well. This can be accomplished by asserting that happiness is a goal, end, and purpose of life, and by making it a right and a duty. As a "good" promoting life, happiness is here not only reduced and disciplined, it is also put to work in the economy of the circulation of goods, and so is wedded to the consumption of evermore merchandise and the accumulation of evermore credit card debt.

But the locution, the *jouissance of the Other* is intriguingly ambiguous in Lacan's seminars: the "Other" can be understood to be not only "the big Other," the phallic domain of discourse, the domain of laws and duties, but also the Other of the exception, the Other of what is the exception to that domain, not inscribed within it, neither castrated nor alienated, *jouissance* in its "*infinitude*," the 'Other than the phallic *jouissance*," namely, the "*jouissance feminine*." The Other can also refer to the "body of the Other, and to a "*jouissance* of the Other," which is "promoted only on the basis of infinity." In the context of a discussion of "phallic *jouissance*," which is the *jouissance* of sexual enjoyment, Lacan shows that the "infinite of *jouissance*" is not infinite in the sense of being mystically and indefinitely endless *jouissance*. Rather, the "infinite" is taken by Lacan in a mathematical sense of being an infinite Cantorian set from which there can be no subtraction or addition.[78] Let us look for a moment at Lacan's remarks on the infinite, found in *Seminar XX, Encore*.

Lacan illustrates his usage of the term "infinitude" by reference to Zeno's paradox of the race between Achilles and the tortoise. Originally, Zeno's paradox was a sort of *reductio ad absurdum* of the ancient identification of time, motion, and space as being discrete series, whereby neither Achilles nor the tortoise can ever take the first step in the race. Nothing gets going; there is no finish line. Zeno's paradox demonstrates that a number, a point of space, has a limit,[79] and between any two countable space points, there is at least one other; there is an infinite series in the "between," making this what is sometimes called a "dense system," or perhaps what Badiou might call a "discontinuous multiple." It is this infinite "betweenness" that makes the race impossible and infinite such that Achilles can never get beyond that first step: although he can pass the tortoise, he can never thus catch up with it except at "infinity" (*infinitude*). For Lacan, this ancient paradox is also the "schema of coming" (*le schème du jouir*). The race has two poles, represented by Achilles and the tortoise. Now since "tortoise" (*tortue*) is a feminine noun, as Lacan's English translator points out, it represents the feminine pole. Earlier in his discussion, Lacan has asserted that in analytic experience, "everything revolves around phallic *jouissance*" (S20: 7/13ff.). With respect to phallic *jouissance*, woman is "not whole" (*pas-tout*). By this, Lacan means that "woman" ("Woman" with a capital W, woman as a universal essence) "does not exist." "Woman," in other words, would be a universal set lacking any existential import. Woman's "sexual organ" is, likewise, of no interest in phallic *jouissance* because the male "pole" (*côte*) of that sexual relationship is really only interested in the *jouissance* of the organ, the phallus. Thus, in the sexual relationship, there is always a failure or fault in the sense that the male pole can never "have" the feminine position. It is never "wholly his" (S20: 8/13). Hence, the superego commandment to "Enjoy!" is not only a correlate of castration, but is also the commandment to enjoy the organ. But, Lacan adds, the consequence of this is that the *jouissance* of the Other, of the body of the Other, the body, namely, of the woman, the feminine "pole," is blocked by phallic *jouissance*, it is an "obstacle" such that the "man does not come," he does not "arrive" (*n'arrive pas*), with the French word *arriver* being a slang term for sexual orgasm.[80] Thus, *jouissance* in this sense is always "promoted" on the basis of an uncrossable infinite. Achilles and the tortoise (Briseis) are in a race, a sexual race in Lacan's reading of it, a race in which one pole, that of Achilles, never "arrives" because he can never catch up with his Briseis, here symbolized by the tortoise, with the female pole (*côte*), in other words, for she is "never wholly his," she is "not whole," there is always something other that "remains," something the phallic *jouissance* cannot catch up with. Between the two poles, the male and the female, there is always this unsurpassable density, the density of the "between." It is a density from which nothing can be either added or taken away and so is not countable. Once again, infinity here has an essentially mathematical derivation. The importance of this is that it distances the infinitude of *jouissance* from meaning, for mathematical definitions are not about meanings. Thus, the infinitude of *jouissance* is written, in Lacan's schemas of the four discourses, and so from within the horizon of the finite, as "object *a*" (*objet petit a*), whereby the letter *a* functions in much the same way as a letter functions in a mathematical formula.

"Object *a*," as the object of fantasy and desire, also marks the play of "semblance" and masquerade in sexual relations, that "paper tiger" one shows to the body of the Other. Here, the density of the "remainder," that which can never be "wholly his," that bit to which Achilles can never quite catch up, is the density of the remainder of castration, which Lacan also calls "object *a*." As such, it constitutes a sort of veil in relation to the real. "*Trompe-l'oeil* is the soul of *petit a*," Lacan says in *Seminar XI* (S11: 112). Like all veils, it also functions as a lure in the way it incites a man to look and see what is on the other side. This, Achilles cannot do. He cannot see "what remains" out of his reach. He cannot see this infinite of the between by which he can never catch his Briseis/tortoise. This between is truly a "supplementary *jouissance*," a *jouissance* "beyond the phallus" (S20: 73–74/68–69), not freed from any reference to the phallus, it is yet the "other side" of phallic *jouissance*; an infinity that cannot be "caught" up with in the horizon of the finite, and which nonetheless is what promotes "phallic *jouissance*," it is an *extraterritorial jouissance*.

What could be more useless than this? Lacan's seminar *Encore* (S20) speaks of this "other side" of *jouissance* in terms of what "serves no purpose" (*ne sert à rien*) (S20: 3/10). This is what he says. He calls it *jouissance* in its "negative instance" (S20: 3/10), feminine *jouissance*. Feminine *jouissance*, even its tamed and trivialized younger cousin, "happiness," must at some point be the antipodes, the "other side," and the end points of both the flourishing and the failure for the whole economy of the circulation of goods, together with the discourse of laws, rights, and duties that maintains that economy. Such *jouissance* is not simply the interdicted (*interdite*), but also the hazardous, unspeakable, and alluring gap, the fissure and point of failure in the articulation of the "well-said" (*bien-dite*) of phallic happiness, where happiness is said (*dite*) to be a "good" and counted among the goods of life, and so given a place and a role to play in a limited economy of desire, the economy of the circulation of goods.

Although Freud maintained himself as close as possible to *jouissance*, he retreated from feminine *jouissance*, Lacan remarks. Perhaps out of timidity, or from a feeling of discomfort as he approached that "point," as Lacan calls it, "where discourse emerges, or even, when it returns there, when it falters," for whatever reason, Freud "abandoned" the question of feminine *jouissance*. He thus worked with a limited, "reduced economy" of *jouissance* (S17: 73/83–84). Here is where Lacan, in his own "getting closer to feminine *jouissance*," in his own act of fidelity to the truth and "*infinitude*" of *jouissance*, by thus not abandoning feminine *jouissance*, by "not giving up on his desire," goes beyond Freud and points the discourse of psychoanalysis—the discourse and the practice—in new directions toward a generalized economy of *jouissance*, *jouissance* in its extraterritoriality.

We can therefore glimpse in these seminars, a doubling of *jouissance*—a double economy of *jouissance*—that of phallic *jouissance* and the "happiness of the phallus," where happiness is a duty and a right, and on the "other side," a *jouissance* phrased in terms of the almost Bataillean categories of the *sans-emploi*, and the "useless negativity," the "out-of-work," or "work-limit," *jouissance* as is figured and marked in the discourse of the seminars as what cannot be put to work, a feminine *jouissance* of expenditure and squandering foreshadowed perhaps in *The Ethics of Psychoanalysis*'s evocation of the tragic image of Antigone.

The example of Antigone provokes the following line of questioning: If *jouissance* in its general economy falls on the side of the unavowable with respect to the laws, moral and juridical, what is its relation to truth and with "evil"?

Let us begin with *jouissance* and truth. Antigone wishes to act in accordance with what she perceives as the indeclinable truth of divine law. She is perhaps driven by a *jouissance*, by the *jouissance* of a death drive. Her resulting act—her suicide that shakes the city to its foundations—seems evil from the perspective of civil law because, as in Hegel's analysis, she seems to promote the welfare of the private and of the family at the expense of the city's public law. The *jouissance* of her death drive turns her into a sort of monster. Let us set this aside for now and return to it later. For now, let us recall another example, famously reviewed in Lacan's seminars, from Kant's moral theory (Sartre also dealt with this in his famous short story "The Wall"), whereby a man, a prisoner, is promised all the *jouissance* he wants if only he will denounce an enemy that "the tyrant fears is disrupting his (own) *jouissance*." Obversely, the prisoner will be executed if he fails to denounce the tyrant's enemy (see S20: 92/85). Kant would demand that no pathological factor be allowed to intervene between a man and his moral duty, whether it is the promise of enjoyment or the threat or fear of death. The man should tell the truth about what he knows regardless of the promise of death or *jouissance*. But, should the man in question tell the tyrant the whole truth, even if it means that by doing so, he will be delivering a potentially innocent man into the hands of the tyrant and so committing a reprehensible, evil act? Wouldn't truth, *jouissance*, and evil here enter into a dangerous liaison? Kant would say that the truth must be told, regardless of the *jouissance* promised. But, Lacan's rejoinder is that truth, the whole truth, can never be told regardless of what is promised or threatened. Another example, also taken from Kant, connects with this: an apparently lusty individual is told that he can have all the *jouissance* (phallic *jouissance*) he wants with a most desirable woman for one night, with the proviso that when his night of *jouissance* is finished (as though *jouissance* could ever be finished), he shall be hanged by the neck until dead. Would he go ahead with it? Or would he set aside his *jouissance* out of concern for his own welfare? How strong is the attraction/repulsion of *jouissance*? Can anything, even truth or the law, whether moral or political, hold up against it? Lacan, of course, affirms that the analyst is always meeting patients for whom *jouissance* is everything. They will gladly transgress the law; they will gladly lie or tell the truth, even to an evil tyrant; they will gladly die for the sake of their *jouissance*. Nothing so pathologically powerful as *jouissance* can ever be set aside in the name of whatever moral, social, or juridical law, or any other asceticism for that matter, or even for the sake of whatever might be promised by way of the future extension of a life to be lived without the brief intensity of *jouissance*. *Jouissance* thus marks a limit, not a mathematical limit but a pathological limit. It is the limit marked by all moral and political law, a limit Kant found necessary to confront, only to set it aside at all cost. With regard to *jouissance* and truth, the truth is that *jouissance*, perhaps because of its being a way of access to the real, the unnamable, unapproachable

real, is only approached on the basis, not only of truth, but also by way
of semblance. *Jouissance* is thus "questioned (*s'interpelle*), evoked, tracked,
and elaborated only on the basis of a semblance" (S20: 92/85). In the
"four discourses" (those of Mastery, of the University, of the Hysteric,
and of the Analyst), *jouissance* is "surplus *jouissance*" (*plus-de-jouir*), (S20:
17/21), namely, the surplus produced in and through work, the work, for
example, of Hegel's slave, who produces a surplus taken up and consumed
in the pleasure of the master. In its role as surplus, *jouissance* is also the
remainder, the overflow of meaning and the symbolic function. In this
"negative instance," it is "object *a*." Looking at the four discourses, one
can see that in the "master's discourse," which is also the discourse of
the unconscious, the master signifier (S_1), that signifier that marks the
point of entry of the subject into the symbolic order, is positioned on
the opposite side from "object *a*," on the opposite side from *jouissance*,
which it evidently must keep at a distance. One must not approach object
a, the surplus and the object of fantasy and desire, too closely. *Jouissance*
will, thus, always maintain this ambiguous relationship with language,
neither inside nor outside, but at the rim. Although Lacan says *jouissance* qua "*jouissance* of the Other sex" cannot be taken as a sign of love
(S20: 17/21), semblance is most fundamental to love. Here, semblance
turns on "object *a*," the object-cause of fantasy and desire. Love is love
of the semblance of being, the semblance being that object that is *a*.[81]
Object *a*, meanwhile, the object of fantasy and desire, is but a construction, something produced in the image of the lover, a semblance of his/
her ego ideal, a narcissistic semblance of the lover in his/her self-image.

As surplus, *jouissance*—at least from the perspective of the 1972–
1973 seminars—is practically on the same level as what Lacan calls *sig-
nifiance*, translated as "signifierness," a term proposed by Lacan's translator,
who invented it in order to translate Lacan's French word. Signifierness
imparts the "nonsensical nature of the signifier," its being apart from
meaning, its having other than meaning effects, in Lacan's words.[82] Thus,
the truth of *jouissance*, a truth perhaps written in the semblances of
"signifierness," puts it at a distance from "meaning." Now, insofar as *jouissance* also relates to the real, Lacan describes it as "access to the real,"
and insofar as the real is inscribed, at least in *Encore*, Lacan's 1972–1973
seminar, on the basis of formalization, mathematical formalization, and
insofar as such formalization itself produces "other than meaning effects,"
and even runs counter to meaning, this would make mathematical formalization perhaps the most advanced instance of "signifierness." Here,
in these dimensions of the "signifierness" of *jouissance* and the real, in

these dimensions always apart from meaning, and in these dimensions of *jouissance* as a limit, we encounter the basis for the symbolic order itself, the basis perhaps of moral law itself, an impasse and pivot upon which everything seems to turn for Lacan.

Does this generalized economy of *jouissance* not also mark a transgressive disavowal, a negation of moral law, such that the basis would also be the transgression of moral law? As a limit, does *jouissance* not also mark a monstrous excess, a beyond of moral law? Would it therefore be tempting to speak of it as "evil"? Let us hasten to say that *jouissance* is not a simple and violent negation of moral law, perhaps its "suspension," its "supplement," it is what both marks a gap in moral law and what would fill that gap; not the existential exception that would confirm the finite horizon of moral law, but the unnamable infinite that opens from within it, the infinite that held old Kant in awe. Evil, to speak in accord with what Badiou has said on these themes, evil would consist in "forcing" *jouissance*, as one might likewise "force" the unnamable, forcing it to stand up and be counted, forcing it to speak when it has nothing to say, redirecting it, putting it to work, in service, for just one example, to the aesthetics, to the violence, and the rage of politics.

For now, we can see in this double economy of *jouissance* the turning, twisting political and economical edge to Lacan's ethical considerations of the knots of desire and the law. This is why Lacan also characterized the ethics of happiness as also being a political question, a political questioning and the questioning of the political. "Happiness has become a political factor," he said in *The Other Side of Psychoanalysis* (S17: 72/83), where "the only happiness is the happiness of the phallus."

In closing this line of thought, let us recall how Lacan has insisted all along that it is not the goal of psychoanalysis to help pave the way for the "bourgeois dream" of attaining human happiness, that it is not the goal of psychoanalysis to ensure the success of phallic *jouissance* to attain the satisfactions of lasting happiness by simply finding out once and for all exactly what it is that *jouissance* wants—what it is that "woman" wants. For Lacan, there is no pregiven positivity of a subject, even as a desiring subject, that would have as its structural opposite an object of desire—not even the semblance of "object *a*"—with a resulting subject—object bifurcation. There is no preestablished subject-object relation in Lacanian analysis; there is no preestablished harmony between a need and any given object such that a need could be satisfied by it (S1: 209). Desire is not pregiven, but constructed in and by the signifying cut, as are its fantasms of happiness. Only in terms of its being guided by the pleasure principle would its goal be to seek satisfaction—happiness—in the attainment of some object. But in truth, desire is defined as lack by Lacan, and so is always seeking to fill out its emptiness; it is always desire for something else, and so defined more by repetition than by satisfaction taken as a *terminus ad quo*. Rather than the *satisfaction/realization* of desire traditional ethics promised under the guise of *Eudaimonia*, well-being, Lacan prefers to speak of desire's *realization*, not as fulfillment—for by the definition of desire, this is impossible anyway—but rather as desire's ceaselessly reproducing itself as lack, being an "indestructible *Wunsch* that pursues repetition, the repetition of signs" (S7: 72). In other words, it is a death drive. The realization of desire obtains in a sliding movement Lacan calls the "metonymy" of desire.

IN CONCLUSION AND SUMMATION

Finally, this: In so many ways and at so many junctures, philosophy may have opened the door on the truth of desire and the subject. But, as Lacan said in his 1969 "Response to Students of Philosophy Concerning the Object of Psychoanalysis,"[83] however philosophy may have wanted to protect that truth, it did so only by slamming the door of truth shut as soon as it had opened it. It is Lacan's self-described task to open that door again, to pry it open using the instruments of Freudian psychoanalysis, in particular, Freud's truth, the truth of the unconscious. Where the discourses of philosophy since Descartes had identified the subject with consciousness, Lacan identifies it with the unconscious, with desire and language. For the discourses of philosophy, for the Cartesian tradition that was so much a part of Lacan's philosophical background and intellectual context, the subject was always a thinking being, where thinking and knowing are in turn identified with seeing, with the transparency of intellectual intuition and ultimately with the embodied gaze. For philosophy, the subject is a thinking substance; it is the transcendental foundation and condition for the possibility of knowledge, the condition for the possibility of, first, a unified science of nature and, through that, the condition for that attainment of an ultimate self-knowledge, a longed-for absolute self-consciousness and a freedom exercised in the presence of beauty. All of this, Lacan maintains, has only served to close the door on the truth of the subject.

Lacan's anti-philosophical gesture is to install his teaching at this coincidence of subjectivity and consciousness and to pry this coincidence open by inscribing within its suture the moments of difference, of alterity, and heterogeneity opened by the truth of unconscious and by the logic of language and desire that Lacan has articulated in his teachings. Especially by way of the "discourse of the analyst" (S17: 31, 33/32, and 36), and the structure of fantasy, Lacan has inscribed across the clarity and symmetry of the philosophical discourse—ultimately, a discourse of certainty founded on the self-transparency of the thinking subject to itself—decisive moments of opacity and asymmetry. This opacity and this asymmetry are first of all introduced by the unconscious and by the identification of the subject with desire, language, and the unconscious. But there is something more: Lacan also introduces a crucial "supposition," which shall turn out to be something other than just another philosophical doubt, for such doubt is always only the flipside of certainty. Unlike the philosophical subject, the Lacanian subject is only "*supposed to know*" (S11: 232), and only "*supposed* to desire" (S11: 253). The Lacanian subject only "supposed to know" and "supposed to desire" subverts the self-certainty of the Cartesian subject. Through its discovery of the unconscious and through the suppositions of knowledge and desire that Lacan has brought to light in the relation between the subject and the Other, psychoanalysis thus introduces a radical and disturbing new asymmetry that breaks open the symmetrical tomb where philosophy had once sealed up the truth of desire. It is this opacity and this asymmetry that shall shatter the philosophical coincidence of subjectivity and consciousness and reopen the door of truth on desire. How so?

First, it is not just knowledge and desire in general that are ultimately in question here. Rather, it is the knowledge and the desire of the analyst as they are in play in the analytic situation of the transference by which the structure of a subject's fundamental fantasy is brought forth that is being emphasized. Everything in the analytic situation turns on the desire of the analyst. It is precisely this desire that must always remain for the analysand the great unknown, something that the analysand can thus only suppose or attribute to the analyst. The subject, in the function of the analyst, thus comes to be in the analytic discourse not one who knows but one who is only "supposed to know." But what does he/she know? The subject is here also the Other who, as an analyst, is supposed to know what it is that will cure the suffering of the patient, the analysand. Lacan answers that the analyst knows "that from which no one can escape . . . quite simply, signification" (S11: 253), where signification is what would emerge from the interpretations of the analyst. But is there not always something else, something always and already active here about which the analyst cannot know and about which he or she is also and irrevocably stupid? Indeed, one of the effects of analytic interpretation is to isolate something rich and complex, linked with the unconscious, something "irreducible," something "non-sensical—composed of non-meanings," "a kernel, a *kern*," in Freud's terminology, "of non-sense" (S11: 250), that may ultimately be identified with the primary master signifier itself, which is also the "the bearer of the infinitization of the value of the subject" (S11: 252). Not only a subject "supposed to know," the analyst is also a subject "supposed to desire." In fact, the two are linked. "The subject is supposed to know, simply by being a subject of desire" (S11: 253). But to desire what? To cure? To care for the soul? What is the truth of the desire of the analyst? Not only the truth of the unconscious, the truth of the desire of the analyst is thus the other great opacity active at the heart of the analytic conversation between the doctor and his/her patient. For the discourse of analysis, as for the structure of fantasy, the object of desire is "object *a*," the object = x, in other words, that unknown, that nullity, that void, that waste, that piece of trash, that something that shall ultimately be disposed of, thrown down or thrown away, but which is yet something that also serves to get desire going. This is precisely the position and the function of the analyst and a key moment of the analytic act. The desire of the analyst must remain for the analysand something unknown or only supposed in the analytic situation, because, in the analytic situation, the analyst occupies the position of master only insofar as he/she is also this "object *a*," this evasive "object x" that triggers the desire of the analysand and ultimately reveals the structure of his/her fundamental fantasy. Likewise, from the perspective of the analyst the analysand can also function as one supposed to know. From the point of view of both the analyst and the analysand, "object *a*" shall thus have no specific contours or configuration; it is whatever it is or whatever it takes to answer the question, "What does the Other, what does the analyst want of me?" This is the question the subject is always asking: "What does the Other want of me?" "What is the desire of the Other?" "How can I fashion myself such that I can become the object of desire for the Other?" Object *a* in this way only temporarily fills in the void, the lack, opened by desire's restless questioning, and in doing so, it keeps desire moving lest it get stuck or frozen into configurations of senseless, death-bound repetition. Meanwhile, on the side of the Other, especially where the analyst occupies this position, likewise we find not a subject that is whole and undivided, but one that is also divided, a subject symbolized as "barred-S." Thus, the desire of the analyst retains this moment of opacity; it is always the unknown x, the self-differencing desire at the heart of the psychoanalytic situation. Because of the role it plays in being the object of desire, the desire of the analyst thus remains such a crucial question and the essential dimension of Lacan's ethics of psychoanalysis. It is also why Lacan makes the question of an ethics of psychoanalysis so central to his teachings, for it is here that he seeks to reopen the door on the truth of the subject slammed shut by the discourses of philosophy, and to do so by marking at the heart of the philosophical discourses on the subject these moments of opacity, asymmetrical moments of lack and desire that shall always prevent that discourse from closing back upon itself. At the heart of philosophy's meditations on desire and subjectivity, Lacan's ethics of psychoanalysis inscribes something that opens philosophy to both its limits and to what exceeds those limits.

Yet, however Lacan says his battle is not for philosophy or positioned on the philosophical front, however it is instead a battle for psychoanalysis and for the psychoanalytic front, it continues nonetheless to have a philosophical effect and to pose questions essential to the future of philosophy. And it may be from within philosophy that the register of the effects of the Lacanian ethics of psychoanalysis can best be assessed and put to work in new directions of thought. Consider, for example, the way Lacan's ethics of psychoanalysis also seems to retain a key philosophical-ethical concept and to pose a key ethical question: that of ethical responsibility. Must not Lacan's subject—whether in the figure of the analyst or the analysand—still bear the weight of a responsibility for his/her desire? Is it not the task of the ethics of psychoanalysis to question the desire of the analyst and ask what it means not only for the analysand but also for the analyst to assume responsibility for his or her own desire? Is such responsibility perhaps something rather like the signification alluded to earlier in the case of the one "supposed to know"? Is it not this desire that cannot be refused (S11: 253)? Thus, to assume a responsibility for one's own desire, at least in the case of the function of the analyst, might also link up—as in the case of Hegel's "master" in the master—slave dialectic—with the assumption of death (S11: 255). It is here, in connection with this question of ethical responsibility in the analytic situation, that we encounter not only the responsibility of the analyst in relation to his/her desire, but also the larger, more generalized question of the transgressive relation between desire and moral law, something Lacan has said he encountered all the time in his analytic practice. Is this not also exemplified in the figure of Antigone who was willing to give up her life rather than give way on her desire? Lacan thus prolongs this traditional philosophical question of ethical responsibility, but he does so in a new way. He does so in terms of the knots of desire and moral law, the (Borromean?) knots of the symbolic, the imaginary and the real, knots tied and undone not only by death but also in and by the structure of fantasy and the object(s) of desire. It is along these lines that Lacan both opposes and enlarges the discourses of philosophy, both ancient and modern, and reopens the door on the truth of desire.

Perhaps we can thus also see a more general ethical perspective and a more general urgency sketched in Lacan's seminars. Perhaps this urgency obtains in relation to the way he shows how the "care of the soul/ self" and the entanglements of moral law and desire are also ultimately bound up with the subjection and the oppressive administration of desire. The question, "What does the Other want of me?" is then positioned at a more general, societal, ethical, and political level. In his seventh seminar, Lacan tells us that this has taken an ominous turn: it has led to the almost universal domination of the economy of the "service of goods" (S7: 303), by which the relationship of each individual to his/her desire is always administrated and so mediated and suppressed. In other words, the economy of the service of goods, in which moral Goods circulate as goods among other goods, results not just in the materialization and the commercialization of desire, but more ominously in "an amputation" of desire; it leads to "a kind of puritanism in the relationship of desire" (S7: 303/350). No doubt it was this puritanism and the sacrifices it implies that provoked Lacan's striking reference to the dramatic situation of Antigone and her confrontation with Creon. By thus situating the subject "in a fundamental relationship" not with the positivity of goods but with the "nullity of death" (S7: 303), Lacan saw, at least in his 1960 seminar, the more general ethical task as that of preparing the subject, through the long and arduous practice of analysis, to not only be able to assume responsibility for his/her own desire, but also to be able to "confront the reality of the human condition."

Seminar VII's most strident moral command is thus heard in the final sessions dating from 1960, not only as a call to assume responsibility for one's desire, but to heed the question, "Have you acted in conformity with your desire?" (S7: 311). In relation to this, the solitary and implacable figure of Antigone will especially stand forth in all her splendor.

5

ANTIGONE, IN HER
UNBEARABLE SPLENDOR

Antigone reveals to us the line of sight that defines desire. This line of sight focuses on an image that possesses a mystery which up till now has never been articulated.

—Jacques Lacan, *Seminar VII*

What we are dealing with is nothing less than the attraction of transgression . . . that obscure and original transgression for which (Freud) found a name at the end of his work, in a word, the death instinct, to the extent that man finds himself anchored deep within . . . its formidable dialectic.

—Jacques Lacan, *Seminar VII*, "The Splendor of Antigone"

In his seventh seminar, *The Ethics of Psychoanalysis*, one of Lacan's declared purposes is to prepare the way toward a new "ethics of psychoanalysis" by first articulating a "demythologization" of the European philosophical ethical tradition. In pursuit of this, he often makes references not only to scientific and clinical observations, but also to literary sources. Why, in this period of his seminars from the late 1950s and early 1960s, when the famous "return to Freud" was at its height, why this appeal to literary, dramatic sources? Why, in a seminar devoted to laying out the groundwork for an "ethics of psychoanalysis," this captivating intersection between psychoanalysis and theater? The following essay takes up this question and shows that Lacan's ethics is also an aesthetics, that his emphasis is not only on the ethical act, but also on "beauty," specifically, a pre-Platonic, Sophoclean beauty: the beauty and the splendor of Antigone. This makes his ethics an ethical-aesthetics, something he situates in terms of his threefold topology of the imaginary, the symbolic, and the real. But this aesthetic dimension is not restricted so much to artistic categories, whereby it might be delimited to the dimensions of the imaginary, nor is it concerned with aesthetic judgment, whereby it might be restricted to the symbolic dimension. Rather, Lacan's seminar develops an ethics of transgression. Beauty thus becomes the almost seismographic register of a movement of transgression that concerns all three of the interrelated dimensions of his psychoanalytic topology, the imaginary, the symbolic, and the real. The following therefore begins with a discussion of the manifold dimensions of Antigone's beauty that Lacan brings forward in his seminar and pursues this in its resonance with the Lacanian ethic as an ethico-aesthetic of transgression, of *jouissance* and "the real." How does this approach contribute toward his task of transforming and demystifying the tradition of European philosophical ethics, which, especially in the late 1950s, had largely become an existential ethics of finitude, an ethics that was essentially a way of "being toward death"?

ANTIGONE'S PARODOS

In his seventh seminar, Lacan referred to a wide range of literary material extending from the courtly love poetry of the troubadours as well as to the novels of the Marquis de Sade. But it is Sophocles' classical tragic drama, *Antigone*, which is most prominent. In the sixth seminar, the reference was to Shakespeare's *Hamlet*, and in the eighth seminar, to Claudel's Sygne de Coûfontaine in *l'Otage*, so tragic drama had a widely important role for Lacan's work in the late 1950s and early 1960s. Such dramatic and literary characters were essential to the development of his thought because, for him, literature had a way of revealing and articulating what he called a "line of sight that defines desire," a "line of sight . . . which up till now has never been articulated" (S7: 247). I shall take this "line of sight" as my theme in the following pages, following its intensity to the moment where splendor, Antigone's transgressive beauty and splendor, coincide with darkness, the darkness of the tomb, the darkness of an impossible, infinite moment "between two deaths."

Antigone, one of Lacan's most well-known referents, was first brought to light in the context of a drama staged in a theater perched at the heart of the city of Athens. Her implacable, indomitable will brought to light a transgressive *jouissance* more closely allied with expenditure and death than with sublimation before the law. She must have been a frightening, monstrous spectacle. The play therefore presented both ethical and political dimensions that were crucial not only for the emerging democracy of classical Athens, but also for modern-day psychoanalysis. At this stage of Lacan's work in the early 1960s, Antigone signified not just the pinnacle and the pivotal ethical act (or "deed," as Hegel's *Phenomenology* calls it, distinguishing a "deed" as action commanded by divine law and so incurring "guilt," from an "act," defined in relation to civil law, and so being identified with "crime"),[1] she was also, from the point of view of Lacan's attempts to develop an ethics of psychoanalysis, a deeply problematic figure. More than just a pathos, she was marked by a "doom" (*Atè*/ἄτη, delusion, ruin, a judicial blindness sent by the gods), as horrifying in its unfolding as it was compelling, the darkness and density of a doom (*Atè*) that was the other side of her singularly radiant splendor.

Antigone has had many starring roles in philosophical texts of the past. In Hegel's matinee, for example, she was one of the shapes or figures through which Spirit had to pass on its path of dialectically attained absolute self-knowledge. She doesn't get very good reviews from Lacan in this role. In *Seminar VII*, Lacan says Hegel is at his weakest when he presents his Antigone. The Hegelian phenomenology of "ethical consciousness" reduces her to playing a transitional role in a dialectic of oppositional nomic discourses—those of divine law and civil law—that ultimately contributes to bringing about a culminating, higher resolution. Moreover, since she is a woman, Hegel also rather stereotypically casts her as naturally having a higher intuitive consciousness of what is ethical, but for good dialectical reasons, she is never allowed to attain a true consciousness of it. Instead, she is tied to the law of the family, which is only inner and implicit, and therefore not exposed to the bright daylight of the real world. Hegel never mentions her climactic moment in the play when she willingly steps into the darkness of the tomb. Instead, he has her watch with ethical resignation as her parents pass away.

In Lacan's late-late show, on the other hand, Antigone's role is both darker and more luminous. Where for Hegel, she was an almost bloodless abstraction, centered only on the universal and throughout remaining estranged from the particularity of desire, for Lacan, on the other hand, she is the scintillating image of desire and the death drive. Far from promising resignation and reconciliation, she epitomizes instead an indelible resistance to reconciliation. In the seventh seminar, she is portrayed as burning a hole through the placid pathways of dialectics. Only with a magician's sleight of hand could Hegel fold her *terribilis splendor* back into the pacifying romance of Absolute Knowledge.

ANTIGONE'S BEAUTY:
ITS SPLENDOR AND PURITY

Of all the characteristics that usually catch the critic's eye—her defiance, her courage, her inflexibility and intransigence, the way she is an allegory of the struggle of the individual against the state, of the feminine, the private, and the family against the public- and masculine-dominated civic duties—for Lacan, it is Antigone's beauty that is "fascinating" and most captivating. Drawing from her famous story something other than a more typically moralizing account, it is above all her beauty that he emphasizes. Not the physical beauty of a pretty face, it is the staggering, swift, and undefeatable radiance of her desire, a desire that brings an entire city to the brink of ruin, that is Lacan's focus.

Like Antigone, Beauty, too, has had many glamorous roles to play in the theater of philosophy, mostly as a lure for desire, as the fantasy propping up desire in its search for a transcendental truth. Was this not her role some twenty-five centuries ago in Plato's *Symposium*, where, ultimately, she was a luminous, Ideal, and true Beauty? In the ephemeral beauty of a rose or a human face, her eternal face would be dimly reflected as though in a mirror. In this way, she was something of a lure for the immortal human soul, drawing it on the rails of its erotic desire for beauty—a desire born from Need and Resource, as Socrates says in the *Symposium*—drawing it like a moth ever upward through the suffering course of its return toward its ultimate destination, the light of an eternal Truth ever shining beyond the icy light of the stars, beyond even the darkness of death.

Now, and after enduring so many conceptual summersaults from Plato down through the Cartesian and Freudian legacies, Beauty alights at last on the Lacanian stage. Gliding in the uncertain, crepuscular light attendant upon the death of the gods and wearing a new mask, she stars in a deathly drama that, despite all, is still Greek: the tragic drama of "the subject's" unending quest for something it can never have, namely, the truth of desire. But her role shall be Janus-faced: both lure and net, both capturing desire and preventing it from attaining access to what Lacan calls its truth in the field of the real.

For the Lacanian theater, where "soul" once was, now "the subject" must be. And be it must in a world from which the immortal gods have all fled. This changes everything, especially the relationship between beauty and desire. No doubt, Plato's determination of the relationship between Beauty and desire is but one—albeit the chief and founding one—among the many philosophical and "pedantic" notions of beauty that, Lacan says, "make the rounds." Typically, he says they allowed for only *a certain relationship* (emphasis mine) between beauty and desire" (S7: 238), one that usually ends up delimiting, prohibiting, denying, forming, or pedagogically shaping desire to fit the needs of the philosophical pursuit of Truth and the higher Good. In several remarkable formulations, Lacan takes steps to distance himself from such "pedantic notions." Most decisively in this regard, it is once again this Janus-faced role for beauty that Lacan emphasizes, this "strange, mysterious relationship" in which beauty functions as both bait and barrier to desire, simultaneously drawing it out and preventing it from ever reaching its object-cause, which Lacan calls, "the Thing." Beauty's appearance "intimidates and stops desire" (S7: 238 and 247). It is both the lure pointing beyond the limits of language and moral-ethical law toward the Thing and the protective barrier against the Thing, what "makes access to [the Thing] difficult . . . a barrier that holds the subject back in front of the unspeakable field of radical desire" (S7: 217, lecture on "The Death Drive," given on May 4, 1960). Antigone's beauty is thus "a beauty that cannot be touched," just as there is "a good that mustn't be touched" (S7: 239). This is "the Thing" for which her beauty is both lure and barrier: the ob-scene Thing that is paradoxically "there" only in being "not-there."

This is the true mystery and paradox of Antigone's beauty. In the course of the seventh seminar, beauty becomes something "elemental" and situated in this way in a field "beyond-the-good." Lacan thus describes Antigone's beauty as a mystery that "up until now has never been articulated" (S7: 237 and 247).

So, while some of the essential elements of the classical storyline are still there, it is a strange, new modern beauty that here stands before us. Implacable, terrifying, and at the same time captivating, the Platonic scheme and its philosophical vocabulary is no longer adequate to describe her or the part she must now play on a stage prepared by psychoanalysis and modern linguistics. Whatever Lacan's interpretation may make of her, Antigone is first of all a pre-Platonic, Sophoclean artistic creation. Plato speaks of the highest art as a *teknopoiein*, a mode of "giving birth," or "procreation, in the beautiful," and certainly the theme of "procreation" is relevant in the case of Antigone. But is Antigone a child of Ideal Beauty? Does she take her measure from it? Or is she a child of something else, a child of incest, a child of something forbidden, something that is both approached and put at a distance in and by artistic creation? Does she take her measure not from the Ideal, but from an unspeakable human, "all-too-human" crime? Likewise, would it be right to say that in her relationship with desire, Antigone's beauty is another instance of what Plato's *Sophist* (235 c–d) calls a *phantastikē*, a semblance, a depiction through images or bodily acts? Is she a likeness that is not really one, the deceptive mimesis of an ideality that is somehow beyond and more primary than the sensory, material world? Lacan takes steps to preclude this. While he does say that beauty is an image of desire and the death drive, there is no mimetic relationship at work here. Beauty, for Lacan, is not a mimetic image of an originary Idea. Beauty does not re-present anything. It does not represent desire or the death drive, for it *is* itself a pulsion, an insistence and a repetition behind which or beyond which there is only a void. Likewise, could we say that Antigone's beauty is an *Erscheinung*, a term found in the aesthetics of German Idealism? Is her beauty but an epiphany only faintly illuminating the limits of the possible for desire or for ethical life, a sign, perhaps an enthusiasm, a sensible appearing distinguished from the grounding dimensions of a supersensible freedom? But the Real, the Thing (*das Ding*)—desire and the death drive do not correspond to such a philosophically delimited dimension of supersensible freedom.

Indeed, what philosophical vocabulary could ever be adequate to what is put in play here? No longer a divine form, no longer an ideal beauty or even the shining sign of a supersensible freedom, Lacan makes recourse instead to a poetic metaphor: beauty is "the cloak of all possible fantasms of human desire. The flowers of desire are contained in this vase [of the beautiful] whose contours we attempt to define" (S7: 295–298). Cloak or vase, as an image, beauty is something like the ever moving curvature of a container having a void at its center.

It is not only beauty's relationship with desire that is here phrased anew, it is also beauty's relationship with death. Hegel's *Phenomenology of Spirit* was famously dismissive of beauty, where she is but an insipid flower. "Lacking strength, Beauty hates the understanding for asking her what it cannot do." And what the understanding cannot but must do is stand up to what is most dreadful, death, in other words. Beauty cannot stand up against the overwhelming power of the negative, Hegel claims.

Lacan's anti-Hegelianism sees this very differently. As he phrased it in 1959, "The function of the beautiful reveals to us the site of man's relationship to his own death, and reveals it to us only in a blinding flash (*éblouissement*)" (S7: 295/342). In Lacan's reading of *Antigone*, beauty is the radiance of an act that—alive—enters the tomb of death. It is the beauty that not only stands up to death but even doubles the stakes: it is a beauty situated "between two deaths." As an image of a transgressive desire, Antigone is ultimately a dynamic image of the death drive that both maintains and disrupts the symbolic order. Her movement at the limit of the symbolic both steps and does not step into a beyond of the death and life that are inscribed within it. But it must also be seen that she embodies more in this than just the usual tragic pathos of finitude and suffering. It is this that the ethic of psychoanalysis attempts to confront and to bring forth in a new way of thinking human finitude in the figures of desire, and death. We shall return to this later on in this essay.

To sum up, the beauty that so captivates Lacan in his reading of the play *Antigone* is thus beauty in its extra-philosophical employment. No longer invested in the philosophical dialectic of Truth, it now finds its place in a new setting: the Lacanian topology. Both image and signifier, "splendor" thus marks the thresholds of the symbolic, the imaginary, and the real / the Thing. Lacking nothing, especially strength, beauty is here stricken by ambivalence. Both determinable and indeterminable, presence and withdrawal, pleasure and pain, attraction and repulsion, it is the uncountable and unapproachable Other of the symbolic order, a beauty in excess of the understanding. As such, the Lacanian theater places Antigone's beauty at the limits of the possible for philosophical discourse dating from the time of Plato. Lacan's Antigone offers us a glimpse of an act carried on the wings of a relentless desire to the point where it accedes to what Lacan here calls "the real," the unnamable, undifferentiated real, the "impossible" that resists and tears at words and images. Here, beauty functions not so much at the imaginary level of consciousness and reality, then, but at a deeper level of the symbolic and its intersections with the unconscious and the real. Rather than concerning itself with the states and experiences of consciousness, we could say by borrowing a phrase from Badiou, that beauty here "knots *letters* and the *real* together . . . in a thinking faced with the void."[2] Between these letters and the real, there is nothing, the void of that impossible, infinite step beyond Antigone takes as she steps alive into the tomb of death.

So, where in the philosophical tradition, beauty may have been an Ideal, or an attribute or quality, or the article of a subjective judgment, for Lacan, it is something dynamic and frightening that obtains at both the symbolic and the imaginary levels and so marks the curvature of a limit where they are knotted with what he calls "the real." In the language of the Lacanian topology, where the domains of the imaginary, the symbolic, and the real overlap, where a *jouissance* casts the image of beauty in its unbearable splendor, Lacan's thinking sutures the poetic image in a way that brings to light a new orientation for beauty with regard to death and desire: beauty as the zero point of the symbolic and the imaginary where words and images fail, where there is a certain exhaustion of language. For example, when in his novel *Petersburg* Andrei Bely is describing the lissome figure of one Sofia Petrovna, he says she has a "splendid shape." But, he considers the phrase a "banality." Immediately, he adds this: when he uses such a phrase, a phrase that in his eyes, at least, is a banality, this is only because he has reached a point where his vocabulary has been "exhausted." He says this humorously, of course. But isn't Lacan's recourse to the phrase "unbearable splendor" to describe Antigone's beauty in a similar situation? Although Lacan's "unbearable splendor" is hardly a banality in his usage, nonetheless, it also marks the limit where vocabularies are "exhausted," where the immeasurable other side of all vocabularies is approached and distanced. Lacan uses other vocabularies to indicate this other side, as when he describes the dark horror of "the Thing," ultimate object-cause of desire, and "the Real," the other side of the symbolic order.

Likewise, as a figure in a Greek tragic drama, a figure presented in the context of one of the great festivals to Dionysus and from within the city walls and in front of its enthralled, gathered citizens, Antigone will be the voice and the image of all that is in transgressive excess and defiance of both the city, its citizens, and the whole network of its symbolic functions that define and delimit it. Transgressively, she is for the city and its citizens something like a force, both fascinating and dangerous, something that must be kept apart, approached at a distance, treated with a ritual respect and only in carefully observed and specific religious and artistic contexts allowed to run its course, appearing, for example, in the modes of phallic images, or in choral dances and ritual sacrifices performed in the center of the public domain: She is an image of the death drive, and of *jouissance* that is attendant upon it. Antigone marks within the symbolic domain an image of the transgression of the symbolic; she is a desire, Lacan remarks, a "*pure* and simple desire of death as such" (S7: 282, emphasis mine). It is in this light that Lacan characterizes the splendor, the *éclat* of her beauty.

Thus, Antigone's beauty is not something to behold in admiration, a sublime-like splendor. Rather, it is the splendor of the potlatch, the purity of the flames of the hecatomb, a splendor and a purity whose value cannot be thus appraised as a good circulating in an economy of goods and of utilitarian values. Lacan sees Antigone as a terrifying image of expenditure, an image of the paradoxical union of pleasure and pain that is *jouissance*. Her splendor bursts from the darkest turnings in the knots of desire and the law. As a transgressive figure, she radiates from the Greek tragic theater a light more ancient, more deeply archaic than the serene light of the philosophers, a light of lucidity and reason emanating from the Good. Antigone's splendor points beyond this; her splendor belongs to the empty darkness of the tomb.

Antigone's beauty is thus a "splendor" (*éclat*), a purifying, cathartic splendor that quickly attains a level of intensity at which an alluring beauty reverts to its opposite, blinding, transporting horror. The chorus, in its last scene with Antigone, reaches this point. Just as she is brought forth to be walled alive in the tomb, they say, "Now I myself am carried beyond the laws at this sight, and I can no longer restrain the stream of tears, when I see Antigone here passing to the bridal chamber where all come to rest" (*Antigone*, line 805). Ultimately and most dreadfully, Creon, the proclaiming voice who seeks the good of the city and who insists on respect for the law, also reaches it as he beholds the bodies of his dead son and wife, suicides both: "Alas, alas! My mind leaps with fear! Why has no one struck me with a two-edged sword? I am compounded (*deilaios*)," "wretched," like paltry dust. (See also Aeschylus, *Choephori*.)

At the limits of language, where a desire attains its identification with pain, Antigone's beauty thus seems at times to be more Sadean than Hegelian, more Sophoclean than Platonic. How could it not be that such splendor is "unbearable"? The very velocity, the steel-like thrust of her act, its *éclat*—a word also defined as the sudden, blinding flash of an explosion, or a burst of laughter, a strikingly Bataillean image—distances her from humanity. She is "insensitive to outrage"; she is cold and almost inhuman. To the chorus of older citizens who suffer where she seems to feel nothing, Antigone seems inhuman. Both a divine-like and agonizing spectacle, she is a swift-paced monster such as they have never seen before, a woman terrifying in her willingness to undergo the suffering, fragmentation, and lacerating loss that comes with the transgression of the limits of the law. Unlike the gentlemen of the chorus, she would never regret the price she must pay. Her *jouissance*, attained only on the other side of the line Lacan evokes in the course of these lectures, comes at the price of this horrifying mutilation and fragmentation of everything the walls of the city would enclose and protect as good, true, and beautiful. In this way, Antigone's beauty does not leave either the thought or the language of the European traditions of humanism intact. Rather, it submits that tradition to a subversion that distances the psychoanalytic definition of ethics from its sheltering warmth.

All of this shows us that new resources are required to articulate the dynamic beauty in its relationship with death and desire.

This is where the "anamorphic image" comes into play. Like the unconscious, Antigone's transgressive, criminal, and unbearable splendor (*éclat*) can only be indirectly or anamorphically apprehended in its effects. Lacan thus also describes her beauty as an "anamorphic image," one that comes into view only when seen from askance, from a certain angle, or off to one side. Antigone's beauty emerges in the way the image of the skull, for example, in Hans Holbein the Younger's portrait *The Ambassadors* becomes recognizable only when viewed from a particular point of view. Likewise, Antigone's beauty snaps into focus only when seen from a point of view Lacan calls "the line of sight of desire." Beyond all death and finitude, she functions as an image, as a movement that congeals for a moment as though across a screen. In this anamorphic play of beauty, the Thing (*das Ding*), the undead Thing, the "object-cause" of desire, like *jouissance*, is "buried at the center of obscurity," buried beyond the reach of the symbolic order in "a field surrounded by a barrier that makes access to it difficult and inaccessible" (S7: 209), both appears and does not appear, is both present and absent. Antigone's drama thus presents in all its beauty and luminosity this dark core of non-appearing at the heart of the human situation.

In her relationship with desire and death, it is thus perhaps best to think of Antigone's beauty not so much as a quality or attribute but rather as a velocity, the velocity of transgression. The implacable swiftness of Antigone's desire, her *pulsion*, is decisive for Lacan's interpretation of the play. In fact, there are two speeds at work here: Creon's, the slow, largely cautious and reactive speed of government, law, and the circulation of practical, secular goods; and on the other hand, the transgressive speed of Antigone's words and deeds, which, as in the race between Achilles and the tortoise, are always a step, an infinite step, beyond.

Yet, in continuity with the doubling and ambivalence that so deeply characterizes the Lacanian articulation of beauty, it must also be said that beauty is not only and purely a velocity, it is also a *point de capiton*, both an act that accelerates and a decisive moment of arrest, a moment of punctuation that arrives with the speed of a blinding clarity, as in the *éblouissement* cited earlier, something that suddenly brings the action of the play to order in a calamitous, punctuating moment of seizure when everything both arrives and collapses in ruin.

This ambivalence also best describes the moment of her *jouissance* in its double transgression of the law and the pleasure principle. Both the law and the pleasure principle would have commanded her to slow down, to abandon her desire, to abandon Polynices' body to the dogs. Both would have commanded her to live, to keep her life in the gay rhythms of light, and so to defy, or at least to avoid death at all cost, to avoid the darkness of the tomb. She refuses all arguments bent on compromise and so quickly and relentlessly moves to her doom. As she does so, she both punctuates and punctures the symbolic order with the empty nothingness of her death. The moment of the *capiton*, in this sense, is not only the moment of the punctuation, in which she reaches the end of the sentence of life, and seizes the "meaning of her life" by gathering into a unity all the signifiers that constitute that life, it is also the moment of the *puncture*, when the needle of desire passes through the limit of death. This moment is the moment Antigone steps "between two deaths," as Lacan calls it. At this moment of *capiton*, Antigone is courageous; she burns with a splendor that provokes the chorus to compare her to a god.

Finally, Antigone's beauty is a beauty not only seen but also heard. We must not only see her and be enthralled by her spectacle, but we must hear her as well, hear her bird-like cries in the storm of dust as she seeks to return her brother to the dead, hear her in those remarkable speeches she makes as she is about to step into the tomb. Hardly the voice of a powerless Beauty, as in Hegel, far from betraying a hidden weakness or softness in her heart, Antigone's voice yet shakes as it lists and measures all that she will be giving up for her measureless desire, the famous inventories of marriage beds and conjugal bliss, the future offspring and future loves she will never know, for all is henceforth lost and now irretrievable to her. We must also hear her as she compares herself to a figure divine, like Tantalus' daughter (*Antigone*, line 825), chained to a rock of death, figure divine, strangely moored beyond the tumult of life and death, and hear her when, at the end of her tether, she stridently scolds the chorus precisely for seeing her as a divine-like presence.

This brings us to the purity of Antigone's beauty, which is most importantly the purity, the almost sacred, saintly, and blessed purity required of anyone who might attempt to step alive into the darkness of death and the tomb.

Her act is pure insofar as it is unclouded by admixtures of doubt, regret, and hesitation or second-guessing. A heroic purity, it is made all the more brilliant by its contrast with her rather lackluster sister, Ismene, who says to Antigone, "But, we're only women. We must be cautious.

The penalty is death, who would risk that? With both of our brothers now dead, hasn't there been enough trouble already?" Antigone's purity, by contrast, is the purity of an indomitable spirit that takes her to her doom, her *Atè*.

In Lacan's formulation, she is driven by her love, she is driven by her desire to the border of *Atè*, ἄτη, an "irreplaceable word" in Lacan's view, one which he claims occurs some twenty times in Sophocles' text, and yet, he says, it still goes unread. In Greek, the word means "bewilderment," "blindness," or "delusion sent by the gods and the disaster that comes of it." In the play *Antigone*, the Chorus speak of *Atè* as Antigone is led away to the tomb: "For in wisdom someone has revealed the famous saying, that evil seems good to him whose mind the god is driving toward disaster (*Atè*); but the small man fares throughout his time without disaster" (lines 610–614, cited by Lacan, S7: 270).

For Lacan, *Atè* "designates the limit that human life can only briefly cross" (S7: 262), a limit where "life can only be lived and thought about from a place where life is already lost" (S7: 280). This is Lacan's reading of the Greek word, ἄτη (*Atè*). "One does or does not approach *Atè*," Lacan writes, "and when one approaches it, it is because of something that is linked to a beginning and a chain of events, namely, that of the misfortune of her family, the Labdacides," for whom a chain of events led from murder of the father to the incestuous relationship of the mother (S7: 264). *Atè* is a limit illuminated in the splendor of desire's transgression. Here, in the image and voice of Antigone, an Antigone "on the other side," Lacan makes visible a desire that is intolerable to see, a "desire of the kind by which even the gods are bound" (S7: 268), a pure desire, desire beyond desire itself and into the drive (*pulsion, Trieb*). For the Lacan of *Seminar VII*, the image of Antigone thus "reveals to us the line of sight that defines desire" (S7: 247). This is the foundation for the imperative he invokes in *Seminar VII*, "Do not give way on your desire" (*ne pas céder sur son désir*), namely, speak the truth of your death-bound desire in the drive, the death drive (*Todestrieb; pulsion de mort*), now seen as reaching *Atè*, going beyond the pleasure principle, toward the extreme of *jouissance*.

This, then, is Lacan's presentation of Antigone, who, in her purity and unbearable splendor, is one who speaks within the city walls the truth of her desire, who will not give way on that desire, who will debate and offer good reasons, but who at the same time will be implacably Other, impossibly outside and in excess of the limits of both its political and ethical laws.

THE ETHIC OF ANTIGONE'S ACT:
DO NOT GIVE WAY ON YOUR DESIRE

Lacan's anti-philosophical gesture with regard to the philosophical tradition of desire and the beautiful thus overlaps with his anti-philosophical gesture of "demystifying" the philosophical-ethical traditions of the good and the beautiful, a tradition that always addressed and yet missed the paradox of desire and the law. The link between beauty and desire is placed on the same grounds as the link between pleasure and the good. Both are essential to Lacan's determination of the ethical subject. The important point is that Lacan places the beautiful within "the field of the beyond-the-good principle" (S7: 238). As such, Antigone is dead to the law and to the city: she is to be excluded, deemed a criminal, and so put to death, submitted to the uncrossable limit of death. And so, anamorphically, we shall have to see the enigma of the beauty of Antigone as the enigma of a woman "between two deaths," an image essentially linked to Lacan's questioning of the philosophical tradition's conception of pleasure and the good. As a figure of transgression, linked with crime, she thus addresses the ethical dimension at the heart psychoanalysis and of *Seminar VII*, the question of the Good and the Beautiful, the question of desire and the law, and of the voice of the law that speaks through the Other.

The ethic communicated in her act, summarized as we shall hear in the voiced command "do not give way on one's desire" can never play a role in a Platonic dialogue intent on seeking the universal essence of Justice and the good for a human being, for Antigone embodies the irreducible *singularity* of desire, a desire—as Kant said of beauty—without a unifying, grasping concept (*ohne Begriff*), a desire for an impossible object of desire. The tradition that commences with Plato, a tradition that Nietzsche might have called "nihilistic," commanded us precisely to give way on desire. It thus maintained a morbid relation between desire and the law, one in which desire was denied, *jouissance* obliterated, and where the death drive, seemingly excluded, was actually put to work building the walls of the city and the systems of knowledge precisely in and by its exclusion. What emerges from this tradition, especially through its incarnations in and as the Christian confessional traditions, is a morbid relation between desire and the law such that desire is always taxed and audited by guilt.

Can one thus see—again, as though "anamorphically"—in the heroic splendor of Antigone's act Lacan's own attempt to articulate an ethic—an ethic of the tragedy *of* psychoanalysis, as Lacoue-Labarthe calls it, an *ésthethique* (both "aesthetic" and "ethic")[3]—on the other side, so to speak, of the great Western tradition in ethics and its "morbid" entanglement of moral law and desire?

If so, wouldn't this ethic, whose imperative is "do not give way on your desire," perhaps be best configured not only in the character of Antigone, but also in Creon? Isn't he the one who in fact gives way on his desire and so incurs the soul-breaking debt of guilt? Isn't he the one who backs down, who has a change of heart, who then hurries to bury the defiled Polynices and so put things back on their proper course only to then arrive at Antigone's tomb, his heart full of contrition and needing forgiveness, alas, too late, and so is then left in ruin, the dead bodies of his wife and son lying at his feet, a man ruined yet somehow purified in and by this very ruin? As embodied and condensed in the image of a severe, inhuman, and transgressive Antigone, on the other hand, we get a rather different understanding of this ethic. Putting aside her own 'pathological desires,' her desire to live and to be happy, putting all of this aside so as to heed to the unwritten laws of the gods she hears from within, laws that threaten the integrity of the city's laws, would Antigone, whose act and whose law would coincide with pain and death, not recall the kind of 'radical evil' Lacan discussed in connection with Kant and Sade? Would this not make Lacan's an ethic of radical evil, or least an ethic that makes the possibility of radical evil one of its most thought provoking questions?

What must be seen is how this Lacanian ethic of psychoanalysis attempts to traverse the fantasmatic framework of traditional ethics by recasting the relationship between the Thing and the law, and so recasting the central concerns and questions of ethics, especially those bearing on the problematic of death and the related urgency of the search for the human good and for lasting human happiness and well-being as the goals of desire. And, too, it must be seen how this Lacanian ethic also recasts the corresponding pathological status so often accorded to desire in its relation to moral law by especially the Kantian moral tradition.

As Lacan phrases it, in the traditional conception of ethics, and here it is in the writings of St. Paul where the Thing is called "sin," there is a dialectical relationship that causes desire "to flare up only in relation to the law, through which it becomes the desire for death" (S7: 83). It is only because of the law that sin and hamartia, which in Lacan's interpretation of the Greek means not only error but also the lack and non-participation characteristic of the Thing, takes on an excessive, hyperbolic character. Lacan's question is this: Does Freudian psychoanalysis still "leave us clinging to that dialectic"? What remains to be explored in the ethic of psychoanalysis is how, "over the centuries, human beings have succeeded in elaborating what transgresses moral law, and so puts them in a relationship to desire that *transgresses interdiction*, and so introduces an erotics that is above morality" (S7: 84/101, translation modified, emphasis mine). So, Lacan's ethics of psychoanalysis, far from being a celebration of the dialectic of interdiction and transgression, where transgression is always cast in terms of sin and guilt, seeks instead an ethic that is the transgression of interdiction itself. Žižek, in commenting on this passage from *Seminar VII*, says that

> the crucial thing here is the last phrase, which clearly indicates that, for Lacan, there is a way of discovering the relationship to *das Ding*, the Thing, somewhere beyond the Law. . . . [Thus], the whole point of the ethics of psychoanalysis is to formulate the possibility of a relationship that avoids the pitfalls of the superego inculpation that accounts for the "morbid" enjoyment of sin, while simultaneously avoiding what Kant called *Schwärmerei*, the obscurantist claim to give voice to (and thus to legitimate one's position by a reference to) a spiritual illumination, a direct insight into the impossible real Thing.[4]

It is these questions and this possible transgression of interdiction that Lacan explores in connection with the figure of Antigone "between two deaths."

Two more quick questions to which we shall have to return: Is Lacan not seeking to prevent the ethic of psychoanalysis from being a kind of morbid ethic of the tragic, an ethic "still clinging" to a pathos of finitude and death, and in doing so, to free it to become an ethic of the real and of *jouissance*? Yet, in its ethical account of *jouissance*, can the ethic of psychoanalysis ever shed the traditional ways and means of sublimation? While it is tempting to describe Lacan's ethic as an ethic of sublimation, this is perhaps not the essential dimension that Lacan sketches in the figure of Antigone. Like *jouissance*, the "impossible to imagine Thing" (S2: 125) requires form or word to make it imaginable or to bring it to expression. At this primary level of the relation of form and signifier to the Thing, Lacan says, is where the problem of sublimation is located (S7: 125). But giving them a form or word, making them imaginable or sayable, also reduces both the Thing and *jouissance* by inscribing them within the limits of the symbolic and the imaginary. Insofar as sublimation would reduce Antigone's *jouissance* to the status of a desire totally captured in and by the symbolic, insofar as sublimation would entail the obliteration of *jouissance* by the signifier, or would give desire a new object or a new form by which it would be, as in the case of the commercial works of art, shaped into something marketable and exchangeable in the economy of goods, and insofar as sublimation would also be in accord with something Lacan would like to avoid, namely, the movement of the Hegelian *Aufhebung*, the dialectical movement that cancels, lifts, and retains the disruptive power of the negative in a higher shape of Absolute Spirit, sublimation is criticized and rejected. Rather, from the point of view of *Seminar VII*, beyond all sublimation there is real, limitless, and indomitable *jouissance*, a *jouissance* of the real that cannot be reinvested in a dialectic of sublimation, hence, an ethic of the real. Limited, sublimated *jouissance* would be a *jouissance* that is measurable, exchangeable, and communicable. But a limitless, immeasurable *jouissance*? It could only be the dissolving of form and name, something unimaginable, something in excess of the ancient philosophical distinction between the ideal and the sensible. But the question remains, how can *jouissance* and this experience be communicated if not by a conventional, limited economy of sublimation? Perhaps this is one of the reasons why Lacan makes recourse to the poetic and anamorphic images he finds in tragic drama, as was discussed earlier in this essay.

BETWEEN TWO DEATHS

Let us continue these questions by considering the way Lacan situates Antigone in all her splendor as a tragic heroine "between two deaths." (The phrase is not really Lacan's; it is something he found in Sade, but Lacan did use it to great effect in his reading of Sophocles' *Antigone*.)

Antigone is a woman brought alive into the realm of death. Hers is the splendor of this "between" of the two deaths. It is in these terms that Lacan brings her transgression, her *jouissance*, to *signifiantisation*.[5] What does it mean to say Antigone stands "between two deaths"?

The first death, of course, is physical, biological death, a death of the body, the death that life brings. Death can also be thought of in terms of the symbolic order: the death that brings life, the death constitutive of the symbolic order, where the symbol or signifier replaces the thing, the symbol being thus the "death" of the thing. One such symbol is the tomb. It signifies death, its dark emptiness making tangible an abyssal death, yet death itself is not there. It is both absent and present in the hollow of the tomb, as was said of the Thing in relation to the vase.

Lacan also envisions a second death, presented not in Freud but in Sade's *Philosophy in the Bedroom*. The "second death," Lacan finds pronounced in Sade's 1795 *Philosophy in the Bedroom*, as the murder of the "second life." This is evoked in long lecture entitled "One More Effort, Frenchmen, if You Are to Be Republicans," abruptly interpolated into the midst of a bedroom drama depicting the most extravagant sexual crimes imaginable. Here, Sade recommends not only that a murderer take the life of the victim, but that he also take his/her "second life." This would be a truly monstrous crime, a "destruction greater than any imaginable," the murder even of "nature's capacity for propagation or destruction" (quoted, S7: 211), "death insofar as it is regarded as the point at which the very cycles of the transformation of nature are annihilated" (S7: 248). It would be the ultimate wiping clean of the slate: the death of death itself, the death that brings on the Sadean eternal punishments envisioned in *Philosophy in the Bedroom*. Creon's condemnation exposes Antigone to this second death. Not only will she die, but all of the children, all of the love that could have come from her bosom, all will also die. Phrased otherwise, insofar as existence (being) itself is identified with the symbolic, this is the global destruction of the symbolic network, the radical annihilation of nature's circular movement of generation and destruction conceivable only in so far as this circular movement is already symbolized and historicized. Absolute death would, thereby, be the death of the symbolic universe as such, the wiping out of all historical tradition opened up by the symbolic order.[6] In passing, we should also note that yet another similar literary reference to this "second death" can be found in Dante's *Inferno*, Canto I, where the poet's guide, Virgil, judges "it best that you should choose to follow me . . . away from here and through an eternal place: To hear the cries of despair, and to behold ancient tormented spirits as they lament in chorus the second death (*la seconda morte*) they must abide."[7] Was this reference from Dante's *Inferno* perhaps an influence on the Sadean notion of a "second death"?

Antigone will be condemned to step alive into the tomb of death, to belong both to death and to life. In this way she is an inverted mirror image of the situation of the dead Polynices, condemned not only to death, but to remain unburied and so among the living. Both are among the dead-undead. But she also echoes Shakespeare's *Hamlet*, who, at least in Lacan's reading, is a character in which his/her act coincides with his/her death.

Like Hamlet, Antigone's work is the work of mourning, and for the fulfillment of rites and obligations to those whose departure from this life has not been accompanied by the rites that it calls for.[8] And, too, somewhat like Hamlet, Antigone receives the instrument of her death from the other: where Hamlet receives the poison-tipped sword from Laertes' hand, so Antigone receives from Creon not the sword but the tomb; he condemns her to death and so to her *jouissance*. But with Antigone, there is always the second death that awaits her.

Now, the second death, the pre-ontological and uncanny domain beyond the "Order of Being," the "between the two deaths," is also the domain of "immortal" life in the sense of what Lacan calls the *lamella*, "the libido *qua* pure life instinct . . . immortal life, irrepressible life" (S11: 197–198), a domain Žižek calls "a domain of monstrous spectral apparitions . . . the domain of the immortal, monstrous 'undead' object-libido," the horrifying "sudden emergence of a life beyond death, the undead-indestructible object, life deprived of all support in the symbolic order."[9] The "second death" is at the center of Lacan's attention in *Seminar VII* not only because of its literary functions and its poetic suggestion. Just as Žižek connects it with "cyber-space," so in the 1959–1960 context of *Seminar VII*, at perhaps the height of the Cold War, with the crossing of ultimate barriers and the "anarchy of forms" on the agenda, with the "sepulchral mounds" gathering and growing "at the limit of the politics of the good," and with the generalized possibility of a second death on a planetary scale, the death of even nature's capacity for regeneration and corruption, the monstrous apparitions of the second death were all very real and frightening possibilities for Lacan, as well. Indeed, as he began his May 18, 1960 lecture, he evoked the cacophony of power and destruction that could be heard beyond the walls of the seminar room. His seminar thus became something of a refuge from the gathering discontents of a planetary civilization on the verge of self-destruction. Lacan thus spoke to his audience of the brutal struggle for power that can still be heard all around us and the stupefying manner in which power conceals and betrays itself in the form of information and promises for doing the greater good that "addresses and captures impotent crowds on whom it is poured forth like a liquor that leaves them dazed as they move toward the slaughter house" (S7: 213). Lacan continues,

The possibility of a second destruction has suddenly become a tangible reality for us, including the threat of anarchy at the level of the chromosomes of a kind that could break the ties of given forms of life. Monsters obsessed a great deal those who up to the eighteenth century still attributed a meaning to the word "Nature." It has been a long time since we accorded any importance to calves with six feet or children with two heads. Yet we may now perhaps see them appear in the thousands. (S7: 232)

Another passage is worth quoting at length:

It is the case that Sade's extraordinary catalogue of horrors, which causes not only the senses and human possibilities but the imagination, too, to flinch, is nothing at all compared to what will, in effect, be seen on a collective scale. The only difference between Sade's exorbitant descriptions and such a catastrophe is that no pleasure will enter into the motivation of the latter. Not perverts but bureaucrats will set things off, and we won't even know if their intentions were good or bad. Things will go off by command; they will be carried through according to regulations, mechanically, down the chain of command, with human wills bent, abolished, overcome, in a task that ceases to have any meaning. That task will be the elimination of an incalculable waste that reveals its constant and final dimension for man. (S7: 233)

So, the context for Lacan's reading of *Antigone* is the terror and discontents of the modern world, the greed for money, the raw struggles for power and domination that push humankind to a kind of apocalyptic limit, edge, or barrier, the crossing of which becomes an ever greater possibility. His concern seems to be for the growing power of the signifier, represented by the power of technological science unchained from any limitations (see S7: 236).

In a sense, the figure of Antigone, which never ceases to captivate and horrify, encapsulates and concentrates these concerns. Antigone does not want to work for the "common good." She is driven by a death drive. Here, the death drive, Antigone's death drive, is at this level, a will to destruction, a will for an Other thing, beyond any instinct for equilibrium, but also a will for that life beyond all death Lacan evokes in *Seminar XI* under the name of the *lamella*. Must it be pointed out that Lacan is obviously not using the term "will" in the Kantian sense of a *Wille*? The term is used only to distinguish the death drive as a "radical desire" in this more precise sense from an instinctual drive for equilibrium. The second death is the unbreachable limit, the unthinkable horror, a law and a love beyond the law in the sense it abandons all desire for equilibrium. Antigone, her beauty, and her splendor are poised between these two deaths. The space of the "between two deaths" is the space of tragedy. It is Antigone's situation and the moving limit that configures her unique beauty. It is from this "between two deaths" that Lacan develops his image of Antigone's beauty and splendor. It is the splendor of her love, the splendor of her desire and her mourning for the impossible object of her desire that takes her to her *Atè* as she approaches but does not transgress this second death. She does not, cannot attain the Thing.

Thinking now of Antigone's beauty and its double relation to desire as both lure and barrier, what is the ultimate object in desire according to *Seminar VII*? Is it beauty? Rather, once again, it is the Thing, *das Ding*, *la Chose*, desire's impossible-to-attain Thing. This pinpoints the tragedy of the play *Antigone*: not that human beings are divided, split; not that rather obvious, overwrought, and conflicted divide between Creon, cast as representing the law of the city and the public domain, and Antigone, cast as representing family and the private domain; but that a human being is defined by desire's insatiable *pulsion* toward what it cannot attain. This desire is the tragedy and radiant heart of the play, *Antigone*.

Lacan uses the term *das Ding* to distinguish it from another term Freud uses, *die Sache* (see SVII: 44–45 and 62–63). The latter is a term Freud uses to refer to the "thing-presentation in the unconscious." This is the *Sachvorstellungen*, the presentation of a thing in the symbolic order. But *das Ding* is the thing in its brute, "dumb reality" (Lacan refers to Harpo Marx, from the Marx brothers, to illustrate this, S7: 55). That is to say, there is no thing (*Sache*)–word (*Wort*) relationship that applies to the Thing qua *das Ding*. In the psychic organization, the whole movement of the *Vorstellung*, governed by the pleasure principle, revolves around the Thing, which, however, appears nowhere in that movement (S7: 57). *Seminar VII* defines *das Ding* in the context of *jouissance* as "the Other, the prehistoric, unforgettable other, that . . . no one will ever reach" (S7: 53).

The goal of desire would seem to aim for the experience of an impossible satisfaction that reproduces an "initial state" by finding the

Thing (*das Ding*), the object again. So, the Thing is also the lost object that must be continually refound, the forbidden object of incestuous desire, namely, the Mother. Lacan writes, "Freud designates the prohibition of incest as the underlying principle of the primordial law, the law of which all other cultural developments are no more than the consequences and ramifications. At the same time, he defines incest as the fundamental desire" (S7: 67). Where "the prohibition of incest is no other than the condition *sine qua non* of speech," *das Ding*, as the lost object of a fundamental desire, is the unspeakable horror, a "beyond the signified" (S7: 54). However it may "present itself to the extent it becomes word (*fait mot*)," it is a word that must "remain silent . . . in response to which no word is spoken." The Thing thus "hits the mark" (*faire mouche*) of words and the limits of words (S7: 55/69).

Yet, the Thing does find its homologue in a shape and a form: the mustard pot, the vase, and the image of woman, the "Lady," the "feminine object" (S7: 126, 149), in the poetry of courtly love. All are forms essentially linked to creation, but, they also essentially enclose and so make visible the "emptiness of a thing in all its crudity, a thing that reveals itself in its nudity to be the thing, her thing, the one . . . found at her very heart in its cruel emptiness" (S7: 163). So, as a feminine object, the Thing is an object-cause of desire, not exactly the object *of* desire, in other words, an object not simply inaccessible but also separated from "him who longs to reach it by all kinds of evil powers . . . ," an object and a "secret," involving a series of "misapprehensions" (S7: 151). Here is where the image of Antigone arises, a "feminine object," an image of the Thing, not "re-presenting" it, but, as was said above, being an image much the same way the shape of a vase or a mustard pot encloses the emptiness within it. She is an image that is also a lure, a beautiful illusion that reveals and hides; her shining beauty is a barrier to what should not be seen.

The counterweight to this drive for the impossible-to-attain-Thing is the Freudian pleasure principle. The Thing is positioned beyond the pleasure principle. Lacan returns to the notion of the pleasure principle in his reading of Antigone. What is its functioning? First, the pleasure principle is indeed a *principle* and not a feeling. It is an operating principle of mental functioning and tied to the reality principle. If pleasure seems to be a matter of intensities or excitations, the actual role of the *pleasure principle* is to avoid such intensities and to maintain excitation at a low level. How does it do this? According to *Seminar VII*,

> the law of the pleasure principle . . . involves flocculation, the
> crystallization into signifying units. A signifying organization
> dominates the psychic apparatus as it is revealed to us in
> the examination of a patient. . . . [Thus,] the function of the
> pleasure principle is, in effect, to lead the subject from signifier
> to signifier, by generating as many signifiers as are required to
> maintain at as low a level as possible the tension that regulates
> the whole functioning of the psychic apparatus. (S7: 118–119)

The image and the imaginary can also play a role here as lure and barrier. Thus, language has both symbolic and imaginary dimensions in the
metonymic movement of desire. As was said before, pain results when
pleasure attains what can only be called an "unbearable" level of intensity,
so it is always a matter of the regulation of intensities. At the symbolic
level, this regulation is given a voice. The pleasure principle enounces its
command: "give way on our desire, keep your pleasure in moderation."
"Avoid excess." "Better to give in to interdiction than to risk castration"
(S7: 307). The transgression of limits, excess in all its forms, is a vice
because it is destructive of balance and self-presence. Equilibrium is the
virtue of pleasure; this is the good pleasure seeks, a good that enables the
subject to live a desire that can never reach the Thing. As a vice, pleasure
crosses a threshold, disrupts or overturns a certain delicate balance of
intensities and becomes pain. Again, this is *jouissance*. Thus, the pleasure
principle is actually opposed to the death drive, for the latter is the
drive that transgresses limits, that always seeks to go beyond the pleasure
principle. The reality principle, Lacan says, "has the closest relationship"
to ethical principles as they emerge from the preconscious as commandments (S7: 74). This pleasure principle is what Antigone violates. She
does not seek the good nor does she seek equilibrium.

Moreover, it is the function of the pleasure principle "to make man
always search for what he has to find again, but which he never will
attain . . ." (S7: 68). The function of the pleasure principle is to be the
law by which the Thing is both sought and kept at a distance (S7: 57).
Pleasure seeks the Thing as a "refound object," a *Wiedergefundene*. The
Thing is what was separated from us at the splitting of the signifying
cut productive of the subject, but was never really lost. Rather, it was as
though buried, enclosed, as though in the tomb of the signifier. And in
the passage from one signifier to another, as pleasure exercises its function
regulating intensity, the Thing was there, that hollow, that emptiness, that
hole. Thus kept at a distance, the Thing becomes presented as a "sovereign

Good." Transgressing the limits of the law in order to attain this Good brings on pain, the extreme disequilibrium, which Lacan calls *jouissance*. "The subject cannot stand the extreme good that *das Ding* may bring" (S7: 73/89). So, the subject cannot "locate himself in relation to the bad," either (S7: 73/89). No matter how the subject "groans, explodes, and curses," nothing is understood and nothing is articulated, even as metaphor. Rather, symptoms are produced, symptoms that are actually the symptoms of a defense against the Thing (S7: 73/89).

So the law and the pleasure principle are given their philosophical, ethical form in the figures of the Aristotelian virtues and in the Kantian categorical imperative. But long before Aristotle, they turned up in an anticipatory, tragic form in certain passages of Sophocles' chorus, and especially in the speeches and proclamations of his Creon, who wants to do the good for all. Creon will be Antigone's counterpart, the one who wants to defend the city against Antigone's baleful desire. Creon thinks only of the good of the city. But, when he promises the good of all as "the law without limits" (see S7: 259), he carries it too far, somewhat in a Kantian or Platonic manner, and this is his hamartia, which Lacan translates as "error of judgment." Lacan tells us, "[Creon's] refusal to allow a sepulcher for Polynices, who is an enemy and a traitor to his country, is founded on the fact that one cannot at the same time honor those who have defended their country and those who have attacked it. From a Kantian point of view, it is a maxim that can be given as a "rule of reason with universal validity." But, "the good cannot reign over all without an excess emerging whose fatal consequences are revealed to us in tragedy" (S7: 259). Antigone will point this out to him from the perspective of her indomitable and *unwritten* Justice (*Dike*). For, at the limit of the law, her *Dike*, her death drive, is always there, like the Thing, a remainder that can never be put behind or contained. Her death drive is the transgression of the limit of the law commanding the pleasure principle and the good for all. Closer to pain and to crime, at least from the standpoint of the city's laws, it takes her near, too near, the Thing in a moment of *jouissance* as she steps alive into the tomb of death.

Thus, there is desire and the drive that always pushes toward and in excess of the limits. This is a "pure desire," the "simple desire of death as such," which the pleasure principle must always oppose. It is precisely this that Antigone incarnates, a "beyond of the pleasure principle," "the pure, the simple desire of death as such." As she steps alive into the tomb, driven there by her passion and her love, she incarnates this "pure," unconditional desire (S7: 282). And what happens to her desire? Qua death drive, it is "the desire of the Other, linked to the desire of the mother" (S7: 283), insofar as desire for the mother is desire for the "maternal thing," which occupies the place of *das Ding*, the Thing (S7: 67). Lacan even claims that "The text [*Antigone*] alludes to the fact that the desire of the mother is the origin of everything," the Mother as Other, as the omnipotent "subject of the first demand."[10] The desire of the mother is the founding desire of the whole structure, the one that brought into the world the unique offspring that are Eteocles, Polynices, Antigone, and Ismene. But this is always "a criminal desire," a desire that was incestuous and in violation of the prohibitions and the laws (S7: 283).

But what this means is that as Other, what Antigone desires is not the Mother as such but the criminal desire of the mother. Antigone's desire is desire for the other's desire. Antigone seeks to be that desire, and in so being, becomes "what she is," a desire without measure. This she could not endure. But where before the law and the limits might have held her back, now she is cut loose from them.

Antigone's desire drives her to this "impasse" at the origins of the tragedy and of human life itself. If we pursue the consequences of what Lacan is saying in his lecture "Antigone between Two Deaths," then it would seem that it was not Polynices, at all, not the brother who was the Thing for Antigone, but it was the mother, the mother as the Other, that Antigone seeks as her "refound object" of desire. Thus, Antigone laments, "When I come there [to Hades], I am confident that I shall come dear to my father, dear to you, my mother, and dear to you my own brother" (*Antigone*: line 895).

We have been prepared for such startling developments since line 90 of the play, where Ismene recognizes that Antigone is "in love with the impossible." Desire without end or closure, desire without mediation, hers is a desire stamped with a destructive character. In the closing, crucial passages of Lacan's reading of *Antigone*, he observes that Antigone has chosen to be the guardian of a criminal desire, the criminal and incestuous desire that lies at the root of her family tree. "The fruit of the incestuous union has split into two brothers, one of whom represents power, the other crime . . . Antigone chooses to be purely and simply the guardian of the being of the criminal as such." The law of the city could have recognized this and pardoned it, but it could not. Antigone's belongs among the condemned. As Lacan writes, she has "sacrificed her own being in order to maintain that essential being which is the family *Atè*" (S7: 283).

One could argue, of course, that Antigone would have better fulfilled her role as guardian of the being of the criminal had she miraculously lived. But between the implacable Creon and her own implacable desire, there is no room for life, only for that minute step taken and not taken beyond the limits of life.

Now we can see how when it comes to the situation of Antigone, for Lacan, the heart of the matter is that her desire is not for the good, the common goods that shelter us from the extremes and that make life comfortable. Hers is a measureless desire for the impossible, a desire to rejoin in death the impossible Thing, that incestuous source from which she springs. She desires something other, something more than her continued social existence. She courts, she pursues death. Lacan thus sees Antigone stepping alive into her tomb as the symbolic image of the death drive in all its destructive, transgressive power, an image pointing beyond the limits of the possible to a "an unspeakable field of radical desire, a field of absolute destruction beyond putrefaction" (S7: 216/256). As such, Antigone's beauty, closer to evil than to the good, is also a sovereign ethical act, a performative, transgressive *éclat* irreducible to a speech act, yet illuminated by the very symbolic order it violates and disrupts. Antigone's beauty is thus an image of transgressive *jouissance*, the transgression of interdiction itself; she is in relation to the Thing "buried at the center of obscurity and inaccessibility." Buried, entombed, a "feminine object," in the end she is in all her untouchable, incandescent radiance, a beauty worth dying for.

Echoing yet another Heraclitean formulation, we could say that, as she steps alive into the tomb "between two deaths," Lacan's Antigone steps and does not step beyond life, beyond the symbolic, and beyond the good governance of the pleasure principle. This is the infinite step taken and not taken. This is where she is most alive and where she finds her center of gravity, not only in the tomb, but more so in the "buried" and obscure Thing Lacan situates beyond the limits of the city walls and the symbolic order, an obscurity toward which she is both drawn and repelled. In her closing remarks to Creon and the Chorus, (lines 890–925), while she may invoke the name of Persephone, receiver of the dead, and remind the gods of her piety, and while she may speak of the unwritten laws of the family as the measure for what she has done, it is the mute Thing that shall answer her prayers from the measureless Other of the real.

TRAVERSING THE SADEAN FANTASY: AN ETHICS OF THE REAL?

Let us now return once again to question the ethic that emerges from Lacan's reading of *Antigone*. It has been characterized as an ethic of the real, and Lacan was clear from the beginning of *Seminar VII* that his concern over the course of that seminar would be for the relation between the symbolic, the imaginary, and the real. Now, right after he speaks of his need to know whether or not he has managed to take a "small step outside ethics" (S7: 19), Lacan begins to show how moral agency actualizes the real, a move that seems on the surface to be homologous with the Kantian ethic in which the moral will makes its object real. "My thesis," Lacan says at that point, "is that the moral law, the moral command, the presence of the moral agency in our activity, insofar as it is structured by the symbolic, is that through which the real is actualized." Likewise, while moral law is not the Thing, yet, we "can only know the Thing by means of the law. I would not have had the idea to covet it [the Thing] if the law hadn't said, 'Thou shalt not covet it.'" Thus, "without the Law, the Thing is dead" (S7: 83–84). To this, Lacan adds another thesis: "the moral law affirms itself in opposition to pleasure . . . ," and finally, "to speak of *the real* in connection with moral law is to call into question the value of what we would normally include in the notion of the ideal" (S7: 20).

In what sense is the word "real" being used here in the context of Lacan's seventh seminar? Certainly, in the sense of the real being opposed to the ideal or to the fictional, it is a material reality, as in the "real" penis as opposed to its symbolization as the phallus. Hegel's formulation "the real is rational" also comes to mind, suggesting thereby that the real responds to logic and reasoning. But the real is also one of the three terms essential to Lacan's psychoanalysis (the Real, the Symbolic, and the Imaginary), in which the real—at least in Lacan's work from the early 1950s—is both opposed to the imaginary and is what resists symbolization; the real as "what is always in its place," the inassimilable, impossible Real. As a pure positivity beyond any series of descriptions, it lacks nothing because it is a hole, a nothing in the midst of the symbolic order, the lack around which that order is structured. Here, the real seems to support the Thing in its "dumb reality" (S7: 55) as what is likewise "beyond the signified." But the real, having no descriptive properties, is thus ultimately known only retroactively by and through the effects, the disturbances it introduces into the symbolic, and so is a way of accounting for those effects. Thus, the burial of Polynices could be seen as the "real," not only in the sense of the real as what is to be actualized by Antigone's "moral agency," but the real in the sense of being what is opposed to the symbolic, as what must not take place, and so is an act in excess of the city's law. A criminal act is to accomplish the tragic destiny of a criminal desire. Since the real lacks for nothing, it is the symbolic that introduces a cut in the real. It is in and through the process of symbolization whereby *jouissance* is excised and so identified with the real that man becomes a man. The world of words thus creates the world of things, Lacan tells us in his lecture "The Function and Field of Speech and Language in Psychoanalysis."[11] Finally, moral agency actualizes the real, gives it a name, a shape, like the mustard pot or the "feminine object." The symbolic surrounds the emptiness within it and actualizes it, makes it appear. Thus, moral agency actualizes the real in and as a certain "being toward death."

Could we say, then, that Antigone is the heroine of an "ethics of the real," as Alenka Zupančič has called it? Would this also be an ethics of contingency and finitude, an ethic that begins with the death of God and affirms the inescapable necessity of human finitude? Is this an ethic intent upon having us realize that we are enclosed in our finitude, that there is no "beyond," there is no life after death, that there is no salvation from death, that the finality of death, the possibility of our being impossible, is the gravity of the human situation we must all be held accountable for and to which we must all face up in one way or another? While Lacan does say that desire "must remain in a fundamental relationship to death" (S7: 303), and while it might seem that this ethic is but a continuation of the kind of analytic of finitude and the pathos of finitude that had prevailed under the influence in the 1950s and 1960s of Heidegger's analysis of *Dasein* and the being-toward-death (*Sein zum Tode*), in fact, it goes much further. As Alenka Zupančič asserts, "the ethics of the real is not an ethics of the finite of finitude."[12] Lacan does say that the "true termination of an analysis" would be when the analysand is able to confront the reality of the human situation, to undergo the anguish and "distress" (Freud's *Hilflosigkeit*) that signal this confrontation of the limit where he/she "touches the end of what he/she is and what he/she is not." Still, such anguish and distress must also be seen as "a protection" against death, that the subject can defend himself against death with death. What is more, the defense against death can also be understood as a defense against something that is not reducible to death in the sense of biological mortality.[13] Distress and anguish are ways of letting death appear, as we have seen in connection with Kojève's reading of Hegel's *Phenomenology*. But death "seen" is no longer the death that kills, but the death that drives life and that is the key to a new way of seeing immortality, the immortality suggested in the "second death," that is also the key to the Lacanian ethic; death as the key not to an infinite desire, the kind of "bad infinite" of a desire never accomplished, but to an infinite *jouissance* linked to the real as Other.[14] The paradox here is to see that the finite and the infinite are not opposed, but that "absence of a beyond, the lack of any exception to the finite, 'infinitizes' the finite."[15]

The key problem, then, is to confront the "human situation" (S7: 303) in this new way and this means that analysis cannot and will not be the guarantor of "the bourgeois dream" by making its patients better able to function happily within the economy of the service of goods, all of which would imply "amputation, sacrifice, indeed a kind of Puritanism in the relationship to desire" (S7: 303). In relation to this, the key ethical question posed in Lacan's last lecture for *Seminar VII*, dated June of 1960, a session entitled "The Paradoxes of Ethics," is this: what standard for human action does Lacanian analysis subscribe to? In the last session of *Seminar VII*, Lacan says that if there is an ethics of psychoanalysis, then it is so only to the extent that psychoanalysis asks, "what is the measure of our action?" (S7: 311). This is really a recasting of Kant's question: "what is the moral worth of an action?" Or of Aristotle's "what is virtue?" and "what is the Good for a human being?"

If not happiness, what is the measure of action? For Lacan, the essential measure of action is given not an imperative but an interrogative form: "Have you acted in conformity with your desire?" (S7: 311ff.). Have you acted, in other words, in conformity not to the law that would set desire aside, that would make it wait, but in conformity with this immeasurable and incommensurable measure that desire is for itself? Desire, measureless desire, is the measure. Again, there seems a Kantian strain to this. Like Kant, the question is not what may or may not be done, not for what objects should or should not be sought, but only for the commandment "Thou Shalt." One never quite knows exactly what is commanded. One only hears, "thou shalt not give way on your desire"; not your desire for this or that object or goal, but do not give way on the lack, on the desire itself—a desire without object—that is your "being," your human situation. This command speaks as a pure enunciation, what Dolar, following Zupančič, calls an "enunciation without a statement."[16] The moral law is a "suspended sentence," commanding nothing but demanding completion, a completion attained only in the act of the subject. Not to give way on one's desire, not to give way on the lack at the center of one's being, this is an ethical, "heroic act." It is along these lines that the Lacanian ethic has occasionally been characterized as advocating a "heroism of the lack."

Again, we can see how Antigone answers the fundamental ethical questions of the measure and the must, the law and the obligation binding human action: "given our condition as men [and women], what must we do in order to act in the right way?" (S7: 19). This is the question that confronts Antigone from the beginning of the action in her drama: what *must* she do? And in doing what she "must," Lacan would say that she is free in that by affirming her desire, she is "autonomous," not determined by any law outside of herself. Thus, Antigone's splendor provides the measure of action: the moment where violation and realization coincide, the moment when she steps into the darkness "between two deaths," the moment that infinitizes the finite. It is the immeasurable moment the drama cannot show, cannot stage, but only report: the moment she enters the real.

It may be her greatest illumination, the radiance, the *energeia*, of her good, but it is also a moment of genuine suffering and loss. Where suffering looms large in this Lacanian ethic of *Seminar VII*, the question arises, "Is this an ethic of the heroism of suffering insofar as *jouissance* comes only with suffering?" Is suffering also the ethical measure of action for Lacan? Is Lacan not locked in the Sadean fantasy here?

Close to the tragic drama, and entangled within its experience, Lacan had to confront the impasse of the Sadean fantasy, which Lacan defines as the fantasy of "eternal suffering" (S7: 261/303). Lacan writes, "In the typical Sadean scenario, suffering doesn't lead the victim to the point where he is dismembered and destroyed. It seems rather that the object of all the torture is to retain the capacity of being an indestructible support [of suffering]" (S7: 261/304). A Sadean freedom obtains here: The suffering subject sustains suffering by separating out from him/herself a double of him/herself "who is made inaccessible to destruction, so as to make it support what, borrowing a term from the realms of aesthetics, one cannot help calling the play of pain (*les jeux de la douleur*). For the space in question is the same as that in which aesthetic phenomena disport themselves, a space of freedom" (S7: 261/303). This becomes the space not only of freedom, but also of *jouissance*, the "conjunction of pain and beauty." Like a truth that is also a lie, Sade's victims are "always adorned not only with all kinds of beauty, but with grace, beauty's finest flower" (S7: 262). The Lacanian ethic and analytic practice seeks a way to "traverse" (a term that appears in *Seminar XI*) this Sadean fantasy, to traverse it in its protective function. For, however linked with suffering, fantasy does actually serve a protective function: it protects the subject from the other's desire by plugging up the gaps, the lack that defines the desire of the other. Fantasy protects by answering the question, "what does the other (and this could be written 'other,' meaning the 'other person' or Other, meaning the symbolic order as such) want of me?" In doing so, fantasy can also congeal and exhibit the ultimately frozen and immobile qualities of the objects to which it is linked, objects that determine the subject's relation to *jouissance* and to language. In other words, it can be the work and consequence of fantasy to turn the subject into an object, a Sadean object of desire. This then becomes the subject's way of answering the question, "what does the other want of me?" The other wants of me that I become its object and in becoming such, I find the shelter I need from the desire of the other. The aforementioned "velocity" of Antigone's beauty and desire resists this objectification. Moreover, insofar as suffering in the Sadean scenario is no more than "the signifier of the limit," the objectification one finds in fantasy is but a "stasis that affirms that that which is cannot return to the void from which it emerged" (S7: 262). Yet, this is also precisely what Antigone will attempt, a return to the void from which she emerged, the void of measureless desire.

But to traverse this fantasy of eternal suffering is not just to find happiness waiting on the other side of suffering. It is something even more malignant than that. It might be to confront and to affirm the hopeless desire that one is, to be the desire that is ultimately the drive, the death drive, a drive without any predetermined goal or destination or object; to be the impossible, unlivable, transgressive drive whose "realization" would attain only in its tireless circling around *the Thing*. There are no safe harbors here. Bound as it is not just to death, the absolute master, but to the sovereignty of the Thing and to the sovereign moment of *jouissance*, Antigone's act, her choice, can be read as lending a tenuous presence to the reef upon which the philosophical-existentialists' slogans of a death-bound authenticity and freedom run aground. This could well have been one of Lacan's targets in his seminars from the late 1950s, when the coffee houses were filled with cigarette smoke and the prattle (and everything from Lacan's remarks suggests that this is indeed how it sounded to him: prattle) of the existentialists, who, in those days, were drawing quite a crowd. But psychoanalysis itself is also endangered by this, its own "end of analysis." Lacan promised nothing. As the "end of analysis," the traversal of the fundamental fantasy is not an act or a "project" undertaken in order that one might "realize" oneself. In any event, how could an analyst give or promise happiness, where happiness is but the *stasis* of small contentments and "personal fulfillment"? Rather, it is "in relation to being that the analyst has to find his operating level,"[17] which is to reverse the structure of fantasy, to have it circle back upon itself, to turn its nullity inside out so as to reconstruct or modify the way fantasy, considered as revolving around an image, for example, is set to work in a signifying structure.[18] This would be to modify the subject's fundamental modes of desire and of defense, and to alter his/her *jouissance*, such that he/she becomes able to "act with one's own being."[19] The figure of Antigone resonates the challenge that this fundamental fantasy presents to the ethics of psychoanalysis, for her beauty, too, is a conjunction of beauty and pain. Must she too not recognize the lack in the Other? Must she not sacrifice her *jouissance*, and find her *jouissance* in some way other than heroic suffering? Does Lacan himself not alter his model of *jouissance* after *Seminar VII*? For *Seminar VII*, *jouissance* is connected with horror. One must go through the "Sadean scenario" and the "second death" in order to understand what is happening with regard to *jouissance*. With *Seminar XI*, one starts with fragmentation in the partial drives until there is integration. Jacques-Alain Miller calls this fourth paradigm of Lacanian *jouissance*, "normal *jouissance*." This is the drive's "normal course" without transgression. Lacan makes the peaceful contemplation of the work of art as a model for *jouissance*. Where *jouissance* becomes closer, more akin to the signifier, there is a new *signifiantisation* of *jouissance* in which the menacing *das Ding* and the "massive *jouissance*" of *Seminar VII* are replaced by the more manageable *objet a*, the libido as "lost object" and "matrix of all lost objects."[20]

But, while it may be that in future seminars Lacan would think of *jouissance* differently than he does in *Seminar VII*—no doubt the Sadean, transgressive *jouissance* will be modified and the links between psychoanalysis and tragedy loosened—nonetheless, both the Sadean perspective and the "dance" of the tragic drama between Creon and Antigone have brought to light core issues to which Lacan kept returning in later years, namely, that the measure and the promise of the ethics of psychoanalysis be the free assent to one's desire.

With such a measure, it is easy to see how the ethics of analysis would not offer the "promise"—and this is precisely the word Lacan uses—of peace and security in life, which, as ethical goals, would be, in Lacan's view, but fantasy objects (new modalities of object *a*) by which the void and the lack of desire could be filled up. It does not seek the moralizing goals of "inner harmony" and normalization (see S7: 302). The Chorus gives voice to such ideals in its final, brief ode that begins: "Good sense is by far the chief part of happiness." But this is the Chorus, the men who first trembled before Creon and trembled again when they saw for themselves what the severity and arrogance of his law made possible. What have these citizens learned? What is their last-man-standing morality? "Stick with good sense." And what is that? "Respect the gods, and keep in mind that boasters will be taught as they grow old the wisdom of knowing one's true place in the scheme of things." But this is a good citizen's morality, a kind of "moral alibi" and "a consent to a moral demand" (Lacan) and not perhaps the true and deeper message of the play. An image, as we have seen, of transgression and the death drive, Lacan's Antigone is driven by something even more terrifying than this, something stronger, more implacable even than a god, something that "renders her pitiless and fearless" and so in excess even of the tragic dimension and its intended evocation and catharsis of fear and pity. Antigone feels neither of these (S7: 264).

Thus, Antigone is the culminating image and measure for Lacan, desire made palpable, made into an image of the transgression of the interdictions whereby death was made to appear as finality and finitude and desire was cast in terms of guilt and avoidance. Antigone embodies the implacable intensity of the death drive that opens desire to a "beyond of the pleasure principle." Thus, she also brings into focus Lacan's attempt to demystify the Platonic and the Aristotelian view of the good, the Supreme Good, and to situate it on the level of the economy of goods, playing the role of something like a lure for desire by which desire may attain its aim but actually miss its true object. Hers is an ethic of *jouissance* as access not to the Good, but to the real.

In summary, the key ethical question of the measure of action is also the question of the field of desire in its relation to moral law. One of the fundamental reasons why Lacan links tragic drama so centrally to the question of ethics is in the way tragic drama inscribes—as though being a topology and a *mathème*—the relationship between action and the desire that inhabits it, and of the fundamental failure of action to catch up with desire (S7: 313). Action is thus inscribed in the space of tragedy and it is within this space that one encounters the "sphere of values," ethical values. But not all is serious and morose here. While the relationship between action and desire seems to function "in the direction of the triumph of death," this must also be seen as the space of the comic, even "derisory play of vision." This may recall Bataille's formulation of death as "imposture," but the point for Lacan is that the comic dwells on the way

> life slips away, runs off, escapes all those barriers that oppose
> it, including precisely those that are the most essential, those
> that are constituted by the agency of the signifier. . . . The
> phallus, [nothing more than a signifier], is the signifier of this

flight. Life goes by, life triumphs, whatever happens. If the comic hero trips up and lands in the soup, the little fellow nevertheless survives. (S7: 314/362)

Lacan's reading of the "space of tragedy" is thus also the space of the comic, which brings to light not just the triumph of death but also the immortal, infinite dimension that inhabits human finitude. This is the "apocalyptic" dimension of tragedy, for Lacan, the truth it uncovers and shows in its very withdrawal, not just the dead bodies that litter the stage as the curtain falls, but the apocalypse of the undead Thing that is, in the action and the splendor, both uncovered and yet veiled in beauty. While this questioning of the relation between action and the desire that inhabits it is also essential to the philosophical ethics of Plato, Aristotle, and Kant, Lacan's tragicomic vision finds itself opposed to that tradition for the way it always expressed an urgency to purge desire, to clean it up, to moderate it, and make it temperate, or to exclude it altogether on the grounds it is "pathological."

THE ETHICAL DIMENSIONS OF CATHARSIS

Here we return to the question with which I began: What is the connection between tragic drama and the ethics of psychoanalysis? The answer lies in the way both tragic drama and psychoanalysis effect a certain *catharsis* of fear and pity. Lacan considered catharsis to be not only the essence of Greek tragic drama but also the link between tragic drama and psychoanalysis. It is also linked to ethical reflection: psychoanalysis, tragic drama, ethics, each in different ways attempts to purge and so purify desire. This is the "tragic sense of life" Lacan will oppose by the comedy he evokes in these last pages of *Seminar VII*. Thus, Lacan will also here submit the function of catharsis to a modification: It is not fear and pity that shall be purged so as to make way for a new level of virtue, happiness, and peace. Such purging is linked with power— "far too human power"—thus making it a morality of the Master (S7: 315). Here again is where the comic dimension comes in, where "the little guy" sets everything in disarray, for it is here that the pathos of finitude, the fear and pity of finitude, wherein desire gives up or gives way on itself, is purged so as to clear the way, or wipe the slate clean, for an affirmation of desire and for the naming of desire that will bring it into being.

Has the drama accomplished what Aristotle deemed to be its essence, namely, a kind of catharsis of the emotions of fear and pity? What is the "true meaning" of this catharsis for Lacan?

To begin with, we must remember something that Lacan had said earlier regarding catharsis and tragic drama. In a reference to Goethe, Lacan remarks how catharsis may not concern the effect of the drama on the audience, which may be too entirely tired or distracted to experience this famous "purging of fear and pity." "Goethe saw the function of fear and pity in the action itself" (S7: 258). It is the characters and the chorus who experience this in the course of their action. But, with regard to Antigone, right through to the end she feels neither fear nor pity. There are some speeches toward the end, as she reaches her *Atè*, where fear and pity seem to cast their chilly shadow, but she walks straight-backed and dry-eyed into the tomb when all is said and done, and without looking back. "This is why she is the real hero" (S7: 258). She seems to have passed to a level beyond fear and pity. This is the point Lacan pursues in his closing lecture: catharsis, as access to desire, means not the purging or the elimination of fear and pity, but the crossing of all fear and pity, the crossing of a limit where "the voice of the hero trembles before nothing" (S7: 322). Thus, catharsis brings to light the true heroic level of the drama, not in a heroism of suffering, but in a crossing of the limit of all fear and pity before which desire might have given way out of regret or hesitation for the cost that would have to be paid to go any further.

In its ethical form, Kant has introduced the "topological milestone that distinguishes moral phenomenon" (S7: 315). Kant's breakthrough was to pose the ethical question in a new way. His ethics no longer asked, "what is permitted?" It no longer asked, "what may or may not be done?" Rather, he put the ethical question in the moral framework of categorical commands and, in doing so, he "managed to reduce the essence of the moral field to something pure" (S7: 317). Thus, he exercised a kind of philosophical catharsis. He purged desire of everything "pathological." He made desire into something purely moral. He purged morality of all desire except for the desire to act out of respect for universal moral law. Kant imposes an unconditional obligation, the unconditional command of reason: "Thou shalt." It would seem that nothing remains to keep us from unconditional respect for moral law, certainly not prudence or self-interest. Lacan continues, "The importance of this field derives from the void that the strict application of the Kantian definition leaves there." And that void is the void of desire at the heart of moral law. Thus, Lacan's reading seems to detect a troubling remainder that resists the Kantian cathartic purification of moral law: at the heart of the unconditional measure of moral law there yet remains an incommensurable measure; at the heart of the finite moral law there remains an irreducible and infinite measure—the void—of desire (S7: 316). Desire may be purged, but the purging leaves behind as its remainder this measureless void that links with an immeasurable burden of guilt. This is the ultimate object of the psychoanalytic catharsis, the purging not of desire, but of this guilt.

In other words, something remains at the center of this Kantian purity that Lacan calls "a need for a space where accounts are kept (*il reste en son point central qu'il faut qu'il y ait quelque part place pour la comptabilisation*)" (S7: 317/366). Here is where we encounter guilt. At the center of the moral field, where we should encounter deathless desire, Kant found the disturbance of a lack, a hole, as it were, a hunger, a need, a desire nothing on earth can satisfy. The soul remains hungry for an afterlife "so that the unrealized harmony may be achieved somewhere or other." This is the dimension of immortal need and of the immortal soul that opens within the heart of the moral field. It is also here that "accounts are kept": "It is this that is signified by the horizon represented by his [Kant's] immortality of the soul" (S7: 317). And it is here, within this field of desire that opens at the center of the moral field, that one encounters guilt in the "bonds of a permanent bookkeeping," a keeping of accounts at the heart of desire. As though it is not enough that a human soul is tortured here on earth, there now opens for Kant an eternity "given over to the keeping of accounts" (S7: 317/366). But, no matter the immortality of the soul, which Lacan thinks of as just a fantasm, no matter the divine presence, the records are still kept in the symbolic order, in the infinity of a desire, in the metonymic movement of the signifier, kept at a point of tension, a break, a splitting, an ambivalence that is the situation for and the definition of the subject. "The traversal of such a fundamental fantasy" structuring desire, as Lacan termed it in *Seminar XI*, would thus seem the psychoanalytic catharsis of the bonding of desire with guilt.

The whole point and meaning of analysis, Lacan declares, "is nothing other than that which supports an unconscious theme, the very articulation of which roots us in a particular destiny, and that destiny demands insistently that the debt be paid, and desire keeps coming back, keeps returning, and situates us once again in a given track, the track of something that is specifically our business" (S7: 319). Thus, the only goods recognized as measuring up and being the measure of action in this ethic of psychoanalysis, which here situates itself at the antipodes of the Kantian and Aristotelian moral and ethical theories, would be the price one pays in this keeping of accounts for access to desire, defined as "the metonymy of our being" (S7: 321). In his reading of the drama *Antigone*, Lacan's emphasis consistently falls on the scenes where, in their actions, the characters pay the price for the access to their desire. Even—or should we say, especially—Creon, must pay, and does pay up to the point where he thinks of himself as a dead man standing among the living, the undead one who has lost everything that was good in life.

"To give way on desire is always accompanied in the destiny of the subject by some betrayal." Here, the distinction between the hero and the ordinary man: the ordinary man is the man who gives up on his desire, and who, in doing so, is returned to the service of goods, returned to the servile, limited economy of goods that serve for some purpose, some other good, serves in the economy of goods that demands that desire wait, that it comes back some other time, or that it always be there managed, pruned, purged, reduced to being like a wind-up toy. Thus, this proposition: "the only thing one can be guilty of is giving ground (*céder*) relative to one's desire" (S7: 321).

And, finally, this proposition: "the access to desire necessitates crossing not only all fear but all pity." The voice of the hero trembles before nothing, especially not before the good of the Other. The hero emerges as the one who has "sacrificed" the castration in and by which s/he was alienated in the Other and separated from the Other and so made into a subject limited, fearful, faded and subjected, submitted to the whims and to the service of the Other, but also a subject placed, comfortable and complacent. Fear and pity are here linked with the subjection of desire. Crossing beyond fear and pity, purging the castration and guilt that comes with every submission to the Other, with every necessary alienation, refusing to give way on his/her desire, the hero's act not only accesses desire, it is also accesses the in-finite.

But this is not limited to tragic drama. There is also a philosophical dimension to such catharsis that can now be brought into view. The catharsis of fear and pity can be linked to a revaluation and a transformation of the philosophical value of desire. From being something endlessly morbid—"pathological," as Kant would say—and fraught with a limitless burden of guilt it is transformed into something affirmative: a limitless affirmation. Might it then be called, in the words of the master himself, Lacan, in his eleventh seminar, a "limitless love?"

EXODUS: ANTIGONE'S LIMITLESS LOVE

Now, in the end I return to questions I posed at the beginning: if not happiness, if not wisdom and "well-being," if the not attainment of Truth, Beauty, and the Good, what then are the moral ends of psychoanalysis as depicted in Antigone's terrifying splendor? What is the "promise offered by analysis," a promise paid in words and interpretations? Is it to effect a heroic transformation, a whole restructuring of the subject's relations to the objects of desire and to the fundamental structuring of desire? Is the subject, heroically not turning its back on desire, also to "traverse the fantasy" that sustains desire, to realize that the fantasy object sustaining desire has nothing behind it, that the "true world is but a fable"? But wouldn't this loss of the ideal go hand in hand with a loss of desire, with the resulting paradox being that in not giving way on my desire, I sacrifice my desire, or better, my desire becomes the sacrifice of my love and the sacrifice of my *jouissance*. It would not bring about a new object of desire in the form of a new sublimation, by which desire would be tradable or salable, but rather would bring about "a change of object *in itself*" (S7: 293), in a renunciation of the object of desire. The change is that, in not giving way on desire, in taking desire literally, "to the letter," one recognizes that "desire is nothing more than the metonymy of the discourse of demand," the unconscious articulation of a signifying series, and for this reason constituted as fundamental alienation" (S7: 293).

Is it not only the tragedy and heroism, but also the ethical dimensions of Antigone's act, her sacrifice without reserve, which are found here? Does she not take her desire to the limit where desire becomes a "limitless love," a concept discussed by Lacan in the closing sections of his *The Four Fundamental Concepts of Psychoanalysis*? Is this act not the core of the ethical act and the ethical life, for Lacan? Is this not the key to understanding both the crucial difference between Antigone and her sister, Ismene, but also the "splendor" of her act? It is the splendor of a "limitless love," a love that infinitizes the finite, to borrow once again a phrase from Alenka Zupančič.[21]

Antigone's "limitless love" must be understood in terms of her sacrifice, which is to say that her sacrifice is an image, something like a sign of the impalpable limits of love. Such love, staged in her act, is not the figure of a sacrifice made to a love of God, nor even to a great intellectual love of God (*Amor intellectualis Dei*), which produces a "serene detachment from human desire," as in the example of Spinoza, also discussed by Lacan in his 1963 seminar (S11: 275), who said that "*desire is the essence of man*" (S11: 275, Lacan's italics), for, as Lacan says of Spinoza's *Amor*, it is an *Amor* that could only be but a love of the *attributes* of God, God's universality, for example, which are only "possible through the function of the signifier" and the "universality of the signifier" (S11: 275), a signifier for which the "subject" is a nonexistence. "This position is not tenable for us," Lacan says (S11: 275).

Nor is her act a sacrifice to the limit-figures of the Other of the law, a purifying sacrifice made in the name of the purity of moral law. Such an act is not only an embrace, in the embrace of death, of the purified body of the law; it is also an act of the sacrificial killing off of the pathological, if not the killing off of desire as such. This sort of love is actually an affirmation of desire taken to a pure state where it becomes identical with the purity of the law, a state that, in Lacan's words, "culminates in the sacrifice . . . of everything that is the object of love in one's human tenderness" (S11: 275). This is the sort of "love" one finds in Kant's moral theory, where unconditional love is an unconditional respect for law, and its act the legislation of the purely rational and metaphysical moral law it respects, such that the law as Other is truly "in us," and more than us, the cruel reign of the biblical fathers becoming interiorized in the even more cruel reign of the superego and its ideals "in us." Schopenhauer was right when he said of Kant that the imperative form that speaks in his rationalistic moral theory is but the heir of the old biblical commandments of Moses and the Decalogue, but now stripped of their biblical foundations, and so made to speak in us, that terrifying voice that commands us to make an impossible sacrifice by purifying ourselves of our real bodies, our real love, and our desires in order that we be capable of embracing the idealized, purely rational body of the moral law.[22] Love is here only another word for renunciation, just as "respect" is another word for subordination, and the moral subject, "the person," another word for subjection before the law, except this time, it is a subjection self-imposed from the grounds of "freedom" taken as but an "Idea of Reason." Such a love, such a self-sacrificing embrace of the purified body of the law, entails, when followed through to the thinking of its limits, the logical affirmation of the Sadean world of radical evil, as Lacan shows in both his seventh seminar and in "Kant with Sade." Such a position amounts to an ethical impasse, and so is not the way out for a subject that has brought to the experience of its own nullity, that has realized that it is but a void; this is not the way out from the aporia of philosophical, ethical love, not another way for a desire that has experienced the loss of all ideals, and so the loss of all desire.[23]

In such dramatic figures as Hamlet, Antigone, and Cygne, Lacan began to find a way, a third way out of the impasses suggested to the ethics of psychoanalysis by the European traditions in ethics as presented in these two philosophical and limited modalities of love and desire. This culminates in the notion of a "limitless love" (see S11: 276), which, at least in the anticipatory context of *Seminar VII*, is suggested by the figure of Antigone's sacrificial act. Antigone's sacrifice does not cleanse or purify the law of the pathological. At the limits of the law, it is a limitless love, as one sees perhaps prefigured in the dramatic action of the play *Antigone*. It is a sacrifice of all the sacrifices of love. It is a transgressive, limitless love in the sense that it renounces its object, renounces renunciation itself, the very renunciation that began with the Fathers and the names of the Father, and gives itself to *jouissance* and to the real of the drive. Is this not the love and the annihilation of the second death? If so, then we can also see in her "limitless love" the phantom figure of her freedom, a freedom for which no sensuous image is ever adequate, in the sense that, through the double death by which she is dead to the symbolic order, she is also no longer represented by a signifier. She is freed, in the language of Lacan's *The Four Fundamental Concepts of Psychoanalysis* (S11: 219), from the aphanisic effect, the effect of "fading," before the binary signifier. Thus, her act is ethical for Lacan insofar as it is an image of the function of freedom and of "the whole business of this term freedom" (S11: 219).

Antigone is, thus, also the image of such a "traversal of fantasy," a phrase from *Seminar XI*, and of the attainment of the drive of all drives, the death drive. Is this not also the paradoxical promise of analysis, to "traverse the fantasy" in this sense of following "the curve of the rise and fall of life," the curve of desire to the other side of the bar separating the subject from the object of fantasy (object *a*) and so regressing from a desire sustained by fantasy into the self-enclosed circuit of the drive in the real? This traversal would effect the displacement of the infinite striving of desire. It would be the catharsis of desire. It would close the gap constitutive of desire in and by regressing to the repetitive, self-enclosed, circular movement of the drive, ever missing its aim, and so find a paradoxical *jouissance* in the real precisely in always missing or surpassing the alleged goals and ideals of human life. This would be a satisfaction realized not in the attainment of the telos and ideals of life, but only in following the paths leading to it, the paths that must always miss the great, good goals. These goals, these ideals, these signifiers have now been displaced. There is no longer any "fading" before them. In other words, are we to give a resounding, Nietzschean "yes" to the Eternal Return of the incalculable real of the drive, now that all the goals are missing and every moment is revealed as a simultaneous doorway between yesterday and tomorrow? But, Lacan asks, "how can a subject who has traversed the fantasy experience the drive? This is the beyond of analysis and has never been approached" (S11: 273).

Are we to attain here a perverted pleasure, a *jouissance*, in this painful, horrifying experience of always missing the goal and finding our pleasure instead only in the pain of this endless circling? Is this the "promise of analysis"? But is this not to promise what we already have, or what we "will already have had," this being the future perfect tense of the promise? Are we not always and already trapped in this drive and if so, does not giving way on our desire only release us to something that is always and already there? Moreover, would the promise of analysis not be the promise of the ultimate horror to attaining a *jouissance* from which there is no escape and no end? Is this not the horror of an infinite life beyond the limits of life and death in the eternal, undead circling of the drive?

Perhaps to attain this would be to attain access to the place both living and dead of the Thing. But, as Lacan concludes *Seminar VII*, what analysis promises and what the subject achieves in analysis is not just that access, but "something else." The subject "counts the votes relative to his own law," a law that is "in the first place always the acceptance of something that began to be articulated before him in previous generations, and which is strictly speaking *Atè*, doom and misfortune." As Lacan writes, "Although this *Atè* does not always reach the tragic level of Antigone's *Atè*, it is nevertheless closely related to misfortune" (S7: 300). This "misfortune" is that of the Oedipal complex, of an impossible desire handed down from one generation to another.

The seventh seminar seemed such a breakthrough. But where do we go from here? No matter how dramatic Lacan's rhetoric may have seemed at the time, with its call not to give way on one's desire, its sense of theater, its evocations of the raptures of heroism and sacrifice and the frightening savagery of the *jouissance* of transgression, it must have also seemed to him that his seminars had reached something of an impasse. Transgression suddenly seemed a dead-end. In the years and seminars that followed, Lacan moved away from the poetry and drama of desire toward a mathematization and toward an increasing insistence on the use of letters and numbers, S_1, S_2, a, the barred S, and so on, all used in varying combinations to formulate and to constitute the four main discourses that comprise the four walls of the human condition.

Jacques-Alain Miller calls this the establishment of a new paradigm of *jouissance* in Lacan's seminars, one worked out in terms of an infinite repetition that is best written mathematically. This develops against the background of a deductive model of thought that can be traced back to Euclid. Mathematics is privileged over poetics. The increasing shift toward the use of *mathèmes* was a shift not only toward a greater rigor and formalization, but also toward a new conception of *jouissance* that sees the relationship between *jouissance* and the binary signifier as primal. This formalization was found in the purity of the mathematical signifier freed from all signifieds. This brought the language of psychoanalysis closer to what Lacan thought to be the language of the unconscious itself and helped him to better understand the "capture" of the subject in and by the symbolic order. In the essays and seminars from the late 1950s and early1960s, desire was identified with the symbolic order, with metaphor and metonymy. Hence, it was always a dead desire, insofar as the sign kills the thing it names. *Jouissance* was what was leftover. It was the forbidden excess of the symbolic order. By 1968, the situation was different: it was no longer the terrifying reign of the Fathers and of the law in the voice that commands prohibition, renunciation, and obedience that had formed the horizon of Lacan's ethical thought in 1960. The new perspectives were developed in a new context of liberation and unlimited *jouissance*. In both Freud and Lacan's work, *jouissance* is identified with repetition: *jouissance* necessitates repetition, "repetition is based on the return of *jouissance*." We have seen this before in the repetition that defines the death drive. The cycles of life are patterns of repetition, as in the repetition of needs and satisfactions. But, in that the repeated can never be anything other, Lacan says, it is also essentially a modality of loss and entropy. As in the death drive, repetition as a way life wears itself down and returns to the inanimate; repetition is a cycle of life whereby life "embraces the disappearance of life" and becomes a return to a point both "on the horizon," and "off the map." Lacan's innovation, and the way he goes beyond Freud's conceptions of repetition, is in the way he further identifies repetition with the repetition of the unary trait, that inaugural point of insertion of the subject into the symbolic order, that decisive "mark" at the origin of the signifier. Here, repetition is directed at *jouissance*. In his later seminars, repetition is thus more strongly located in the domain of the signifier than it ever was in Freud's work (see S17: 253/181 and 45/51). Repetition, signifying relations, now supplant transgressions. This is an advance from the articulations of the earlier seminars. With this comes a new emphasis on the body, both the body (*corps*) of the subject and the body of the signifier, where *jouissance* is in the "glory of the mark," something attained in between the gesture of the marking and the body to be marked (S7: 49). Lacan here marks and remarks on the play of repetition in the *corps* and the *encore* (again). The symbolic order, which had been the habitat for the semblances of truth, the death drive, and the moral law in the earlier formulations, now, rather than excluding *jouissance* as impossible excess, conveys it.[24] If language is a crystal, *jouissance* is the refraction that emerges through it. In a "paradigm shift," *jouissance*, which, in *The Ethics of Psychoanalysis*, had been articulated in terms of loss, expenditure, and transgression of the law, now comes to be identified not only with loss, but also with a "surplus" produced in and by the symbolic order, the surplus of repetition. "Enjoy!" "Enjoy More!" But whose *jouissance* is this? Is it a *jouissance* of the body? Or the *jouissance* of the Other? Who or what is the subject of this *jouissance*? Is there not a connection here between a new ethics and a possible politics of *jouissance*? These are some of the questions Lacan confronts in his seventeenth seminar, *The Other Side (Envers) of Psychoanalysis*, and the twentieth seminar, *Encore*, which are the subjects of the next essay.

6

THE DESIRE FOR HAPPINESS AND THE PROMISE OF ANALYSIS

Aristotle and Lacan on the Ethics of Desire

The goal is that *jouissance* be avowed, precisely insofar as it may be unavowable. The truth sought is the one that is unavowable with respect to the law that regulates *jouissance*.

—Jacques Lacan, *Encore*

I have no intention of making criticisms of the society in which we live here. It is no better and no worse than any other. Human society has always been a folly. It's none the worse for that.

—Jacques Lacan, *My Teaching*

One of the last sessions in *The Ethics of Psychoanalysis*, given at the very end of June in 1960, is entitled "The Demand for Happiness and the Promise of Analysis." One of the upshots of Lacan's teachings, and particularly when it comes to his discussion of the "promises" and the "ends" of analysis, is a striking devaluation of the very possibility of the promise of ethics. Analysis does not promise to respond favorably to the subject's "demand" for happiness. Quite to the contrary, it brings about a dissolution of the subject. Analysis seems the devaluation of whatever promise or promises the great European traditions in ethical and political theory has made or could have made with regard to the "end(s)" of human life: The promise of the good, first of all, the promise of the reign of the good, the promise toward which human eyes weary of suffering could turn with the hope of the just rewards of a just and proper life, the rewards that come with governance, the good governance, of the soul and the city. It is Lacan's claim that the promise of a healing truth that waits at the end of a proper caring for the soul, a promise at once ethical and political, is

187

at its end. With the "death of Man and God" and the "demystification" of the essentialist and performative values of the European traditions in philosophical ethics, comes the end of the promise. The contractual, philosophical basis for the possibility of any such promise being made by an analyst, by a teacher, politician, or master, the promise of the Good, the True, and the Beautiful, and the reign of truth and justice that abides in this age of civilization and its discontents, seems to have been undermined and falsified by events. It also seems that ethical and political discourses have reached an impasse; their classical forms inherited from Socrates onward down into the systems of the university discourses seem exhausted, or at least condemned to survive only in somewhat embalmed, truncated academic forms. Is there no way out of this? Is there nothing new to say?

By no means, however, are the European philosophical traditions in ethics and politics, for example, dead and finished for Lacan. Were that the case, he would not have spent so much time challenging and questioning them. As we have seen, "truth" is a lively and central question for Lacan. Like the classical tradition in which it is given voice, it has a powerful role and an important place in Lacan's teachings. For Lacan's concerns in raising the question of truth were not only to raise the question of the foundations and theoretical conditions for the possibility of an ethics of psychoanalysis in particular, but also to approach a new and more generalized "ethics for our time." Is this also the link to the articulation of a "politics" for our time? Not the politics of the institutions of psychoanalysis, the almost theological politics of admissions and "excommunications," as Lacan called them, nor the money politics of politicians and state governments; the level of Lacan's questioning is directed at the great politics of the great promises, the kind of politics that at one time stood a chance of becoming a "master science." Little wonder, then, Lacan was always so indifferent to conventional politics—an indifference that is perhaps another aspect of his alleged anti-philosophy. Such ethics and politics was always a discourse of promises and more promises that could never be kept. Can we perhaps find something more in his teachings than this, something new, a different way, perhaps, of questioning the political?

THE PASSION FOR THE REAL

If psychoanalysis is not to be a religion, with its own priests, monasteries, and confessional booths, if it is not be a science, not at least in the sense that "biology" is a science, if psychoanalysis is to be perhaps more than a science, if psychoanalysis is an ethic, how can it become what it is? What shall be the ethical and political space of this level of thinking in psychoanalysis such that it confronts the enigmas and violence of not only individuals in distress, but also of "civilization" as such and its worsening "discontents"?

This would mean calling into question the limits and the relations between the classical forms of ethics and politics and attempting to articulate both an ethics and a politics that goes beyond them. Machiavelli's path-breaking book *The Prince* was perhaps the first book to describe a politics stripped of any teleological ethical concerns. It thus became the first book to mark an absolute break between ethics and politics. In doing so, it also more accurately reflected what was indeed happening in the real politics of his time. Since that book's publication in 1532, there has been an effort to rethink the relations between ethics and politics, an effort to find a new basis for linking ethics and politics. Beyond the debates between the opposed classical vocabularies and working concepts of ethics and morality, with Greek *eudaimonic* virtue on one side and Kantian moral duties and rights on the other, Lacan seeks a new way of theorizing and articulating the possibilities for an ethics and a politics of psychoanalysis.

In his analyses of the Church and the Army, Freud's 1921 *Group Psychology and the Analysis of the Ego*, became another path-breaking book in this regard. It offered a new way of mapping and conceiving social relations in terms of the vertical relationship of the group vis-à-vis the leader qua ego ideal at the top, intersected by the horizontal relationships of community, of egos on a par with one another in the group. It pointed the way to a new psychoanalytic approach to articulating social relations and power structures in society. But Lacan took this a step further. Especially in the late 1960s, he began to conceive of both ethical and political structures and relations in terms of "discourses," the four discourses of mastery, of the university, of hysteria, and of analysis. These are also the discourses for the four "impossibles" of governance, education, desire, and analysis. These four discourses put the Freudian horizontal and vertical dimensions of social relations on a new footing. For Lacan's "discourse" theory, the commanding dominance implied in the vertical relation is developed not in terms of the personality of the leader, but as a discursive structure with its master signifiers. Here, the verticality can be seen in Lacan's schema whereby the divided subject (S barred) is below, and the master signifier is above the line separating them. This recalls the diagram for metaphor and for the logic of paradigmatic substitutions discussed in his earlier seminars. The horizontal relations, meanwhile, appear not only at the level of the imaginary relations between one ego and another, but also at the level of the generalized structure of fantasy, which is not only structurally articulated, but which also appears from within the very same master's discourse at the level of its truth, the master signifier having as its truth the barred Subject in relation to object *a*. Insofar as object *a* is an object-cause of desire, this would put it on the "horizontal" level of metonymic displacements and syntaxes that occur across the chain of signifiers structuring desire, something also prominent in Lacan's earlier seminars and now given a new articulation in the seventeenth seminar. Object *a* in this way can and must also be seen as being a key social link. Thus, fantasy and the structure of fantasy would be perceived by Lacan's discourse theory as having an important social and political role to play. In his new schemas of the "four discourses" and in his emerging articulation of a "feminine *jouissance*," Lacan also articulated at a new level a relation to "Other-ness" that unfolds in his seventeenth seminar as "the other side of psychoanalysis." My hypothesis is that especially in these later seminars Lacan began to explore more explicitly the links between ethical and political life, and in doing so he not only oriented social and political analysis in terms of a theory of four prevalent discourses that form the four walls of all ethical and political relations but he also called into question the limits and relations between ethical and political life by bringing them into a confrontation with *jouissance* and the real. Lacan had always defined the subject as both the effect of signification and, as such, a response to the real (*réponse du réel*) ("l'Étourdit," *Scilicet* 4: 15). His later seminars advance this conception further by opening it to a wider stage of political dimensions.

Perhaps the essential directions to pursue are already contained in the complexities of the relationship Lacan articulates between desire and language up to the time of his seventh seminar. But his teachings on *jouissance* and the real go farther than this. Certainly, the ethics of psychoanalysis was focused on a theoretical and practical concern for the "desire of the analyst" and for the "ends of analysis." But this was not the end. The new concepts and vocabularies Lacan's teaching invented as it made its way—and it seems that the invention of new concepts, especially in the field of ethics, is one of his seminars' most important philosophical legacies—certainly had the more generalized effect of opening the conceptualization and articulation of the human situation in the world today to new dimensions and new possibilities, to the promise of an "encounter with the real," as he had called it in *Seminar VII*. Lacan's seminars promised this encounter that "must always be missed." How did he keep this promise in his later seminars? In this sense, then, Lacan's seminars on the ethics and the politics of psychoanalysis always had so much promise, and even now, they are still so promising.

But where does this promise lead? In what directions and with what aims do we follow this Acteon in his encounter with Diana? It is to seek a way out of what Lacan perceived as the impasse of the European traditions and discourses on ethics, the impasses of the doctrines of "know thyself," of "moral virtues" that promised to answer to the demands of happiness and the good? Does it take us beyond the impasse of "moral duties" and of the legislated power of "moral law," the ultimate foundations for which lie in the freedom that obtains only as the sublime idea of a pure reason? What kind of "man," what kind of world would come of this?

While Lacan's ethics of psychoanalysis did not promise new foundations or ideals, it does offer something else. One could account for this "something else," which marks the slippage and the distance that Lacan puts between his teachings on ethics and those of the European classical traditions in ethical and political discourse, in the following way: Where for the classical European tradition, the primary passion was a passion for the Good, the True, the Just, the Beautiful, and so on, in Lacan, there is something one is almost tempted to call a "passion for the real," to use a phrase from Badiou's book *The Century*,[1] and in particular, a passion for the *jouissance*, for the "limitless love," that is access to the real. Perhaps this was the true promise offered by the ethics of psychoanalysis, not the promise of happiness and the satisfaction of desire, but what Lacan called "an encounter with the real" (S11: 53), an encounter with the real of desire and the drives. But, insofar as the real is the "*inassimilable*," the encounter with the real is something that must always and necessarily be "missed" (S11: 55, Lacan's italics). There is literally no-thing there to encounter. At best, the real is summoned only through a play of masks and veils, the screens of fantasy, and of object *a*, a screen behind which the real is nothing but a hole in the Other. Hence, the recognition one finds in Lacan's teaching on both ethics and politics for the primacy of semblance, an irreducible semblance, in every encounter with the real, as in every attempt to attain, to name, and so to contain, the real, for it certainly has its disruptive effects. We have seen this already in Lacan's reading of the play *Antigone*. My purpose now shall be to show how Lacan's later seminars, particularly the seventeenth seminar, *The Other Side of Psychoanalysis* (1969–1970), and the twentieth seminar, *Encore, On Feminine Sexuality: The Limits of Love and Knowledge* (1972–1973), carried these questions and perspectives forward and developed them further.

So, a "passion for the real." And why not? If Badiou is right, a similar "passion for the real" characterizes the twentieth century more generally. Badiou traces it through theater, politics, art, and Lacanian psychoanalysis. Such a passion for the real at one time might have hoped for an act, an artistic, ethical, and political act, that, in its purity or in the flexing of a gesture purified of any care or concern for self-interest, would indeed bring the real into view in all its violent and thrilling immediacy, would bring it out from under the veiling shadows of morality and law so as to let it shine in all its captivating splendor. At one time, such a passion for the real might have been confused with a love of truth. Alas, for Lacan, the real is but a nullity, an absence of meaning. There is therefore nothing in it; there is no truth in this sense to reveal. In any case, a passion for the real could have taken a potentially disastrous course. As one of its more frightening manifestations, it could have become an ethics and a politics somehow "beyond good and evil," a politics and an ethics of pure acts, "happenings" disconnected from either Law or Idea, purely aesthetic outbursts and iconoclastic conflagrations, a riot of means over the ends, and the pathological over duty and respect. But, with the encounter with the real being always and essentially missed, such a politics of the raw and direct encounter with the real can only be regarded as something dangerously misguided. After all, perhaps the leading function of the play of semblances in every encounter with the real is to keep the real at a distance, to neutralize or "sublimate" its effects. Hence, in Badiou's words, the twentieth century is shaped by its "commitment," whether in theater or ethical-political discourse, to "thinking" the real in its relation to semblance, the relationship, for just a first example, between "real violence and semblance, between face and mask, between nudity and disguise."[2] As we have seen in Lacan's reading of Sophocles' *Antigone*, this is the sort of question being raised in the evocation of the splendorous, violent, and tragic dimensions of Antigone's act, when her "limitless love" is brought to life as the theatrical *mimesis* of an action, as a semblance for the encounter with the real. Its splendor enacts an encounter in which death itself and the disasters of incestuous relationships darkly stalk the stage. They are both there and not there in the figure of her beauty, both captivating lure and barrier to the real, and in the interplay of the sublimation both limited and general of a passion for the real. The shiver of violence that runs through the play, the violence of Antigone's act, the "between-two-deaths," is played out in the gap between the semblance and the real. There is always a need, in short, to both approach and repel the real, something Badiou says that Brecht put at the heart of his theory of theater.[3] This is the question, this is the situation of the question, that Lacan's teachings on ethics address, but now, it is in terms of *jouissance* in its relation to the real and to the modes of semblance, of a *jouissance* situated in the gap between semblance and the real. It shall be a question, therefore, of seeing how *jouissance* becomes in Lacan's seventeenth and twentieth seminars a link between the ethical and the political dimensions. More specifically, and more acutely, the situation confronted in *The Other Side of Psychoanalysis*, an ethical and political situation of the post-1968 turbulence that Lacan will characterize as "shameless," is a situation in which the real, in which fantasy and object *a* in relation to the real, have come to occupy the position of the master signifiers, and in which a generalized destitution of the prevailing "master signifiers," the signifiers for all the ends and purposes of man and society, has become an inverted ideal. Surely, this is the "other side" of the ethics and the politics that Lacan is exploring in his presentation of the "four discourses" in *Seminar XVII*. What are the ethical and political consequences of an age in which *jouissance* and the passion for the real have become "ideals," political, ethical ideals, and made the objects of an intense promise?

MEASURING THE DISTANCE BETWEEN ARISTOTLE AND LACAN

On the other side of the chasm of history that separates us from the ancient world, far from the modern "passion for the real," we find the classical tradition of the "care for the soul." Its passion was not for the real, but for tranquility and well-being. Such care seems quite literally a world apart from the ruckus of modern life.

What could this have to do with Lacan and contemporary psychoanalysis?

While it is common knowledge that Aristotle has had a major impact on such twentieth-century thinkers as Heidegger, it must have come as something of a surprise to Lacan's audiences in his seminars in the 1950s to hear Aristotle's name invoked so often in the context of lectures on Freud and psychoanalysis. One would have expected to hear the names of Hegel and Marx, and especially those of Ferdinand Saussure and Roman Jakobson, given the general structuralist inclination of Lacan's thought in those years. But to so often invoke the name and ideas of Aristotle must have seemed unusual. Yet, it was indeed especially Aristotle's ethics that continued to interest Lacan throughout several of his seminars, especially *Seminar VII* (1959–1960), entitled *The Ethics of Psychoanalysis*. On several occasions during the course of that and other seminars, Lacan called upon his audience to go back and read Aristotle, telling them that Aristotle's ideas and general approach to ethics are useful and certainly not lacking in interest for the practice of analysis. But, while in full appreciation for the classical value of Aristotle's work, and while also pointing out the importance of Brentano's 1887 lectures on Aristotle for Freud (who had attended them), Lacan also told his seminar that his purpose was to measure the distance covered since Aristotle and to show in part how much an ethics of psychoanalysis would differ from the classical values of Aristotle's ethics. It seems that Lacan's strategy might have been to show the profile of his own thought precisely by showing just how much it differed from Aristotle's. Lacan commented, for example, in his seventh seminar that the ethics of psychoanalysis is characterized by "an effacement, a setting aside, a withdrawal, the absence of a dimension that one only has to mention in order to realize how much separates us from all ethical thought that preceded us" (S7: 10/19–20). This dimension is the concern for the formation of good habits. This is what ethical life is, for Aristotle, good habits and good character. The formation of good habits is essential if human desire is to attain its Good, defined as well-being (*eudaimonia*).

But the Lacanian doctrine of "separation" and his use of the word "repetition" are deeply rooted in the supposition of the unconscious, something Aristotle was unaware of. This marks the essential wedge or distance between Lacan and Aristotle with regard to the scope and direction of ethical life. The term "repetition," for example, is a word that also has considerable force in Aristotle's conception of "habit" (the Greek *ethos*, a word derived from a Greek verb meaning to repeat)[4] and is connected to the formation of character and good habits. But it has a completely different sense in psychoanalysis where it is connected to the death drive. The distance between Lacan and Aristotle can also be measured in their shared meditation on the fact that human beings are always seemingly directed toward or guided by a conception of their own good. Human desire is always oriented toward the attainment of "the good." Even to desire pain is to desire it in some sense as one's own good. But, Aristotle and Lacan differ in the way each evaluates "the good": for Aristotle, the ultimate ethical good is *eudaimonia* (well-being), the realization of human potential, whereas for Lacan, even this highest of goods still circulates in an economy of goods where it has but a fantasmatic role to play in and as something employed to plug or to fill the lack that defines desire. Moreover, Aristotle defines desire as a natural appetite that can be shaped into a desire for the highest of goods. The Lacanian conception of desire owes nothing to nature. It is linguistically informed, the restless, unappeasable metonymy of being. Psychoanalysis does not therefore shape or train desire. While it may seem that desire for Lacan is a desire for the impossible, ultimately, it is always a desire for *jouissance* in the real, a desire therefore linked not with well-being, but with transgression.

Hence, there is a nexus, a crosscurrent and a confrontation between the texts of Aristotle, Freud, and Lacan that is both important and provocative for anyone today seeking to understand the possibilities and the basis for ethical thought. It shall be expressly my purpose to explore this nexus in the following pages, beginning with a brief outline of Aristotle's key ideas in his *Nicomachean Ethics* and then to proceed to a discussion of Lacan's critical reading of Aristotle, showing just how Lacan might have had good reason for beginning with Aristotle's ethics. My emphasis shall be on Lacan's seventh seminar on the ethics of psychoanalysis and the role that *jouissance* plays in both that seminar and *Seminar XVII*, entitled "Other Side," the "Envers," of psychoanalysis. I shall be comparing this with the role that *eudaimonia* (happiness) plays in both Aristotle's ethics and his politics. Just as *eudaimonia* is an important link between Aristotle's ethics and his politics—it is the common ideal, goal, or telos for both the desire of the singular individual and for the political space of the community, the *polis*—so *jouissance* plays a similar linking role in Lacan's seventh, seventeenth, and twentieth seminars. It shall be my thesis that Lacan's is an ethic of *jouissance* just as Aristotle's was an ethic of *eudaimonia*. What links, what separates these two discourses on ethics and politics?

I shall begin with an overall sketch of Aristotle's ethics, showing the importance of *eudaimonia* for that ethical framework, and then proceed to a discussion of ethics and politics of *jouissance* in Lacan's seminars, stressing how from *Seminars VII* and *XVII*, Lacan changed the way he understood the relationship between *jouissance* and the three key structural orders, the Symbolic (the Law), the Imaginary, and the Real, by which he defined both the structure of the ethical subject and the political domain. Two literary figures, Sophocles' Antigone, presented *in Seminar*

VII, and Claudel's Sygne, from *Seminar VIII*, make cameo appearances as signifying images by which Lacan points out the role of *jouissance* in ethical life and what he calls, in connection with this, the "tragic dimensions"[5] of ethics, something Lacan suggests is necessarily foreclosed in Aristotle's *Nicomachean Ethics*. Following a discussion of Lacan's usage of the terms "the real" and *jouissance*, I then turn to a discussion of the "four discourses" of *Seminar XVII*, and show the relation between especially two of these discourses, that of the "master's discourse," where Lacan situates Aristotle's *Ethics*, and that of the "analyst's discourse," where we will find Lacan's presentation of the ethical and political "ends," the "termination" of psychoanalysis conceived in part as the traversal of the ethical and political fantasms of "happiness."

ARISTOTLE: AN ETHICS AND POLITICS OF *EUDAIMONIA*

Jacob Klein taught that both Plato and Aristotle are philosophers of the Good, but they differed in the way each conceived the "manner of being" of the Good.[6] For Plato, the Good was detached from time and history. This is not the case for Aristotle. Rather, the Good is conceived as the realization or actualization of human potential, which Aristotle designates by the word *energeia*, meaning activity. Aristotle's thesis is that there were many ways of talking about the Good: the goods of political life, the goods of money, health, pleasure, and so on. But, the chief Good, the Good toward which all the others tend as toward their end, and the only Good he was ultimately interested in, was a Good realizable in a human lifetime, one that would be the flourishing of that life. Aristotle's word for this is *eudaimonia*, which is commonly and badly translated as "happiness," but which might be better phrased as "well-being." To say that happiness is a chief good, Aristotle says, amounts to a truism. He therefore specifies it in terms of the "human function." The human function is not just to live, but, is first "an activity of soul (*psuché*, meaning 'breath,' and 'soul,' the principle of life) which follows or implies a rational principle." The human function is a "certain kind of life," in other words, one that implies or requires a human psychology. Happiness as the highest good for a human life would be the best and most noble exercise of the human function as the exercise of the highest capacities of the human soul. In other words, it would be "an activity of soul in accordance with virtue (*arête*), and if there are more than one virtue, in accordance with the best and most complete."[7] Happiness is then identified with a way of life that is the best exercise of the human faculty of reason, and so the complete satisfaction of human potentiality. It is the noble, good activity (*energeia*) by which human potentiality (potency) is realized in activity. Aristotle's is an ethic not just of particular actions, but of a whole life conceived of as activity.

Aristotle did not define this sort of Good as being mathematically determinable. Hence, there is no exact and ideal science for ethical life. Rather than mathematics, biology was a master science for ethical life. Ethical life was thought along the lines of biological development from the state of the seed to that of the fully grown plant-bearing flower and fruit.

How could a human being realize the promise of "happiness," an English word that very poorly translates Aristotle's term *eudaimonia* (well-being)? Only by the taming of desire through the inculcation of good habits (*ethos*). Good habits are best exemplified in the capacity for making a good choice (*prohairesis*) of the mean(s) by which the "right" and "good end" (*telos*) of *eudaimonia* could be achieved. However "relative to each" ethical choice may be, it is nonetheless determined by a rational principle, or as a prudent man (the *phronismos*) would counsel. But the ethical life is not a theoretical life, although rational principles and good deliberation play key roles in establishing it. It remains a practical life, a life of action, of doings and deeds. Thus, Aristotle consistently conceives of ethics along the lines of virtue, conceived not as an ideal Form, but meaning right or best performance of the human function, a way of being at work, *energeia*. "Happiness" (*eudaimonia*), which Aristotle thought of as the ultimate goal and Good of all human activity and an end complete and self-sufficient unto itself, was not just a disposition or mental state, but, once again, as a way of life, an activity (*energeia*), a comprehensive life, difficult to achieve, that would include the goods of the worldly life, the material goods of prosperity and political honors and friendships, the goods of the body, such as pleasure, health and beauty, and the goods of the soul, namely, the virtues of wisdom (*sophia*), courage, and temperance, or moderation (*sōphrosynē*). While the life of the statesman and the life of the philosopher are thought to best exemplify the life of excellence, Aristotle comes down on the side of the philosophical life as being the best, for the life of the statesman, he says, is too busy, too distracted, and so most tied to the life of contingencies. Hence, the most complete form of well-being (*eudaimonia*) was the life of contemplation in the exercise of theoretical wisdom.

Lacan maintains that the Aristotelian ideal of the contemplative life is based on the gaze, as object *a*, "one of four *supports* that constitute the cause of desire" (S20: 95/87). But surely, something is awry in this because for Lacan's 1964 *Seminar XI*, there is a split between the eye and the gaze that takes Lacan's understanding of the gaze rather far afield from what obtains in Aristotelian contemplation. The Lacanian gaze is situated not in the eye, but in the Other. It is the gaze of the Other. The gaze is on the side of the object of the scopic drive. Perhaps what Lacan means is that when a subject contemplates, as Aristotle's uses the term, it contemplates, or sees an object, in this case an object of thought, and that object is always and already gazing back at the subject. This would make the act of contemplation a subjection of the thinking subject rather than its highest form of *energeia*. Is this Aristotelian contemplation? Here is what Aristotle says in his *De Anima*: Thinking is, *like* perception, *like* the act of seeing, a passive affection in which what thinks and what is thought are identical.[8] Does the object of contemplation, the "divine in things," gaze back at the contemplating subject? This hardly seems to be Aristotle's contention. Rather, it is only in the contemplative life that what is divine in us, namely, mind or *nous*, attains an almost mystical union with what is divine in things, that being what is most eminently knowable and divine in them. Thus, it is only through the contemplative life that a human being can attain—as much as is possible for a mortal being—something like an immortal, divine life, when the soul exercises and so actualizes its being as a thinking soul and thus becomes complete in itself, tirelessly, and lastingly complete. Such *eudaimonic* activity best realizes the human function, which, according to Aristotle, is to live a life in accordance with what is best and highest and most divine-like in the human soul, and it is virtue that is highest, especially the intellectual virtue of wisdom, which is the right activity of *nous* or mind. It is only through the taming of desire, the moderation of physical desire, that this can be realized. A life of untamed physical desires would only bring about a life of physical and psychological ruin, misery, dependencies, and the consequent debilitation and enslavement of the intellect.

But the crux to this ethical program lies not in the theoretical but in the moral virtues of moderation, courage, and the like. It is in this domain that the formation of "good habits" is most important. Hence, ethical life, the life of the virtues, for Aristotle is not just the mental exercise of knowledge. It is also practice, insight, and the kind of psychological, physical balance that is worked out over a lifetime of being in situations calling for moderation or courage. In this sense, virtue, the choice of the middle amount between extremes, is something relative to each person and so cannot be determined in abstraction from the individual. Yet, it must not be forgotten that determining the middle amount is not entirely up to the individual, but is something that can and must also be determined by a rational principle, *logos*, *episteme*, or by the counsel of a prudent man. In other words, it is not up to Johnny to decide what is good for Johnny. It is the master's voice that must guide him. Desire must conform to order.

So, with such relativism not aside, let us insist, then, on the pedagogical and discursive elements in Aristotle's conception of ethical life, the role played by the right, straight, and true discourse, the *orthos logos*, the discursive practice that sets forth the arguments and the order of what has to be done, that thereby persuades desire by providing it with its ideals of pleasure and fear. It is the discourse that teaches, guides, and thereby helps to shape desire, establishing the practical logic of its ends and goals. It is the teaching that shows the way and makes the promises by which desire can become something praiseworthy and honorable in the eyes of others, rather than being a source of shame. It is the words of the master toward which Aristotle's hearers turn as they seek the counsel necessary to the realization and satisfaction of a man's deepest desire, his desire for "happiness." And when it comes to desire, the master—whether philosopher or priestess—always counsels "nothing in excess" (*Meden agan*), the same words inscribed in gold over the entrance to the Temple of Apollo at Delphi, seat of the Delphic Oracle. Avoid excess, the prudent master counsels, especially the kind of excess that overrides pleasure and mingles with pain, the kind of excess that goes beyond the human limit, an excess of pleasure that Lacan will call *jouissance*. It is this which must be resisted and from which the ethical life must separate itself. What Lacan will articulate as *jouissance* appears in Aristotle's ethic as something disruptive and destructive, and so forbidden. Aristotle condemns such *jouissance* in the most extreme terms: excess is vicious, shameful, bestial, and monstrous. It is this dimension of Aristotle's ethics that Lacan emphasizes in *Seminar VII*, for it shows the relation of the symbolic order and of desire in Aristotle to be one of exclusion. Moreover, the symbolic order, the *orthos logos*, is something imposed on desire from outside. Desire, while amenable to discourse, is nonetheless seen by Aristotle as somehow beyond the symbolic order of words and laws. Desire is natural, whether linked to appetite or to intellectual desire. "All men by nature desire to know," as the first lines of Aristotle's *Metaphysics* say. The symbolic order is something to which desire must always conform or be condemned. Desire is always a desire for something; it is a potentiality always seeking its realization in things or in pleasure. Words can inform desire of its proper goals and ends whereby it attains satisfaction. But it seems that raw, physical desire, the stuff of the moral virtues, is ultimately bestial for Aristotle, something the human being shares with animal being. Hence, it is always problematic, for it is the dimension of appetites and fears in the human soul. It is always a force, therefore, that must be trained and shaped by good upbringing, and something that always requires the examinations and regimens of a good doctor of souls. Hence, we may conclude by observing that for Aristotle, this is what makes desire something biological. It is the element of life, the *psyche*, the *animus* by which the living are distinguished from the dead and the inanimate.

In summary, it is truly a practical wisdom, a *Phronesis*, that Aristotle is defining in his ethics, a practical relation of thought and habit to desire, the sort of wisdom exemplified in realizing the proper balance between good habits and right thought, a balance between having the right, rational, and providential ends, the right desires, in other words, and at the same time, the practical skill of right deliberation concerning the best means and ways of realizing those ends and satisfying the desire for health, wealth, and "happiness." This is the substance of Aristotle's *orthos logos* on desire. Virtue for Aristotle is thus both means and end, a means toward the realization of *eudaimonia*, happiness or well-being, and an end in itself, something right to desire and toward which desire should tend; virtue is set forth as something chosen, something desirable for itself as an end and not just as an instrument for attaining something further. This is especially the case with *eudaimonia*, happiness, the happiness of the contemplative life, truly a life enjoyed only by the master, and the ultimate telos whereby desire, whether intellectual or moral, attains full satisfaction. But the Aristotelian ethical life has the political community as its setting. Ethics is a part of politics for Aristotle. There is an essential link, then, between the good, the *eudaimonia*, for the individual and the good for the community.

As Aristotle says in his *Politics*, regarding the question of whether or not the happiness (*eudaimonia*) of the individual is the same as that of the state, "there can be no doubt . . . they are the same."[9] It is *eudaimonia* that plays the pivotal role in determining the overall goals of both ethical and political life for Aristotle. It is what defines the ethical and political space of human life. *Eudaimonia* is the necessary condition for the polis, the city-state, the political community, insofar as it is what the members of the polis hold in common, that in which they share equally, that telos or goal upon which all the like-minded men that constitute the polis have in common, namely, a desire for happiness, "the highest good."[10]

Now, while Aristotle's *Politics*, as its title might indicate, is indeed concerned with a conventional sense of the word "politics," meaning by that the constitutions of governments and the political activity and affairs of statesmanship, there is another level active in Aristotle's thought, one that goes beyond politics, a level that one might call "the political." This is a level concerned with determining the structure and ideals of political life that opens, shapes, or makes possible the social, economic space of politics. As Chantal Mouffe expresses it, "the political cannot be restricted to a certain type of institution, or envisaged as constituting a specific sphere or level of society. It must be conceived as a dimension that is inherent to every human society and that determines our very ontological condition."[11] For Aristotle, the political was that level of his discourse concerned with the articulation of the highest ideals and goals of both ethical and political life, namely, the desire for *eudaimonia*. It is also this level that we shall be emphasizing in our reading of Lacan, whereby there is not only a concern for the "ethics of psychoanalysis," the various practical and professional dimensions of the doctor-patient relationship, but also for the "ethical" and for the "political," both of which are conceived in terms of desire, *jouissance*, and the real as the structural, ontological dimensions of ethical and political life.

Is Aristotle's ethics, based as it is on the assertion of *eudaimonia* as the end, goal, and destination for desire, not the "other side" of psychoanalysis, the "other side" of *jouissance*, in the sense of being the other scene of ethical and political fantasms, that "other side" whereby fantasms become "master signifiers"? Is it not the function of this "other side" to be the target in the Lacanian ethics and politics of psychoanalysis of subversion and "de-mystification"? And is it not subversion that brings forward all that is positive in any potential Lacanian ethics and politics?

I would like to see how *jouissance*, while far from being an ethical-political ideal for Lacan, and while undergoing changes in its overall articulation in Lacan's seminars, plays a homologous yet inverted role linking the ethics and the politics of Lacanian psychoanalysis. I shall pursue this through Lacan's later seminars, especially the seventeenth seminar and the twentieth, *Encore, On Feminine Sexuality: The Limits of Love and Knowledge* (1972–1973).

LACAN: AN ETHICS AND
POLITICS OF *JOUISSANCE*

Like Aristotle, Lacan's ethics of psychoanalysis is not just an academic body of knowledge or a grand theory, but a praxis. Thus, his work is situated not only in relation to that of Aristotle's ethics, but also in relation to Freud and Marx. Like those authors, Lacan's concern is to address the causes of human suffering and a human need for transgression. He confronts this in both the individuals who come to him as patients and in what might loosely be called the "ills" of society at large, Freud's "civilization and its discontents," a text and a topic that overshadows much of Lacan's seventh seminar on ethics. Whereas for Aristotle, ethics was a set of counsels, supported by arguments, on how one might make the best choice in life of the various means toward the overall goal of life, which was to realize human potentiality and to attain *eudaimonia* ("happiness," as the term is translated), the Lacanian ethics of psychoanalysis confronts a different situation. Here, the analyst is constantly confronted by patients who do not just desire happiness, they demand it, just as they demand love, just as they demand that the analyst know the answer to the question that haunts them: "What do I really want?" "What will bring an end to my suffering?" "What does the world want me to be?" But, Lacan's ethics of psychoanalysis is obviously not concerned with the limited and practical task of elaborating techniques for helping people, his patients, namely, to determine the best means by which they could attain happiness. Rather, the scope of the seminars was much broader and more philosophically inclined. Lacan most often seems more concerned in his seminars with showing the ethical and political effects of the Freudian discovery of the unconscious. This was at the heart of Lacan's "return to Freud." Following upon Freud's discovery of the unconscious and following the related discoveries of linguistics, nothing can ever be the same again for ethical-political discourse. Henceforth, these new horizons shall completely recast the whole problematic of ethical and political thought.

This new orientation established by Freud's discovery of the unconscious establishes Lacan's ethics of psychoanalysis as the "other side" of Aristotle's ethics. What does this mean, to be the "other side"? It means there is a respect paid to Aristotle's work. Its value is recognized and deeply appreciated. But Lacan will challenge it, enlarge upon it, alter its framework, and supplement its lack of contact with the human unconscious. Thus, in his 1960 seminar, Lacan said that, indeed, he seeks to demystify the classical ethical tradition of the Good, the True, and the

Beautiful. For Lacan the Good is not, as it was for Plato, a transcendental and timeless source, nor is it, as it was for Aristotle, the realization of human potentiality. Rather, the Good is but "a good," a value circulating in the economy of what Lacan calls "the service of goods." Its role in the structure of human desire is thus one of Lacan's major concerns in his meditations on ethics.

Just as Aristotle's ethics is dominated by the word *eudaimonia*, defined as the ethical Good realizable in a human life, so Lacan's ethics of psychoanalysis is dominated by the word *jouissance*. But, *jouissance* is not a new formulation of the human good, nor is it an ethical ideal, but something at the core of human experience that almost escapes definition. By naming it, Lacan made it a new artifact of ethical discourse, and in doing so, he completely recasts the theoretical and practical understanding of the analytic situation in particular and the ethical and political dimensions of the "human condition" more generally.

As for Aristotle, so, too, for Lacan, there are many ways of talking about the Good with no one sense assumed as primary or privileged. But what are the senses of "the Good" in the context of analysis? Is it the Good of the analyst? Is the analyst taken as a paradigm of the Good insofar as the analyst is the "one who knows"? Is the purpose of analysis to get the patient-analysand to identify with the analyst through transference and so to adopt the analyst's notions of the Good? Or would it be the Good of the patient, his desire for sexual satisfaction, his ideals of happiness, perhaps, that are at the heart of the relationships and situations that may be among the causes of the patient's suffering? Could it be an objective Good? Could the purpose of analysis be to normalize the patient, to have the patient conform to or adopt the predominant social ideals of the Good, happiness, for example, attained through the pursuit of the goods of wealth and health? Could the purpose, the promise, and the destination of analysis be to bring the patient to the point where he or she may exercise a Good Will?

These are some of the questions Lacan's seminars posed, and, over the course of his seminars, in *Seminar VII*, for example, on *The Ethics of Psychoanalysis*, he saw the moral and ethical dimensions of human life in a new light, one that emanates not only from the philosophical tradition of Plato's Good, but also from the pages of Greek tragedy, that strangely beautiful but dark light—"the splendor," as Lacan calls it—that radiates from the tragic heroine, Antigone.

It is therefore my working thesis that Lacan's is an ethic not of the Good, but of *jouissance* and "the real," which, although it names not so much an impossible beyond or excess of the Good, nonetheless ultimately marks something unattainable, a limit, a suspension, a point of failure, perhaps, that coincides with a point of intensity. They are key terms for the seminars I shall be considering in the following pages, which convened from 1959–1960 to 1972–1973, where Lacan took up the question of the aims and the promise of the ethics of psychoanalysis, thinking this question through in terms of the ambiguous, knotted relationship of desire and the limits of love, knowledge, and moral-ethical law. How are these terms defined over the course of these seminars?

Let us begin with Lacan's use of the term, "the real." Where especially the Platonic tradition of ethical thought has tended toward the Ideal, toward what could well seem a transcendental "unreal," Lacan thus proposes a shift in direction and a change of attitude. He will go "more deeply" into the real. For him, "the question of ethics," he writes, "is to be articulated from the point of view of the location of man in relation to the real" (S7: 11–12/20–21). "Moral action," Lacan teaches, is "grafted (*entée*) onto the real." It introduces something new into the real and thereby opens a path in which the point of our presence is sanctioned" (S7: 21/30). This new usage of the term "the real" also completely recasts the relations of identity and difference between the Real and the Rational, and points out Lacan's indebted adversity to Hegel, for whom the Real is the Rational.

First the term "the real" is situated and defined in Lacan's triad of the Imaginary, the Symbolic, and the Real. It must be differentiated from both its conventional and its technical meanings, where it is taken to be "reality," the sort of "reality" referred to in Freud's notion of "the reality principle," or as a "scientific reality," as a "social reality," or, in the parlance of everyday, natural consciousness, simply what is "out there," the empirically factual, "reality" as the totality of the objects of thought and perception.

Lacan rejects the idea that reality is an unproblematic given. Reality is not just a perceptual object but also a construct linked with fantasy. This much was observed by Freud in connection with dreams and with the way when dreams fail in their task to protect sleep, reality, or rather the "reality principle," intervenes. Waking up to reality, one continues in a sense to dream. Thus, reality is fantasy for Lacan. While we do receive data through sense perception, but with the exception of this supposed pure data, reality is fantasy.[12] Reality is thus rooted in the structure of desire and functions to satisfy the pleasure principle whereby tensions and excitations are maintained at a manageable level.

This fantasmatic dimension of reality also applies to the "reality" of the sexual relationship, sexual complementarity, which Lacan shows to depend for the integrity of its functioning on semblance and "fantasmatic propping."[13]

Yet, Lacan's use of the term "real" is also said to compare with Freud's use of the phrase "psychic reality," which designates not the inner world of dreams, but a deeper inner core that Laplanche and Pontalis characterize as "heterogeneous" to the symbolic order and "resistant" to it. "Heterogeneity" and "resistance" thus make up the "nucleus" "more real than the majority of psychic phenomenon."[14]

In *Seminar VII*, Lacan places the "real" in opposition to what is conventionally meant by the English word "fictitious." As Lacan shows in connection with his reading of Jeremy Bentham, "fictitious" does not necessarily mean "that which deceives." Rather, Lacan identifies the fictitious with the symbolic, thus distinguishing the real once again from the symbolic. Whereas the early seminars in the 1950s did place the real outside or beyond the symbolic order, where it designated a pure positivity of being without lack or negativity, which are in turn introduced by the symbolic order, Lacan's later seminars situated the real in terms—which would be the terms of presentation—of the symbolic order. Thus, Lacan's striking thesis from the 1960 seminar: "(T)he moral law, the moral command, the presence of the moral agency in our activity, insofar as it is structured by the symbolic, is that through which the real is 'presentified,' or brought to presence (*se présentifie*), or, as the reflexive construction in French has it, it could 'present itself'—the real as such, the weight of the real (*le poids du reel*)" (S7: 20/28). There is no real without the symbolic. For the Lacan of *Seminar XX*, the real is called "the mystery of the speaking body, the mystery of the unconscious," but only insofar as it is a "logical obstacle" within the symbolic. In this sense, "the real is the impossible" (S20: 131, 119 and 122/142). But the real is not reducible to being a non-representable other outside the symbolic, because making it such would actually include it within the symbolic by representing it precisely as its non-representable beyond. Rather, the real is the internal limit of the symbolic order, the internal limit of representability, its "traumatic core," as Žižek colorfully phrases it. As such, the real is thus the "extimate" core of the symbolic, that point where the limit between inside and outside is rendered problematic. It names both that gap, that empty place at the heart of the symbolic and the attempt to close it or fill it through the naming of what is unnamable. The real is thus the figure of the limit Lacan's ethics and politics would wish to enter more deeply.[15]

Hence, the real has a double relation with the symbolic: it is both brought to presence in being named as the unnamable by the symbolic, and, it is also cut off, rejected by the symbolic. The real is both nameable and unnamable, is both inside and outside the symbolic. Hence, a gap or cut always marks the encounter with the real.

Likewise with desire, which Lacan says elliptically, "precisely because desire is articulated that it is not articulable . . . in the discourse that suits it, which is ethical and not psychological."[16]

Quite in connection with this, Lacan also speaks of the real of *jouissance*—a *jouissance* of the body—something necessarily cut off, rejected, sacrificed in the becoming of subjectivity and the assumption of a position in the symbolic order. This is how one becomes what one is: one must sacrifice what one "is" (the real) so that one might become what one "is" (in the symbolic order). The real qua *jouissance* is thus the extimate limit of all subjective interiority and identity.

Four summary major propositions need to be made at this point:

First, the real marks both the extimacy and the subversion of the symbolic order.

Second, and, at the same time, it marks the need for the series of substitutions and displacements called upon to fill this gap, to suture this wound marked by the real at the heart of the symbolic. Hence, the role for the Thing (*das Ding*) and for "object *a*" (*objet petit a*) in Lacan's seminars. They are both lures and barriers to the real.

Third, this "tropological substitution" (Laclau) demonstrates the independence of the signifier in relation to the signified. Saussurean isomorphism between signifier and signified is abandoned in the assertion of the primacy of the signifier. Signification, signifier, sign are all considered to be signifiers. It is here that we should locate the materiality of the signifier and not just at the phonemic level. This makes Lacan's ethics a "materialism" rather than an "idealism."

Fourth, with this, a search for meaning is displaced in favor of a questioning of truth, which is identified with the signifier. Lacan is not concerned with the meaning of desire or of the unconscious, but with truth as *aletheia*. Truth is articulated by way of the signifier, and at the same time, it is also the limit of articulation. Truth slides under the signifier, as is indicated by the presence of the bar in Lacan's schemas for the four discourses where the position of truth is shown to be below the bar separating truth from agency. As discussed in an earlier essay, one of the consequences of this is to show that truth is a lie, what can only be half-said *(mi-dire)*.[17] In these ways, Freudian psychoanalysis marks "the return of truth to the field of science at the same time as it comes to the fore in the field of its praxis—repressed, it reappears there."[18] It is in terms of propositions such as these that Lacan develops an ethical and political discourse that avoids all essentialism, the assertion of an ultimate and abiding conceptual substance above and beyond language, as one finds in the ethical-political discourses of Plato and Aristotle. For Lacan, there is rather a permanent sliding of the signified, whether it is Truth or the Good, under the signifier.

Let us turn now to Lacan's "sliding" use of the term *jouissance*. It is in terms of *jouissance*—and in *Seminar VII*, what he calls the "Thing" (*das Ding*, a term he uses to designate a hole in the symbolic order and the impossible object-cause of desire, and which he later replaced with the *mathème objet petit a*)—that Lacan's ethics tends "more deeply into the real." *Jouissance* is an immensely complicated and varied topic in Lacan's seminars, so I will limit my discussion to the connotations of this term as they apply to our comparison of Lacan and Aristotle.

One of the first topics to emerge in Lacan's seminar entitled *The Ethics of Psychoanalysis* is pleasure. Pleasure is certainly an important issue in Aristotle's ethics. While *eudaimonia*, the ethical Good, is certainly pleasurable, it is not to be identified with pleasure. So, first, what is the relationship of *jouissance* and pleasure in Lacan's seminars?

Following Freud in this regard, pleasure, for Lacan, is not a feeling, but a principle. As such, it is tied to another principle, the Freudian "reality principle." In Freud's *Interpretation of Dreams* (1900), pleasure is identified with the symbolic order (once again, this is its fictitious bearing) and so with a law that seeks to limit pleasure. The pleasure principle thus becomes the "unpleasure principle" insofar as pleasure always seeks to maintain a state of balance or homeostasis. Pleasure's principle is to maintain a lower, more comfortable level of excitation (S2: 79–80). Unpleasure, pain, marks the rise in the level of excitation to the point where pleasure becomes too much and so turns into its seeming opposite, pain. Pleasure is thus, a "restitutive tendency" (S2: 79–80). *Jouissance* is this limit-figure or beyond of pleasure. It is even opposed to pleasure, and so to desire. *Jouissance* goes beyond the "pleasure principle." Still following Freud, Lacan also links both pleasure and *jouissance* to repetition, the figure of the return, and so to the death drive, the "repetitive tendency," and to all else that not only is the secret beauty and the mystery of life, but also what ultimately "goes against life" (S17: 45/51).

In his *Ethics of Psychoanalysis*, Lacan articulates a notion of *jouissance* that applies to the individual much in the way *eudaimonia* concerned the individual in Aristotle's ethics. But, Lacanian *jouissance* seems the other, far side of the Aristotelian *eudaimonia*. *Jouissance* is what *eudaimonia* must resist and refuse. Chiefly, the difference lies in this: For Aristotle, the ethical-political subject is ultimately but a conscious being consciously seeking pleasure in moderation, whereas for Lacan, the horizon of ethical and political thought is the Freudian discovery of the unconscious, especially as it intersects with structural linguistics. Pleasure, taken to be a "principle" by Lacan, is thus rooted in deeper structures of the unconscious and is not restricted to feelings or sensations.

But Lacan and Aristotle share a common concern for the relation between discourse, desire, and the moral-ethical law by which pleasure is contained, limited, or excluded altogether. The Aristotelian discourse of the master, the wise man (the *phronismos*), can help to shape and to bring about a change in life through the education and formation of desire. Lacan calls this the "hygiene of desire." The master's words provide the student with the arguments and counsels persuading him that the life of ethical and political justice is the right one. Coupled, as this must be, with good starting points and diligent practice, *ethos*, or habit, on the part of the "hearer," desire is thereby discursively defined and thus inclined toward the Good, qua rational *eudaimonia*. The words of the master seek to inform, to contain, and so to bring about the good government of desire, which is first encountered as a biological force identified with appetite and *eros*. Thus, in accordance with the guidelines laid down by the dominant notion of the "proper function" of a human being, the moderation of desire is enacted.

At first sight, this task of the philosopher bears comparison to the work of the analyst. Indeed, Lacan calls Socrates the first analyst. Like the philosopher's discourse, through nothing but words, the analyst also brings about a change in the suffering condition of the patient, the analysand, such that the fantasies or symptoms that were blocking the patient's life and causing suffering and frustration, could unravel and fall away. The discourse of analysis, which is nothing but talk, really, thus brings about an effect, a change in the way a patient lives. But this change is structural. Yet, it is something a patient cannot do on his/her own. Self-analysis never works. So, the problem confronted by Aristotle and Lacan alike is that of the relation of language and law to desire and to *jouissance*. How can speech, either the arguments of the ethicist or the discourse of analysis, shape and have an effect on human souls? What happens here such that desire submits itself to moral-ethical law? For Aristotle, the words are those of the master, the *orthos logos*. He lectures, the hearers listen.

His words, coupled with proper habits, *hexis*, on the part of the hearer, guide the latter toward the proper formation of desire. For Lacanian psychoanalysis, the situation is reversed. The patient speaks. The analyst mostly listens. Since desire is already structured like a language, the effect of the talking cure does not seek to contain, shape, and govern desire but rather to alter the very structure desire takes in an individual patient and that causes him/her to suffer. Accordingly, the Lacanian intervention is at another level, that of the unconscious. Persuasion, rhetoric, does not play a role since it is the patient who does the talking, not the analyst, though he may be taken to be the "one who knows." It is only through the other, through the patient's relation with the analyst, that language can have an effect. Éric Laurent thus describes the psychoanalytic act as involving two partners, the analyst and analysand. The latter speaks about his suffering, his symptom, which "is hooked into the materiality of the unconscious, made out of things that have been said to him, that have hurt him and that are impossible to say and so cause him suffering." The analyst punctuates what the analysand says and allows him "to weave the thread of his unconscious." The powers of language and its truth effects are thus called "interpretation," which is the actual power of the unconscious. Interpretation works on both sides, that of the analyst and the analysand, although each of these two sides has a different relationship to the unconscious.[19] The crucial dimensions of the unconscious, of fantasy, and of the transference between analyst and analysand at work in the analytic act are all understandably missing in Aristotle's account of the relation between the *phronismos*, the man of practical wisdom, and his interlocutor. So, Lacan's conception of the analytic act may well be taken as supplementing the classical relation between the classical philosopher of ethics and his interlocutor(s).

Thus, where the Aristotelian ideal of *eudaimonia* connoted a unity and justice of the soul (with the soul being defined as the animating principle of life), and the completion, realization, and actualization of life, Lacan spoke instead of a divided subject, divided between conscious and unconscious registers. And where Aristotle would thus link *eudaimonia* strictly with conscious desire and the objects of such desire, the desire for health, wealth, and wisdom, for example, Lacan articulates a concept of *jouissance* that is closer to the drives where it is not the attainment of the object that counts, but rather missing the object and circling around it. Unlike Aristotelian *eudaimonia*, Lacanian *jouissance* is divided or distributed between conscious and unconscious levels. As suggested by Jacques-Alain Miller in a 1993–1994 seminar entitled "Donc," and in his "The Sinthome, a Mixture of Symptom and Fantasy,"[20] it seems there are two subjects operative in Lacan's seminars, a subject of the signifier and a subject of *jouissance*,[21] a distinction that parallels the distinction between the subject of the statement and the subject of the enunciation, or the diremption between thought, qua discourse, and being. The subject of *jouissance* would have to be a mythical subject. It has its counterpart not in the signifier but in the void. The subject of *jouissance* is the subject of what, for lack of a better word, one might call a "complete" *jouissance*, as in the *jouissance* of the primal unity with the mother, that the great, mythic, and amorphous *jouissance* that briefly obtained only to be cut off by the intervention of the symbolic and the consequent dividing (barring) of the subject in its dolorous ascension to being as a desiring subject defined by lack. As such, the subject of *jouissance* becomes something of a lost subject, the subject of a lost fullness of *jouissance* that, however sought, can never be restored except in and through fantasy. Nothing more than a metaphor for such lost plenitude and unity, fantasy is a lost unity redeemed only to be lost again in its very redemption. This situates the analytic experience in terms of what Lacan calls "a deeper meaning of action," something he is also tempted to call the tragic sense of life, a tragic dimension that is also comedic and so set apart, or set at a distance from the more serious and pedagogical horizons of Aristotle's ethics. This "space of tragedy" functions in the direction of the triumph of death, Lacan says. Thus, it also describes the diremptive dimensions of the life of a subject supported by the signifier (S7: 313).

But, again, *jouissance* is a crucial link between the ethics and the politics of psychoanalysis, just as *eudaimonia* was for Aristotle a link between ethics and politics. This is well established over the course of Lacan's seminars from the late 1950s through the early 1970s. There are two basic stages to this relation between the ethics and politics of *jouissance* for us to consider.

First, in Lacan's seventh seminar (1959–1960), entitled *The Ethics of Psychoanalysis*, there seems little place for politics because *jouissance* is transgressive, situated in terms of a brutal violation of the symbolic order, a kind of absolute access to the real and so as a transgressive, sovereign outside or beyond of the autonomous symbolic order. As exemplified in the image of Sophocles' *Antigone*, *jouissance* is a singularly destructive and sacrificial act, but seems at first sight to remain an individual, ethical act and not a political one.

Why is it not political? Structurally, this is because of the way at this stage in his seminars Lacan positioned and conceived the relationship between *jouissance* and the symbolic order in terms of transgression.

As exemplified by Antigone's act, an act that "refuses to give way on its desire," as Lacan would say, the ethical subject is thus rare, formed by a violent breach. It is, thus, not a common but an exceptional individual, so not ostensibly political. In the play, the character Antigone, qua ethical subject, is interpellated, called forth individually by the gods and by divine law, not by the common human voice of political law.

But, as Jacques-Alain Miller has shown,[22] there is a second stage in this development. In the later seminars, in *Seminar XVII*, for example, the relationship between *jouissance* and the symbolic order changes. Here, Lacan scorns the word "transgression," calling it "lewd." By the 1970s, in *Seminar XX*, *jouissance* is identified with the signifier, with the body of the letter. Lacan calls this *jouissance* a "*dit*-mension of the body in the speaking being . . . where it speaks, it enjoys." This is also the *dit*-mension of the unconscious, a *jouissance* of the unconscious. "The unconscious," Lacan says, in an apparent reversal of his earlier proposition, "is the not the fact that being thinks . . . the unconscious is the fact that being, by speaking, enjoys, and . . . wants to know nothing more about it at all" (S20: 105/96). There are multiple plays in *Encore* on this *dit*-mension: "*dit*-mension," *dit* (said) from the French *dire* (to say); also linked with *Dimanche*, Sunday, day of leisure and of what, according to Lacan, Kojève called the completion of absolute knowledge, and so a kind of holiday, Hegel's holiday, which puts him on "the winning side," *du côté du manche*. Insofar as it is *mi-dire*, half-said, it is not only the side of *jouissance*, but also the side of truth, which Lacan defines as the subject (S) of the divided Other (A, *Autre*, barred), the Other as lack.[23]

Let us now sketch the migrations of Lacan's thought on *jouissance* through these two general stages of his seminars, and see how by *Seminar XVII* (1969–1970), the articulation of *jouissance* had been significantly transformed from what it was in the days of *Seminar VII* (1959–1960).

Throughout the seminars, Lacanian *jouissance* can refer to the extremes of sexual pleasure and desire, with connotations of orgasmic fullness and masturbatory pleasure. But *jouissance* is also opposed to pleasure in the sense of going beyond the pleasure principle. *Jouissance* is pleasure mingled with pain, and so it constitutes a necessarily rejected "beyond" of the pleasure principle. In this sense, *jouissance* might be compared to the Freudian notion of the libido. *Jouissance* is here identified with a unity and fullness of being that however impossible to achieve, nonetheless remains an object-cause of desire and so the basis of fantasy.

But, *jouissance* is not restricted to these sexual-biological dimensions. It can also be located at the level of the body of the signifier, as in *Seminar XX*, where the signifier "is situated at the level of enjoying substance (*substance jouissance*)," the *dit*-mension. But, even though he often utilizes Aristotle's vocabulary, there are differences between his use of this vocabulary and Aristotle's. Lacan's use of the term "substance," for example, refers to form as structure, as in structural linguistics. This only remotely compares with the notion of substance in Aristotle's ethics, where substance (*ousia*) would be spoken of in terms of form as *ousia* and of the *eudaimonia* of the soul as *energeia* and *entelechia*. This is the language of potency and act, which is certainly missing in Lacan. *Jouissance* is not actualization of a potentiality (See S20: 24/27). In *Seminar XX* (1972–1973), the signifier is the cause of *jouissance*, a material cause. Considered as a "final cause," the signifier brings *jouissance* to a halt. This is "the other pole" of the signifier, "its stopping action (*coup d'arrêt*) and it is there (*est là*) at the origin of the signifier as it is in the direct address of the moral command" (S20: 24/27).

Seminar VII (1959–1960), where *jouissance* is identified with the path toward death, foreshadows Lacan's notion of the death drive, which he insists also obtains at the level of the symbolic order. This thematic continues into *Seminar XVII* (S17: 18/18), where Lacan also speaks of the death drive in connection with repetition and the symbolic order. Quoting an eighteenth-century French doctor, Marie Francois Xavier Bichat, Lacan says in this text that life is "the totality of forces that resists death." Thus, Lacan implores us to

> read what Freud says about life's resistance to the decline into Nirvana (death, the zero point of excitations), as the death drive was otherwise described at the time he introduced it. No doubt, at the heart of analytic experience, which is an experience of discourse (and not biology), he gives thought to this decline toward a return to the inanimate. . . . What is this, if not the true sense to what we find in the notion of instinct, which is that it implies knowledge?

But, as Lacan continues, this "ancestral knowledge" of life's deepest dimensions is what Freud calls a "beyond" of "the pleasure principle." It is what overturns the pleasure principle by which life maintains a state of equilibrium. This "ancestral knowledge" of the death drive "brings life to a halt at a certain limit on the path to *jouissance*. For the path toward death—this is what is at issue—it's a discourse—the path toward death is nothing other than what is called *jouissance*" (S17: 18/18).

In *Seminar XX*, Lacan speaks of a "phallic *jouissance*," the *jouissance* of the phallic part of the body. But phallic *jouissance* also has "*another* satisfaction," the "satisfaction of speech," a *jouissance* of the word. This is certainly active in Aristotle's *Ethics* and in the words, counsels, and speeches of the master to his "hearers." In Lacan, this is the satisfaction that links *jouissance* to a slippage in a chain of signifiers stretching from *jouissance* to justice. Through a play of metaphor, the signifier *jouissance* slides off the tongue of speech to form new constellations and correspondences. Phallic *jouissance* is the *jouissance* of the "just enough" and of "justice," which further links it with Aristotle and his "notion of justice," and from there to the "just barely (*justesse*)." Lacan: "This already justifies what Aristotle contributes with the notion of justice as the bare mean (*le juste milieu*), [and] the barely successful (*réussite de justesse*)" (S20: 64/61). This play of phallic *jouissance* and its "other satisfaction" justifies in Lacan's view the presence of Aristotle's texts at Lacan's seminars.

But why is this "phallic"? Certainly, as was just pointed out, the articulation tends to follow Freud, for whom there is only one libido, and that is a masculine, phallic libido. But it is more to the point to say that *jouissance* is here essentially tied with the phallic function in language, the alienation brought about by castration and language, the renouncement of a primary, unspeakable *jouissance*, that of the mother, the renouncement of the one who one makes demands, the mother who gives orders and who thereby establishes the child's dependence, and so the one who becomes the "privileged site of prohibitions." Renouncement, castration, in other words, is the essential factor in the formation of subjectivity and the necessary assumption of one's place in the symbolic order. This is its phallic dimension and the grounds of sexual difference: unlike "woman," "man," the "virile" male is "a creature of discourse" (S17: 55/62). Thus, phallic *jouissance* is also a symbolic *jouissance*. It is in this space of speech, in this phallic *jouissance* that finds its satisfaction in the speech, the *dit*, of the master, as we find Aristotle's ethics and politics.

In addition to this, and thus contributing to the surplus of connotations for the term *jouissance*, Lacan evokes yet another *jouissance*, which he calls "feminine *jouissance*," a *jouissance* which, "up to now," has been but a crack, fault, or failure in phallic *jouissance*.

What is the relation of phallic and feminine *jouissance*? I discussed this in an earlier essay, but let me approach this question again from yet another angle.

Woman (*La femme*) is first of all a signifier "whose place it is indispensable to mark" and that "cannot be left empty" (S20: 73/68). But "Woman" is also something that cannot be talked about because "Woman" as such does not exist. "Woman" (*la*) is a signifier that is essential yet it "cannot signify anything" because there is no referent. " 'Woman' is not-whole" (S20: 73/68). Thus, "there is no woman except as something excluded by the nature of things, which is the nature of words (*Il n'y a de femme qu'exclue par la nature des choses qui est la nature des mots*)." So, nothing can be said about *La femme* (S20: 73/68). In her being "not-whole," her *jouissance*, when compared to phallic, sexual *jouissance*, is something "supplementary," and not merely "complementary" (S20: 73/68). That is to say that with regards to the phallus, "she" has a different relationship with the phallus, a "different way of keeping it for herself." "She" is not wholly within the phallic function, Lacan says, but that does not mean "she"—*elle*, who doesn't exist and who signifies nothing—is "not there at all." "She" is always something "more, (*en plus*)" (S20: 74/69). But this excess, this surplus, this supplement is not transgressive. Nor is it something "she" possesses. It is an *en plus* of *jouissance*, a *jouissance* of the body about which nothing can be known or said, and which therefore "puts us on the path of ex-istence," something that might well turn out to be the mystical path toward the "God-face" (S20: 77/71).

Where *jouissance* is sexual and so phallic, Lacan says *jouissance* "does not relate to the Other as such" (S20: 9/14), which would be to the Other as the heterological locus of the Other sex. The man, the speaking man, only thinks he approaches "woman." What he really approaches is his own fantasy of woman, object *a*, as Lacan calls it, the fantasy object by which he, the speaking man, actually fills in the loss constituent to his desire, by which he fills in or plugs up the yawning chasm of lack that breathes life into his own desire. Phallic *jouissance* is only about the phallus. But, in excess of this phallic and sexual *jouissance*, Lacan is saying in the later seminars, another *jouissance*, feminine *jouissance*, is announced precisely as the *jouissance* of the Other, the *jouissance* of the excluded. Feminine *jouissance* is hence said to be heterologically ineffable, suggesting that where the Other is not just the other sex but is rather the phallic order of speech and the law, it shall be excluded from this sense of the Other. Perhaps it is with feminine *jouissance* that a psychoanalytic ethic of speech would reach its limit, its impasse. Feminine *jouissance* is in a relation of exclusion from the "nature of things," which is the nature of words, because it is first of all somehow in excess of the phallus, being the supplement, the surplus in the phallic figure of the limit. At the limit: this would also place feminine *jouissance* at the infinite insofar as Lacan links the figure of the limit with the infinite, as in the case of a number, which has a limit and to that extent is infinite (S20: 8/14). As such, feminine *jouissance* is a *jouissance of* the Other, not a *jouissance in* relation to the Other. The words "feminine *jouissance*" then name the flow of a *jouissance* that up to now has only been experienced as the fault, the moment *sans-emploi* of the phallic, masculine *jouissance*, an ineffable moment that can be neither possessed nor known. Feminine *jouissance* thus marks the limits of language and knowledge and in this way is linked with the real and the unconscious.

Thus, an essential link with masquerade. Let's read a text from Lacan's *Seminar XVII*: "Woman lends herself to *jouissance* by daring the mask of repetition." (The death drive?) "She presents herself here as what she is, as the institution of masquerade." Then, Lacan adds, "She teaches her little one to parade." (But who is this "little one"? The little phallus yet to come? He can only hope to be what she, the M(O)ther, wants.) To continue reading Lacan, "She tends toward surplus *jouissance* because she, the woman, plunges her roots, like a flower, down into *jouissance* itself. The means of *jouissance* are open on the principle that he (the little one?) has renounced this closed, foreign *jouissance*, renounced the mother."[24] Phallic *jouissance* has as its shadow play, as its surplus, this little masked drama, the "institution of masquerade" in which "Woman" (*La femme*) "lends herself to *jouissance*." This lending is so as to train the little one to parade. A kind of orthopedics of desire, one could suppose, is enacted as she teaches her little one to parade. But the point is this: the way toward *jouissance*, phallic *jouissance*, the only *jouissance* that allows for "happiness," is through the M(O)ther, through the renunciation of the M(O)ther and through the renunciation of feminine *jouissance*. It's not just the prohibition against the mother on stage here, there is also her dominance; she is a mother who makes demands, gives orders, and reduces the child to dependency (S17: 78/89–90).

But this woman who gives the orders and trains her little one to parade is not the whole of feminine *jouissance*, for feminine *jouissance* is the *jouissance* of the not-whole, the *jouissance* of the signifier that "cannot signify anything." The problem is to prevent feminine *jouissance* from falling back into the whole, which is why it cannot be the complement (in the logical sense of this term) of phallic *jouissance*, for were it the complement rather than the supplement of phallic *jouissance*, it would, indeed, fall back into the whole (S20: 73/68). Preventing this "not-whole" from falling back into the whole is necessary if feminine *jouissance* is to continue in its essential task of being both the conditioning and the contesting supplement—that dangerous supplement—of phallic *jouissance*. The not-whole of feminine *jouissance* is essential for the wholeness promised at the horizon of phallic *jouissance*. The masked actions of "Woman" "lending herself to *jouissance*"—and the mask covers precisely this not-whole of the woman, the fact she is a signifier signifying nothing, an emptiness, a nullity, a crack or point of failure that supplements the order of phallic *jouissance*—are conditioned and directed by the phallic function, which is to forbid. To order, to forbid, dominance and mastery, these are essential dimensions of the ethical and political regimes of phallic *jouissance*. These are also regimes of "enjoyment." The masked "Woman" conditions the coming into being of the phallic function and its *jouissance*, as the text from *Seminar XVII* has suggested. The "daring of the mask" is essential to her motherly role in the child's ascension to phallic enjoyment. "Woman" moves by way of the mask and the masquerade. Feminine *jouissance* supplements and facilitates the lack introduced by castration, being the not-whole present only in and through the daring of the mask. This recalls how the "rending power of the negative," of death, is brought to presence and put to work in Hegel's dialectic only in and as masked, given form and a shape or configuration in the dialectic of Spirit. It is the mask that sets "Woman" apart as something excluded, but it is also what puts her to work opening the way toward *jouissance*, what allows and facilitates her role in relation to phallic *jouissance* as the woman who gives the orders and trains her little one to parade. Her part is thereby to enact the very renunciation necessary to the establishment of the regime of phallic *jouissance*. Phallic *jouissance* must pass by way of the M(O)ther, it must pass by way of the renunciation of feminine *jouissance* and endure her domination if it is to find its way toward "enjoyment," and it is phallic *jouissance* and phallic *jouissance* alone that allows for happiness defined as enjoyment. Feminine *jouissance*—the not-whole—in this regard is the *envers*, the other side of phallic *jouissance*. It is the conditioning supplement by which phallic *jouissance* arises and by which it achieves its illusory wholeness. It is the silence that makes possible the approaches of "the man who speaks." This means that feminine *jouissance* is not the transgression of phallic *jouissance* but its conditioning and disruptive supplement, the intimacy of the phallic that is also its extimacy.

Thus, the double economy of *jouissance*, of phallic and feminine *jouissance*, woven together in a single two-sided fabric, a single, but open texture, comes into view: one side phallic and linked with the letter and the prohibited union with the mother and so to an unspeakable supplement; the other side, a feminine *jouissance* "before the letter," identified with the *dit*-mension of an embodied masked drama at the edge of the symbolic, the real, and the imaginary. A double economy of *jouissance*, situated at the intersection of these topographic domains and opening infinitely. Feminine *jouissance*, in her political and ethical role, is both limit and the supplementary excess of limits. As such, it must itself be a double function, simultaneously the inside and the outside, the redemption and the reduction of phallic *jouissance*, the restoration of and resistance to a lost primal unity with the Mother. Feminine *jouissance* is thus something other than the desperate search for a transgressive *jouissance* that awaits on the impossible, forbidden other side of limits, the side of an Other with which there is no and can be no relation. Feminine *jouissance* is the other side of phallic *jouissance* in much the same way Lacan's discourse is the "other side of psychoanalysis."

Feminine *jouissance* thus essentially transforms the Lacanian concept of *jouissance* and its relation with the "real." Feminine *jouissance*, through the masquerade, is a newly articulated "encounter with the real." But this encounter is no longer carried on the back of transgression. The relation with truth is even more essential. The association of truth with "Woman," with the goddess Diana, recurs in these pages from the seventeenth seminar where truth is said to be the "dear little sister of *jouissance*" (S17: 174/203), situated between "us" and the real.

Just as it has with truth, so *jouissance* has an essential link with knowledge, especially "unconscious knowledge," the sort of knowledge the subject does not know that it knows, knowledge as a "means of *jouissance*." Although one can never know or salt the tail of the "bird of truth" of the unconscious, it can be enjoyed. *Jouissance*—feminine *jouissance*—can be the way one enjoys one's unconscious.

Whether concerning *jouissance* in its relations with the real, with truth, or with knowledge, it is the dimension and the *dit*-mensions of language, of discourse, that must again be emphasized. But where the earlier seminars so often discussed language in terms of structural linguistics and situated psychoanalysis in terms of this wider, more theoretical horizon, the seventeenth seminar narrows the focus somewhat and makes it at once more political by situating *jouissance* in terms of four specific discourses: mastery, knowledge, hysteria, and analysis. "We are beings," Lacan says, "born of surplus *jouissance*, as a result of the use of language . . . of language that uses us" (S17: 66/75). How is the subject—how is *jouissance*—inscribed in and "used by" the institutions of mastery, knowledge, hysteria, and psychoanalytic practice? The new political dimensions unleashed by the transformation of his conception of *jouissance* emphasize this link, this political link between discourse and *jouissance*. Access to the political passes only by way of *jouissance*, perhaps by way of the modes of exclusion and renunciation of feminine *jouissance*. As Lacan says in *Seminar XVII*, "The intrusion into the political can only be made by recognizing that the only discourse there is, and not just analytic discourse, is the discourse of *jouissance*, at least when one is hoping for the work of truth from it" (S17: 78).

Insofar as *jouissance* is situated in terms of the symbolic order itself, the being of signifiers, and with production, as an excess or remainder of production, Lacan's analysis in his seventeenth seminar develops further the role *jouissance* plays not only in the fantasies of the individual person, but in capitalism and contemporary life more generally. Lacan thus compares *jouissance*—the surplus of feminine *jouissance*—to the Marxian notion of a "surplus of value." For the lost unity, for renounced *jouissance*, a whole series of substitutions are made, which Lacan marks with the *mathème objet petit a*, whereby the gap introduced by renouncement is not so much totally closed, healed, or filled in, for this is impossible, as it is forgotten. "(T)he lack of forgetting is the same thing as the lack in being, since being is nothing other than forgetting," Lacan claims (S17: 52). Forgotten in the sense of "covered over," the gap ever re-opens, like an unsutured wound. Thus, the various object-causes of desire, the attainment of which never bring the satisfaction and the happiness they would seem to promise, can never be enough. This is a logic that is as social as it is individual. The lack—the not-whole—always remains. There is always a need for something more. Desire, defined not by biology but by the symbolic order, can thus still be articulated in terms of the plays of metaphor and metonymy. Thus, for this new stage of political and ethical thought that emerges with the seminars of the late 1960s, Lacan's teaching was a mode of resistance to and subversion of the political and economic fantasies that too readily and too easily promise a happiness that can never be realized, or that papers over the very real suffering of individuals in society that is always the dark underbelly of such "happiness."

Moving in this new direction whereby *jouissance* is increasingly situated in terms of discourse, and as the supplementary and surplus *dit*-mension of discourse, Lacan can also show how the philosophical discourses on ethics and politics are all essentially *phallic*. Their architecture is founded on the necessity of systematic exclusions, training, and discipline. Shall they not be likewise conditioned and subverted by the feminine? And what has Woman, masked woman, to say to this "little one," the philosopher? Could she train him/her to parade? Wouldn't feminine *jouissance* always fail in any dialogue with the philosopher, for she has nothing to say? Is the feminine *jouissance* not Lacan's anti-philosophy in yet another guise? For all these reasons and more, feminine *jouissance* in and as "supplement" and "surplus" never appears as such among the four discourses Lacan presents in *Seminar XVII*. How could it? It is non-discursive in the sense of being never said. It moves under the play of masks. But its role shall be stronger than ever. Indeed, this doubling of the phallic by the feminine in matters of *jouissance* introduces a political perspective, a new political *dit*-mension, that was not so clearly present before. From the standpoint of the seventh seminar, transgression led to the tomb. *Jouissance* threatened to congeal, its conceptual flows curdled and scabbed over by the sheer weight of the mortifying drama of transgression. In the later seminars, there seems a new dynamic, lighter, more intangible and elusive, more akin to the movements of a dancer across a wider stage. The ponderous impasse encountered in *Seminar VII* gives way to a new, more verbally playful way of diagramming the levels and labyrinths of human desire. A fourfold discourse is introduced, a schema ever open to new readings and interpretations, ever new ways of articulation and adjustment. And whence the "measure of Man" that once was taken in terms of the fourfold relation of gods and men, earth and sky? It now becomes a measure taken in new ways of spanning the world-forming discourses of mastery and subjection, of knowledge and love, of the hysteric and the analyst. This second stage of Lacan's thought is developed at length in *Seminar XVII, The Other Side of Psychoanalysis* (1970).

THE FOUR DISCOURSES

Lacan's "four discourses" show four different but interrelated ways in which discourse dominates society. The four discourses are thus the discourse of the Master, the University, the Hysteric, and the Analyst. These are the discourses for what Freud called the three "impossible professions" (Lacan, S17) of modern life: to govern, to educate, and to psychoanalyze (i.e., "to cure") (*regieren, erziehen, kurieren*) (S17: 166/193). The discourse of the hysteric, meanwhile, may be said to be the discourse of desire and protest, the discourse that is always saying, "This is not it, no, this is not it." Since Lacan says it is always seeking a master, it is the discourse that produces the discourse of the master. As one commentator phrases it, these four discourses are the way "Lacan demonstrates how differently structured discourses mobilize, order, repress, and produce four key psychological factors—knowledge/belief, values/ideals, self-division/alienation, and *jouissance*/enjoyment—in ways that produce the four fundamental social effects of educating/indoctrinating, governing/brain washing, desiring/protesting, and analyzing/revolutionizing."[25] This summary has the merit of also emphasizing how these four discourses show the ethical-political links between the individual-ethical dimension and the political dimensions of society. Understanding the basic schemas for these four discourses will help us to see how Lacan situates *jouissance* at this stage of his ethic of *jouissance*, whereby *jouissance* is no longer strictly identified with the heroic transgression of the law and as access to the Thing (*das Ding*) and to the unspeakable Real.

Thus, there are four positions for each of the four discourses and four terms: S_1, S_2, S barred, and object *a* (*objet petit a*). The basic four positions name functions:

Agent	Other/work		S_1	S_2
$\rightarrow$			$\rightarrow$	
Truth	Production		S barred	*a*

Before going any further, Lacan's remark from *Seminar XX* (1972–1973) should be cited: It was not in vain, he says, "that I came up with the inscriptions (*l'écriture*) *a*, the barred S signifier. . . . Their very writing constitutes a medium (*support*) that goes beyond speech, without going beyond language's actual effects" (S20: 93/86).

The left-hand side of the inscription is being qua the subject speaking or sending a message, hence, the direction of the arrow. The right-hand side is that of the Other, of work and of meaning, and so marks the position the subject receiving the message must assume.

Filling in these slots with the terms of the master discourse, at the top two positions, those above the bar, we have S_1, the master signifier, on the left, and S_2, the string of signifiers, discourse, on the right. S_1 is the unary master signifier, which here occupies the position of the agent. S_2 is also said to occupy the position of the slave, so the master-slave relationship is here symbolized as a relation between different polarities of a single discourse, as Hegel himself showed, rather than as existential, extra-discursive moments. The master discourse is thus a discourse of power, it is the discursive structure of power and of conflict. Moreover, Lacan says, "there is no better way to pin down the master signifier, S_1 . . . than by identifying it with death" (S17: 170/198), with the "visiting card [of death] by which a signifier represents a subject for another signifier" (S17: 180/209).

A master signifier (S_1) is any signifier—it could be the phallus, or the Name-of-the-Father (*le nom du père and le 'non' de père*), the dead father, "who keeps *jouissance* in reserve" (S17: 123/143), or just a word, or a part of a word, a phonemic element, even the shine on a woman's nose, it could be something completely nonsensical—any signifier that, at the psychological level, plays a dominant role in establishing the subject's primary position of identity. At the ethical, social, and political levels, the master signifiers are important not only for the way they structure the identity and direction of the subject but for the way they "dominate and govern anything that any given moment is capable of emerging as speech" (see S17: 166/194). They thus dominate, anchor, and justify claims and demands of the political and ethical message. The master signifier is taken by those receiving its ethical and political message as a value beyond question, a value that "goes without saying." Such signifiers might be the Good, Happiness, Freedom, Capital, and so on.[26]

The master signifier is always something repeated, insisted upon in the sense that "repetition is fundamentally the insistence of speech," hence, its connection with the death drive (S3: 242). A patient, for example, may be constantly repeating the same word, making the same reference, or gesture, repeating it, insisting upon it, always returning to it; or the patient's discourse may halt before such signifiers as though the master signifier marks blockage. The patient cannot get around this so keeps returning to it over and over again. The work of analysis is to break this blockage so that the patient can "get on with his/her life." As a unary signifier, or unary trait (*trait unaire*), the master signifier is the "simplest form of mark," the "origin of the signifier," and "the means of *jouissance*" (S17: 46–49/52–54). In the diagram developed in *Seminar XI*, S_1 would be situated in the overlap between Being, the domain of S barred, and "Meaning," that is, "the Other" (see S11: 211). Lacan's diagram shows this overlap to be a dimension of non-meaning. For there to be meaning, there must be a linkage that Lacan calls the articulation of the master signifier with the chain of other, secondary signifiers $(S_1–S_2)$, whereby S2 then becomes identified with knowledge.

The teaching of *Seminar XVII* is that *jouissance* is thus identified with the point of inscription of the signifier. In his earlier seminars, Lacan conceived the symbolic order as autonomous and self-contained and *jouissance* was opposed to it. But, with *Seminar XVII*, the signifying chain inscribes, articulates the barred subject, insofar as it conveys truth, death, and desire, but, most importantly, it conveys *jouissance*.[27]

This is important for what I've been calling the second stage of Lacan's ethical-political *jouissance* because it shows once again that *jouissance* is here identified with language, with the signifier, rather than as a transgressive, sacrificial excess or beyond of the symbolic order. Identified with repetition and the unconscious, it is also linked with the real, defined as what does not deceive and what always returns to the same place. Reality is deceptive. It misleads and deceives. But the real always returns to the same place. The repetition of *jouissance* is in this return of the real. A few years later, in *Seminar XX*, Lacan says this is a *jouissance* that "shouldn't be/could never fail (*qu'il ne faudrait pas*)—in the conditional tense" (S20: 59/56). Not phallic *jouissance*, Lacan says, "were there another *jouissance* than phallic *jouissance*, it shouldn't be/could never fail to be that one" (S20: 59/56). This "other one," impossible from the outset because "there is no other than phallic *jouissance*" (S20: 60/56), is "the one that makes (woman) not-whole"; it is "feminine *jouissance*."

Although the master signifier is crucial for establishing a subject's identity as a speaking being, this cannot occur until it is articulated into the symbolic order. S_1 must link with S_2 for the subject to "open," to attain the level of a human being, that is to say, a speaking being. In Lacan's phrasing, this is to accept castration. And, since there is an open number of ways in which this articulation can occur, unique to each individual, there is a balance in Lacan's analysis between the claims of the universalism of structure and the pluralism of articulations. In any event, the master signifier is the signifier for a subject, shown below the bar, as the subject of the unconsciousness, a divided, castrated subject. It is a subject barred. It is never presented, "never in the present," but is only represented by a signifier for another signifier.[28] Again, it is only as an effect of the link, the "altogether initial one between S_1 and S_2," that this "fault we call the subject" can open (S17: 88). It should also be noted here that the top left and right positions provide the basic structure for the subject of the statement (the enunciated), while the bottom two positions, that of S barred and object *a* exhibit the unconscious structure for the subject of enunciation. Thus, the divided subject is the truth of the master signifier, and the master signifier is the agent for the divided subject by which that subject is represented for another signifier (S_2). It is also through S_1 that the "*défilés* of the signifier" (Lacan), S_2, can gain purchase on the subject. But, as Lacan says, the subject represented by the master signifier is not univocal. It is represented, undoubtedly, but it is also not represented. At this level something remains hidden in relation to this very same signifier. Thus, the truth of the subject, the truth of the subject's desire, which is the truth of the unconscious, cannot be fully said, but only half-said (*mi-dire*), and is always the truth that is also a lie.

This structure of barred S in relation to meaning, S_2, mediated, or represented by S_1 that marks the initial lack whereby the subject is both represented and not represented by the master signifier, is the structure of alienation. An example illustrates the point: A subject may be identified by a master signifier such as "bad boy" (Éric Laurent's example).[29] Even though he may have other given names, "bad boy," which is perhaps what his mother or his father used to call him, is the master signifier around which his identity is anchored. That's what he is, a bad boy. But "bad boy" does not exhaust the subject. The subject is always more than a univocal "bad boy." There is thus always a degree of remainder, something lost, refused, set aside, from which the subject is alienated, insofar as representation by the signifier is never complete. Not all of the subject can be present in the Other of the symbolic order. The subject is alienated insofar as it is a speaking subject and must speak in order to make its demands and pursue its desires, which themselves have the linguistic structure of metaphor and metonymy, or of alienation and separation.[30] The inaccessible remainder, the inaccessible loss, the inaccessible *jouissance* is the *jouissance* of the real. Thus, the master signifiers are related not only to repetition and to *jouissance* but also to death, the absolute master.

The lower level is the structure of separation, the level of the divided subject in relation to object *a*. Here, there is another level of loss and lack. Object *a*, which in the master's discourse occupies the position of production, marks the lack and loss produced by inscription of the subject in discourse, the symbolic order, the big Other. Thus, *Seminar XI* sees the spool and its cotton thread deployed in the game of the reiterated *fort-da* Freud's grandson played whenever his mother left him alone as a striking instance of object *a* operating at the level of separation. Here, it marks not only the primacy and emergence of signification, but also the primacy of the gulf, the gap, the "ditch" opened by the separation from and the absence of the mother. One can only "play at jumping across this ditch" separating the child from the mother, and this is where the play of the spool and its thread come in. As object *a*, the spool and its thread, repetitively thrown in a centrifugal arc when the mother is gone, is not just an image of the mother reduced to a little ball, but is a "small part of the subject," Lacan says, "that detached itself from him while remaining his" (S11: 62). Deployment of the spool makes up for her disappearance by making him, the grandson, and his spool the agents of it; he also expects her return through the repetition of the *fort-da*. And, Lacan adds, that this is to say, "in imitation of Aristotle, that man thinks with his object." The signifier marks the emergence of the subject and his body, and that it "is in the object to which the opposition is applied in act, the spool, that we must designate the subject." This "object" is thus object *a* (S11: 62).

With *jouissance* and repetition, with the *jouissance* that always seeks repetition and always seeks to return to the same place, with this repetition, there is also a loss of *jouissance*; there is entropy. "And," Lacan says, "it is in the place of this loss introduced by repetition that we see the function of the lost object emerge, of what I am calling the *a*" (S20: 48). This is also the structure of fantasy that brings *jouissance*: The divided subject in relation to the *lost object*, always seeking its return, and the subject of the drive in relation to object *a* as the site of an *absolute loss*. I will return to this shortly.

This is where we should mark the pertinence of Aristophanes' myth of the origins of love, recounted in Plato's *Symposium* as being the search for one's lost "other half." And, by extension, this desire for completion could also characterize the Aristotelian ethic and its Good qua *eudaimonia*, defined as the teleological object of desire, the realization of the unity and wholeness of ethical-political life, which would have to include friendship, and a love qua *philia*, for the friend as not just the other half, but as "another self." In both cases, as far as Lacan is concerned, we are working at the level of the imaginary. But the difference, for Lacan, is that where the Aristophanic lover searches for his/her other half as one's *sexual* other half, Lacan's notion of separation and the symbolically defined structure of fantasy shows the subject's search to be "for that part of himself lost forever," a part "constituted by the fact that he is only a sexed being, and that he is no longer immortal" (S11: 205). In this sense, object *a* is the object-cause of desire, and arises with castration and inscription in the symbolic order.

Regarding the position of *jouissance* in the master's discourse, it can be seen from the diagram that *jouissance* is positioned as object *a* on the lower right-hand side of the schema at the level of production. It has "castled" (Miller's word), it has taken the same place, as S_1, the unary trait, in the master's discourse. *Jouissance*, meanwhile, is both produced and at the same time expended if not excluded altogether by the master's discourse on the grounds that it represents a loss and a surplus; thus *jouissance* becomes surplus *jouissance*, *plus-de-jouir*. *Seminar XVII* thus links it with the function of surplus value in Marx.

Here is the root of the surplus of *jouissance* produced in capitalistic societies. *Seminar XVII* says that work does not produce knowledge. Rather, work, like the "master discourse," precisely in and through its necessary avoidance of "absolute *jouissance*," produces a surplus of *jouissance*. There is something like a thermodynamics at work here. Lacan describes the master signifiers as the place from which "discourse is ordered." It is the

place or position from which "the dominant is issued." It is the place of
"the Good," or the place of "the law" (*la loi*) first in the sense of something articulated, the law as signifier, as structure of *jouissance*, the law
that constitutes the law in another sense as *le droit*, in the sense of duty,
rights, and law" (S17: 43). It is around and toward (*pros hen*) the master
signifier that the Aristotelian ethic is organized and projected. Now this
position of the dominant, this position of the law (*la loi*), in the master
discourse also blocks and rejects *jouissance*, damming it up, so to speak.
This rejection is an effect of discourse. In doing so, in damming up *jouissance*, it produces a residue, a surplus, a dynamic, which is productive of
further signifiers, thus making it a surplus that propels the repetition of
jouissance and so links it with disruption and death. The energetics of the
blockage or resistance is productive of the surplus. It is here that we see
"object *a* (*l'objet petit a*) emerge, which we have nailed down as surplus
jouissance" (S17: 79/91). This is also Lacan's theory, derived from Marx,
of the accumulation of capital. He goes on to expand his illustration of
this "thermodynamics" of the master signifier: " 'S$_1$' [the master signifier
in the master's discourse], is the dam. The second 'S' is the pond that
receives it and turns the turbine. There is no other meaning to the con-
servation of energy than this mark of an instrumentation that signifies the
power of the master" (S17: 80/92). Once a higher level has been passed,
surplus *jouissance* is no longer simply surplus, something leftover, but is
reinscribed as a value in the totality of whatever it is that is accumulating
from out of an essentially transformed nature. What Marx denounces in
surplus value is the spoliation of *jouissance*. And yet, this surplus value
is a memorial to surplus *jouissance*, the equivalent of surplus *jouissance*.

This links the *jouissance* of the libido with "contemporary life" qua
consumer society, wherein *jouissance*, as metaphor for the lost, ruinous,
and renounced *jouissance*, is dribbled out like chocolates from a sampler
box, "petty trifles," "little bits of *jouissance*" that Lacan calls *lichettes* (S17:
108/124; the English translation of the text uses the word "morsels,"
but *lichettes* might also mean "little licks," from *licher*, to lick).[31] Lacan:
" 'Consumer society' derives its meaning from the fact that what makes it
the 'element' . . . described as human is made the homogenous equivalent
of whatever surplus *jouissance* is produced by our industry—an imitation
surplus *jouissance*, in a word. Moreover, that can catch on. One can do
a semblance of surplus *jouissance*—it draws quite a crowd" (S17: 81/93).

The work of the master's discourse at S$_2$ thus produces *jouissance*
qua excess, qua surplus. This surplus, or anything else that might have
once traumatized or threatened the stability and smooth operation of

the system productive of goods and values, is continuously reinvested back into that system and so returned to us, the consumer of values and goods, in a new form, one now quantified and bearing new commercial values. The surplus of *jouissance* thus takes on a variety of new metaphorical, substitutional formats that seek to plug the gaps opened in the symbolic order, and in doing so, only ends up insisting upon those gaps and so further propelling desire like the turn of a turbine. What was once disruptive comes back as an ingredient in trifles, as the new "life styles," whereby intoxication is rendered as "happiness you can drink" and the unspeakable, unknowable modulations of *jouissance* are made to speak in the general "blah-blah of satisfaction," as Lacan calls it. *Jouissance* is thus reduced to being the happiness of having the newest and next best thing, the signs of success, "a status symbol," a material fantasy offered for sale in the fantasmagoria of capitalism. This does indeed "draw quite a crowd." But this system, productive of surplus, also seems to entail entropy and loss, and it is at the point of loss that we have access to *jouissance*, as Lacan explains in *Seminar XVII*. "Knowledge produces entropy," he says, "the dimension of entropy gives body to the fact that there is surplus *jouissance* to be recovered. . . . This entropy, this point of loss, is the sole point . . . at which we have access to the nature of *jouissance*" (S17: 49–50). One might also speak of this whole process as the hidden death drive of capitalism. No wonder it draws quite a crowd. Nothing is more fascinating than death. Is this, indeed, the modern masquerade of *jouissance* qua commercialized *eudaimonia*?

Object *a*, identified as the object-cause of desire and as *jouissance*, fills in for the refused, lost, and ruinous *jouissance* of the real spoken of earlier. It is perhaps another route by which *jouissance* is both approached and reproached. In fact, object *a* marks what cannot be attained by either desire or the drives. The drives circle around it, an image of the eternal return. In the two-circle Venn diagram used by Jacques-Alain Miller to show the structure of separation, object *a* marking a lack, the lack of the desire of the Other, is positioned in the same place the master, unary signifier, S_1, occupied in the structure of alienation, that is to say, precisely at the overlap between the Subject and the Other, with the signifying chain S_1—S_2 being positioned in the zone of the Other. Here, object *a* is located in the fantasy that brings *jouissance* (barred S in relation to *a*) and shown to be clearly outside the sectors of the diagram containing the set of articulation, S_1—S_2. Where desire is desire of the Other, object *a* is the answer the subject gives to the question, "What does the Other want from me?" The subject can then even shape itself or condition itself such that it becomes this *a* that it believes the Other wants it to be. It thus assumes its role in the various and specific fantasies of the subject that bring *jouissance*.

In the analytic act of interpreting desire, the subject undergoes a traversal of fantasy such that the new resulting structure has object *a* in relation to the barred Subject. Thus, in the discourse of analysis, it is object *a* that takes the position of the agent, the dominant position of mastery. This is the position of the analyst and it is from there that new master signifiers are produced and desire unlocked and inscribed in a new way, with a resulting structural alteration in the barred subject, which is now in the position of the Other and the site of work. But, as one can see, the resulting structure is also the structure of the fantasy of perversion. The discourse of the analyst and the structure of perversion overlap.

This structure of the analytic act returns us to the question of the relation of ethics and politics in Lacan's seminars. At this stage of the seminars, what might constitute an ethical and a political act for Lacan? Just as ethics was a part of politics, for Aristotle, how is the ethical act embraced by the political in Lacan's teachings? What are the consequences of these teachings of the four discourses for Lacan's articulation of the ethical and political act(s)?

First, there is a way of seeing the ethical-political act as an act of contestation and "resistance," "resistance by logic," that opens a new way of being, perhaps a being in "fidelity to truth," as Badiou phrases it, a way of not "giving way" or "giving up" on desire, but which, in any case, Lacan situates in relation to the real and *jouissance*.

Seminar VII uses Antigone's act as the exemplar of such an ethical act qua transgression. Such an act would effectively break with the teleological horizon for the singularity and finitude of human desire traditionally named by the great signifiers of the Good, the True, and the Beautiful, toward the impossible infinite of the real. In this case, the ethical act is a sovereign, transgressive act as the opening, the traumatic tear in the law of the symbolic order, that point of excess and overflow that marks and inscribes the limits of the law. *Jouissance*, as access to the real, is here such a limit. Which is why Lacan, at least in *Seminar VII*, also seems to identify it with the death drive and with the double death that Antigone undergoes in transgressing the city's laws: her act brings not only a biological death, but also the death by transgression of the symbolic order. The ethical-political act is here a momentary affirmation and suspension of the power of the law, and radical reconfiguration of the city's symbolic order that Creon was determined to defend, the introduction of a gap in the city walls.

Yet, it isn't just the violence that stands out in her act. There is also the assumption of desire, a taking of a love and a truth to their limits, but always as the assumption of a responsibility. Herein lies the freedom of Antigone's act: not that it escapes the grip of necessity and establishes a new regime of events, but rather that it freely assumes the necessities that determined it. Freedom, like meaning, is thus retroactively constituted, a *point de capiton*, as Lacan would say, that punctures and punctuates the stream of necessities and conditions in which it was already embedded, suddenly giving it a sense, a freedom, as in the baleful moment of Antigone's act. This is thematic in all of the dramatic, tragic figures Lacan singles out at this stage of his seminars as exemplars of the ethical act: Antigone, certainly, but also Oedipus, Lear, Hamlet, Sygne. As tragedies, these are not just plays that dramatize the character as gripped by implacable fate, for they freely pursue and assume responsibility for the necessity of the chaos they bring into the world, and it is only in the freedom of their act that the cruelty of their fate is revealed in its structural articulation.

But is there an ethical-political act in terms of the model of the traversal of fantasy? In this case, we turn to *Seminar XVII*, where we see that Lacan defined ethics in a new way whereby "act" is distinguished from "action," from *actionnaire*, and from *activiste* (S17: 125/146). Here, there can only be an act, Lacan says, "in a context *replete* [my emphasis] with everything involving the signifier's effect" (S20: 125/146). The "ethical act" is thus distinguished not in terms of the categories of pre-symbolic decisions or in terms of a choice of means whereby an ideal and one's human "being" could be realized in the highest sense of its functions, but rather in terms of a total transformation of one's being. This would be an act that opens the "replete" of the signifier, and in so doing, effects a structural transformation of desire.

On these grounds, we can compare the act to perversion. Just as perversion is not defined by Lacan as an "act" in the sense of being an "aberration" in relation to social norms or "natural criteria," but as a "structure" (S1: 221), so the ethical act must also be thought also as a "structure." This is an unconditioned ethical act. It does not enter the world as an exemplary accordance of an individual action with moral norms, whether that is the happiness of the individual or even what serves the well-being of the political community. Nor is its worth evaluated in terms of respect for moral law. Rather, it is a transformation of structure. Lacan's conception of the transformational ethical-psychoanalytic act might thus be comparable to the Nietzschean "transvaluation of all values." The ethical act at the center of Lacanian psychoanalysis is the transformation of the very framework of a subject's world experience, a revolutionary disturbance of the fantasmatic core of the structure of desire, a dislocation of the fantasmatic object-cause of desire. He calls this a "traversal of the fundamental fantasy" that structures desire and gives it its course.

The traversal of fantasy does not entail giving up one's illusions and getting back to reality. Instead, it is a deeper, more intimate confrontation with object *a* and its relation with the real and the truth of desire. A reversal of structure results in the subjectifying of object *a* as the object-cause of desire. But it must be noted that "to traverse" in this sense pertains only to what Lacan calls "the inverted ladder of desire," and not to the drive. On the "inverted ladder of desire," where desire is defined as desire of the Other, object *a* is part-object, a pure sign, a misrecognized effect or a metaphoric replacement for the primal lost object, and so, a route of return for *jouissance*. But as for the drive, which never attains its object but attains it only in missing it, object *a* is something radically less; it is loss itself; it is a "hole," a void around which the drive circles. Where "lack" is a spatial metaphor, Žižek suggests, "loss" is the collapse of space itself, a kind of black hole of the drive; not a void actually, but a hyper-density that absorbs everything. This is object *a* as pure loss.[32] It is thus a paradoxical hyper-density as loss. Thus, there is an inherent ambiguity in object *a* that must be taken into account in any discussion of the traversal of fantasy. It is one Lacan also spoke of in *Seminar VII* in connection with the beauty and splendor of Antigone: like beauty, object *a* is both lure and barrier to the real. Hence, it is in the traversal of fantasy that the ethics and politics of analysis enters more deeply into the real, as Lacan said was his purpose in *Seminar VII*, through taking object *a* as both lost object and as loss itself.

It must also be noted that before the traversal of the fantasy, the separated object *a* can become overpowering and opposing; the subject fades or undergoes what Lacan calls an "aphanisis" before it. One gives way, as Lacan's expression has it, on one's desire. Again, this obtains when object *a* is taken as both lure and barrier to the real. But when *a* is subjectified in the traversal, the subject assumes the object-cause of its desire. It thus assumes the lack and loss that it "is." To traverse is thereby to become what one "is."

Lacan's concept of the traversal of fantasy suggests that the political act can also take the form not of a violent revolutionary act, motivated, for example, by the eighteenth-century political ideology of Fraternity,

Liberty, and Equality, but as a critique of ideology itself and as a cultural criticism. What, in Lacanian terms, would this be?

First, the surprising possibility is that the "traversal of fantasy" could be said to be crucial to the very structure of modern commodity-culture democracy, whereby what were once merely the fantasmatic ideological object-causes of a political-hysterical desire for freedom, for self-determination and *eudaimonia*, for example, are no longer perceived as just fantasms, object-causes of political desire, but are now assumed and come to constitute the very political institutions of the agent-position of democratic political life. Antagonism, pluralism, and difference, crucial to democracy, are thus put in the position of object *a* qua traversed by the divided subject. As was suggested earlier, would this not place democratic commodity cultures as having the structure of perversion? Capitalism and democracy in their new globalized forms become not just a permanent revolution, but a permanent, ongoing traversal and resurrection of political fantasies, for only fantasy and its various modes of object *a* can constitute the kinds of transient consensus necessary for the functioning of "majority rule" in democratic and pluralistic societies in which the erstwhile coordinating master signifiers have been largely overturned or sharply devalued. The social link in today's capitalistic democracies is no longer the master signifiers but object *a*.[33]

But let us take this further by briefly considering what Lacan's teachings suggest for the task of ideology critique. Let us begin with the idea that ideology means more than "false consciousness" and deception, more than just not knowing the truth of reality because masking is not necessarily coupled with a process of unmasking. Ideological critique is not just correcting what we know. What must be seen is that ideological illusions do not always obtain on the side of knowledge, but rather on the side of what people are unconsciously doing. This is what the psychoanalytic critique can open up for us. Following Žižek here, ideology is thus a misrecognition on the part of the desiring subject of "its own effective conditions," a distance, a divergence between the so-called social reality and our distorted representations, our false consciousness of it. In other words, ideology plays the role of a fantasy in the discordance between the "what we are doing" and "what we think we are doing." As Karl Marx phrased it, "they do not know it, but they are doing it" ("*Sie wissen das nicht, aber sie tun es*").[34] These two levels might correspond to the levels of alienation and separation discussed earlier. "What we think we are doing" would be at the level of alienation, where we have the positions of agency and work, of the senders and receivers of messages, while what we are doing would correspond to the level of separation, where we have the positions of truth and production, of the barred subject and object *a*, the basic fantasy structure of the master discourse. Allow me to quote Žižek's examples: At the level of knowledge, one may well know that one's ideal of Freedom, that the freedom from hunger and ignorance, for example, may still mask or even require particular modes of exploitation, yet one continues to live by this ideal nonetheless. Or, in commodity exchange,

> when individuals use money, they know very well that there is nothing magical about it—money, in its materiality—is simply as an expression of social relations. The everyday spontaneous ideology reduces money to a simple sign giving the individual possessing it a right to a certain part of the social produce. So, on an everyday level the individuals know very well that there are relations between people behind the relations between things. The problem is that in their social activity itself, in what they are doing, they are acting as if money, in its material reality, is the immediate embodiment of wealth as such. They are fetishistic in practice, not in theory. What they "do not know," what they misrecognize, is the fact that in their social reality itself, in their social activity—in the act of commodity exchange—they are guided by the fetishistic illusion.[35]

Lacan's schemas from *Seminar XVII* thus enable us to see the political, social, and economic fantasies and fetishisms that guide and propel desire at the level of doing rather than just at the level of conceptual knowing. Thus, we are made aware of just how deeply such ideologies structure social reality. They do not remain subjective, conceptual, and interior, but also have an objective, intersubjective, and unconscious dimension that obtains at the level of doing and not just at the level of conscious knowing.

But, a more general question lingers: can the gap between what we think we are doing and what we are in fact doing ever be closed by the psychoanalytic critique? Does psychoanalytic discourse offer a way of resisting the political ideologies that generate not only socially stabilizing modes of enjoyment (*eudaimonia*), but also repression and mutilation? Would a subversion of the master signifiers of ideology, the signifiers of a utopian totalitarianism, for example, where antagonism, negativity, and pluralism are repulsed, ever suffice? Could it ever finish the job?

By looking again at Lacan's schemas, one can see that the analyst's discourse subverts the master signifiers by replacing them with object *a*, which now becomes an open space where nothing is asserted. But, this works an effect on the Other as a barred Subject, not as an individual but as liberal-democratic consumer society, with the effect being the production of new master signifiers: in the analyst's discourse, object *a* is in the position of the dominant agent, the barred Subject is in the position of the Other as interpellated receiver, and S_1 is in the position of production. Hence, the whole necessary process returns full circle as individual master signifiers are subverted but not the overall necessary role and position of master signifiers as such. They are produced anew. Moreover, give the analyst's discourse a counterclockwise quarter of a turn and you have the discourse of the hysteric, the divided subject that does not know what she wants, now occupying the position of the master who is always and endlessly seeking a new master signifier.

How can the subversion of the master signifiers in the political and social arena ever be completed? Is this even desirable? Is this the ethics and politics of psychoanalysis? Wouldn't Lacan's focus on the symbolic order limit any more direct political role psychoanalysis might play? Must it not resign itself to being but a mode of cultural-criticism rather than an agent of more direct politically subversive action? Is this ever enough? By this time, Lacan was becoming more and more skeptical about the possibilities of transgression and subversion as key forms of ethical and political action. Consistent with the logic of its dialectic, transgression illuminates and also strengthens the limits it crosses. In his view, while resistance to "mastery" and "subjection" of all kinds is necessary and even admirable, all too often it is also but the obverse, the "other side," of an insistence on the necessity of there being new masters. The icy distance he maintained with the noisy insolence of the activists, agitators, and revolutionaries who attended his seminars in the late 1960s and early 1970s resounds in something he said to them: "You are only looking for new masters, and you shall find them." But perhaps "mastery" itself had taken new forms and required new strategies. Mastery no longer prohibits. It has realized that success is better assured when "everything is permitted." So what new modalities of political action did Lacan envision? What was "subversion" to become for him?

By the 1970s, a second stage, as I am calling it, of ethical and political discourse emerged in Lacan's teaching. The model of *jouissance* as the transgression of prohibitions was changed. With the emerging globalization of capitalism and democracy and the student riots that accompanied the arrival of these phenomena, with the work stoppages and numerous other political-social crises that made up the atmosphere of the times, Lacan began to articulate subversion in new ways. With the cultural decline of the Oedipal paradigm whereby the subject was integrated into the paternal law and the symbolic order by way of castration, and with the rise of a culture that is already polymorphously perverse, a discourse of shame took on a new political edge in Lacan's later seminars.

Perhaps Lacan saw that psychoanalysis had no need of introducing perversion as the model for subversion, for we are already perverse. Perversion, whereby object *a* occupies the position of the agent in the schema of the four discourses, already stages the secret political-ethical fantasies that kick-start desire and sustain public discourse, with administered *bourgeois* life, the barred, divided Subject, being wholly interpellated by the daily capitalist commands "Enjoy Yourself!" "Seek Happiness!" This describes the post-political, post-ideological world of hedonistic consumerism.

Lacan's seminars from this period thus speak of shame. It seems the new purpose of the analytic discourse is to make its hearers feel shame in the midst of a shameless age. Lacan's teaching in the 1970s sought thereby not just to ironically restore a sense of honor for thinking and for the role and position of the master signifier, but also to make visible the horizon of a post-ideological age in which so many of the old master signifiers that had loomed large over all matters human were now missing, junked, or sharply discounted in the naked pursuit of power and gain in a consumerist society.

Shame is an effect of the master signifier; it is produced by what Lacan calls "the dominant position" of the signifier (S_1 in the "Discourse of the Master"). To speak in a way that must now seem old-fashioned and out-of-date, shame is produced in the subversion of the master signifier. By abandoning it, by placing oneself outside of the system organized around it, the systems of science and education, the university system, for example, such that one is no longer under its tutelage, no longer shaped by its master values of culture and knowledge, one's act could be seen by the gaze of the social order as something impudent and shameful. And insofar as shame is produced by the system's adherence to the master signifier, it, in some way, still belongs to it, is still captured by the gaze of the system, the obscene, shame-producing gaze of the Big Other, and so it becomes an act that is shameful.

But to update this and to say this is a shameless age is to say this is an age when the gaze of the Big Other has been eclipsed. It is an age of the twilight of the master signifiers, which is not to say that "everything is possible." For in an age and time when nothing is prohibited, nothing is permitted. There is no longer anything for which one deserves to die.[36] As Lacan told his audience in those shameless days (June 1970) of the student protests and upheavals at Vincennes, the "obscene" and "vain scene" of the University of Paris VIII campus, it is indeed unusual "to die of shame" (see S17: 180/209), to truly undergo the death of the master signifiers, in the *jouissance* of the abandonment of fidelity, in the release of oneself from the self-imposed tutelage of such master signifiers as shame's opposites, "honor" or "honesty," or "glory."[37] Such abandonment would have to be beyond shamelessness, an excess of honor and honesty. But is there any shameful position outside of the system's adherence to the master signifiers? Is shame still a possibility? Is Lacan's an ethic that would teach his hearers and his readers how to get beyond guilt, but still be capable of feeling shame, an ethic that would ironically seek not subversion, but the maintenance and the production of master signifiers? In a shameless age, it is life itself that is devalued, said to be meaningless. To feel shame: this occurs only in the light of the honor of the signifier and the honor of thinking and of life itself. This would be a new thinking of European nihilism and the Nietzschean ethical thematic of the "de-valuation of the highest values." Could there yet be something worth dying for? Not in the sense of a cause greater than life, but in the sense of one's own singularity and whatever it is—that unquantifiable, uncountable master signifier, S_1—that holds one's life up against all that would crush and mutilate it. It is this singular honor that Lacan finds in the tragic figures of Antigone and Oedipus at Colonus: blind, an outcast with only his daughter at his side, yet still not lacking, even demanding, as Lacan says, "the honors due his rank" (S7: 304). It is also the singular honor seen in King Lear (see S7: 305) and Claudel's Sygne, who, in the end, like Lear, having lost everything else, has still not lost the enigmatic power of her honor. Alone, betrayed, they do not die like dogs, they do not merely "kick the bucket," but die what Lacan calls "a true death" in which they erase their own being, subtracting themselves, as it were, "from the order of the world" (S7: 306). But they were one and all aristocrats, and no doubt their aristocratic values, like that of Aristotelian magnanimity, has been eclipsed in an age of "cash and carry" politics, when greed, far from being located in the register of vices where Aristotle had placed it in his category of virtues, now itself becomes something of a virtue: "Greed is Good," as Miller says, quoting a slogan from the 1980s film *Wall Street*, a slogan he says typifies an age that produces not shame, but impudence.[38]

But, the upshot of these mutations of Lacan's way of articulating the real and *jouissance* shows that the ethics of psychoanalysis will not be producing new maxims, new imperatives, new prescriptives useful to the realization of the human potential for happiness and the Good. Until *Seminar XX*, at least, it is an ethics for which there is no "Other of the Other," no grand Other, no transcendental signifier that would either condition, justify, or ground ethical or political action, or finally bring the slippage of language and the symbolic order to a halt. There is no final point of arrest, no signifier that could ultimately and finally justify the human condition. It is instead an ethic, a practice and a teaching, "embraced (*étreint*)," as Lacan says, "by the manipulations of the signifier and its possible articulations." For Lacan, these are "the givens, the datum, the materials (*les données*) of psychoanalysis" (S17: 45/50). But let me stand corrected here. There is indeed one imperative heard in *Seminar VII* that still resonates: "Do not give way on your desire." Giving way on one's desire, which in this context might be interpreted as allowing one's desire to be shaped, defined, and manipulated by the fantasies of consumer society, is perhaps the one thing for which one can still feel guilt and a sense of shame.

Perhaps, in an ironic twist, Lacan can be read as not just the subversion of Aristotle and the classical tradition of ethics, but its "other side," its updated and modern version, an Aristotle for the twenty-first century that would take into account the Freudian discovery of the unconscious and the breakthroughs of modern linguistics, which would then be able to traverse the fantasy of *eudaimonia* and see it and assume it for what it is, the ethical-political ideology of the master who does not have to work. Do not Lacan and Aristotle both address the core of human suffering? Would not the category of shame, for example, be something completely comprehensible to Aristotle, who, after all, lived in what cultural historians are fond of calling a "shame culture"? Lacan's concept of desire is in some ways classical, especially when compared to that of Deleuze, for example. Unlike Deleuze, for which there is no object-cause of desire, where desire is prior to its objects, and is a positive and productive force that exceeds its objects in a proliferating flow, and where there is henceforth no need for either castration or a fundamental lack, for Lacan, desire, as in Aristotle, is sustained by an object-cause. And this is not just some lost cause external to desire, the Mother, for example, upon which desire would remain transfixed upon the ultimately unsatisfying replacement objects. Rather, it is a purely formal cause, forever eluding our grasp; it is the invisible hand of desire, always directing desire from within.

Hence, all that Aristotle condemned as bestial and monstrous returns for Lacan as the very subject matter and the level of human suffering he had to confront on a daily basis in his capacity as a psy-choanalyst. As he says in *Seminar VII*, the analyst confronts on a daily basis the human need for transgression. This situates the Lacanian eth-ics essentially in a dimension Aristotle could not have seen, namely, the decidedly inhuman dimensions of the unconscious, and of the implacable demands of the superego that can be even more effective than the moral law at policing an individual's behavior and choices in life. From the early seminars, Lacan's ethic was thus linked to something no doubt unnamable and quite in excess of the classical ideals of the Good, the True, and the Beautiful, something Lacan voiced in various ways, using new, even poetic words: "*Jouissance* and the real," "the death drive," "the Thing," "*objet petit a*," "lack," and so forth. For Lacan, the ethical ideals of happiness, the desire for wholeness and completion, all function as terms in what he calls the fundamental fantasy of ethical and political discourse, which are but metaphors of object *a* whereby the hole, the lack at the heart of the human situation, a lack opened in the real insofar as that "human situ-ation" is situated in and by the symbolic order, is plugged by forgetting, and whereby it begins its play as a fantasy, something that kick-starts desire, but is quite unknown to it, as was shown in the "discordance" noted earlier between what "people are effectively doing and what they think they are doing."[39] Aristotelian "happiness" has a necessary function in this sense of playing the role of the object-cause of desire in the fantasy of wholeness and healing, for this fantasy is perhaps the only way to make livable an insatiable desire always and already captured by death, and by *jouissance* as "access to the real."

Beyond Aristotle's *eudaimonic* ethics, Lacan's new "ethics of psy-choanalysis" thus also subverts one of the most ancient of Greek ethical ideals, inscribed in stone at the Temple of Apollo, the seat of the Delphic Oracle, at Delphi: *Gnothi seauton*, "know thyself." Aristotle's ethics and politics certainly speak from within that tradition. But for Lacan, this maxim has lost its compelling force. What "self" comes to light in the Lacanian ethics except one that is divided between thinking and being? Is that still an ethical self? Perhaps, but an ethical self that would be rare, one formed performatively by the resistance of an individual life to a life of shame, not only because shame is not a life worth living, as Socrates says of "the unexamined life," but more so because it is not a life worth dying for, in the sense that it would be a life that has given way on its desire (see S17: 181/210).

And what reflexive "knowledge" would the ethic of psychoanalysis produce and what is the relation of such knowledge to truth, to love, to guilt and shame, and to the classical philosophical tradition of ethics and politics? The closing sessions of *Seminar VII* answer this by saying that the termination of analysis is when the subject truly confronts the "reality of the human condition," which is death. Thus, the promise, the termination of analysis is not *eudaimonia* but distress and the destitution of the subject, that is to say, in that "state in which man is in that relationship to himself, which is his own death" (S7: 304). In one of his more important formulations, dating from his sixteenth and seventeenth seminars, Lacan also answers this question when he says that "knowledge is the *jouissance* of the Other (*savoir de l'Autre*)" (S17: 14/12), a symbolic knowledge, the knowledge of the truth of desire.

We are left with this conclusion: that ultimately there is no "self-knowledge" for Lacanian psychoanalysis, at least not in the sense of the term proposed by the great European tradition of the "care of the soul." For sure, "self-knowledge" does not obtain at the level of the unconscious, because not only is there no self or soul to know at that level, but also because the unconscious cannot be an object of knowledge, but can only be something that is known, a "known unbeknown," as Fink expresses it.[40] Ultimately, it is an unconscious knowledge (*savoir*), a knowledge "cut in two," as Lacan says,[41] knowledge as *jouissance* of the Other, the Other that is more my self than myself. For Lacan, this is the ethics of today, the ethics of the gap, the fissure, the *spaltung*, as he calls it, that will always break and open the heart of human life. And as for the politics of *jouissance*? Well, wouldn't that have to be the politics of the always incomplete, the split and antagonistically barred big Other, the politics of the bleeding heart of democratic life and the economy of "the service of goods" (S7: 303)? Such an ethics and a politics must always seek the delicate balance between the excesses of *jouissance* on one side, bringing about a society of psychotic perversion, and, on the other, the icy triumph of totalitarian master signifiers, whereby *jouissance* is embalmed in the desiccated regime of perpetual peace. And wouldn't the attainment of such a delicate balance be its ironic "virtue," its virtue beyond all virtue, its "limitless" virtue, and its practical wisdom? Virtue as *jouissance*, not of the soul, but of the body, a new "*dit*-mension" of virtue qua *jouissance* that may be thought as being the "other side," the *envers* of the virtues of moderation and the moral law: not the place where when he/she speaks, he/she commands/obeys, but where in the position of the master, "*it* speaks, *it* enjoys." *Encore*: again, when it speaks it does so from where object *a* and the unary trait are one, where the subject of the signifier and the subject of *jouissance* meet in the enjoyment of the *sinthome*.

7

TO CONCLUDE /
NOT TO CONCLUDE

We qualify sadness as depression, because we give it soul for support, or the psychological tension of Pierre Janet, the philosopher. But it isn't a state of soul, it is simply a moral failing, as Dante, and even Spinoza, said: a sin, which means a moral weakness, which is, ultimately, located only in relation to thought, that is, in the duty to be Well-spoken, to find one's way in dealing with the unconscious, with the structure.

—Jacques Lacan, *Television*

And in the margins to Lacan's statement, this by Jacques-Alain Miller:

There is no ethic beside that of the Well-spoken.

This essay is intended as the conclusion for this series of essays. It attempts a positive formulation of Lacan's ethics as an ethics that must be "well-spoken," and shows what this means against the background of a Lacanian anti-philosophy, an issue brought into focus by reading Alain Badiou's "Formules de *l'Étourdit*." I shall close this essay by turning to something Lacan discussed in *Seminar VII, The Ethics of Psychoanalysis*: the "promise" of psychoanalysis. How is this a promise "Well-spoken"? The main textual referents shall be Lacan's *l'Étourdit*, plus his seminars and texts from the early 1970s, and the aforementioned essay by Alain Badiou.[1]

IS AN ETHICS "WELL-SPOKEN"
AN ANTI-PHILOSOPHY?
BADIOU ON LACAN'S *L'ÉTOURDIT*

In its classical formulations, the European philosophical traditions of ethics were always "Well-spoken." They spoke eloquently of the Good, of human happiness, and of high purposes in life. But this was because, at least in its classical forms, the philosophical traditions of ethics had something to back them up: there was Truth, there was a higher Purpose, and there was the ideal of the realization of human potentials. Life had a meaning and a direction. But this era is over. These idealistic armatures have been pulled away. The classical era of ethical eloquence, that way of "saying" the ethical good, that way of phrasing ethics in the modes of judgment and prescription, that time has passed.

Lacan's ethics of psychoanalysis must be seen in this light as attempting to find a new way of taking ethics seriously. It does not offer the hope of finding new meaning in life, nor does it offer a program for the formation of good habits and positive thinking. It disdains the very idea of formulating a meta-language on truth. Nor is it a new critique of practical reason. Rather, it seeks an ethics, where, yes, ultimate Truth and Knowledge, the twin pillars of ethical life, have been devalued. They are henceforth merely something "said." This accords with the Nietzschean title "How the True World Became a Fable," a mythos; the true world has become something "said." In other words, Truth and Knowledge shall be taken to be "effects" rather than "conditions." Truth and Knowledge are no longer said to exist in the Real, but rather in the dimension of the Other, the domain of the Symbolic order, which, for Lacan, is also the dimension of the unconscious. Hence, we must find our way toward this unconscious, we must find our way of dealing with it, for it is there, always there. We must find our way through the thickets of tradition toward this new way of "saying" ethical life.

No doubt, it was Freud and his "discovery" of the unconscious that marked the threshold for this new ethical articulation. But, and not in spite of all of Lacan's misgivings about this, perhaps we can and must also credit Nietzsche for being a path breaker in this regard, for it was Nietzsche who first saw that ethical statements are but evaluations, perspectives, and as such, rooted deeply in a genealogy and a legacy of passions, instincts, fears, and wild aspirations that had never before been brought to articulation. Ethics, for Lacan, indeed, his whole teaching, must be seen as an effect of the unconscious, as the effect of an encounter with the Real, the Real as *nihil*, as void, gap, wound, impasse, and not as a repository of transcendent values and truths, or as the habitat of the Beautiful and the Good. We must also credit Nietzsche for his insights into the nihilism of "our era." For this what we are also talking about here, how this time of twilight, this era of the destitution of the True World, is experienced as an era of "nihilism," as the era of the death of the gods and the wiping clean of the horizons wherein Man had traditionally found his place, his home, and his direction. It was Nietzsche who most acutely saw and said how this, our modern era, is a time of wandering and homelessness. In the widening deserts and gathering darkness of this nihilistic age, it might well seem that today humanity wanders without direction, like those lost members of the Achilpa tribe discussed in Mircea Eliade's book *The Sacred and the Profane*, who, their god-given sacred staff broken and their orientations lost, simply decided to lie down in the desert and die.[2] This age of nihilism is thus also an age of triumphant "anti-humanism." If classical Greek humanism found its signature slogan in the thesis "Man is the measure of all things," this has taken on a new meaning in the age of contemporary nihilism. Now steeped as never before in an awareness of his/her own finitude, "death-bound," living in a senseless universe abandoned as much by the gods as by all ultimate reasons for hope and salvation, a being that must withstand its own ruin, Man is now more than ever the measure of all things, a being bound with destitution. Again, no doubt the Freudian discovery of the unconscious has contributed to this, for Man is now also suddenly a stranger to himself, divided from within. The "self-knowledge" promised by the humanistic European traditions of ethics, especially the ethics of the care of the soul, has been recast by Freud's legacy. After Freud, self-knowledge is now regarded as a knowledge that obtains in the registers of the imaginary, the register of the ego. The classical formulas of self-knowledge can now be seen as modes of self-deception insofar as self-knowledge, and here Lacan uses the word *connaissance*, is not only a mode of recognition, self-recognition, but is also and necessarily a mode of *méconnaissance*, of misrecognition. We can never know ourselves as we truly are. This has been central to the teachings of Lacan's seminars, and it is the situation from which that teaching began. This, then, is the context, the horizon of nihilism from which Lacan's ethics also speaks. Where Hölderlin once asked, "What are poets for in a destitute time?" perhaps we can hear Lacan asking something similar of ethics: What is an ethics for in a destitute time and how is it possible in an age of destitution?

We must not conclude from this that there is no ethics at all to be found in Lacan's *The Ethics of Psychoanalysis*, or that his ethics is an "anti-ethics" and therefore part and parcel of his more general anti-philosophy. Nor does Lacan's ethics follow the pattern of a "negative theology" whereby we find what we are looking for only by saying what it is not. Rather, it seems an interesting possibility to suggest there is a sort of "purloined letter" of ethics to be found in Lacan's seminars.

The subject matter and direction of Lacan's thought on ethics is noth-ing hidden or esoteric. Rather, it is something like the letter in Poe's *The Purloined Letter*. We should seek this "letter"; we seek the instance and the insistence on the ethical letter circulating in Lacan's seminars somewhere out in the open, not hidden, like a secret or a hidden truth waiting to be brought forth, but as something lying in the open all around us. It is to be found in the way desire is talked about in the four discourses Lacan outlines, the discourse of Mastery, of the University, the Hysteric, and the discourse of the Analyst. Lacan's ethic of psychoanaly-sis is to be found in the way desire is said in each of these discourses, the way each of these turns into the other, and the way Lacan works through, makes the "tour" through these ways desire is said (*dit*). For, after all, it is desire that humans most want to talk about, all the ways we can be driven mad by desiring too much, by desiring endlessly, one thing after another, driven mad by the paranoid fears that our desires will be blocked or frustrated, or by ceaselessly wanting to know what the Other—what other people, what "life"—expects of us and wants of us so we might be more desirable and lovable; we are driven mad, in short by never knowing what our desire is in the first place. Perhaps we must look for the key directions of Lacan's ethics in connection with the very desire to put a stop to this madness, the desire to cure and to care for our souls, and perhaps we shall hear its refrain in the question, "Can we learn to outgrow our madness?"

We must hear in this how Lacan distances himself from any ethics that posits an abiding truth of the Real. We must also see how he discards any attempt at a universalistic articulation of ethics. True, there does seem to be the suggestion at least of an "ethics of our time" sketched in his teachings. But the important point is to see that Lacan is nonetheless not proposing anything like a universal ethics, or an even an ethics in general. All of these attempts culminate in philosophical absolutist articulations and in categorical imperatives of moral law. As was shown in an earlier essay in this series, this is only a way of bringing the terror of the real into moral law, embedding it there as something both Good, and at the same time, radically evil. And this is precisely due to its attempts to command universally. For Lacan, it can never be a matter of determin-ing a transcendental perspective on ethical life that would be true for all and for every act. It can never be a matter of determining a rational principle that would enable us to judge the moral worth of each and every act or describe the rational or emotional sources from which each and every moral action springs. Rather, the ethics of psychoanalysis shall only be concerned with the particular, with the individual. Even Lacan's prescription from *Seminar VII*, "Do not give way on your desire," has its particular address. It shall be most eminently a concern for what obtains in a particular act, the psychoanalytic act, which is, after all, a speech act, and a particular way of making truth speak. Earlier essays have explored Lacan's teachings on truth in psychoanalytic practice and now it is time to take these studies a step further with regard to a specific psychoanalytic act called "the pass," which is something that Lacan instituted and approached in so many ways and through so many textual and experiential ways, as the act wherein desire is said and—if it is "Well-said"—it is thus transformed. In short, it is an act whereby one finds one's way in dealing with desire and the unconscious.

And how does this relate to philosophy? This is my question. In this regard, I would like to return full circle to a question that has overshadowed each and every one of the essays in this collection, namely, is Lacan's questioning of the limits and foundations of ethics of psychoanalysis an anti-philosophy? Or is it a new way of saying the ethical, a way that possibly brings with it the essentials required for a new way of formulating the relations of language and desire, a new way of articulating truth and the real, a new way of saying ethics that shall have an important bearing on philosophy? Lacan's teachings regarding this act—the analytic act, which once again, is essentially a speech act—must be seen therefore not only as a rejection of philosophy but rather as having a decisive and creative effect upon it. It shall orient the way ethics is said in new directions and toward new dimensions, thereby opening philosophy to new possibilities of articulation. An ethics "Well-spoken," even for philosophy, must be an ethics that finds its way of dealing with the unconscious. Henceforth it must also be not only the saying and the what is said of the truth of the human situation, but it must also leave a place, a silence, perhaps, for what can only remain unsaid in that situation. These are my themes.

It is in light of these perspectives that Badiou's reading of Lacan's *l'Étourdit* becomes especially pertinent.

PHILOSOPHY, UNIVOCITY

If nihilism is the horizon of philosophy today, must not the philosopher also be a nihilist? Badiou's reading of *l'Étourdit* sets this context aside. Among the conditions for philosophy, he does not name nihilism. The philosopher must be a scientist, *savant(e)*, poet, *artiste*, a political militant, un *militant(e) politique*, and a lover, *amant(e)*, but not a nihilist. Never mind. Perhaps nihilism itself is out of date by now.

But for Badiou it is also because philosophers still believe in something: they believe in truth qua sense (*sens*), the meaning of being as the identity of thinking and being. The philosopher is a lover of truth, one who seeks the truth of love. Lacan may be in this tradition. How can he therefore be typecast as an anti-philosopher?

In his construction of philosophy, the "true nature" of ontological philosophy "from Aristotle to Deleuze" is defined by a fundamental conception and a fundamental task, to think and to know (*savoir*) the univocity of being.[3] Philosophy is still Parmenidean according to this construction of it and its history. For Badiou, philosophy has never experienced the destitution of this task. A few pages later, he also attributes to philosophy a second defining orientation, namely, that for the "philosophical operation," there must be a *sens*, a meaning and a direction, both of and for truth (*il y a un sens de la vérité*).[4] Philosophy, in short, belongs to the domain of the univocity of being and to the idea that truth still has a meaning. Hence, philosophy's privileging of the paradigm of mathematics, as in Plato and the Pythagoreans. The mathematical paradigm best secures univocity. Insofar as mathematics can provide precision in measure and taking the measure, it can also serve Plato and the Pythagoreans as a model science or proto-science, where, for them, ethics has as its task the determination of the harmony and balance of the soul. Such harmony of the soul is akin to a musical harmony, and as such, it is mathematically determinable, something Aristotle and his school denied.

Now, the whole context and problematic of nihilism notwithstanding, it is Badiou's claim that philosophy is still a tradition of "wisdom" (*sagesse*). In its traditional form, it offers a crucial "consolation." In its wisdom, in its univocity and its love of truth, philosophy can offer a truth of the real (*une vérité du réel*). In speaking of the real, we are referring not to the real in the sense of being "reality," something encountered in experience as the real world, but rather to the Lacanian Real, the real that Lacan has insisted upon in its topological relations with the Symbolic and the Imaginary as what is disruptive and an impasse for univocity and truth. In the Lacanian topology, while having no phenomenal aspect, while never appearing as such in experience, the real appears only in its disruptive effect. This is all that can be known about it. The real is both the paradoxical limit for univocity and truth and, at the same time, that toward which univocity and truth, that toward which the whole apparatus of the symbolic order is directed and against which it runs aground. Philosophy's claim—especially, let us add, the claim implicit to the philosophy Lacan never ceased engaging with in his seminars, namely, Hegel's philosophy, the philosophy of Absolute Knowledge, the philosophy of the system of Truth—this philosophy's claim is that the real—that "death," for example—can be reduced without remainder to meaning (*sens*) and that there is a truth of the real that can be known insofar as truth is identified with *sens* qua "meaning and/or direction."

For Badiou's reading of Lacan, it is here, in this crucial relation to the Real, that Lacan's anti-philosophy unfolds, which is not the same as characterizing Lacan as being specifically anti-Hegelian, which he is not. Rather, Lacanian anti-philosophy would consist more broadly in the attempt to reduce philosophy's overall ontologizing of language; it would consist in the attempt to critically reduce philosophy's claim to know the truth and to say the truth, the whole truth, as *sens*; it would consist in critically reducing philosophy's claim that the real is the rational, that it can be reduced to meaning and truth. It would critically oppose philosophy's claim that there can be a "truth of the real," and that this truth can be known.

In Badiou's essay, the term "formula," as stated in its title "Formules de *l'Étourdit*," is itself equivocal. It has two referents: first, that found in the formulas of sexuality, for example, or in the *mathème* (the "algorithm") of fantasy (barred S in relation to *objet petit a*), and second, it has a "poetic sense," as in Badiou's example from a quotation by the poet Rimbaud, "*J'ai trouvé le lieu et la formule*" (translated by Scott Savaino as "The place and the wording came to me").[5] The formula here is the poetic "wording," perhaps the poetic saying, rather than being an algorithm.

Lacan's "Well-spoken" ethic must speak from the space between these two dimensions of the "formula." It must find its way between univocity and equivocity, between poetics and the rigor of the *mathème*. Indeed, this is what one encounters all the time in Lacan's seminars as he moves between the precision of formulas and the plays of *lalangue*, as he moves between the references to the poets and references to the scientists and mathematicians.

However anti-philosophical it may be, the Lacanian discourse can be read as actually sharing something important with philosophy. For both, philosophy and Lacanian analytic discourse, univocity is brought into view only by escaping equivocation and polyvocity. Philosophy's operation brackets the equivocity of being so as to bring to light the underlying logic of univocity. This is the very strategy at work, for example, in the early Platonic dialogues where there is a search for definitions that must work through the many ways of saying "justice," for example, or "courage," or "love" (qua *éros*). All must be defined in terms of their turning toward the One of univocity, the One of ultimate Truth and Knowledge. This is the whole point of the Socratic *elenchus* defined as the testing of opinions for their truth, for their ability to stand and be thought as knowledge and not as just another opinion. Likewise, for Lacan, psychoanalysis operates in the domain of equivocation, the equivocation of the signifier and the plurality and conflict of interpretations. Although the overall trajectory of the cure must pass through the domain of the equivocal, the ultimate point of the analytic discourse is to bore a hole, so to speak, through the equivocal such that the "void of univocity" (*le vide de l'univocité*) might be brought to the surface of discourse.[6]

So, as it turns out, both philosophy and Lacanian analysis must operate between univocity and the domain of equivocity (*le royaume de l'équivoque*). Like philosophy, Lacan, too, is trying to find his way from the equivocation of words and language to the purity of the formulas of univocity. Hence, where Lacan's anti-philosophy might seem at first simply to oppose philosophy's aspirations to be the only or premier discourse of the univocity of being, it would seem that the discourse of analysis itself aspires in its own way to attain univocity. The difference is that for Lacan, there is no univocity of being. Univocity obtains only at the level of the formulation. Hence, it is only a possible regulative ideal. Nevertheless, the pursuit of univocity is why Lacan so readily took to the formalism of structural analysis, why he found the structural anthropology of Lévi-Strauss to be so promising, and why he spent so much of his time in his seminars developing first his understanding of the proper force of the semiology of the signifier and his graphs of desire; it is also perhaps the reason why his topology, with its Borromean knots, structurally linked the domains of the imaginary, the symbolic, and the real; why he developed the schemas for the four discourses; and finally why he articulated his *mathèmes*. But there is this important difference: for Lacan, univocity offers not a more rigorous ontology but rather a more rigorous "transmissibility" of whatever knowledge can be said to arise in and through the analytic act, a knowledge that can only be described as the register of the effect of the real, an effect of the unconscious.

Univocity thereby offers to psychoanalysis an important link not only with philosophy, but also with science. With univocity, the act becomes something with a scientific profile. Univocity is something achieved in the many confirming repetitions of the act; it is something built up, inductively, as it were, through confirming instances whereby piece by piece the equivocations of the medium of the act, namely, language, are reduced, bracketed, so to speak, and their univocal residue brought to formalization. While this may sound suspiciously like a phenomenological reduction, it must be said that the reduction is not a reduction *to* meaning, but a reduction *of* meaning, a reduction of the equivalence between truth and *sens*.

So, while Lacan may share in philosophy's pursuit of univocity, its direction, "the direction of the cure," one might say, is completely at odds with the direction of philosophy's "love of truth" and so with any sense of sharing in the consolations of philosophy. While the search for univocity might condition the discourse of analysis, condition the *mathème*, and condition the fluency of that discourse, yet, were it a true univocity, the "void of univocity," to borrow Badiou's characterization, it could still not be brought to appearance, it could still not be said in the wholeness of its truth, for, in taking the form of a "saying," it would require language, and thus only be returned back through the hole into the domain of meanings and equivocation. This is why Lacan adopted the *mathème*, which, without reference to meaning, answers the question, "How can univocity be well-spoken?"

This recalls something just alluded to earlier about the differences between Lacan and philosophy. Philosophy and Lacanian psychoanalysis have very different ways of speaking about the One.

Philosophy, at least philosophy as constructed in Badiou's essay, holds that the One is One in a strict sense: the well-rounded, spherical One as articulated in Parmenides' poem, or the One named in Aristophanes' discourse from Plato's *Symposium*, the original condition and now also the destiny and the desired point of return and reunion of the two erotic halves hence sundered and wandering in search of their "other half." This is the logic of love, the longing to return to the One. The One here is the goal and of the fantasm of love, be it the love of truth or erotic love. Even these two loves, erotic love and the love of truth, must be seen, therefore, as but two sides of the same coin. The One of the philosopher is thus the spherical unity of thought and being, of truth and *sens*, the unity of the male and female, whereas the One of Lacanian psychoanalysis is the aspherical One of difference.

For Lacan, the One, the Uni of the Univocity, is not one. It is the One of difference. There is no one "Name-of-the-Father," for example. Rather, it must always be phrased as the *Names*-of-the Fathers, which is Lacan's formulation in *Seminar XI, The Four Fundamental Concepts of Psychoanalysis*. Multiplicity, equivocity, it seems, is ultimately irreducible

for Lacan. Moreover, the One is the One of "pure difference." This is
the one of the signifier that is defined by difference. Hence, where the
assertion of univocity is the assertion of the One, it is not the assertion
of a countable One so much as it is the assertion of a One that can be
counted on, counted on to always be there, the One as the "pure difference" of the real. The proposition of the One at the heart of Lacan's
ethics and his politics, $Y a d' l'Un$, the univocity that comes forth through
the hole cut through equivocation, repeats the classical assertion of the
unity of thought and being only so as to exceed it, to displace it, to find
within its intimacy that "gap" of extimacy, and to show the "knowledge"
following from it to ultimately be but something like a myth, a fable
told in order to fill that "gap" and so miss the real. No doubt one could
also find a necessity in Lacan's $Y a d' l'Un$, the "such a thing as One,"
if, that is to say, one follows Lacan's definition of "necessary" as asserted
in his *Encore*: the One is necessary in the sense that "it never stops *not
being* written (*ne cesse pas de s'écrire*)" (S20: 59/55). It is this thinking of
the One as *faille* (gap, or fault) that marks the rigor of the difference, the
"pure difference," not only between Lacan and philosophy, but between
Lacan and the other discourses and therapies of psychology, as well,
behaviorism, for example, which, according to Lacan is but a continuation of the classical European tradition rather than a break from it. This
"gap" at the heart of the univocity that the cutting through equivocation
brings forth is thus the gap, the difference, the void, as Badiou phrases it,
from which the promise of psychoanalysis is made, a promise not for the
consolation of a truth of the real, but for the ultimate confrontation of
death, of the void of the real, a promise of the affirmation of the human
condition rather than a sneaking way of attaining revenge against it in
and by opposing its multiplicity to the mastery and univocity of the One
as the whole of truth and knowledge.

Now, the pursuit of univocity in the analytic discourse is also the
pursuit of a knowledge (*savoir*) that is transmissible, a knowledge that
can be taught and passed on. For Lacan, this knowledge takes the form
of a "correct formalization" (*formalisation correcte*) of the analytic act.[7]
The correct formalization only comes forth in the hole bored through
the domain of equivocation, a hole bored through equivocation so as to
escape equivocation. Analogously, formalization only comes forth in the
analytic act insofar as it bores a hole through the real, again, so as to
escape it. For philosophy, love, the philosopher's love of truth, was the
drill bit by which this hole was cut through the real, but for philosophy,
the drill bit produced not a hole but the discovery of a rich vein of

truth—*sens* glittering in the darkness of the real. For philosophy there is a truth of the real that can be retrieved and stated in a discourse of truth and univocity once it has been brought to the surface and has escaped the equivocity of words and language. But, it is Lacan's experience that any attempt to bore through the real, as though one is searching for an underlying and preexisting vein of truth qua *sens* (meaning) in the real, any attempt to bore a hole through the domain of equivocity in search of an ultimate univocity, always comes up against an impenetrable wall, a wall Lacan calls the "wall of the impossible" real. This is said to be impossible because it is irreducible, undecidable, indeterminable, indemonstrable, and ultimately inconsolable.[8]

We could say that Lacan goes deeper into the real, something he has been maintaining since *Seminar VII*, than does philosophy. Philosophy's "moral failing," to use the language of the passage from *Television* quoted in the epigraph, its weakness, is the way it cannot find its way toward the real except by the familiar routes of truth. Trapped, as Badiou expresses it, in its love of truth, hypnotized by the specular mirror reflection between truth and *sens*, philosophy ends up shirking its "duty," and so breaks up the triplet of truth-knowledge-the real. "Truth," the famous "love of truth" and the "love of wisdom," thereby become easy alibis. Philosophy's assertion of univocity covers over the real, ignores it, is ignorant of it, or puts it to work as a moment in a *Parousia* of truth.

Psychoanalysis takes the real, the wall of the impossible real, very seriously. Yet, as far as psychoanalysis goes, we must also say that in light of the real, the desired letter of the "correct formalization" never arrives. From its very source in univocity it must also always miss its destination, always come up against its limits, against the wall of its own impossibility, and against its own determining negation.

THE TRIPLET TRUTH–KNOWLEDGE–THE REAL

The pivot for understanding what is at stake in Lacan's anti-philosophy is to see how philosophy and psychoanalysis offer very different ways of reading and inscribing what Badiou calls "the triplet of truth-knowledge-real" (*vérité-savoir-réel*). Philosophy and psychoanalysis share this triplet. It is the frontier between their two discourses.[9] But, and here is the crucial difference between Lacan and philosophy in Badiou's eyes, philosophy tends to break up this triplet. Philosophy, defined as a love of truth and as what would seek to find this truth in the real, breaks up this triplet into twos: there is a truth *sens* of the real, and then there is a knowledge of truth. Moreover in Badiou's view, it is characteristic of philosophy to think in terms of oppositions. For Badiou's reading of *l'Étourdit*, Lacan's anti-philosophy consists not only in his defense of the triplet, truth–knowledge–the real, but also in his rejection of this oppositional thinking characteristic of philosophy. This is the crux of Lacanian anti-philosophy.

Let us consider a primary example: Hegel. Badiou claims that what Lacan could never settle for in his engagement with Hegel, the so-called Absolute Master, was the way Hegel, like all philosophers, had to think in terms of oppositions and the way the third was introduced only as a moment of resolution, a moment of synthesis of an oppositional pair, the synthesis and the consolation of opposition. The third always arises for the philosopher from the two in their opposition. First, there is the thesis, then the moment of its anti-thesis, and finally the sublation of their opposition in the moment of synthesis. Without recourse to a Hegelian dialectic, Lacan wants to maintain the triplet wherever he finds it, whether in the topology of the imaginary, the symbolic, and the real, or in the triplet, truth–knowledge–the real. For Lacan, this triplet does not emerge across a dialectic of oppositions. It is primary. It is foundational. This is Badiou's reading of *l'Étourdit*.[10]

Psychoanalysis maintains this triplet by saying that one cannot name truth without also entailing knowledge and the real. One cannot name knowledge without entailing truth and the real. One cannot name the real without evoking truth and knowledge. The key to the maintenance of the triplet is to deny that there is a truth qua sense (*sens*) of the real. If there were, then the pair truth and knowledge could emerge independently of the real. There is a truth of the real and then there is knowledge of this truth. For Lacan, there is no "truth" as such of the real; hence, there is no knowledge, as such, of the real. This is his first and foundational thesis. There is no originary sense (*sens*) qua "meaning and direction" for the real because there is no truth of the real. If there were a truth and a *sens* in or of the real, analysis, like philosophy, would ultimately be hermeneutics, and one can well see how this would dissolve the triplet. But, analysis is not hermeneutical because it does not make philosophy's claim that there is a truth qua *sens* in and of the real.

In the psychoanalytic maintenance of the triplet, therefore, truth and knowledge are bound with the real insofar as Lacan thinks of them not as preexisting in the real, but as effects of the real. A saying is always produced as an effect of the real. Knowledge (*savoir*) is always produced as an effect of the real. Phrased otherwise, insofar as Lacan identifies knowledge qua *savoir* as identified with the symbolic order and the subject's relation to the symbolic order, as the diagram introduced in *Encore* shows (S20: 90/83), knowledge in this sense as the symbolic order is a vector directed toward the real, but not something found in the real.

For Badiou's reading of Lacan, "knowledge" is an effect of the real, a consequence of the function of the real. What is the "function" of the real? How can we formulate the real in its relations to truth and knowledge? Thinking philosophically, if the real is not to be identified with the domain of truth-*sens*, it would have to belong to the opposite of sens, namely, non-*sens*. Philosophy works in terms of twos, rather than triplets, thus, where there is a truth qua *sens* of the real, its opposite would have to be non-sense (non-*sens*). The real, in these terms, would be non-*sens*. Philosophy has other ways of phrasing this: the real is noumenal; it is unknowable because it lacks all phenomenality. Lacan's *l'Étourdit* rejects this: the real is neither reducible noumenally nor phenomenally because it must be thought in relation to the symbolic order, in relation to language. The oppositional pair, *sens* and non-*sens*, must not delimit it. Rather, there is no truth-*sens* of the real because for Lacan it is the ab-*sens* of truth and knowledge. This restores the triplet. Truth and knowledge are both absent in the real. What could one say about the real if one cannot say that there is truth and knowledge of the real? For Lacan, there is a third term, a third way. The real is the register in the regimes of truth and knowledge of ab-*sens*. Again, the triplet returns. The wall of the real is encountered not as non-*sens*, not as the mere opposite of the pair *sens* and truth, and certainly not as a noumenal dimension and as a limit-figure in a phenomenology of knowledge and thinking, but rather as the absence of relation; it is the *ab-sens*, as the terminology of *l'Étourdit* has it, the subtraction, the withdrawal and nullity of sense. *Ab-sens* means an absence of a decisively important relation, an absence that therefore "makes no sense."

Again, we encounter the real as the impossible at the heart of the symbolic order. The real as nullity, as void of sense, as ab-*sens*, is the absence, the impossibility of a relation. Insofar as thinking for philosophy is the thinking of relations, thinking runs aground or runs up against the wall of the impossible real because at the heart of the real there is an impossible relation that must be thought. Lacan rather famously calls this the impossibility of a sexual relation. This returns to what was posited earlier regarding Lacan's doctrine of the One. The One is pure difference. The impossibility of a sexual relation is the concrete and universal instance of the not-One of Oneness. It is the fundamental form for psychoanalysis of the One as difference. It is the impossible relation that opens the philosophical sphere of the One to an aspherical dimension of the One as difference. We shall be returning to this.

But before going any further, allow me to expand a bit on the usage of the term "knowledge" in Badiou's reading of Lacan. Badiou has said that the triplet truth–knowledge–the real forms the frontier or the borderline between philosophy and Lacanian psychoanalysis. This suggests that the triplet is something they both have in common although they have different ways of articulating it. Part of the Lacanian antiphilosophy, or the Lacanian "extimacy of philosophy," as I am attempting to articulate it, concerns the fact that Lacan uses these terms "truth," "knowledge," and the "real" in very different ways than philosophy does. Earlier essays in this volume have already discussed Lacan's use of the terms "the truth" and "the real," but what about his use of the term "knowledge"? Allow me to comment on this before continuing in our reading of Badiou's essay.

In his twentieth seminar, *Encore*, Lacan says that prior to Descartes, "the question of knowledge had never been raised." Furthermore, it was only with the arrival of psychoanalysis that the question "What is knowledge?" was raised anew. He also says that it is in relation to the connections between knowledge and the signifier, and knowledge and *jouissance* that psychoanalysis has succeeded in raising this question in a new way (see S20: 96/88). But Lacan's new way of posing the question "What is knowledge?" is also one of the ways in which Lacan increases the distance of the frontier between psychoanalysis and philosophy.

Knowledge has a double sense for Lacan: it can mean *savoir* or *connaissance*. Knowledge qua *savoir* is usually identified with the symbolic, knowledge located in the Other, whereas knowledge as *connaissance* is identified with the imaginary, with the fields of self-knowledge and knowledge of other people, for example. Knowledge qua *savoir* itself has a double sense in Lacan's teachings: there is knowledge of the subject in the sense of being knowledge about the subject, a knowledge that posits the Other, the symbolic Other, as its locus, knowledge that is transmissible and related to learning, the knowledge that obtains at the level of the university discourse. But, there is also another knowledge, another scene active in the analytic act, a "knowledge" (*savoir*) that Lacan says the subject knows nothing about, a knowledge that, paradoxically, the subject does not know that it knows, a knowledge which also has its locus in the Other, but in the Other in the sense of the Other of the unconscious, also identified with the order of signifiers insofar as the unconscious is "structured like a language." In connection with especially the latter sense of knowledge, the knowledge in the Other, Lacan adds that "the subject results"—could one not say that the subject is an effect?—"from the fact that this knowledge must be learned, and even have a price put on it . . . it is its cost that values it, not as exchange but as use" (S20: 96/89). And here is where there is a connection between knowledge and *jouissance* in that the knowledge, as Lacan says, is "difficult" not only to acquire but also to enjoy (*jouir*). The "conquest," the learning of knowledge, a learning connected with learning how to use the signifier, is renewed in its exercise and is "always directed toward its *jouissance*," something Lacan illustrates in a diagram he provides in *Encore* where the symbolic order is shown as a vector directed toward the real and passing beneath the "open set" of *jouissance*, which is thus situated in a space between the imaginary, the symbolic, and the real (see S20: 96–97/89 and 90/83).

The division that defines the divided subject (symbolized as the barred S) is a division, a barrier, between the subject and knowledge in this latter sense of the term as being an unconscious knowledge that the subject somehow both knows and does not know. One of the goals of psychoanalysis is somehow to formalize what is going on at the level of the unconscious knowledge (*savoir*) that the subject does not know that it knows. This is a knowledge roughly analogous to the kind of knowledge structural anthropology attempts to bring out from the deep structures of mythology, a knowledge of elementary kinship rules, for example, that is active and in use, but not "enjoyed" in that it is not brought forth to speech; it is not talked about.

Looking at one of Lacan's early graphs from the mid-1950s, "schema L" (see S2: 243–245), introduced to illustrate the problems raised by the relations between the ego and the other, language and speech, we can see that the symbolic relation between the Other ('A'/*Autre*), the unconscious, and the subject, the analytic subject, symbolized by S in this early graph, is blocked by the vector of the imaginary. The imaginary is the domain of the ego and its imaginary and narcissistic relations with its others (*autres*), its fellow beings. Why is this said to be imaginary? Because those others (Lacan would use a small letter "o" here) are not really the Other, not the Other that is both a radical alterity and, insofar as it is the Other of the symbolic order, is the Other that Lacan says is "made for truth" (S17: 187/217). The others are but reflections of the imaginary ego, "shadows," as Lacan calls them, which arise in the narcissistic mirror-play of the ego. The "true Other," the radical alterity that transcends imaginary relations, is separated from the subject (S) by speech. The subject, Lacan says, is thus "separated from the Others, the true ones, by the wall of language. . . . The subject doesn't know what it is saying, and for the best of reasons, because he doesn't know what he is" (S20: 244).

For Badiou, and for the Lacan of *l'Étourdit* and other work from the early 1970s, what is irreducible in psychoanalysis is the encounter with the function of the real as radical alterity, now formulated as the ab-*sens* of truth. Here, the encounter with the real is the encounter with the real qua the "wall of the impossible." The real is what cannot be known in the sense that it transcends both the imaginary and the symbolic. The irreducible alterity of the real, the irreducible impossibility of the real is now formulated in terms of the impossibility of the sexual relation. To bring this impossibility to the level of science whereby it could be formalized the locus of language would require traversing the equivocity and the vector of the imaginary such that it could be inscribed in the Other, the Other that is "made for truth," and given the form of a *mathème*. This would seem to be one of the goals of the Lacanian psychoanalysis. Thus, the passage from equivocation to univocity named in Badiou's essay is not only a passage from the imaginary to the symbolic order. It is also the passage from the knowledge that is unknown, an unconscious knowledge, to the level of a knowledge that can be said to be 'known.' This must encounter a barrier, the wall of the impossible real.

How does knowledge concern ethics? Is the locus of the Lacanian ethics not only within the Other, but also within the locus of the other, other persons, one's fellow human beings? Unconscious knowledge, it should also be recalled, is not localized as the property of a particular subject, but is an intersubjective symbolic order with localized configurations. Lacan does speak of *the* "subject-supposed-to-know" (*le sujet supposé savoir*), meaning the particular subject as embroiled in the illusion that it possesses *savoir*, that it knows the truth. This can also be knowledge in the sense of a *connaissance*, the self-knowledge one finds as the ultimate goal of the philosophical ethic of the care of the soul/self. Self-knowledge would here be imaginary, a self-knowledge one finds in Aristotle's ethics that is realized only across or through the ego's imaginary relations with its others, its fellows, its "friends," as Aristotle calls them. The ethics of psychoanalysis rejects this and especially warns against its occurrence in the analytic situation. First of all, the ethics well-said would be one propelled beyond the level of the imaginary and toward the level of the symbolic and toward *jouissance*. Therefore, the ethics of psychoanalysis will be situated first and most importantly in relation with the symbolic order, the Other, in other words, the "big Other"; it will be situated at the level of the relation with language and the unconscious. It will obtain at the level of the triplet, of truth, knowledge (*savoir*), and the real, but with the additional idea that truth, knowledge, and the real are, as a triplet, bound with *jouissance*. An ethics well-said will thus not be an ethics concerned with the imaginary relations that obtain between the ego and its others, its fellow beings, as is the case with most ethical discourses from the history of European philosophy. Here, too, in this placement of ethics at the level of the symbolic, and in terms of *jouissance*, rather than the imaginary, we encounter the Lacanian anti-philosophy. This does not mean that such imaginary relations have no place or role to play whatsoever, for, at an elementary level, the analytic situation itself is still an encounter between two egos. But the primary orientation concerns the Other of the unconscious. The ethics of psychoanalysis is concerned with finding one's way in dealing with the unconscious. This changes everything in the so-called face-to-face encounter of the analytic situation.

In the analytic situation, the analyst must likewise occupy the position of the Other, not the other. Lacan does say that in the transference active in and necessary to the analytic situation, the analyst must indeed seem to the analysand (the patient) to be the one who embodies knowledge (see S11: chapter 18, 230ff.). The analyst plays the role in the analytic situation as the "subject-supposed-to-know" in the sense that the analysand can take the analyst to be the one, to be the Other, who knows what is ailing him, who knows, what the analysand does not know, namely, the true meaning, the signification, of what the analysand is saying and therefore the truth of the analysand's desire. This embroils the analysand in the effort of trying to seek out what it is this Other wants or expects of him/her so that the analysand can give the analyst whatever he/she wants or whatever it might take so that this knowledge can be revealed. Then, retroactively, as it were, the truth of all those nasty little other details, all the slips and gaffs and so on that punctuated the saying of the analysand and so frustrated it, can be brought forth in their true meaning and be alleviated. But, the analyst must never in this situation deceive him/herself into thinking that he/she really does know. The analyst can even allow the analysand to play the role of the one-supposed-to-know, to allow the analysand the imaginary illusion that he/she knows what he/she is talking about, just to get him/her to say anything with the idea it will be alright, that the analysand will hit upon the truth. But as for the role of the analyst, it is crucial that the analyst avoids these imaginary situations and maintains the division, the split, between what he/she is or is not as an analyst and what he/she knows (*savoir*). This is shown in the schema for the discourse of the analyst wherein the position of the analyst, indicated as *a*, sits above the bar of truth, which is identified as S_2, the knowledge presumed by the analyst but separated from him/her. The end of analysis comes only with the analyst being cast down from this position, being thrown down as the subject-supposed-to-know such that the analyst becomes a piece of trash, so to speak. We shall be returning to this subject-supposed-to-know in connection with the moment of destitution experienced in the analytic act.

Psychoanalysis, in its practice, in and through the practice of the transference, must constantly find its way in dealing with the unconscious. It must find its way in dealing with a knowledge that is not known, a knowledge of the unconscious as based on the signifier as such (S20: 96/89). This elusive knowledge would indeed be knowledge about the truth of the subject's desire, but a truth that must not be taken to be a "meaning" of desire, as the philosopher might have it, a truth that would somehow explain desire and be its ultimate direction, or goal, its *sens*, but rather truth as the structure of desire that obtains in and through the signifier, a structure that comes to light retroactively, for example, in the function of the real in the relation to the fundamental fantasy that sparks desire. It is a truth that emerges in other words, as an effect of the encounter with the nullity of the real, and that is present in analysis in and as the act of saying when the truth of desire speaks, when that structure is brought forth from the equivocity of the imaginary self-knowledge (*connaissance* as *méconnaissance*) to formalization as *savoir*.

Badiou's discussion of knowledge and truth seems to gloss over these important manifold usages in Lacan's discourse whereby knowledge is double: it has levels of both *connaissance* (the imaginary) and of *savoir* (the symbolic order).

But it also misses something else just touched upon: *jouissance* in its connections with truth and knowledge. In thinking of thinking as what aims at meaning, at truth-*sens*, he thus misses what Colette Soler has called the chief anti-cognitivist, and therefore perhaps the chief moment of the Lacanian anti-philosophy, whereby thinking is identified with *jouissance*.[11] Badiou's reading could be reformulated to take this into account. It is not only that truth-*sens* does not obtain in the real, but also that truth is linked with *jouissance*, and so with semblance. Truth is thus never reached except by "twisted pathways" (S20: 95/88). Lacan's diagram from

Encore shows *jouissance* as an "open set" obtaining between semblance, a result of the vector of the symbolic, and the real, in a way analogous to the way the imaginary came between the Other and the Subject in the L-schema referred to earlier. The "true" is like *objet petit a* (object *a*) in the structure of fantasy; it can be taken for being something substantial, it can be taken as truth-*sens*, for example, and in this function, it is what makes "men always run headlong down the same pathways," but, in the end, it, truth qua object *a*, dissolves, unable "to sustain itself in approaching the real" (S20: 95/88).

To get back to what Soler is saying, insofar as thinking is the thinking of truth as object *a*, as an imaginary truth-*sens*, it cannot be identified with knowledge. Knowledge as formalized knowledge, knowledge as symbolized and formulated in the *mathème*, *savoir*, in other words, knowledge that must arise by boring a hole through the equivocations that obtain in the register of the imaginary (the level of *connaissance*), must always come up against something that is irreducible, a barrier that obtains at the level of a knowledge that is not-known, that cannot be known, which is not only the real of the unconscious, but which is also a *jouissance* that Lacan also links with the unconscious. The unconscious is thus not a unity of being and thinking, but, insofar as it is the unconscious of a speaking being, is identified with desire and *jouissance*; "the unconscious is the fact that being, by speaking, enjoys," and, "wants to know nothing about it" (S20:104–105/95–96).

Badiou never mentions this *jouissance* perhaps because he finds its role to be so limited in Lacan's text, *l'Étourdit*. It is there, it is named, but its function is more strongly developed in *Encore* (S20), a seminar contemporary with *l'Étourdit*. I am rather insisting upon this because of the essential relations, discussed in earlier essays in this volume, that *jouissance* has with the ethics of psychoanalysis. I have described Lacan's ethic as an ethics of *jouissance*. In this, it is an ethics of the encounter with the real, and a way of dealing with the unconscious. An ethics well-said will therefore be an ethics of *jouissance*. It is an ethics that begins with the fact that insofar as a human being is a speaking being, it is a being that enjoys, and so a being that cannot be totally reduced to an epistemological univocity of the *mathème*. In its *jouissance*, it is also in excess of univocity.

Now, let us return to what was said earlier about the real qua *ab-sens* of truth and knowledge.

Philosophy says there is a knowledge of truth qua *sens* in the real. Lacan's inverts this in his schema of the analyst's discourse wherein knowledge is placed in the position of truth only when it is a knowledge on the side of the unconscious, which, too, is knowledge as a function of the real and so as a knowledge unknown-to-the-subject.[12] Again, we encounter the necessary enforcement of the binding of the truth–knowledge–the real in Lacan's discourse by which thinking, insofar as it is a *jouissance*, cannot be a knowledge of the real. It can only be the register of the effect of the real. So, we would again encounter Badiou's conclusion that there is no knowledge *of* the real, but now by a different route, the articulation of thinking in its relations with *jouissance*. *There is no knowledge of the real, there is only the function of the real in knowledge, which is not the same thing.*[13]

There is no truth of the real, there is no *sens* of the real, nor is there knowledge of the real. This is because the real must be thought as ab-*sens* and ab-*sens* in turn must be thought as the impossibility of the sexual relation. *L'Étourdit* maintains that the real constitutes "the wall of the impossible." This is why in his diagrams of the four discourses found in *Encore* (S20), in the discourse of mastery and of the university, the very discourses where Lacan places the discourse of philosophy, Lacan shows the vector of impossibility as obtaining between S_1 and S_2, between the position of the master signifier and knowledge. There is no way of breaking through the wall of the impossible so as to reach and obtain a truth of the real, since it does not exist, and so there is no way to reach knowledge of that truth (see S20:16/21). How can this impossibility be understood? The real as *ab-sens* of truth, as the impossible, must be thought as the absence, or the impossibility of a sexual relation. Thus, a completed formula arises in Lacan's *l'Étourdit*: *sens ab-sexe*.[14] There is knowledge of the real only insofar as there is a function of the real within it, and the function of the real is to comprise the "wall of the impossible" in this sense.

As was said before, it is Badiou's claim that philosophy cannot think this *ab-sens* of the real as the absence of the sexual relation. Prisoner of the couple truth-*sens*, philosophy thus breaks up the triplet truth–knowledge–the real and so misses an important rule of knowledge whereby truth-*sens* is linked with knowledge only insofar as knowledge is a function of the real, "that function that produces the formula, 'there is no sexual relation.'"[15]

Let us pause here for a moment. Badiou claims that in saying there is no truth of the real, Lacan is working even against what he himself has said prior to *l'Étourdit* regarding the role and place of truth in analytic discourse. In truth, Badiou probably goes too far in this, for

Lacan did not cease to problematize the relations of truth, knowledge, and the real. Nor does he in fact abandon his ways of phrasing truth in its relations with knowledge and the real as "half-said" (*mi-dire*), and since we never find him ever saying that there is truth qua sense of the real, so, the allegedly new position, articulated in *l'Étourdit*, is now only returning upon these themes in new ways rather than being something completely different. Lacan has always situated truth at the level of the saying: "I, truth, speak!" Truth, as saying and as an effect of the real, is never whole, insofar as the One itself is not whole but is always not-One, the One of difference. What is new, perhaps, is the linking of thinking, the linking of truth and knowledge to *jouissance*, which seems to become particularly prominent in the seminars and texts from the early 1970s. *Seminar XX, Encore*, speaks of truth as being the sister of *jouissance*, which would situate truth in relation to the real on the grounds that *jouissance* is precisely an "access to" qua an "effect of" the function of the real. So, there is truth, but not, as the philosopher—at least not in Badiou's construction of the philosopher—might have it: there is no absolute truth, there is no univocity of truth, there is no whole-truth embedded in the real as its sense (*sens*), its meaning and direction.

To illustrate this point, it could be added that Lacan says the same thing about dreams: the dream does not have a meaning or sense built into it. There is no mystery to a dream, resolved by discovering its true meaning. Rather, the sense of a dream is "read in what is said about it" (S20: 96/88). It is the way the dream is talked about, the way it is structured in "the said" that is important, the way in the analytic situation and in the saying of the dream by the analysand there is a constant interplay between the said (*dit*), the saying (*dire*), and the non-said (*non-dit*). This is the interplay, the play of masks, of semblances, and of *pseudos* proper to the saying of truth.

What is more, *Encore*, it should be recalled, speaks of an "indisputable truth," namely, "that there's no such thing as a sexual relationship" (S20: 12/17). This means that there is a truth only in the saying or only in the formulation of the real as a function, as an effect of the real.

Again, Badiou's claim is that philosophy asserts there is a truth of the real because for philosophy there is a *sens* of the real. But, in keeping with *l'Étourdit*, Badiou underlines Lacan's claim that the real, qua the impossibility of a sexual relation, cannot be reduced to either sense or nonsense (*sens*/non-*sens*); it exceeds this opposition and so exceeds philosophical discourse which always turns between these two poles: there is either sense or nonsense. For philosophy, that's the given spectrum of possibilities. For Lacan, on the other hand, there is something more: there is the "impossible" third term Lacan introduces into the philosophical opposition of *sens*–non-*sens*: there is the real as ab-*sens*, the absence of sense, the exteriority of the opposition of sense and nonsense. Thus, with the real consisting here of the impossibility of the sexual relation, Lacan provides a positive formulation of the ab-*sens* of the real as *sexe* ab-*sens*. Badiou's claim is that there is no truth here because there is no *sens* (meaning) for this impossible real. The real is the impossibility of a sexual relation, an impossibility that exceeds both sense and its opposite non-sense and so attains a third possibility, ab-*sens*, which Lacan writes as the *sens* ab-*sexe* of the real.

That a sexual relation is impossible does not mean, of course, that there are no acts of sexual intercourse. Rather, as far as psychoanalysis is concerned, there are two dimensions to this: First, while there may not be a private language, *jouissance* is "private." *Jouissance* is one's own affair, so to speak. Sexual partners never quite know what the other wants. One has to ask in so many ways: "What turns you on?" Sexual partners may conjoin, but sexual *jouissance* does not. In this sense, *amour* is narcissistic. "The real is narcissistic," as Badiou says of Lacan, the sexual bond is imaginary.[16] Second, and at the root of this, the sexual relation—as a relation—is a relation of signifiers, following upon Lacan's definition of the subject as represented by a signifier to another signifier. "Man" and "woman," the masculine and the feminine, are not so much biological, genital beings as they are signifying elements. And, as Lacan shows in his formulation of this, they are articulated in incommensurable ways in relation to the phallus and to the phallic function that is the key element in their sexual articulation, producing thereby the different modalities of *jouissance*, phallic and feminine. This is important and relevant to our discussion because, as matters turn out, the rock of the real, the impossible real, has this truth at its primary effect, for the real qua *ab-sens* is the impossibility of a relation, namely, the sexual relation, and so, in Lacanian terms, one must think and say—in a way that only can be described as "well-said"—that the real is *ab-sens* and so is also *ab-sexe*, or, in its brief formulation, *sens ab-sexe*.[17]

To sum up: from the standpoint of Lacan's text, *L'Étourdit* (1972), three terms, constituting a triplet, are at the heart of an ethics that is "well-said": the said (*dit*), the saying (*dire*), and the non-said (*non-dit*). This triplet must be maintained in its unity. The saying can only be in relation to the said (*dit*) and the non-said (*non-dit*). These three parallel the triplet of truth, knowledge, and the real. To this, there is a third triplet: *sens*, non-*sens*, and the ab-*sens*, that, likewise must be maintained in its unity. Where philosophy, trapped in its pursuit of the pair truth-*sens*, can only oppose *sens* to non-*sens*, ab-*sens* arises as the negation of this oppositional pair, as a third term that arises not from their dialectical opposition but as something given as the between of *sens* and non-*sens*. *Sens* and non-*sens*, the philosophical opposition is now to be seen as the effect of ab-*sens*, as the effect of the real qua *sens*-ab-*sexe*. These triplets thus chart the Lacanian anti-philosophy.

I think that something crucial for our understanding of Lacan's anti-philosophy follows from this: The conception and articulation of an alleged Lacanian "anti-philosophy" must not be allowed to fall back upon the philosophical way of thinking in oppositions, as in the philosophical opposition of *sens*–non-*sens*, for example. Otherwise, this anti-philosophy would be but another route of return for Lacan's discourse back into the fold of philosophical saying. Maintaining the triplets of the true-knowledge–the real, the triplet of *sens*–non-*sens*–*sens* ab-*sexe*, and that of *dit*–non-*dit*–*dire*, of the symbolic, the imaginary, and the real, maintaining these triplets thus serves to locate at the heart of philosophy's discourse, in the intimacy of its pairs of truth and *sens*, and in its oppositions of *sens* and non-*sens*, a discourse that is both intimate and ex-timate to it. The ethics well-said is the saying of this extimacy as an effect of all that must remain non-said, namely, the impossible real. Thus, the well-said of the ethics of psychoanalysis is one that holds to the triplet of the said, *dit*, the saying, *dire*, and the non-said, *non-dit*. Truth is what is said, but it is also the saying (*dire*), or more precisely, the half-saying (*mi-dire*), where both the saying and the non-said, the *non-dit*, are effects of the real. As such, they are not reducible either to non-*sens* nor to *sens*. Rather, they obtain as *sens* ab-*sexe*. These triplets structure the ethics and politics of Lacanian psychoanalysis.

We thus have a) the fourfold discourses from *Seminar XVII* (the discourse of the master, of the university, of the hysteric, and the analyst); b) the triplets of truth, knowledge, and the real, of the said, the saying, and the non-said, of *sens*, non-*sens*, and ab-*sens*; and c) in the middle of it all, we will also have the two: not the two of the knowledge and the known, not the oppositional pair of *sens* and non-*sens* not even the pair of the philosopher and the truth, or of the analyst and the real, but "them two," them two lovers, man and woman, "them two" ways of being inscribed in relation to the phallus and the phallic function, them two in the impossibility of their non-relation, the impossibility of their ever coming together to form One, the impossible sexual relation between them, the *sexe-sens*, as Lacan formulates it, the "wall of the impossible" that is at the heart of every ethics said to be "well-said." Thus, we have the four, the two, and the three. Now, as it turns out, are these not also ways of saying the One which is not One? Are they are also the three steps of the enigma the sphinx poses to Oedipus, the enigma that "man" is for himself? Is this enigma not at the heart of the ethics of psychoanalysis? Is this not the enigma that maintains the gap and the overlap between philosophy and the anti-philosophy of Lacanian psychoanalysis? What can be said in answer to this?

TOWARDS AN ETHICS WELL-SAID OF THE PSYCHOANALYTIC ACT: THE PASS

In connection with this concern for univocity, and in connection with the question of the "transmissibility" of the analytic discourse, we now have the opportunity to consider something important that emerges in Badiou's discussion of Lacan's alleged anti-philosophy: Lacan's anti-philosophy importantly turns on the question of the psychoanalytic "pass" (*passe*) that Badiou describes as one of Lacan's most intriguing inventions.

The pass is both an act and a procedure. Something happens in the pass, but it is also something repeatable because authorized; the pass is this procedure of authorization. Let's begin with the pass taken as a procedure of authorization. Generally speaking, one becomes an analyst only after having gone through the pass, which is an essential part of the training of an analyst. The analyst must prove him/herself by taking the curriculum of the EFP (the École Freudienne de Paris, founded by Lacan in 1964), by going through analysis, and then testifying about his/her analysis before witnesses. The pass was therefore the institutional framework establishing the practice of psychoanalysis, defining its ends, purposes, goals, techniques, and so on.[18] As an officially recognized procedure, the pass has a date and a history: it was instituted in 1967, three years after Lacan founded the École Freudienne de Paris, the EFP.

No doubt because of its claims to enact a "cure," psychoanalysis in France was always required to have an officially recognized and established status. The analyst is a doctor or a psychologist. Because of all the heterogeneous proliferation of cures and therapies, from primal scream therapies to group therapies, it is little wonder that official intervention was required.[19] The institution of the pass addressed these concerns.

But it also addressed the concern for the univocity and transmissibility of psychoanalytic truth and knowledge. The pass underwrites transmissibility. Whatever knowledge and truth psychoanalysis formalizes in its *mathèmes*, it is witnessed and authorized in and through the pass. The pass was not, therefore, just a murky existential moment, the personal experience of having gone through analysis; the ends and goals of analysis also had to be institutionally theorized and defined. "Transmissibility" here refers to the requirement that knowledge and truth withstand a process of certification whereby what occurs in the analytic act is rendered capable and worthy of being transmitted by being recognized and certified by a school, the Lacanian school of psychoanalysis, for example.

Badiou observes that the pass is a process of selection that would probably result in many unworthy philosophemes being dumped, thrown away, as of being of no value in accounting for the effect of real on discourse and formalization. Philosophy's claim, for example, that there is a truth of the real, would no doubt be one such castoff. Deciding which formulas will be retained and which will be cast off is an issue decided by the authorizing organs of the École.

As Badiou writes, the pass also allows one to speak of the psychoanalytic act as having taken place "somewhere," and to have done so in a way that cannot be said of philosophy. Does one speak of a philosophic act in the way one speaks of an analytic act, in the light, let us say, of specific parameters, established guidelines, recognized precedents, and orientations? The frontier issue, therefore, between psychoanalysis and philosophy, an issue that Badiou sees as defining Lacanian anti-philosophy is this: while there is a "pass" for psychoanalysis, philosophy does not and cannot have the pass. "Deep down," Badiou says, Lacan was convinced that philosophy, with its teacher-disciple, master-slave structure (as shown in Lacan's schema for the discourse of the master, and as exemplified in the *Meno* dialogue, in Socrates' dialogue with the slave boy), "does not have a pass." Not only does philosophy seemingly lack the corresponding institutional armatures and power structures that one finds in the psychoanalytic schools and associations, institutions that could conceivably define and determine the veracity and usefulness of a philosophical pass and that could lay down the law and say whether or not a philosophical act had taken place, but Lacan might also say that philosophy does not "pass through," in the sense that it does not pass through to the end of analysis, that while the philosopher, in doing philosophy, may call various ideas and opinions into question, neither the philosopher nor philosophy pass through. In other words, philosophy does not traverse the fantasy fundamental to its desire. As a practice and a discourse, philosophy does not succeed in passing through from its place in the discourse of the master to the discourse of the analyst. It does not traverse the fantasy of mastery, the structure of which is exhibited in the schema for the discourse of mastery. Philosophy does not traverse this structure.

What would it mean for philosophy to traverse the structure of the fantasy? What is the fantasy philosophy must traverse? First, let us recall that the structure of fantasy is given in the *mathème* $ ◊ *a*. This is read as formulating the relation (a relation of inclusion or exclusion, symbolized by the "punch," the diamond shaped punch between the poles of the barred S and *a*) of the divided subject, symbolized by the barred S, to *petit objet a*, the object-cause of the subject's desire. *Objet a* symbolizes the ever moving fantasm that sparks desire by being taken as something that could fill the gap, the void, the lack, at the heart of desire. *Objet a* stands in and so supplements the lack cut into being in the ascension of the subject into the symbolic order (the lack produced in and by the "signifying cut"), where the subject comes into being as a being defined according to the logic of the signifier. The effect of object *a* is to fill the nullity at the heart of the real; it is a way of dealing with the *ab-sens* of the real, the impossibility of a sexual relation. Another way of looking at this symbol is to see *objet petit a* as a kind of zero point, a point always displaced in relation to itself. While in its guises, *objet a* can take form as an object of desire, it must also be understood in the *mathème* of the fantasy as representing the null point of *ab-sens* opening between *sens* and non-*sens*, a point of perpetual displacement of *sens*.

Now Lacan positions the discourse of philosophy in the master's discourse, where we also find the *mathème* of fantasy inscribed below the lines separating the level of S_1 in relation to S_2.[20] What is philosophy's fundamental fantasy that constitutes the framework of its desire? If Badiou is correct, philosophy's fundamental fantasy, the fundamental object-cause of its desire, would have to be the love of truth, where truth is something transcendent that could be discovered in the real and brought to the surface by interpretation, dialogue, or whatever. In the structure of the philosophical fantasy, truth would occupy the position of *objet petit a*. This is a fantasy because there is no truth qua *sens* of the real. Philosophy's fundamental supposition that there is a truth-*sens* of the real, is, for Lacan, a fantasy. As an object *a* in the fantasy, truth both supplements the hole bored through the real and is the very drill bit for that hole. Truth is taken to be the sense of the real and not but one of the effects of the real. Truth, in its fantasmatic role, fills the lack at the heart of philosophy's love, its desire for truth. Truth is the object-cause for the divided subject of philosophy, namely, the classical philosopher, defined as the one who loves truth, as the one who desires to know and to have the consolation of truth, the whole truth. This is the fundamental fantasy that classical philosophy—the version of philosophy constructed in and by Badiou's essay—cannot traverse without losing itself as philosophy. Quoting Rimbaud's poem "À une raison," Lacan says that "love is a sign that one is changing reasons . . . in other words, one changes discourses" (S20: 16/21). But philosophy's love of truth has the effect of foreclosing the possibility of its changing discourses. Philosophy's love of truth is not just another reason. The traversal of the fantasy of the love of truth would be the extimacy of philosophy. This is the pass, the passing through of the fantasy of truth that philosophy cannot make.

To return to our discussion of the pass, the importance of the moment of authorization is not only in the way it situates Lacan's discourse in relation to philosophy, but also the way it situates the ethics of psychoanalysis, indeed the question of what it means for a psychoanalytic ethic to be "well-said," in the context of essentially political institutions, and so in terms of the protocols of institutionalized modes of legitimation and excommunication, the latter term only hinting at the analogies that could be drawn between the psychoanalytic institutions and the priestly institutions of religion. This places the whole issue of what would or would not count as "knowledge" and what would or would not count as an ethics well-said in the context of the four discourses, especially in those of philosophy (the discourse of the master), and science (the university discourse), as discourses having an institutional framework or context. This places the whole issue of identifying what counts as an act for psychoanalysis in the context of the question of the relations of institutions of power and knowledge. The univocity of an ethics well-said might then be determined according to what the psychoanalytic institutions would allow it to be. Here, the ethics of psychoanalysis, the ethics of the pass, thus meets up with the politics of psychoanalysis and the politics of the pass, as Lacan himself personally experienced.[21]

This also hooks up with the classical philosophical tradition of ethics. Again, it is Lacan's thesis that philosophy lacks the pass whereby whatever univocity it attains could be "authorized" and count as transmissible. A search for univocity can certainly be said to characterize the ideal of the Pythagorean and Platonic ethic. Was not its purpose to bring forth correct definitions of ethical acts by which they could be distinguished from their opposites, and by which they could be said to be acts based on truth and knowledge, making ethics a properly theoretical discourse, and so making it one that could, indeed, be taught? Was this not an ideal examined and ultimately rejected in Plato's *Meno* dialogue, for example? No doubt, this task was left unrealized. Plato's dialogue left the whole promise of a consolation of philosophy and the resolution of the *elenchus* somewhat in abeyance as the philosopher and his interlocutors finally had to settle for something decidedly less than knowledge when it comes to the question of determining the essence of an ethical act. It had to settle for something Plato called true opinion, something therefore much less than an exact or correct formalization of the ethical act. Even Aristotle's ethics did not promise anything approaching "correct formalizations." Instead, he based his ethics not only on a rational principle or on the hope for the precision of a univocity with regard to the overall problematic of determining the "right amount," but he also let the matter ultimately rest on the good counsels of the prudent man. Yet, lacking the pass, none of this was settled by way of committee, but only in terms of the logic of the arguments proffered in the philosophical search for the True, the Good, and the Beautiful. It was settled in ways internal to the discourse itself in its passing through opinion and the many ways the good has been said toward the univocity of the correct definition of the essence of the ethical act. But while one could say a tradition is established in this, the tradition and the discipline of the question, perhaps, but it would be difficult to say if any positive knowledge had been passed on or passed down. Philosophy, in this instance, and unlike psychoanalysis, seems more the discipline of the question, rather than the discipline of univocity and truth as Badiou makes it out to be. But, to get back to what we were saying about philosophy's "fantasy," namely, its love of truth, this situates it not only at the level of the question but also at the level where the most important questions are not being asked, or being left unsaid.

A well-spoken ethic of the analytic act must thus speak not only from the between of equivocity and univocity, it must also speak from the standpoint of a turning of the four discourses, and from the turning by which one passes from the powerlessness of the imaginary and the domain of equivocation toward the symbolic and toward the "wall of the impossible" real. The ethics well-spoken shall be an ethics of this pass, the pass qua the turning, the *é-tour-dit*, the eternal turning of the said from the discourse of philosophy and the discourse of mastery toward the saying of the discourse of analysis.

Beginning, one could say, from the impossible real, or by reference to it, Lacan's anti-philosophy is the turning of the discourse of philosophy, which Lacan calls the discourse of mastery, such that it is overturned, such that it runs aground so to speak on the reef of the real as *ab-sens* and as the wall of the impossible. The turning of the four discourses, from the master's discourse to the discourse to the analyst, is a turning of the way the ethical is said in the discourse of philosophy, a turning from inside the movement of that discourse, a movement Lacan's topology shows to be likened to that of the surface of a *torus* or a Möbius strip. This is not, therefore a purely theoretical or conceptual overturning of philosophy. Nor is it a turning of philosophy toward its "beyond" or its Other taken to be a sort of noumenal reality or something simply unsayable. Nor is it a turning against the discourse of philosophy from a position somehow outside or exterior to it, as one finds in radical skepticism. Rather, this is the turning of the discourse proclaiming the possibility of a truth of the real and of a knowledge of truth, the ethical-moral discourse of philosophy, namely, such that it can be "well-said." This is the turning by which philosophy would be able to find its way in dealing with the unconscious and with the real as the impossibility of the sexual relation. This turning would be the "pass" of philosophy by which philosophy would confront the impasse of the love of truth.

But, it is in the fact that the pass must be considered as not just a theoretical procedure but also as an *act* that the chief anti-philosophical moment of Lacanian psychoanalysis can best be situated. The act is the enactment of the triplet in its unity of truth–knowledge–the real. There is a unity of word and act such that the truth and knowledge that are put to work in their usage and *jouissance* in the course of the act are effects of the real as *sexe ab-sens*. It is not just in its word and the theory, but also in its "act" that psychoanalysis is disentangled from philosophy. It is in the psychoanalytic act of the pass where word seamlessly conjoins with act. The act in question is the analytic act as importantly and essentially defined in terms of the "transference."

Anti-philosophy though it may be, the Lacanian discourse crossed the frontier between philosophy and psychoanalysis in his eighth seminar, entitled *The Transference*. Lacan spent nearly all of *Seminar VIII*, from 1960, developing a reading of Plato's *Symposium* as a way of approaching the complexities of the transference, especially for the way it structures the "doctor"-patient/analysand relationship. There is the famous unity of word and deed (*logos* and *ergon*) at work in the Socratic dialogue that no doubt catches the eye of the psychoanalyst. The psychoanalytic act is, likewise, a unity of word and "deed." But, in light of what was said before, it is the unity of truth-*sens* that is also in play in the philosophical discourse: the word as a deed is directed at the real insofar as it has a truth-*sens*, here ultimately taking shape as the True, the Beautiful, and the Good.

According to Lacan's reading of the *Symposium*, Socrates, in his dialectical relations with Agathon and especially Alcibiades, shows himself
to be not only one of the first philosophers but one of the first analysts,
as well. "Almost an analyst," it must be said, for he is still captive to the
philosophical opposition of truth-sense and non-sense, he is still captive
to the philosophical fantasy of the love of truth. So, he is not yet well-said;
he has not yet found a way of dealing with the unconscious. Nonetheless,
the psychoanalyst can find much food for thought in this dialogue. It is
in the context of his reading of the *Symposium*, for example, that Lacan
was able to articulate one of his new formulas, that of the *agalma*, a first,
preliminary version of *objet petit a* where it is combined with the phallus,
making it a somewhat mysterious object-cause of desire. This is the role
Socrates must play; he must be the *agalma* for the desire of Alcibiades
so that he, Alcibiades, can attain the true object of his desire, which is
Agathon. Although he is fond of saying that he is ignorant, that his
whole philosophy commences with an awareness of ignorance, Socrates
must also ironically play the role of the subject-supposed-to-know. He
knows the true word that is the ultimate sense, the ultimate "what" that
would answer the philosophical-ethical questions, "What is love? What is
desire? What is *eros*?" But, again, this dialectic of desire is precisely that,
a dialectic of the desire that aims at the unity of the One, a dialectical
of the love of the Beautiful as the ultimate figure of *vérité-sens*. The
Beautiful, Truth in and as the Beautiful, is the ultimate form taken by
the real in and as *objet petit a* in the structure of the fantasy. Socrates is
the locus where the fantasy is enacted. It is in his being, at least in the
gaze of Alcibiades, the very embodiment of the beautiful that he is in the
position of *objet a*. He is the stand-in for the radiance of the Beautiful
and the ultimate object of desire, but, from the standpoint of the analyst,
he is what marks and supplements the void of the real as it shines forth
on the brilliant surfaces of the Socratic word and deed as the *jouissance*
of word and deed, as the truth effect of the real.

But, and let us anticipate my closing thoughts in saying this: just as
jouissance is the excess of the pleasure principle, and so linked not only
with pleasure but also with pain, even death, so *jouissance* as truth effect
of the real not only has the philosophical effect of displacing truth, but
it also has the practical effect, enacted in the analytic act, of being the
destitution, the *désêtre* (a Lacanian neologism that might be translated as
"unbeing") of the subject. It may seem that Socrates, too, must withstand
his own destitution. But, this comes as a moment of the ultimate care
of the soul, whereby the soul is released unto the death that will free it

for its unity with truth-*sens*. Hence, the fantasy enacted in the Socratic philosophical act attains its most brilliant moment, not as a moment of destitution, but as a moment of salvation.

A rather different measure of destitution is at work in the analytic act of the pass: it is the very turning of the Subject to its overturning, the opening of the dialectic of truth and its opposition of *sens* and non-*sens* to *jouissance* as the effect of an encounter with the nullity of the real. Thus, the Socratic dialogue is a beautiful dialogue, but it is not a dialogue "well-spoken," for it fails to find its way "in dealing with the unconscious." Thus, the beautiful Socratic way of speaking the ethics of philosophy as a care of the soul, is a saying that purifies the soul of the pathological, purifies it of all but the love of truth-*sens*. The philosophical saying thus prepares the soul for death, prepares it to find its immortality in the way it transcends finitude and makes death the ultimate purification, and so the ultimate affirmation of the fantasy of philosophy insofar as death is the way the soul is finally released from the equivocations of embodied life so as to find the true object of its desire, the beautiful univocity, the beautiful consolations of eternal truth. It is this fantasy that is traversed in the inconsolable destitution of the subject enacted in the psychoanalytic act of the "pass." We shall return to this.

But first, let us turn to consider the temporality, the double temporality, of the analytic act of the pass in Lacanian psychoanalysis.

The analytic act, in withstanding destitution, thus finds its way to deal with the unconscious as a way through the impasse of the philosophical opposition between the finite and the infinite, which almost mirrors the opposition of *sens* and non-*sens*. This couple, the finite and the infinite, breaks the unity of another triplet evident in the psychoanalytic act of the pass: the triplet of the finite, the infinite, and what I shall call the "in-finite," which is a radical finitude, exterior to the opposition of body and soul, of death and immortality. Philosophy typically puts the finite and the infinite in an oppositional relation: death and immortality, becoming and being. While Hegel found a dialectical way around this opposition, it is certainly there in Plato. How does Lacan address this?

In Badiou's reading of *l'Étourdit*, the analytic act, the pass, must find its way from equivocity to univocity. But this is not just a movement as between two static structures. The analytic act, the pass, is a seamless moment, apparently mysterious, of interpretation and anxiety. In this way, it is an act that "does not deceive." In other words, it is not just a matter of bringing forth an exact formalization; it is not just the proffering of a truth that would be convincing. There is also the considerable anxiety of the act that must be passed through. There is the experiential moment of ennui experienced as destitution that must be confronted. In a strong sense, the pass is also a moment of decision that Badiou compares to the moments of decision in Kierkegaard's ascension through the aesthetic to the ethical and finally to the religious stages, for example;[22] it is the seamless moment of word and act in which the real is encountered in its power to produce a decisive transformation, the moment of the act and the *mathème*. This is the moment of "the pass" whereby the analysand becomes an analyst, passing as though from Kierkegaard's ethical to the religious stage. It is the moment when the real enters the integral transmissibility (*intégrale transmissibilité*) of the *dire* of the act. Again, this is the moment that is at the center of any ethic well-spoken. An ethic well-spoken consists of these two united aspects of formalization and act.

Thus, Badiou writes, there are two "demands" at work in the analytic act and what he calls "an ethics of the cure": first, a demand to direct and to produce a correct, precise formalization, what Lacan also calls a correct interpretation; second, the moment of anxiety and destitution, as the effect of the encounter with the truth of the real. This is also to be demanded of the analytic act: it must produce a transformation of desire in and as the traversal of the fantasy of desire. But, due to the proximity to the real of the unconscious enacted in the traversal, it has anxiety as its effect, and so is something that requires caution: it must be doled out, so to speak, in "dosages." Again, these two are always interlaced with one another. Thus, there are also two temporalities at work here: the temporality of a correct formalization, tempted perhaps by "haste," and the temporality of anxiety.

The temporal vector of the correct formalization passes from the imaginary to the level of the signifier and the level of the formula, the *mathème*. Formalization, Badiou says, is the production of a field of capture (*un champ de capture*) in which an encounter with the real becomes a real possibility. But it also implies a temporality of haste Badiou identifies with the love of truth in which one is tempted to act too hastily so as to bring the analysis quickly to a close and so to terminate it precipitously. This is the risk at stake.

Here is where the other exigency arises: anxiety. Anxiety is the *affect*, as Badiou calls it, of this encounter with the real in the triplet truth-knowledge-real. Anxiety is the existential guarantee, the living moment of authorization of the encounter with the real. That anxiety must be "measured" in "dosages" implies a temporality by which the falling due of the real (*l'échéance du réel*) is constantly deferred. The real demands payment, truth and knowledge are ways of payment, but so is anxiety. And there is always a debt to be paid. Lacan has said that the only "goods" he recognizes are not just the ethical goods named by the philosophers, but rather the goods one pays in the encounter with the real, making the encounter with the real seem almost akin to an act of sacrifice in which one might have to give up too much, as has been shown in Lacan's reading of the tragedy *Antigone*. No doubt there is a need to defer these payments, to avoid paying them all at once, to maintain, as it were, some distance from the real and from the encounter with guilt and the *ab-sens* of sexuality. Anxiety, the act that underwrites the *mathème*, thus sits at the edge of *sens* and non-*sens* and there is on the part of the analyst a temptation to maintain this edge rather than plunge over it. Anxiety can demand too much.

Likewise, the cool of formalization can demand a hasty and brilliant finish to the analytic session so as to avoid, at least on the part of the analyst, his/her own destitution, haste itself thereby also being a deferral of destitution.

The Lacanian act, the ethic of the cure, as these passages suggest, must therefore balance itself between these two, the temporality of formalization and the temporality of anxiety. The ethical call is to find the way between these two temporalities of haste and stagnation, of formalization and restraint, to find the right pacing: On the one hand not to give in to the temptations of haste, the "brilliant finish," and, on the other, not to allow anxiety either to overwhelm or for the sessions to go on interminably and so to stagnate in the constant play of deferrals. These two temporalities active in the analytic situation thus reference Freud's title *Analysis Terminable and Interminable*, or, as the French translation has it, *Analyse finie et analyse infinie*.

The ethic well-said finds the balance between the temporalities of concluding and not concluding of the session. It is a way of always being, in its relation to the exteriority of the *ab-sens* of the real, at the borders of *sens* and non-*sens*, which are the same insofar as they both avoid *sexe ab-sens*. These two temporalities under discussion here could perhaps be seen as the temporalities of the ethics of psychoanalysis, the temporalities of the fold of the finite and the infinite in the analytic session. Badiou's main point in these passages is to show that the analytic act, punctuated in terms of these two reciprocal temporalities, holds to the triplet of truth, knowledge, and the real. The discourse of philosophy, on the other hand, might have broken this triplet apart were it to assert the two, Truth, the whole truth, Eternal Truth, and knowledge, the knowledge of things that can be otherwise. Hegel attempted to dialectically unify these in his *Phenomenology of Spirit* where time and history were brought to their closure and completion in and as Absolute Knowledge. But, this system probably only succeeded in further widening the gap between time and Absolute Truth. In any event, Truth and Knowledge thus became classical philosophy's ways of revenge against time and passing away. The promise of the philosophy of the care of the self is the overcoming of time in the promise of the eternal. In this way, philosophy has maintained both a revenge against time and against the real, thereby maintaining an ignorance that seems proper to philosophy, an ignorance of the *ab-sens* of the real, plugging up its staggering, temporalizing lack with the assertion of an eternal Truth and Knowledge.

Can these two temporalities of the analytic session, that of the infinite and the finite, to retain the French translation of Freud's essay, be transposed and made analogues for the temporalities of the ethics of philosophy? Let us propose something a little daring and adventurous here. Let us assert that there are two very general temporalities for the ethics of philosophy, that of the infinite and the finite, and that what they have in common is that both are forms of nihilism; that in different ways, one classical and one modern, they comprise a horizon of nihilism for ethical thought. The philosophical temporality of the infinite—the temporality of the care of the soul—would be that which inflates the truth-*sens* couple such that it becomes eternal, becomes an eternal Truth and the ultimate object of desire for the soul. We have touched on this already as being the algorithm of the fantasy of philosophy. The effect of this is to turn philosophy, qua care, into the preparation for death; to view the body as the prison of the soul, and to assert that the proper domain of the soul is the divine, the eternal, an abode of a truth somehow infinite, somehow timeless, where suffering comes to an end when the soul bids its farewell to coming into being and passing away. Death shall not have the last word. But, Nietzsche has well shown this to be a mode of nihilism in the sense of its being a form of revenge against life, revenge against time and passing away. Thus, for Badiou, this is where the disjunction between philosophy and analysis and a definitive form of Lacanian anti-philosophy arises. Philosophy always sees itself has having no temporal demand whatsoever. *Truth-sens* shall always be there, like an ancient landscape. Philosophy has "all the time in the world," and is always taking its time.[23] But in the analytic act, as Badiou understands it, through the doubling of the temporality of the *mathème* and the temporality of anxiety, the triplet knowledge–truth–the real, is maintained.

On the other hand, in terms of the modern experience of nihilism, we have the ethics of finitude, an ethics for which there are no truths, an ethics that draws breath from the vacuum left by the death of God, that takes its anxiety-ridden start from a being-unto-death. It becomes an ethics of the absurd, or an ethics of authenticity in the face of death. Here, death has the last word. But this, too, tries to break apart the triplet of truth–knowledge–the real by extinguishing its terms in an acid bath of pessimism and skepticism. That this is a form of nihilism can be seen in its emphasis on death and on the destitution of truth. Life has no meaning. Everything ultimately dissolves without remainder. The reign of truth-*sens* is over and there is nothing in its stead but a chasm of loss and catastrophe. Perhaps this modality of nihilism comes with the collapse of the fantasy that sustained the desire for truth in philosophy. With the collapse of the fantasy of the love of truth that had energized philosophy and that gave it its hope and its sense of promise, there comes a destitution of being, a destitution of philosophy experienced as the shadow of nihilism. Perhaps the thrust of Lacan's anti-philosophy and of the ethics of psychoanalysis, is to find a way out of these two impasses. Lacan's struggle to articulate and to defend his invention of the pass may have as its philosophical effect a way out of the impasse that results from these two nihilistic temporalities of the ethics of philosophy. Hence, the ethics of psychoanalysis would be neither an ethics of the infinite, in the sense just sketched, nor an ethics of existential finitude, but something exterior to this opposition, an ethics of the in-finite, or, to phrase it in a way symmetrical with what has been said about ab-*sens* as the between of *sens* and non-*sens*, perhaps this would be an ethics of the in-finite, an ethics of the real and of *jouissance* that is neither finite nor infinite, neither death nor an eternal life, but what opens between this philosophical-religious opposition that has sustained so much of the European tradition of ethics, especially the tradition of the care of the soul.

Lacan did not bequeath us very much as to how this ethics might finally take shape, but it has the merit of at least pointing in the direction of a new way of conducting a genealogy of morals, a way that would show how the truths and values of ethics are not inscribed in either the eternal stars, nor in the darkness of death, but in the strange and ever-troubling light of desire and language. In its affirmation of desire, we would have an affirmation of life, an overcoming of the revenge hosted against life and passing away. The ethical saying, the ethics well-spoken, would be an affirmation that would trace the values and truths of ethical life not back to the couple of truth and *sens*, either as eternal forms or as what must withstand its own destitution, but as the effects of the *ab-sens* of the real. In this way, ethics finds its way in dealing with the unconscious.

Let us carry this a step further. Badiou's essay has thus evoked the two temporalities of analysis, that of the finite and of the infinite. We now come to something of a climax in the process and the drama of analysis, the moment of its end, the moment of the end of analysis where interpretation and anxiety converge in a moment of destiny and destitution (*désêtre*). This is a moment neither finite nor infinite, an end, a term neither terminable nor interminable, but something of a third, perhaps, the in-finite moment of a catastrophe in the double sense of the word, being both a moment of destitution, of a downturn, and of a strophe, a turning of desire into another dimension, another possibility. I have already touched upon this earlier, in connection with Lacan's reading of Plato's *Symposium*, and once again, my purpose is only to think this moment in connection with its relation to philosophy.

Because of its connection with anxiety and destitution, because the way the ethos of psychoanalysis wraps itself around the kernel of our being, around the *ex nihilo* that subsists at the heart of the human being like an impenetrable void (S8: 13), because the analytic act is also a tragic act, it does not attempt to project onto this void or onto this tragedy any healing sovereign Good. And, like an act in a tragic drama, here, too, the hero, the analyst, in this case, falls in the end "like a piece of trash (*déchet*)."[24] In coming to the being of desire, in coming to know and coming to the being of knowledge, the analyst must, at the end of analysis, "withdraw: *sicut palea*, as [Saint] Thomas said of his work at the end of his life, like muck."[25] Likewise, the analysand, who, in the pass, must withstand the collapse of the fantasy that has sustained his/her desire, must also, in the end, undergo something like a destitution of his/her desire, framed as it was by the logic of castration and the fantasy that was built up around it. Through the pass, the analysand who would be an analyst must come to traverse the fantasy that sustains desire, must come through this to the truth of his/her desire, a truth experienced as destitution. The experience of the impasse of the unconscious and of the desire of the Other is a crucial moment in the pass. Lacan formulates this impasse as the *irpas*, a neologism suggesting both "to go through" and "not gone through." It is a reference to the real as the truth of the unconscious as a pure desire articulated as a *désirpas*, a "desire-not," a desire for which there is ultimately no interpretation or solution—no way out—because unconscious desire is a desire that will always remain. The impasse of the pass is the encounter with the real as absence of meaning. To undergo the destitution is in part to encounter the impasse of the real as unconscious desire. Here is the ordeal of the subjective destitution, which, being both a pass and an impasse, is necessary for any analyst-to-be.[26]

Perhaps the summarizing difference between the context of ethical nihilism and the psychoanalytic act turns on the different registers of destitution in each: whereas nihilism is the experience of the destitution of the highest values, for analysis, for the ordeal of the pass, on the other hand, there is a destitution of the analysand who would become, through the experience of the pass, an analyst. Such destitution is not a consequence of the downfall of truth, but of the downfall of the fantasy sustaining desire. It is an effect of the affirmation, not the negation of desire, an affirmation that carries desire to its limit at which it sustains its own destitution.

But something more must be said about this most acute moment in the analytic act in its relation to philosophy and anti-philosophy, something I touched upon briefly before. Lacan has often indicated how essential the role of the subject-supposed-to-know is for the philosopher. He found it in Descartes where the desire for certainty—and Lacan emphasizes the word "desire" here—has God as its guarantor: it is God that is the subject-supposed-to-know. Likewise, in the Platonic dialogues, Socrates, as we have seen in connection with the *Symposium*, has played this role. We can also see this at work in another dialogue, the *Meno*, where Lacan dwells on Socrates' dialogue with the slave boy and the search for a component of knowledge in ethical life that might compare with the knowledge obtained in mathematics. Insofar as ethical virtue for the Platonic-Socratic tradition is ideally identified with theoretical knowledge, with knowing in a strong and precise sense what one is doing, it must avoid the experience of the collapse of the subject-supposed-to-know. Lacanian analysis would strongly differ from philosophy precisely on this point. In the analytic act, the analyst—and here lies its ethical moment—must offer him/herself as the medium (*objet a*)—in this case, as the subject-supposed-to-know—through which the subject undergoes its own destitution, its *désêtre*. The analytic act enacts the deflation, the destitution of the subject-supposed-to-know. In the experience of the pass, and as a result of the traversal of the fantasy sustaining desire, Lacan writes, "the subject sees his own self-assurance sink, a self-assurance that stemmed from the fantasy in which everybody's opening onto the real is constituted." This collapse, this ultimate grasp of desire places the analyst in his/her relation to knowledge in the grasp of *désêtre*.[27] In this destitution, in this collapse of the analyst as the subject-supposed to know, the psychoanalytic act thus clears the way for the subject to proceed not toward an eternal truth as a guide for life and action, but toward the truth of his/her own particular, time-bound, death-bound desire, a path therefore also linked with destitution, anxiety, and the encounter with death. To discover, in other words, the truth of the fantasy that upholds desire and that upholds castration and alienation is to discover that there is no truth and no universe of discourse that can provide the analysand with the knowledge and the answers he/she needs. To undergo the terrible experience of destitution is to encounter the real as something impossible because not symbolizable, something that eludes knowledge, that eludes truth, and that makes a hole or an opening into it. Thus, unlike the God of the philosophers, unlike the Socratic dialectician, the analyst must not offer him/herself in the temporalities of the analytic act as the measure of reality. Rather, as the subject-supposed-to-know, and so as the one embodying the Other, in short, the position of the analyst forms something like a third party between the living person of the analyst (the analyst qua other rather than being the Other) and the analysand, a third party that is also a pivot around which the transference and the analytic act turns. The *désêtre* is the deflation of this subject-supposed-to-know such that the analysand renounces the desire to find approval or love in the Other as compensation for all the sacrifices he or she has had to endure in the course of analysis. At this point, the subject attains a boundary or limit of desire whereby the analysand no longer needs to situate his/her desire in terms of the Other, in terms, that is to say, of a need for approval from the analyst the Other, but is now, following upon the deflation of the analyst as a subject-supposed-to-know, and for the first time left to determine for him/herself what possibilities are left for his/her own desire.[28]

The ethics of psychoanalysis thus offers a commentary on the position of the analyst and on the desire of the analyst in the analytic act. Throughout the ordeal of the ends of analysis, the analyst must maintain a reticence; the analyst must not offer consolations or reassuring guarantees. This is the ethical exigency of analysis. The analyst must not be the measure of reality. Such reticence is the eloquence of the ethic well-said.

How different this seems when compared to the eloquence of the philosopher—Socrates, for example—in the philosophical dialogue. Does he ever maintain his own reticence? Does the philosopher ever face or encounter his/her own destitution in the philosophical dialogue? For the philosopher, at least for the Pythagorean-Socratic philosopher of the care of the soul, there is no encounter with destitution. There is risk, as is clear in the early Platonic dialogues that pertain to the last days of Socrates, but it is one that the philosopher engages assured that all will turn out well in the end. This is the promise of philosophy, at least in its classical form, a promise that psychoanalysis cannot offer, that in the end, even death and destitution shall ultimately bring no chilling sting.

TO CONCLUDE / NOT TO CONCLUDE

So, whence the promise of psychoanalysis? We can perhaps conclude with the assurance, as though it were another Sunday (*Dimanche*), when we seem to have all the time in the world, that the accursed share of this pathway of truth that Lacan opens before us, this thinking of the One as "gap," as fault, better prepares us for the stratagems and the lures of semblance; perhaps it better arms us against the hypnotizing enthrall of the false goods circulating in the economy of goods, and better arms us, as well, against the vanity of our own demands—the "regressive demands," as Lacan called them (S7: 300)—for love and for Oneness, demands that preoccupy and entrance us to the point that one might take oneself to be little more than a sacrifice for their attainment. But this is only the beginning, for the thinking of the One is also the thinking of the end and the promise of analysis. And, in the end, perhaps the one and only end of analysis, when the promise of analysis attains its end and its Oneness, there is but a "pass," as Lacan called it, whereby the analysand him/herself becomes an analyst and everything must always begin again in the seemingly eternal turning, the *É-tour-dit* of the said, the saying and the non-said. Is this not the ultimate promise of an ethics well-said, that it not give way, no matter what, on desire? But, in making this "pass," one must, as though it were one's duty, confront the real, the but half-said truth of the human situation, which is not only death, as in the Hegelian dialectic, but also desire that "leads us to aim at the One," at the "gap" (*faille*). Or, as Lacan said in his seminar on the ethics of psychoanalysis, "at the end of analysis the subject should reach and should know the domain and the level of the experience of absolute disarray," a level of distress and anguish, in which a danger is allowed to appear (S7: 304/351). This touches on the limit for man, it touches on the hole, the "gap" in his being; "it touches the end of what he is and what he is not" (S7: 304/351). And who would deny that to accomplish just this much is not, after all, a little thing? Yet, again (*Encore*), is it not also a very philosophical thing?

In closing, let me return to something I touched upon in an earlier essay in this series. In the context of a discussion of the transference, and in connection with the avowal of *jouissance* that is a constant
in Lacan's discourse—a *jouissance* articulated against a background of
the experience of the limits of language, of law, of death and sexuality,
all the limit-figures, in short, of the defile, of the rank and file, of the
signifier that defines the being and the limits of the human experience
in the world—in connection with all of this and in the context of the
analytic experience of the transference, something new arises in Lacan's
discourse, something glittering and tantalizing—is it perhaps a new ideal,
a new value?—something that many in his audiences and many among
his readers had thought he had downgraded to the status of an illusion
returns to form perhaps the most radical horizon of his ethics of psychoanalysis: namely, love.

All the best of the philosophers spoke highly of love: Socrates, Plato,
Spinoza, Kant, Nietzsche, and Kierkegaard. But for them love was always
but a vehicle whereby something transcendent could be brought into view,
the transcendence of the Good, of the Law, of God and Truth. Freud,
too, put it to work in the transference as its virtual engine: doctor love,
the identification of the patient with the analyst, love as an illusion, love
as a narcissistic relation of the patient to an object. But for all of these,
love was always bound with an object, and always situated within the
law, the law of the pleasure principle, the law of narcissism, where love is
but the way by which one makes oneself lovable to and before the other.

But, in his final, closing remarks of *Seminar XI* on *The Four Fundamental Concepts of Psychoanalysis*, Lacan evoked another love, another
domain, and another possibility of love. He called it a limitless love, a
love that has renounced its object, a love outside the limits of the law.
A love linked to *jouissance*, but not the *jouissance* of the sexual body,
where *jouissance* is limited to being one's own, but to a pure *jouissance* at
the limit of both the ego and the imaginary as well the subject and the
symbolic, a *jouissance*—a "love"—that arises from the limit-experience,
from the very impasse of the impossibility of the sexual relation, a *jouissance* that surges from the "impenetrable void," "the kernel" of "our being"
(S8: 13), a love that begins as an encounter with the *ab-sens* of the real,
and that surges in this place of non-relation as an address to the other,
a *jouissance*, a love that, beyond all narcissism, addresses the other not in
a fantasmatic and narcissistic search for unity with the other, but that
addresses the being of the other in its inviolable difference and from
the *ab-sens* of the real. And it would have to be said that this would

be a "love"—hitherto unthought by philosophy—at the limits of both imaginary and the symbolic orders, a love that has perhaps an ontological bearing, and that has its temporality not in the infinite, nor in the finite, but in what I am here approaching as the in-finite.

So, perhaps when Lacan tells us, "Do not give way on your desire," he might also be telling us, "Do not give up on love, not give up on this pure, limitless *jouissance*, do not give up on your *sinthome*." *Sinthome*: a curious, archaic word, an "ancient way of writing the symptom" (S23:11), but that differs from a symptom in that it is uninterpretable, not a message from the unconscious, structured like a language, but a particular trace of *jouissance*. It is a word Lacan began using in the 1970s as he moved away from the model of linguistics toward a new topology and new ways of visualizing the Borromean knots tying the symbolic, the imaginary, the real to one another and to the symptom; it is a word and a name that designated new pathways in Lacan's thought, a new articulation, in an almost Joycean tumult of language, of the unanalyzable dimensions of *jouissance*, dimensions in excess of the efficacy of the symbolic and the imaginary. Uninterpretable, it is what thus also survives destitution, for there is no neurotic fantasy to traverse. As pronounced in Lacan's last words on the subject, from his 1974–1975 seminar, it is also what "allows us to live," neither finite nor infinite, but as the in-finite *jouissance* of a limitless love. And this is why Lacan considered himself to be a lifelong lover of love and why he installed himself—as one can see in his eighth seminar—in all the ambiguities and equivocations of the philosophies of love. Love in this sense of being a "limitless love" would have its ethical force in being both an avowal of life and of truth, where truth is not so much a *sens* as it is a "fidelity," to borrow a term from Badiou, that does not give way on desire, that does not give way on the One as difference, and the chance encounter with the being of the other that arises from within it. Would this be, then, not just a love of truth, but the truth of a love that would begin from the ultimate intimacy at the heart of philosophy and be the ultimate extimacy of philosophy?[29] Is love in this sense of being a "limitless love" not that in-finitesimal something that marks the difference between the ethics of psychoanalysis and the ethics of the care of the soul? Is this not what marks the distance between Lacan and the morality of the law that would have set all love aside as pathological for fear it might have had a role to play in determining the law? What limitless love is this? Is it not what takes the analytic act to a new level of ethical life, to a level that, until the discovery of the unconscious, could perhaps never have been glimpsed by the philosophers? But now that it is there, does it not transform philosophy and psychoanalysis alike?

The metaphysical and ontological targets of Lacan's anti-philosophy might well seem to be something of the past, configurations of philosophical thought long gone by. But Lacan's demystification of the tradition of the care of the soul, rather than being the ruin of philosophy, can be seen instead as laying the groundwork for a new way of philosophizing, for a new way of thinking what it is to be a mortal, speaking human being in this world. It may be the preparation for a new way of articulating what it means to "take care" and "to cure," a way that is neither an ethics of finitude, an ethics promising the authenticity of a resolution toward death, nor an ethics of the infinite, an ethics of Truth that would pretend to have all the time both in this world and whatever might lie beyond it, but an ethics of the in-finite, an ethics of the *ab-sens* of the real, an ethics of a *jouissance* that cannot be restricted to the opposition of the finite and the infinite.

Would it be hasty to conclude on these grounds that perhaps what we find across Lacan's seminars is not so much a thinking that exhausts itself in opposing the fantasms of a philosophy that no one really holds any longer, like a coin no longer in circulation, not so much an anti-philosophy, in other words, that would be but the other side of a philosophical tradition now fading into the growing shadows of an age of nihilism, but rather, from the intimacy of thought, it risks the opening, the extimacy of philosophy toward an in-finite thinking? Would it be hasty to conclude that Lacan offers the adumbrations of a new departure, the outlines of a new ethics and a new way of thinking and speaking, a new way of taking up the question of what it is to be a human being, both desiring and speaking from the heart of the real? And rather than concluding this thought in haste, would it not be the duty of the thinker to begin again, to affirm again the possibilities sketched across a lifetime of work of an ethics that takes its start not from the spirit of revenge against life, but from *jouissance* and the real, an ethics, as Lacan said, that would now be—and perhaps for the very first time—"well-said"?

NOTES

INTRODUCTION

1. The distinction between the French terms for knowledge active in Lacan's seminars, *savoir* and *connaissance*, with its correlate *méconnaissance* (misrecognition), is discussed in the seventh essay in this collection. *Savoir* pertains to the symbolic order. It is the ultimate target of psychoanalysis, the unconscious knowledge of the truth of desire, a knowledge that is blocked, obscured, or covered over by the work of *connaissance* (the register of philosophical self-knowledge), which obtains at the level of the imaginary and the conscious ego.

2. This is an oblique reference to Hölderlin's "The Meaning of Tragedies," in Friedrich Hölderlin, *Essays and Letters*, edited and translated with an introduction by Jeremy Adler and Charlie Louth (London: Penguin Books, 2009), 316, and to interpretations of this famous passage by Philippe Lacoue-Labarthe, for example, in his "Hölderlin's Theater," in *Philosophy and Tragedy*, edited by Miguel de Beistegui and Simon Sparks (London and New York: Routledge, 2000), 119. The reference to the "double death" stems from Lacan's seminar, *The Ethics of Psychoanalysis, 1959–1960*, edited by Jacques-Alain Miller and translated by Dennis Porter (New York: W.W. Norton and Co.), the session dated June 8, 1960 and entitled "Antigone between Two Deaths," 270ff.

3. In order "to withstand the test of commentary," the question with regard to the task Lacan's reading of Freud sets for itself is, paraphrasing Lacan, "not simply to situate, but to gauge whether the answer (the text) gives to the questions he raises has or has not been superseded by the answer one finds in his work to current questions." My own modification of this is to seek the questions, not the answers, Lacan's texts suggests for contemporary concerns. See Lacan, "The Freudian Thing," *Écrits*, 336/404.

ESSAY 1. TOWARD AN ETHICS OF PSYCHOANALYSIS

1. Marcelle Marini, *Jacques Lacan: The French Context*, translated by Anne Tomiche (New Brunswick: Rutgers University Press, 1992), 20ff., where one will

find an informative account of the complicated context surrounding the publication of Lacan's seminars.

2. Sigmund Freud, *An Autobiographical Study*, translated and edited by James Strachey (New York: Norton, 1952 [1925]), 57. On page 67 of that work, Freud says that the only philosophers he read were Schopenhauer, whom he credits with anticipating some of the discoveries of psychoanalysis, such as the dominance of the emotions, the "supreme importance of sexuality, and the mechanisms of repression, and Nietzsche, who, likewise, was prescient of psychoanalysis.

3. Again, I refer the reader to Marcelle Marini's *Jacques Lacan: The French Context*, 230–231.

4. Anonymous, "l'Infinie et la castration," *Scilicet* 5 (1975), 75–77. *Scilicet* is a review journal published by the École Freudienne. It was a collection under the direction of Jacques Lacan.

5. Ibid., 76.

6. Ibid., 78–79.

7. Ibid., 75.

8. Ibid., 85–86. See also Lacan's remarks in *l'Étourdit*, also published in *Scilicet* 4 (1973), 5–31. The concluding essay in this collection returns to this theme of the in-finite.

9. Jacques Lacan, *Écrits*, translated by Bruce Fink (New York: W.W. Norton & Company, 2006), 269/324.

10. Ibid., 270/324.

11. Ibid.

12. Ibid.

13. Jacques Lacan, "l'Étourdit," *Scilicet* 4 (1973), 5–52, also quoted in Dylan Evans, *Dictionary of Lacanian Psychoanalysis* (East Sussex: Routledge, 1996), 208. For the distinction between continuous and discontinuous transformation, see Evans, *Dictionary of Lacanian Psychoanalysis*, 208.

14. J. Laplanche and J. B. Pontalis, *The Language of Psychoanalysis*, translated by Donald Nicholson-Smith (New York: W.W. Norton & Company, 1973), 127.

15. Lacan, *Écrits*, 270/325.

16. Ibid., 275/331.

17. Ibid., 274/330.

ESSAY 2. PHILOSOPHY'S PREPARATION FOR DEATH

1. Lacan, *Écrits*, 536/642.

2. Alain Badiou, "Lacan and the Presocratics," in *Lacan: The Silent Partners*, edited by Slavoj Žižek (New York and London: Verso: 2006), 7.

3. Badiou, "Lacan and the Presocratics," 13.

4. Slavoj Žižek, *The Ticklish Subject* (London and New York: Verso, 2000), 154.

5. Maurice Blanchot, *The Space of Literature*, translated by Ann Smock (Lincoln: University of Nebraska Press, 1982), 38.

6. Jean-Claude Milner, "Lacan et la science moderne," in *Lacan avec les philosophes*, 344. (The author has added the dash in the word "infinite" for emphasis.)

7. Alexandre Kojève, *Introduction to the Reading of Hegel*, edited by Alan Bloom, translated by H. Nichols Jr. (New York and London: Basic Books, 1969), 5.

8. Lacan, "Reply to Jean Hyppolite," *Écrits*, 319/382.

9. Evans, *Dictionary of Lacanian Psychoanalysis*, 17.

10. Slavoj Žižek, "A Hair of the Dog That Bit You," in *Lacanian Theory of Discourse* (New York: New York University Press, 1994), 47.

11. Lacan, "The Direction of the Treatment and the Principles of Its Power," 1958, *Écrits*, 524/628.

12. Lacan, "The Subversion of the Subject and the Dialectic of Desire," *Écrits*, 686/810.

13. Lacan, "Response to Hyppolite," *Écrits*, 320/383.

14. Lacan, "The Subversion of the Subject and the Dialectic of Desire," *Écrits*, 692/817.

15. Ibid., 692/817.

16. Ibid., 693/818.

17. Ibid.

18. A later Lacan would turn against this and assert there is no Other of the Other.

19. Lacan, "Introduction to Jean Hyppolite's Commentary on Freud's *Verneinung*," *Écrits*, 316/380.

20. Slavoj Žižek, "Hegel with Lacan, or the Subject and Its Cause," in *Reading Seminars I and II*, edited by Richard Feldstein, Bruce Fink, and Maire Jaanus (Albany: State University of New York Press, 1996), 398.

21. Lacan, "The Function and Field of Speech and Language in Psycho-analysis," *Écrits*, 260/316–264/321.

22. Ibid.

23. Ibid., 264/321.

24. Ibid., 264/321.

ESSAY 3. THE "TRUTH ABOUT TRUTH"

1. On "retroaction," see Lacan's 1960 essay, "The Subversion of the Subject and the Dialectic of Desire in the Freudian Unconscious," *Écrits*, 681–682/805. For a discussion of Freud's *Nachträglichkeit*, see Laplanche and Pontalis, *The Language of Psychoanalysis*, especially page 112.

2. Nancy, "Manque de rien," in *Lacan avec les philosophes*, 201–206.

3. An important source for this thesis concerning truth is Nancy's "Manque de rien."

4. Ibid., 202.

5. Lacan, *Écrits*, 337/405.

6. Lacan, "The Signification of the Phallus," *Écrits*, 581–583/692–694: "The phallus is the privileged signifier of (the) mark in which the role of Logos is wedded to the advent of desire."

7. Éric Laurent, "Alienation and Separation (I)," in *Reading Seminar XI: Freud's Four Fundamental Concepts*, edited by Richard Feldstein, Bruce Fink, and Maire Jaanus (Albany: State University of New York Press, 1995), 22–23.

8. Ibid.

9. See Lacan, "The Instance of the Letter in the Unconscious," May, 1957, *Écrits*, 504–505, and, Jean-Luc Nancy and Philippe Lacoue-Labarthe, *The Title of the Letter* (Albany: State University of New York Press), 65.

10. Lacan, "The Subversion of the Subject," *Écrits*, 685/808.

11. Lacan, "The Function and Field of Speech and Language in Psychoanalysis," 1953, *Écrits*, 237/287, and "Logical Time and the Assertion of Anticipated Certainty," 1945, *Écrits*,169ff./207ff.

12. Nancy and Lacoue-Labarthe, *The Title of the Letter*, 82.

13. Lacan, "Position of the Unconscious," *Écrits*, 704/830.

14. Ibid.

15. Jacques Lacan, *The Four Fundamental Concepts of Psychoanalysis*, edited by Jacques-Alain Miller, translated by Alan Sheridan (New York: W.W. Norton & Company, 1978), especially chapter 16, "The Subject and the Other: Alienation," from the seminar session of the May 27, 1964, and page 144, from the seminar session of April 22, 1964.

16. Diagrammed:

$$\frac{S_1 \text{ (agent)} \quad \rightarrow \quad S_2 \text{ (the signify chain, the field of knowledge, the Other)},}{\text{(S barred)} \qquad \text{(truth) } \lozenge \ a \ (\textit{objet petit a}, \text{ position of loss and } \textit{jouissance})}$$

17. Lacan, "Position of the Unconscious," *Ècrits*, 713/841.

18. Lacan, "The Subversion of the Subject and the Dialectic of Desire," *Ècrits*, 691/185.

19. Ibid.

20. Ibid., 715/843.

21. Ibid.

22. Ibid., 719/848.

23. Ibid.

24. Ibid., 717/846.

25. Ibid., 712/840.

26. To diagram this without the requisite Venn circles:

1) The level of "alienation":

Where $ is within the circle of Being, S_1, the unary trait, is within the rim, the overlap between the Venn circle for $ (Being) and S_1, the Venn circle identifying the set "Meaning." The ^ designates the position of the "rim" of the unconscious, the overlap of Being and Meaning.

$$\$ \rightarrow (S_1, \text{ the lack}) \;\wedge\; S_2$$

2) The level of "separation": Again, the same two circles, one for Being, one for Meaning. This is a *vel*. The overlap, the position of the "rim," the "punch" (symbolized by the V or the ^) marks the position of the lack, which at the level of alienation is identified with the unary trait, or master signifier marking the subject, subjectifying him/her, and at the level of alienation is identified with object *a*, or with the "Thing," as it was named in the seventh seminar on ethics. Thus, $ (Being) in a relation of inclusion and exclusion with object *a* (lack) **v** ($S_1 \rightarrow S_2$) (the signifying chain, Meaning).

This follows Laurent, "Alienation and Separation," 19–38.

27. Lacan, "Position of the Unconscious," *Écrits*, 712/839.

28. Ibid., 718/847.

29. Ibid., 720/849.

30. Ibid.

31. Certainty, Cartesian certainty, is possible for Lacan not at the level of being, the level of the statement, marked as $S_1 \rightarrow S_2$, the level of the *ego cogito*, the level of the "I am," the level Lacan will later identify as that of the Master, in Hegel's master-slave dialectic, but at the level of S barred, at the level of the thinking unconscious, the level of the subject of the unconscious, perhaps identified with the position of the slave in Hegel's master-slave dialectic.

32. Colette Soler, "The Subject and the Other (II)," in *Reading Seminar XI: Freud's Four Fundamental Concepts*, edited by Richard Feldstein, Bruce Fink, and Maire Jaanus (Albany: State University of New York Press, 1995), 49.

33. Lacan, "The Position of the Unconscious," *Écrits*, 714/842.

34. Laurent, "Alienation and Separation (I)," in *Reading Seminar XI*, 25.

35. Lacan, "Position of the Unconscious," *Écrits*, 715/843.

36. Soler, "The Subject and the Other II," 49; Lacan, *Seminar XI*, 188, and "Position of the Unconscious," *Écrits*, 715/183, for the use of the term *velle*.

37. Soler, "The Subject and the Other II," 49.

38. To quote Lacan's 1960 "The Subversion of the Subject and the Dialectic of Desire," "man's desire is the Other's desire . . ." The subject is addressed by the Other, "What do you want?" ("*Chè vuoi?*"), and this question "best leads the subject to the path of his own desire" in the analytic situation in which it is Other qua analyst that the subject asks, "even without knowing it . . . 'What do you want from me?'" *Écrits*, 690/815.

39. Soler, "The Subject and the Other (II)," in *Reading Seminar XI*, 49.

40. Lacan, "Position of the Unconscious," *Écrits*, 707/834.

41. Ibid.

42. On the "indestructible," see, for example, Sigmund Freud, *The Standard Edition of the Complete Psychological Works*, Volume V (1900–1901), translated by James Strachey (London: Vintage, The Hogarth Press, 2001), 577.

43. Nancy, "Manque de rien," 204–205.

44. Alain Badiou, *Infinite Thought: Truth and the Return of Philosophy*, translated and edited by Oliver Feltham and Justin Clemens (London and New York: Continuum, 2004), 85.

45. Ibid.

46. Jacques Lacan, *Television: A Challenge to the Psychoanalytic Establishment*, translated by Denis Hollier, Rosalind Krauss, and Annette Michelson, edited by Joan Copjec (New York: W.W. Norton & Company, 1990), 83, also quoted in Evans, *Dictionary of Lacanian Psychoanalysis*, 217.

47. Lacan, Seminar of May, 1973, quoted by Badiou, *Infinite Thought*, 86.

48. Lacan, "Seminar on *The Purloined Letter*," *Écrits*, 13/20.

49. Badiou, *Infinite Thought*, 86.

50. Evans, *Dictionary of Lacanian Psychoanalysis*, 175.

51. Lacan, "Seminar on *The Purloined Letter*," *Écrits*, 10/16.

52. Lacan, "Instance of the Letter," *Écrits*, 435/524.

53. Nancy and Lacoue-Labarthe, *The Title of the Letter*, 30–31.

54. Mikkel Borch-Jacobsen, *Lacan: The Absolute Master*, translated by Douglas Brick (Stanford: Stanford University Press, 1991), 125.

55. Lacan, "The Instance of the Letter," *Écrits*, 437/526.

56. Nancy and Lacoue-Labarthe, *The Title of the Letter*, 68.

57. Lacan, "The Freudian Thing," *Écrits*, 358/431.

58. Lacan, *Écrits*, 358/431, and "The Signification of the Phallus," 578/689.

59. See, for example, Jacques Lacan, *The Seminar of Jacques Lacan, Book I, Freud's Papers on Technique, 1953–1954*, edited by Jacques-Alain Miller, translated by John Forrester (New York: W.W. Norton & Company, 1988), 49ff., and "Psychoanalysis and Its Teaching," *Écrits*, 373/447 and 379/454. See also "Introduction to Jean Hyppolite's Commentary on Freud's *Verneinung*" in *Écrits*.

60. See Freud, "Psychopathology of Everyday Life," *Standard Edition*, Vol. VI, translated and edited by James Strachey (London: Hogarth Press, 1960), 1–7.

61. Lacan, "Psychoanalysis and Its Teaching," *Écrits*, 373/447.

62. Lacan, "The Freudian Thing," *Écrits*, 358/431.

63. Lacan, *Écrits*, 340/409.

64. Jacques Derrida, "The Purveyor of Truth," in *The Purloined Poe*, edited by John P. Muller and William J. Richardson (Baltimore: Johns Hopkins University Press, 1988), 185.

65. See Barbara Johnson, "The Frame of Reference: Poe, Lacan, Derrida," in *The Purloined Poe*, 217.

66. Derrida, "The Purveyor of Truth," in *The Purloined Poe*, 185.

67. Lacan, "The Freudian Thing," September 1955, *Écrits*, 343/412 and 362/436.

68. Ibid.

69. Lacan, *Écrits*, 337/405.

70. Lacan, "Science and Truth," *Écrits*, 737/868–869.

71. Lacan, "Psychoanalysis and Its Teaching," *Écrits*, 366/439.

72. Freud, *The Ego and the Id*, translated by Joan Riviere, edited and revised by James Strachey (New York: Norton Library, 1960), 42–43.

73. Lacan, "Position of the Unconscious," *Écrits*, 708/835.

74. Lacan, "The Instance of the Letter in the Unconscious," *Écrits*, 419/502.

75. Ibid.

76. See Lacan, *Écrits*, 430–431/517–518, and Nancy and Lacoue-Labarthe, *The Title of the Letter*, 68/83.

77. Lacan, "Position of the Unconscious," *Écrits*, 708–709/835–836.

78. Ibid.

79. Lacan, "The Direction of the Treatment and the Principles of Its Power," *Écrits*, 525/641.

80. Lacan, "Psychoanalysis and Its Teaching, *Écrits*, 379/316.

81. Badiou, *Infinite Thought*, 58.

82. Lacan, "Psychoanalysis and Its Teaching," *Écrits*, 1957, 366/438–439.

83. Theodor Adorno, *Minima Moralia*, translated by E. F. N. Jephcott (London: New Left Books, 1974), 59.

84. Badiou, *Infinite Thought*, 82.

85. Ibid., 84.

ESSAY 4. THE KNOTS OF MORAL LAW AND DESIRE

1. See, for example, Lacan, "Science and Truth," 1965–1966, *Écrits*, 734/865, and see *Seminar VII*, 7.

2. Also quoted by Bruce Fink, *The Lacanian Subject: Between Language and Jouissance* (Princeton: Princeton University Press, 1995), 35.

3. Lacan, *Television*, 107.

4. Ibid., 6.

5. See also Lacan, "Response to Hyppolite's Commentary on Freud's *Verneinung*," *Écrits*, 322–324/386–689.

6. Lacan, *Television*, 108.

7. Ibid.

8. Lacan, *Écrits*, "Seminar on *The Purloined Letter*," 6/11.

9. See also Lacan, "Response to Hyppolite's Commentary on Freud's *Verneinung*," *Écrits*, 322–324/386–389, and Slavoj Žižek, *Looking Awry* (Cambridge, MA, and London: MIT Press, 1991), 135–137.

10. Lacan, "The Subversion of the Subject and the Dialectic of Desire," *Écrits*, 678/801.

11. Lacan, *Television*, 108.

12. See also Lacan, *Écrits*, 677/800.

13. Lacan, *Écrits*, 693/818.

14. Žižek, *Looking Awry*, 137.

15. Lacan, *Television*, 107–108.

16. Lacan, "The Freudian Thing," *Écrits*, 347/417.

17. Lacan, "Seminar on *The Purloined Letter*," *Écrits*, 10/16.

18. See also Evans, *Dictionary of Lacanian Psychoanalysis*, 218.

19. We've seen this already in our discussion of truth and lie, but there is another instance of this in Lacan. In *Seminar VII* and in his work in the early 1960s, Lacan gave the use of the French *ne* as an example or instance in which the subject of the unconscious manifests itself ambiguously and indirectly. This is not quite the same *ne* that appears in *ne pas*. *Ne* is a negative particle. It emerges only when I speak, not when I am spoken. Take it out, and the enunciation loses its force (*Écrits*, 667/800, and S7: 64). This *ne* is not such a definite negation as it is a "discordance" (Damourette and Pichon, *Des mots a la pensée*, quoted in Fink, *The Lacanian Subject*, 38), a kind of submerged negation (the Freudian *Verneinung*) used after verbs of fearing and certain conjunctions, for example, when the "subject enunciates his own fear" (S7: 64). It is, thus, "an enunciation that denounces itself" (*Écrits*: 678/802). It introduces a "hesitation, ambiguity, or uncertainty," seemingly denying what it asserts, whereby the speaker wishes for what he/she fears or seems discordant from what he/she is doing or wishing for ("Je crains qu'il ne vienne"—"I'm afraid he is coming" [S7: 305]). As such, it only roughly corresponds with the way the English word "but" can be used, as in, "I will not deny *but* that it is a difficult thing." So, the discourse of the unconscious subject, this "other agency," manifests itself by likewise being a discordance, an interruption or slip of the tongue within "the conscious or ego discourse." Fink, *The Lacanian Subject*, 39.

20. Lacan, "Position of the Unconscious," *Écrits*, 708/835.

21. Jacques-Alain Miller, "An Introduction to Seminars I and II: Lacan's Orientation Prior to 1953 (I)," in *Reading Seminars I and II*, edited by Richard Feldstein, Bruce Fink, and Maire Jaanus (Albany: State University of New York Press, 1996),10.

22. Lacan, *Écrits*, 677–678/800–801.

23. Lacan, *Écrits*, 678/801.

24. Lacan, *Écrits*, 654/775.

25. Lacan, "Logical Time and the Assertion of Anticipated Certainty," 1945, *Écrits*, 170/207–208.

26. Evans, *Dictionary of Lacanian Psychoanalysis*, 195.

27. Nancy and Lacoue-Labarthe, *The Title of the Letter*, 116.

28. Evans, *Dictionary of Lacanian Psychoanalysis*, 196.

29. Kojève, op. cit., 1969, 3–5.

30. Lacan, "The Subversion of the Subject and the Dialectic of Desire," *Écrits*, 689/814.

31. Lacan, "The Signification of the Phallus," *Écrits*, 579/690.

32. Ibid.

33. Ibid.

34. Ibid.

35. Lacan, *Écrits*, 681/804.

36. Lacan, *Écrits*, 679/802.

37. Lacan, *Écrits*, 431/518.

38. Lacan, *Écrits*, 262/319.

39. Lacan, *Écrits*, 719/848.

40. Lacan, "Position of the Unconscious," *Écrits*, 719/848.

41. Jacques-Alain Miller, "Paradigms of *Jouissance*," *lacanian ink* 17 (2000): 17.

42. Ibid., 21.

43. I refer to a very helpful and suggestive essay by Philippe Van Haute, "Death and Sublimation in Lacan's Reading of *Antigone*," in *Levinas and Lacan: The Missed Encounter*, edited by Sarah Harasym (Albany: State University of New York Press, 1995), 98.

44. Miller, "Paradigms of *Jouissance*," 20.

45. Ibid.

46. Alenka Zupančič, "Ethics and Tragedy in Lacan," in *Cambridge Companion to Lacan*, edited by Jean-Michel Rabaté (Cambridge: Cambridge University Press, 2002), 187.

47. Žižek, *The Ticklish Subject*, 153.

48. Immanuel Kant, *Religion within the Boundaries of Mere Reason, and Other Writings*, translated and edited by Allen Wood and George di Giovanni (London: Cambridge University Press,1998). See part 1, "Concerning the indwelling of the evil principle alongside the good, or, Of the radical evil in human nature."

49. Kant, *Religion within the Boundaries of Mere Reason*, 6: 21. Emphasis mine.

50. Ibid., 6: 23, the note.

51. Slavoj Žižek, "A Hair of the Dog That Bit You," in *Lacanian Theory of Discourse*, edited by Mark Bracher et al. (New York: New York University Press, 1994), 51.

52. Kant, *Religion within the Boundaries of Mere Reason*, 6: 37.

53. Žižek, "A Hair of the Dog That Bit You," 49.

54. Ibid.

55. Kant, *Religion within the Boundaries of Mere Reason*, 6: 46–47.

56. Lacan, see "Kant with Sade," 645/765.

57. On "reciprocity," see "Kant avec Sade," *Écrits*, 649/770.

58. Miller, "Paradigms of *Jouissance*," 20.

59. Ibid.

60. Lacan, *Écrits*, 650/771.

61. Miller, "An Introduction to Seminars I and II: Lacan's Orientation Prior to 1953 (III)," in *Reading Seminars I and I*, 222 and 234.

62. Miller, "A Discussion of Lacan's 'Kant with Sade,'" in *Reading Seminars I and II*, 220.

63. Alain Badiou, *Ethics: An Essay on the Understanding of Evil*, translated by Peter Hallward (London/New York: Verso, 2001), 37.

64. Lacan, *Écrits*, 645/765.

65. Miller, "A Discussion of Lacan's 'Kant with Sade,'" 219.

66. Lacan, *Écrits*, 648–650/769–771.

67. Žižek, *Looking Awry*, 159.

68. See also Evans, *Dictionary of Lacanian Psychoanalysis*, 60.

69. Lacan, "Desire and the Interpretation of Desire in *Hamlet*," from the seminar dated April 1959, translated in *Literature and Psychoanalysis*, edited by Shoshana Felman, Yale French Studies, Number 55/56 (New Haven: Yale University Press, 1977), 20.

70. Lacan, "The Subversion of the Subject," *Écrits*, 690/815.

71. Lacan, "Desire and the Interpretation of Desire in *Hamlet*," 15.

72. Žižek, *Looking Awry*, 158.

73. Lacan, "The Subversion of the Subject," 1960, *Écrits*, 696/821.

74. Ibid.

75. Žižek, *Looking Awry*, 137.

76. Lacan, "The Subversion of the Subject," 1960, *Écrits*, 696/821.

77. Ibid., 697/822.

78. On the "infinity" of *jouissance*, see Lacan's 1972–1973 seminar, *Encore, On Feminine Sexuality: The Limits of Love and Knowledge*, edited by Jacques-Alain Miller, translated by Bruce Fink (New York: W.W. Norton & Company, 1988), 8/13. I quote, "'Enjoy!' is a correlate of castration, the latter being the sign with which an avowal dresses itself up (*se pare*), the avowal that *jouissance* of the Other, of the body of the Other, is promoted only on the basis of infinity (*infinitude*)," and page 103. I am also indebted to Zupančič's commentary on this, "The Perforated Sheet," in *Sexuation: SIC 3*, edited by Renata Salecl (Durham and London: Duke University Press, 2000), 282–296. See Lacan's *The Other Side of Psychoanalysis*, 71, for just one important passage relating to *jouissance feminine*, and also *Encore*, especially the seminar of January 20, 1973.

79. Lacan defines the "limit" in *Seminar XX, Encore* as "that which is defined as greater than one point and less than another, but in no case equal either to the point of departure or the point of arrival" (9/15).

80. See the translator, Bruce Fink's, helpful notes, *Seminar XX, Encore* (7), notes 27–30.

81. See Lacan, *Seminar XX, Encore*, "Love is addressed to the semblance" (17 and 92/85).

82. I refer to *Seminar XX, Encore*, 18–19, the translator's note 12.

83. See Lacan, *Television*, 108, which has provided much of the background for the remarks found on these concluding pages.

ESSAY 5. ANTIGONE, IN HER UNBEARABLE SPLENDOR

1. G.W.F. Hegel, *Phenomenology of Spirit*, translated by A. V. Miller (Oxford: Clarendon Press, 1977), from the section on "Spirit," paragraph 468, page 282.

2. Badiou, *Infinite Thought*, 88–89.

3. Philippe Lacoue-Labarthe, "De l'éthique: à propos d'Antigone," in *Lacan avec les philosophes*, (Paris: Albin Michel, 1991), 23/31.

4. Žižek, *The Ticklish Subject*, 153.

5. This is Miller's term, as used in his "Paradigms of *Jouissance*."

6. Slavoj Žižek, *The Sublime Object of Ideology* (London and New York: Verso, 1989), 135.

7. Dante, *The Inferno*, translated by Robert Pinsky (New York: Farrar, Straus, and Giroux, 1994), 9.

8. Lacan, "Desire and the Interpretation of Desire in *Hamlet*," 38.

9. Žižek, *The Ticklish Subject*, 154, see also *Seminar XI*, 197–198.

10. See also Lacan, "Desire and Interpretation of Desire in *Hamlet*," 12.

11. Lacan, *Écrits*, 228–229/276–277.

12. Alenka Zupančič, *Ethics of the Real* (London: Verso, 2000), 249.

13. Ibid., 249–250.

14. See Lacan, *Seminar VII*, 303–304, and Zupančič, *Ethics of the Real*, 250.

15. Zupančič, *Ethics of the Real*, 249.

16. Mladen Dolar, *A Voice and Nothing More* (Cambridge: MIT Press, 2006), 98, and Zupančič, *Ethics of the Real*, 164.

17. Lacan, *Écrits*, 513/615.

18. Lacan, "The Direction of the Treatment and the Principles of Its Power," 1958, *Écrits*, 533/638.

19. Lacan, *Écrits*, 512/613.

20. Miller, "Paradigms of *Jouissance*," 23–26.

21. Zupančič, *Ethics of the Real*, 249, and see Essay 4 in the present volume.

22. Arthur Schopenhauer, *On the Basis of Morality* (*Über das Fundament der Moral*), translated by E.F.J. Payne (Indianapolis and Cambridge: Hackett Publishing Co., 1995), 56–57.

23. I refer the reader to a lecture given by Anne Dunand on "The Ends of Analysis," published in *Reading Seminar XI*, 248–249 especially. This was especially helpful in formulating the analysis contained on these pages.

24. See Miller, "Paradigms of *Jouissance*," 33.

ESSAY 6. THE DESIRE FOR HAPPINESS AND THE PROMISE OF ANALYSIS: ARISTOTLE AND LACAN ON THE ETHICS OF DESIRE

1. Alain Badiou, *The Century*, translated by Alberto Toscano (Cambridge: Polity Press, 2007).

2. Ibid., 48.

3. Ibid., 48–49.

4. See *Seminar VII, The Ethics of Psychoanalysis*, p. 10, the translator's footnote for the reference to the two Greek terms for ethos, with two different Greek spellings, one using the Greek letter *eta* with *tonos*, and the other the letter *epsilon* with *psili* and *oxia* diacritical marks, whereby one has an active voice, meaning the capacity to form habits through the repetition of virtuous actions, and the other a passive voice, being a capacity to be acted upon.

5. Lacan writes in Seminar Seven, "Antigone is a tragedy, and tragedy is in the forefront of our experiences as analysts—something confirmed by the reference Freud found in Oedipus Rex as well as in other tragedies." (S7: 243/285).

6. Klein, Jacob, *Commentary on Plato's Meno* (Chapel Hill: University of North Carolina Press, 1965).

7. Aristotle, *Nicomachean Ethics*, I.7, 1097b 22–1098a 18, translated by W. D. Ross and revised by J. O. Urmson, in *The Complete Works of Aristotle* (Princeton: Princeton University Press, Bollingen Series LXXI, vol. 2, 1984), 1734.

8. Aristotle, *de Anima*, translated by J. A. Smith, in *The Complete Works of Aristotle*, (Princeton: Princeton University Press, Bollingen Series LXXI, vol. 2, 1984), Book IV, 429–430.

9. Aristotle, *Politics*, Book VII, 2, 1324a, translated by B. Jowett, in *The Complete Works of Aristotle* (Princeton: Princeton University Press, Bollingen Series LXXI, vol. 2, 1984), 2102.

10. Aristotle, *Politics*, VII, 8, 1328a 25–40.

11. Chantal Mouffe, *The Return of the Political* (London and New York: Verso, 1993), 3; also quoted, in Yannis Stavrakakis, *Lacan and the Political* (London and New York: Routledge, 1999), 72.

12. Miller, Jacques-Alain, "Context and Concepts," in *Reading Seminar XI*, 12.

13. Barnard, Suzanne, "Introduction," in *Reading Seminar XX*, 9.

14. Laplanche and J.-B. Pontalis, *The Language of Psychoanalysis*, 1988: 315; quoted in Žižek, *The Ticklish Subject*, 270.

15. Ernesto Laclau and Chantel Mouffe, "Identity and Hegemony," in *Contingency, Hegemony, Universality* (London and New York: Verso, 2000), 68.

16. Lacan, *Écrits*, "The Subversion of the Subject and the Dialectic of Desire," (1960), *Écrits*, 681/804.

17. Laclau and Mouffe, "Identity and Hegemony," 68–70. See the schema at endnote 16 for Essay Four, "The 'Truth about Truth.'"

18. Lacan, *Écrits*, "The Subversion of the Subject," 1960, 677/799.

19. Éric Laurent, "Guiding Principles of Any Psychoanalytic Act" (1997/2006), http://www.lacan.com. (accessed June 2009).

20. Miller, J-A., "The Sinthome, a Mixture of Symptom and Fantasy," in *The Later Lacan* (Albany: State University of New York Press, 2007), 55–72. I refer the reader to this publication, part of a seminar Miller gave at the Department of Psychoanalysis, Paris VIII, for a fuller treatment of this distinction.

21. Quoted from Fink, "Knowledge and *Jouissance*," *Reading Seminar XX*, 22.

22. Miller, "Paradigms of *Jouissance*," *Lacanian ink 17*, 2000, 43–48.

23. See *Encore* (S20), 90 for Lacan's diagram of position of Truth in relation to the imaginary, the symbolic, and the real, also note Lacan's mathème for Truth; and also see 106/97 and the seminar of March 8, 1973, "On the Baroque," and pp. 105/96, 114–15/103–4.

24. See Lacan, S17, 78/89-90, and Fink, *The Lacanian Subject*, 60.

25. Mark Bracher, "On the Psychological and Social Functions of Language," in *Lacanian Theory of Discourse*, 109.

26. Ibid., 112.

27. See Miller, "Paradigms of *Jouissance*," 33. Miller says that in the *L'envers de la psychanalyse*, *jouissance* is the "inserting point of the signifying apparatus."

28. Ibid., 30.

29. See Laurent, "Alienation and Separation," in *Reading Seminar XI*, op. cit., 25.

30. Laurent, "Alienation and Separation," 25.

31. See also Miller, "Paradigms of *Jouissance*," 37.

32. For a full discussion of the distinction here being made between object *a* as the object-cause of desire, and object *a* as the object of the drive, see Jacques-Alain Miller, "*Le nom-du-père, s'enpasser, s'en servir,*" online at http://www.lacan.com; and Slavoj Žižek, "Object *a* in Social Links," SIC 6, 2006: 117 and in his books *Parallax View* (London and New York: Verso, 2007), and *In Defense of Lost Causes* (London and New York: Verso, 2008).

33. See Žižek, who quotes A-J. Miller on this, "Object *a* in Social Links," in *Jacques Lacan and the Other Side of Psychoanalysis*, SIC 6, edited by Justin Clemens and Russell Grigg (Durham and London: Duke University Press, 2006), 110, and see Žižek, *In Praise of Lost Causes*, 325.

34. Quoted in Žižek, *The Sublime Object of Ideology*, 30.

35. Žižek, *The Sublime Object of Ideology*, 31.

36. Miller, J-A., "On Shame," SIC 6, *Reflections on Seminar XVII*, 15–27.

37. See also Dominick Hoens, "Toward a New Perversion: Psychoanalysis," in SIC 6, *Reflections on Seminar XVII, edited by Justin Clemens and Russell Grigg* (Durham and London: Duke University Press), 96.

38. Jacques-Alain Miller, "On Shame," SIC 6, *Reflections on Seminar XVII*, 23–26.

39. See Žižek's article, "Object *a* in Social Links," SIC 6, *Reflections on Seminar XVII*, 2006.

40. Bruce Fink, *Lacan to the Letter* (Minneapolis: University of Minnesota Press, 2004), 109.

41. Lacan, "Radiophone," in *Autre écrits* (Paris: Éditions du Seuil, 2001), 432.

ESSAY 7. TO CONCLUDE / NOT CONCLUDE

1. Alain Badiou, "Formules de *l'Étourdit*," in *Il n'y a pas de rapport sexuel* (Paris: Ouvertures Fayard, 2010), 101–134, translated by Scott Savaino, "The Formulas of *l'Étourdit*," in *lacanian ink* 27 (2006): 80–96. My references are to the French edition. My reflections here have been especially helped and inspired by Badiou's "Formules de *l'Étourdit*," by Lacan's later seminars, *XVII* through *XX*, and his *l'Étourdit*, the two versions, one published in *Scilicet* 4 (1973): 5–52, and the other in *Autres écrits* (Paris: Seuil, 2001), 449–497, and also by Colette Soler's "Lacan en antiphilosophe," *Filozofski Vestnik* 27, 2 (2006): 121–144. Finally I would like to acknowledge my debt to Christian Fierens' very helpful reading of *l'Étourdit*, *Lecture de l'Étourdit: Lacan 1972* (Paris: l'Harmattan, 2002).

2. Mircea Eliade, *The Sacred and the Profane*, translated by Walter R. Trask (New York: Harper Torchbooks, 1961), 33.

3. Badiou, "Formules de *l'Étourdit*," 102.

4. Ibid., 108.

5. Ibid., 101, and "The Formulas of *l'Étourdit*," 80.

6. Badiou, "Formules de *l'Étourdit*," 104.

7. Ibid.

8. See Lacan, *l'Étourdit*, *Scilicet* 4 (1973): 8, and Christian Fierens' *Lecture de l'Étourdit: Lacan 1972* (Paris: L'Harmattan, 2002), 61.

9. Badiou, "Formules de *l'Étourdit*," 108.

10. Ibid., 125.

11. Soler, "Lacan en antiphilosophe," 127.

12. I refer to the schema for the discourse of analysis where we have *objet petit a* in the position of command, and S_2 beneath the bar separating them in the position of truth. The schema also shows a vector passing from S_1, on the side of production, toward S_2, in the position of truth. If the phallus is the master signifier (S_1), then it passes into the truth of the unconscious, the knowledge supporting the role of the analyst qua master. This is thus a knowledge as bearing the effect of the function of the real, the function of a constitutive lack, a lack carried in the signifier of the phallus. See *Seminar XX*, 21/16.

13. Badiou, "Formules de *l'Étourdit*," 122.

14. Ibid., 112.

15. Ibid., 113–114.

16. Alain Badiou, *Éloge de l'amour* (Paris: Flammarion, 2009), 27.

17. See Badiou's discussion of this, "Formules de *l'Étourdit*," 110–111.

18. There is an informative discussion of the process of the pass in Dylan Evans' *Dictionary of Lacanian Psychoanalysis*, 135. Dylan writes, "the procedure was as follows: the person seeking the pass (*le passant*) tells two witnesses (*le passeurs*), who must be in analysis at the time, about his own analysis and its conclusion, and these two witnesses then relay this account to a jury of seven. The jury then decides, on the basis of the two accounts, whether to award the pass to the candidate. There were no preestablished criteria to guide the jury, since the pass was based on the principle that each person's analysis is unique. If the candidate was successful, he was awarded the title of A.E. (*Analyste de L'École*). Unsuccessful candidates were not prevented from seeking the pass again if they wished to."

19. There are many descriptions of this situation: I refer to the reader to Marcelle Marini's book, for example, *Jacques Lacan: The French Context*, 13ff., for a succinct and accurate account of this, and to *Psychoanalytic Politics*, by Sherry Turkle, especially the chapter entitled "Psychoanalytic Societies and Psychoanalytic Science" (New York: Guilford Press, 1992), 119–141. One other reference should be added: Jean-Claude Milner's *L'Œuvre claire: Lacan, la science, la philosophie* (Paris: Seuil, 1995). The description of Lacan's work as an anti-philosophy, he writes, dates from 1975 and the reorganization of the Department of Psychoanalysis at University of Paris VIII. It resurged in 1980, on the occasion of a *polémique* engaged by Althusser. See Milner, *L'Œuvre claire*, 146.

20. The schema for the master's discourse is:

$$\frac{S_1}{S} \rightarrow \frac{S_2}{a}$$

21. Again, I refer the reader to Marini, *Jacques Lacan: The French Context*.

22. Badiou, "Formules de *l'Étourdit*," 131.

23. Ibid., 135.

24. Ibid., 134.

25. Jacques Lacan, "Proposition du 9 Octobre 1967 sur le psychanalyste de l'École," *Scilicet* 1 (1968), quoted in Marini, *Jacques Lacan: The French Context*, 210.

26. Ibid., 209.

27. See Lacan, "L'acte psychanalytique," in *Autres écrits*, 375ff.

28. See Anne Dunand, "The End of Analysis (I) and (II)," in *Reading Seminar XI*, 251–256. Her discussion was very helpful to my formulations of these ideas.

29. These concluding thoughts, perhaps unheard of in the literature on Lacan, have been inspired not only by *Seminar XI*, but also by Badiou's *Éloge de l'amour*, 27–29, and by Lacan's *Séminaire, livre XXIII, Le sinthome* (Paris: Seuil, 2005), the session of April 13, 1976, 119–139. I also refer to Evans, *Dictionary of Lacanian Psychoanalysis*, 188–189, for his discussion of the *sinthome*. See also the essays included in Véronique Vorus and Bogdan Wolf, eds., *The Later*

Lacan (Albany: State University of New York Press, 2007), for detailed studies of the clinical dimensions of the *sinthome* and its relevance to the "treatment" of psychosis.

REFERENCES

WORKS BY JACQUES LACAN

The Seminars

Seminar I *Le Séminaire, livre I: Les écrits techniques de Freud.* Texte établi par Jacques-Alain Miller. Paris: Seuil, 1975. (English translation: *The Seminar of Jacques Lacan, Book I: Freud's Papers on Technique: 1953–1954.* Translated by John Forrester. New York: Norton, 1988.)

Seminar II *Le Séminaire, livre II: Le moi dans la théorie de Freud et dans la technique de la psychanalyse, 1954–1955.* Texte établi par Jacques-Alain Miller. Paris: Seuil, 1978. (English translation: *The Seminar of Jacques Lacan, Book II: The Ego in Freud's Theory and in the Technique of Psychoanalysis, 1954–1955.* Translated by Sylvana Tomaselli. Notes by John Forrester. New York: Norton, 1991.)

Seminar III *Le Séminaire, livre III: Les Psychoses, 1955–1956.* Texte établi par Jacques-Alain Miller. Paris: Seuil, 1981. (English translation: *The Seminar of Jacques Lacan, Book III: The Psychoses, 1955–1956.* Translated by Russell Grigg. New York: Norton, 1993.)

Seminar IV *Le Séminaire, livre IV: La relation d'objet, 1956–1957.* Texte établi par Jacques-Alain Miller. Paris: Seuil, 1994.

Seminar V *Le Séminaire, livre V: Les Formations de l'inconscient, 1957–1958.* Texte établi par Jacques-Alain Miller. Paris: Seuil, 1998.

Seminar VI Le désir et son interpretation, 1958–1959. Unpublished. (English translation, "Desire and the Interpretation of Desire in *Hamlet.*" Translated by James Hulbert, in *Literature and Psychoanalysis: The Question of Reading: Otherwise.* Yale French Studies, Number 55/56, edited by Shoshana Felman, 1977.

Seminar VII *Le Séminaire, livre VII: L'éthique de la psychanalyse, 1959–1960.* Texte établi par Jacques-Alain Miller. Paris: Seuil, 1986. (English translation: *The Seminar of Jacques Lacan, Book VII: The Ethics of Psychoanalysis: 1959–1960.* Translated by Dennis Porter. New York: Norton, 1992.)

Seminar VIII *Le Séminaire, livre VIII: Le transfert, 1960–1961.* Texte établi par Jacques-Alain Miller. Paris: Seuil, 1991.

Seminar X *Le Séminaire, livre X. L'angoisse, 1962–1963*. Texte établi par Jacques-Alain Miller. Paris: Seuil, 2004.

Seminar XI *Le Séminaire, livre XI: Les quatre concepts fondamentaux de la psych-analyse, 1964*. Texte établi par Jacques-Alain Miller. Paris: Seuil, 1973. (English translation: *The Four Fundamental Concepts of Psychoanalysis*. Translated by Alan Sheridan. New York: Norton, 1978.)

Seminar XVII *Le Séminaire, livre XVII: L'envers de la psychanalyse, 1969–1970*. Texte établi par Jacques-Alain Miller. Paris: Seuil, 1991. (English translation: *The Seminar of Jacques Lacan, Book XVII, The Other Side of Psycho-analysis, 1969–1970*. Edited by Jacques-Alain Miller, translated by Russell Grigg. New York: Norton & Company, 2007).

Seminar XVIII *D'un discours qui ne serait pas du semblant, 1970–1971*. Texte établi par Jacques-Alain Miller. Paris: Seuil, 2006.

Seminar XX *Le Séminaire, livre XX: Encore, 1972–1973*. Texte établi par Jacques-Alain Miller. Paris: Seuil, 1975. (English translation: *The Seminar of Jacques Lacan, Book XX: Encore, On Feminine Sexuality: The Limits of Love and Knowledge*. Translated by Bruce Fink. New York: Norton, 1998.)

Seminar XXIII *Le Séminaire, livre XXIII: Le sinthome, 1975–1976*. Texte établi par Jacques-Alain Miller. Paris: Seuil, 2005.

ADDITIONAL WORKS BY JACQUES LACAN

Lacan, Jacques. *Écrits*. Paris: Seuil, 1966 and 1999. English translation: *Écrits: The First Complete Edition in English*. Translated by Bruce Fink. New York: Norton, 2002 and 2006.

———. "Radiophone." In *Autres écrits* Paris: Seuil, (1968), 403–448.

———. *l'Étourdit*. Scilicet 4 (1973), 5–52.

———. . . . *ou pire*. Scilicet 5 (1975), 5–10.

———. *Télévision*. Paris: Seuil, 1974. (English translation: *Television: A Challenge to the Psychoanalytic Establishment*. Translated by Denis Hollier, Rosalind Krauss, and Annette Michelson. Edited by Joan Copjec. New York: Norton, 1990.)

———. *Autre écrits*. Paris: Seuil, 2001.

———. *My Teaching*. Translated by David Macey. London: Verso, 2008.

ADDITIONAL REFERENCES

Anonymous. "L'infini et la castration." *Scilicet* 4 (1973), 75–133.

Aristotle. *On the Soul*. Translated by W. S. Hett. Cambridge: Harvard University Press, The Loeb Classical Library, 1975.

———. *Politics*. Translated by Benjamin Jowett. *The Complete Works of Aristotle*. Princeton: Princeton University Press, Bollingen Series LXXI, Vol. 2, 1984.

Badiou, Alain. "Lacan et Platon: le mathème est-il une idée?" In *Lacan avec les philosophes*, 133–154. Paris: Albin Michel, 1991.

———. *Manifesto for Philosophy*. Translated and edited by Norman Madarasz. Albany: State University of New York Press, 1999.

———. *Ethics: An Understanding of Evil*. Translated and introduced by Peter Hallward. London: Verso, 2001.

———. *Saint Paul: The Foundation of Universalism*. Translated by Ray Brassier. Stanford: Stanford University Press, 2003.

———. *Infinite Thought: Truth and the Return of Philosophy*. Translated and edited by Oliver Feltham and Justin Clemens. London: Continuum, 2004.

———. *Theoretical Writings*. Translated and edited by Ray Brassier and Alberto Toscano. London: Continuum, 2005.

———. *Metapolitics*. Translated by Jason Barker. London: Verso, 2005.

———. *Being and Event*. Translated by Oliver Feltham. London: Continuum, 2005.

———. "Lacan and the Presocratics." In *Lacan: The Silent Partners*, edited by Slavoj Žižek, 7–16. New York: Verso, 2006.

———. *The Century*. Translated by Alberto Toscano. Malden, MA: Polity Press, 2007.

———. *Éloge de l'amour*, with Nicolas Truong. Paris: Flammarion, 2009.

———. *Le fini et l'infini*. Paris: Bayard, 2010.

Badiou, Alain, and Barbara Cassin. *Il n'y a pas de rapport sexuel: Deux leçons sur l'Étourdit de Lacan*. Paris: Librairie Arthème Fayard, 2010.

Barnard, Suzanne, and Bruce Fink, eds. *Reading Seminar XX: Lacan's Major Work on Love, Knowledge, and Feminine Sexuality*. Albany: State University of New York Press, 2002.

Bely, Andrei. *Petersburg*. Translated, annotated, and introduced by Robert A. Maguire and John E. Malmstad. Bloomington and Indianapolis: Indiana University Press, 1978.

Blanchot, Maurice. *The Space of Literature*. Translated by Ann Smock. Lincoln: University of Nebraska Press, 1982.

Borch-Jacobsen, Mikkel. *Lacan: The Absolute Master*. Translated by Douglas Brick. Stanford: Stanford University Press, 1991.

Bowie, Malcolm. *Lacan*. London: Fontana Press, 1991.

Bracher, Mark, et al., eds. *Lacanian Theory of Discourse*. New York: New York University Press, 1994.

———. "On the Psychological and Social Functions of Language: Lacan's Theory of the Four Discourses." In *Lacanian Theory of Discourse*, edited by Mark Bracher, et al., 107–128. New York: New York University Press, 1994.

Chaumon, Franck. *La loi, le subject et la jouissance*. Paris: Éditions Michalon, 2004.

Chiesa, Lorenzo. *Subjectivity and Otherness: A Philosophical Reading of Lacan*. Cambridge: MIT Press, 2007.

Cixous, Hélène. "Attacks of the Castle." Translated by Eric Prenowitz. In *Rethinking Architecture*, edited by Neil Leach, 303–307. London: Routledge, 1997.

Copjec, Joan, ed. *Radical Evil*. London: Verso, 1996.

———. *Imagine There's No Woman*. Cambridge: MIT Press, 2002.

Dante. *Inferno*. Translated by Robert Pinsky. New York: Farrar, Straus and Giroux, 1994.

de Certeau, Michel. "Lacan: An Ethics of Speech." Translated by Marie-Rose Logan. In *Heterologies, Discourse on the Other*, 47–64. Minneapolis: University of Minnesota Press, 1986.

Declerq, Frédérique, and Paul Verhaeghe. "Lacan's Analytic Goal: Le Sinthome or the Feminine Way." In *Re-inventing the Symptom*, edited by Luke Thurston, 59–83. New York: The Other Press, 2002.

Deleuze, Gilles. *Logique du sens*. Paris: Les Éditions de Minuit, 1969.

———. "How Do We Recognize Structuralism?" In *Desert Islands and Other Texts, 1953–1974*. Cambridge: Semiotext(e), 2004.

Derrida, Jacques. "The Purveyor of Truth." Translated by Alan Bass. In *The Purloined Poe*, edited by John P. Muller and William J. Richardson, 173–212. Baltimore and London: Johns Hopkins University Press, 1988.

———. *Resistances of Psychoanalysis*. Translated by Peggy Kamuf, Pascale-Anne Brault, and Michael Naas. Stanford: Stanford University Press, 1998.

Dolar, Mladen. *A Voice and Nothing More*. Cambridge: MIT Press, 2006.

Dunand, Anne. "The End of Analysis (I) and (II)." In *Reading Seminar XI*, edited by Richard Feldstein, Bruce Fink, and Maire Jaanus, 243–256. Albany: State University of New York Press, 1995.

———. "The End of Analysis (II)." In *Reading Seminar XI* edited by Richard Feldstein, Bruce Fink, and Maire Jaanus, 251–258. Albany: State University of New York Press, 1995.

Eleb, Danielle. *Figures du Destin: Aristote, Freud et Lacan ou la rencontre du réel*. Paris: Éditions Érès, 2004.

Evans, Dylan. *Dictionary of Lacanian Psychoanalysis*. London: Routledge, 1996 and 2005.

Feldstein, Richard, Bruce Fink, and Maire Jaanus, eds. *Reading Seminar XI: Freud's Four Fundamental Concepts*. Albany: State University of New York Press, 1995.

Fierens, Christian. *Lecture de l'Étourdit: Lacan 1972*. Paris: l'Harmattan, 2002.

Fink, Bruce. *The Lacanian Subject: Between Language and Jouissance*. Princeton: Princeton University Press, 1995.

———. "Knowledge and *Jouissance*." In *Reading Seminar XX*, edited by Suzanne Barnard and Bruce Fink, 21–46. Albany: State University of New York Press, 2002.

———. *Lacan to the Letter*. Minneapolis: University of Minnesota Press, 2004.

Freeman, Kathleen, trans. *Ancilla to the Pre-Socratic Philosophers*. Cambridge: Harvard University Press, 1977.

Freud, Sigmund. *An Autobiographical Study*. Translated and edited by James Strachey. New York: Norton, 1952 [1925].

———. *The Interpretation of Dreams*. In *The Standard Edition*, Volumes IV and V. Translated and edited by James Strachey, 1–621. London: Hogarth Press, 1953 [1900].

———. *Three Essays on the Theory of Sexuality*. In *The Standard Edition*, Volume VII. Translated and edited by James Strachey, 125–244. London: Hogarth Press, 1953 [1905].

———. *Beyond the Pleasure Principle*. In *The Standard Edition*, Volume XVII. Translated and edited by James Strachey, 3–64. London: Hogarth Press, 1955 [1920].

———. *Group Psychology and the Analysis of the Ego*. In *The Standard Edition*, Volume XVIII. Translated and edited by James Strachey, 69–143. London: Hogarth Press, 1955 [1921].

———. *Jokes and Their Relation to the Unconscious*. In *The Standard Edition*, Volume VIII. Translated and edited by James Strachey, 3–181. London: Hogarth Press, 1960 [1950].

———. *The Psychopathology of Everyday Life*. In *The Standard Edition*, Volume VI. Translated and edited by James Strachey, 1–310. London: Hogarth Press, 1960 [1901].

———. "A Child Is Being Beaten: A Contribution to the Study of the Origin of Sexual Perversions." In *The Standard Edition*, Volume XVII. Translated and edited by James Strachey, 179–204. London: Hogarth Press, 1961 [1919].

———. "Negation." In *The Standard Edition*, Volume XIX. Translated and edited by James Strachey, 235–239. London: Hogarth Press, 1961 [1925].

———. "Repression." In *The Standard Edition*, Volume XIV. Translated and edited by James Strachey, 146–158. London: Hogarth Press, 1961 [1915].

———. "The Unconscious." In *The Standard Edition*, Volume XIV. Translated and edited by James Strachey, 166–215. London: Hogarth Press, 1961 [1915].

———. *Civilization and Its Discontents*. Translated by James Strachey. New York: Norton, 1961 [1930].

———. *Introductory Lectures on Psycho-Analysis*. In *The Standard Edition*, Volume XV. Translated and edited by James Strachey, 3–239. London: Hogarth Press, 1963 [1915–1917].

———. *The Ego and the Id*. Translated by Joan Riviere. Revised and edited by James Strachey. New York: The Norton Library, 1960 [1923].

———. *Moses and Monotheism: Three Essays*. In *The Standard Edition*, Volume XXII. Translated and edited by James Strachey, 3–137. London: Hogarth Press, 1964 [1939].

Gasché, Rodolphe. *Europe, or the Infinite Task*. Stanford: Stanford University Press, 2009.

Grigg, Russell. *Lacan, Language, and Philosophy*. Albany: State University of New York Press, 2008.

Harasym, Sarah, ed. *Lévinas and Lacan: The Missed Encounter*. Albany: State University of New York Press, 1998.

Hegel, G.W.F. *Phenomenology of Spirit*. Translated by A.V. Miller. Oxford: Clarendon Press, 1977 [1807].

Hoens, Dominick. "Toward a New Perversion: Psychoanalysis." In *Reflections on Seminar XVII: Jacques Lacan and the Other Side of Psychoanalysis. SIC 6*, edited by Justin Clemens and Russell Grigg. Durham and London: Duke University Press, 2006.

Hölderlin, Friedrich. *Poems and Fragments*. Translated by Michael Hamburger. Fourth Bilingual Edition. London: Anvil Poetry, 2008.

———. *Essays and Letters*. Translated and edited by Jeremy Adler and Charlie Louth. London: Penguin Books, 2009.

Huson, Timothy. "Truth and Contradiction, Reading Hegel with Lacan." In *Lacan: The Silent Partners*, edited by Slavoj Žižek, 56–78. London: Verso, 2006.

Johnson, Barbara. "The Frame of Reference: Poe, Lacan, Derrida." In *The Purloined Poe*, edited by John P. Muller and William J. Richardson, 213–251. Baltimore and London: Johns Hopkins University Press, 1988.

Juranville, Alan. *Lacan et la philosophie*. Paris: Presses Universitaires de France, 2003.

———. "The Lacanian Thing." In *Lacan in the German-Speaking World*, translated by Elizabeth Stewart, edited by Elizabeth Stewart, Maire Jaanus, and Richard Feldstein, 79–100. Albany: State University of New York Press, 2004.

Kant, Immanuel. *Practical Philosophy*. Translated and edited by Mary J. Gregor. Cambridge: Cambridge University Press, 1996.

———. *Religion within the Boundaries of Mere Reason, and Other Writings*. Translated and edited by Allen Wood and George di Giovanni. Cambridge: Cambridge University Press, 1998 [1792].

Kesel, Marc de. *Eros and Ethics*. Translation from the Dutch funded by NWO, the state institute funding scientific research in The Netherlands. Albany: State University of New York Press, 2009.

Kojève, Alexandre. *Introduction to the Reading of Hegel*. Translated by James H. Nichols, Jr. Edited by Alan Bloom. New York: Basic Books, Inc., 1969.

Lacoue-Labarthe, Philippe. "De l'éthique: à propos d'Antigone." In *Lacan avec les philosophes*, 21–36. Paris: Albin Michel, 1991.

———. "Hölderlin's Theater." In *Philosophy and Tragedy*, edited by Miguel de Beistegui and Simon Sparks, 117–138. London and New York: Routledge, 2000.

Lacoue-Labarthe, Philippe, and Jean-Luc Nancy. *The Title of the Letter: A Reading of Lacan*. Translated by François Raffoul and David Pettigrew. Albany: State University of New York Press, 1992.

———. *Retreating the Political*. London: Routledge, 1997.

Laplanche, J., and J. B. Pontalis. *The Language of Psychoanalysis*. Translated by Donald Nicholson-Smith. New York: Norton, 1973.

Laurent, Éric. "Alienation and Separation (I)." In *Reading Seminar XI*, edited by Richard Feldstein, Bruce Fink, and Maire Jaanus, 19–28. Albany: State University of New York Press, 1995.

———. "Alienation and Separation (II)." In *Reading Seminar XI*, edited by Richard Feldstein, Bruce Fink, and Maire Jaanus, 29–38. Albany: State University of New York Press, 1995.

———. "Symptom and Discourse." In *Reflections on Seminar XVII: Jacques Lacan and the Other Side of Psychoanalysis*. *SIC 6*, edited by Justin Clemens and Russell Grigg, 229–253. Durham and London: Duke University Press, 2006.

Lévi-Strauss, Claude. *Structural Anthropology*. Translated by Claire Jacobson and Brooke Grundfest Schoepf. New York: Basic Books, 1963.

Marini, Marcelle. *Jacques Lacan: The French Context*. Translated by Anne Tomiche. New Brunswick: Rutgers University Press, 1992.

Miller, Jacques-Alain. "Extimité." Text established by Elizabeth Doisneau. Translated by Françoise Massardier-Kenney. In *Lacanian Theory of Discourse*, edited by Mark Bracher, et al., 74–87. New York: New York University Press, 1994.

———. "An Introduction to Seminars I and II: Lacan's Orientation Prior to 1953 (I)." In *Reading Seminars I and II*, edited by Richard Feldstein, Bruce Fink, and Maire Jaanus, 3–14. Albany: State University of New York Press, 1996.

———. "An Introduction to Seminars I and II: Lacan's Orientation Prior to 1953 (II)." In *Reading Seminars I and II*, edited by Richard Feldstein, Bruce Fink, and Maire Jaanus, 15–26. Albany: State University of New York Press, 1996.

———. "A Discussion of Lacan's 'Kant with Sade.'" In *Reading Seminars I and II*, edited by Richard Feldstein, Bruce Fink, and Maire Jaanus, 212–240. Albany: State University of New York Press, 1996.

———. "On Perversion." In *Reading Seminars I and II*, edited by Richard Feldstein, Bruce Fink, and Maire Jaanus, 306–322. Albany: State University of New York Press, 1996.

———. "Commentary on Lacan's Text." In *Reading Seminars I and II*, edited by Richard Feldstein, Bruce Fink, and Maire Jaanus, 422–428. Albany: State University of New York Press, 1996.

———. "Paradigms of Lacanian *Jouissance*." Translated by Jorge Jauregui. *lacanian ink 17* (2000): 8–47.

———. "On Shame." Translated by Russell Grigg. In *Reflections on Seminar XVII: Jacques Lacan and the Other Side of Psychoanalysis*. *SIC 6*, edited by Justin Clemens and Russell Grigg, 11–28. Durham and London: Duke University Press, 2006.

———. "The *Sinthome*, a Mixture of Symptom and Fantasy." In *The Later Lacan*, edited by Véronique Voruz and Bogdan Wolf, 55–72. Albany: State University of New York Press, 2007.

Milner, Jean-Claude. "Lacan et la science moderne." In *Lacan avec les philosophes*, 333–351. Paris: Albin Michel, 1991.

———. *L'Œuvre Claire, Lacan, la science, la philosophie*. Paris: Seuil, 1995.

Muller, John P., and William J. Richardson, eds. *The Purloined Poe: Lacan, Derrida, and Psychoanalytic Reading*. Baltimore and London: Johns Hopkins University Press, 1988.

Nancy, Jean-Luc. "Manque de rien." In *Lacan avec les philosophes*, 201–206. Paris: Albin Michel, 1991.

Patoçka, Jan. *Liberté et sacrifice*. Translated from the Czech and German by Erika Abrams. Paris: Jérôme Millon, 1990.

———. *Heretical Essays in the History of Philosophy*. Translated by Erazim Kohák. Chicago: Open Court, 1996.

———. *Plato and Europe*. Translated by Petr Lom. Stanford: Stanford University Press, 2002.

———. *L'Europe après Europe*. Translated from the German and Czech under the direction of Erika Abrams. Paris: Éditions Verdier, 2007.

Plato. *Sophist*. Translated by F. M. Cornford. In *Plato: The Collected Dialogues*. Edited by Edith Hamilton and Huntington Cairns. Princeton: Princeton University Press, 1971.

———. *Symposium*. Translated with an introduction and notes by Alexander Nehamas and Paul Woodruff. Indianapolis and Cambridge: Hackett, 1989.

Rabaté, Jean-Michel. *Jacques Lacan*. New York: Palgrave, 2001.

Reinhard, Kenneth. "Toward a Political Theology of the Neighbor." In *The Neighbor: Three Inquiries in Political Theology*, edited by Slavoj Žižek, 11–75. Chicago: University of Chicago Press, 2005.

Sade, Marquis de. *Philosophy in the Bedroom*. In *The Marquis de Sade: The Complete Justine, Philosophy in the Bedroom, and Other Writings*, compiled and translated by Richard Seaver and Austryn Wainhouse, 177–370. New York: Grove Press, 1965 [1795].

Safouan, Moustapha. *Lacaniana: Les seminaries de Jacques Lacan*. Paris: Librairie Arthème Fayard, 2001.

Santer, Eric. "Miracles Happen: Benjamin, Rosenzweig, Freud, and the Matter of the Neighbor." In *The Neighbor: Three Inquiries in Political Theology*, edited by Slavoj Žižek, 76–133. Chicago: University of Chicago Press, 2005.

Schopenhauer, Arthur. *On the Basis of Morality*. Translated by E.F.J. Payne. Indianapolis and Cambridge, UK: Hackett, 1995 [1837].

Soler, Colette. "The Symbolic Order (I)." In *Reading Seminars I and II: Lacan's Return to Freud*, ed. Richard Feldstein, Bruce Fink, and Maire Jaanus, 39–46. Albany: State University of New York Press, 1996.

———. "The Symbolic Order (II). In *Reading Seminars I and II: Lacan's Return to Freud*, edited by Richard Feldstein, Bruce Fink, and Maire Jaanus, 47–55. Albany: State University of New York Press, 1996.

———. "Lacan en antiphilosophe." *Filozofski Vestnik* 27, 2 (2006): 121–144.

Sophocles. *Antigone*. Translated by David Greene. Chicago: University of Chicago Press, 1991.

———. *Antigone*. Translated by Hugh Lloyd-Jones. Cambridge: Harvard University Press, The Loeb Classical Library, 1994.

Stavrakakis, Yannis. *Lacan and the Political*. London and New York: Routledge, 1999.

Stewart, Elizabeth, Maire Jaanus, and Richard Feldstein, eds. *Lacan in the German-Speaking World.* Albany: State University of New York Press, 2004.

Turkle, Sherry. *Psychoanalytic Politics,* second edition. New York and London: Guilford Press, 1992.

Van Haute, Philippe. "Death and Sublimation in Lacan's Reading of Antigone." In *Levinas and Lacan: The Missed Encounter,* edited by Sarah Harasym, 102–120. Albany: State University of New York Press, 1995.

Žižek, Slavoj. *The Sublime Object of Ideology.* London: Verso, 1989.

———. *Looking Awry: An Introduction to Jacques Lacan Through Popular Culture.* Cambridge: MIT Press, 1991.

———. *Enjoy Your Symptom!* New York: Routledge, 1992.

———. *Tarrying with the Negative.* Durham: Duke University Press, 1993.

———. "A Hair of the Dog That Bit You." In *Lacanian Theory of Discourse,* edited by Mark Bracher, et al., 46–73. New York: New York University Press, 1994.

———. *The Indivisible Remainder: On Schelling and Related Matters.* London: Verso, 1996.

———. "There Is No Sexual Relationship." In *Gaze and Voice as Love Objects. SIC 1,* edited by Slavoj Žižek and Renata Salecl, 208–249. Durham and London: Duke University Press, 1996.

———. "Hegel with Lacan, of the Subject and Its Cause." In *Reading Seminars I and II,* edited by Richard Feldstein, Bruce Fink, and Maire Jaanus, 397–416. Albany: State University of New York Press, 1996.

———. "Four Discourses, Four Subjects." In *Cogito and the Unconscious. SIC 2,* edited by Slavoj Žižek, 74–116. Durham and London: Duke University Press, 1998.

———. *The Ticklish Subject.* London: Verso, 1999.

———. *Welcome to the Desert of the Real.* London: Verso, 2002.

———. "Neighbors and Other Monsters: A Plea for Ethical Violence." In *The Neighbor: Three Inquiries in Political Theology,* edited by Slavoj Žižek, 134–190. Chicago: University of Chicago Press, 2005.

———, ed. *Lacan: The Silent Partners.* London: Verso, 2006.

———. "Object *a* in Social Links." In *Reflections on Seminar XVII: Jacques Lacan and the Other Side of Psychoanalysis. SIC 6,* edited by Justin Clemens and Russell Grigg, 107–128. Durham and London: Duke University Press, 2006.

———. *In Defense of Lost Causes.* London: Verso, 2008.

Zupančič, Alenka. "The Case of the Perforated Sheet." In *Sexuation. SIC 3,* edited by Renata Salecl, 282–296. Durham and London: Duke University Press, 2000.

———. *Ethics of the Real.* London: Verso, 2000.

———. "Ethics and Tragedy in Lacan." In *The Cambridge Companion to Lacan,* edited by Jean-Michel Rabaté, 173–190. Cambridge: Cambridge University Press, 2003.

WEB SITES

James Lovelock. "We Can't Save the Planet." Interview on the BBC (March 30, 2010). http://news.bbc.co.uk/today/hi/today/newsid_8594000/8594561.stm, interview (accessed April 2, 2010).

http://filozofskivestnikonline.com/index.php/journal/index (accessed March 2011).

http://www.lacan.com (accessed June 2009).

Young, Liane, Joan Albert Camprodon, Marc Hauser, Alvaro Pascual-Leone, and Rebecca Saxe. "Disruption of the right temporoparietal junction with transcranial magnetic stimulation reduces the role of beliefs in moral judgements." PNAS 2010 107 (15) 6753-6758; published ahead of print March 29, 2010, doi:10.1073/pnas.0914826107. http://www.pnas.org/content/107/6.toc (accessed April 8, 2010).

INDEX